LUTZ EDZARD

Language as a Medium of Legal Norms

Schriften zum Völkerrecht

Band 131

Language as a Medium of Legal Norms

Implications of the Use of Arabic as a Language in the United Nations System

By

Lutz Edzard

Duncker & Humblot · Berlin

Die Deutsche Bibliothek – CIP-Einheitsaufnahme

Edzard, Lutz:
Language as a medium of legal norms : implications of the use of Arabic as a language in the United Nations System / by Lutz Edzard. – Berlin : Duncker und Humblot, 1998
(Schriften zum Völkerrecht ; Bd. 131)
ISBN 3-428-09307-0

Fotoprint: Berliner Buchdruckerei Union GmbH, Berlin
Printed in Germany

ISSN 0582-0251
ISBN 3-428-09307-0

Gedruckt auf alterungsbeständigem (säurefreiem) Papier
entsprechend ISO 9706 ♾

Dem Andenken von Martin Zupančič

Preface

This study emanates from research carried out by the author in his capacity as a research associate at the Department of International Law at Munich University in 1994/95 and half of 1996. During twelve months of this time frame, the author was also a visiting scholar at the Translation and Editorial Division of the United Nations, New York. The research was undertaken in the framework of the project "Linguistische Konfliktprävention"/"Arabische Vertragssprache" at the Department of International Law at Munich University. This project, under the direction of Professor *Bruno Simma,* was funded by the Deutsche Forschungsgemeinschaft (German Research Council). The collection of data took place at the United Nations headquarters in New York, assisted by staff members in the Treaty Section, Office of Legal Affairs, and in the Translation and Editorial Division, Office of Conference Services, and by Arab diplomats accredited at the United Nations. The goal was to verify hypotheses on the role of language as a medium of legal norms in interviews with Arab and non-Arab staff members and diplomats, the topic being the use of Arabic in international legal documents. The author is greatly indebted to Professor *Bruno Simma,* University of Munich, and Professor *Stefan Wild,* University of Bonn, both of whom read earlier drafts of parts of this book, and also wishes to thank the following persons for their help and advice with the project: Professor *Michael Carter,* then at New York University, Professor *Ann Mayer,* University of Pennsylvania, *Reinhard Schlagintweit,* Dr. *Hubert Lang,* Dr. *Aref Hajjaj* and *Wolfgang Dik,* Auswärtiges Amt (German Foreign Office), Professor *Hilmar Krüger,* University of Cologne and Bundesstelle für Außenhandelsinformation (Federal Office of Foreign Trade Information), *Federico Riesco,* United Nations, Office of Conference Services, *Mahmud Suqi, Samir Khouri,* and *Ali Shadi,* United Nations, Arabic Translation Service, *Elisabeth Warburton,* United Nations, English Translation Service, *Marc Labelle,* United Nations, Office of Legal Affairs, Treaty Section, *Rima Bordcosh,* United Nations, Department of Public Information, and H.E. Ambassador *Adnan Abu Odeh,* then at the Permanent Mission of Jordan to the United Nations. Special thanks are due to *Orin Gensler* for valuable comments on content and style of this study.

Thanks also to *Berit Bein*, *Alexandra Köhnken*, and *Christian Szyska* who helped with proofreading and indexing the manuscript. Needless to say that responsibility for the format and the content of this study remains solely with the author.

Bonn, March 1998 *Lutz Edzard*

Table of Contents

Chapter Four

Application of the theory of interpretation to the realm of war and peace

Chapter Five

Application of the theory of interpretation to the realm of human rights

Chapter Six

Case study: application of the theory of interpretation to the definition of "ethnic, religious, and linguistic minorities" in UN documents

Chapter Seven

Conclusion

Appendix

Analytical catalogue of data and sources

References

Index

Tables

Abbreviations

Bgbl. II	Bundesgesetzblatt, Teil II
CAT	Convention against Torture and other Cruel, Inhuman or Degrading Treatment or Punishment
CEDAW	Convention on the Elimination of All Forms of Discrimination against Women
CERD	(International) Convention on the Elimination of All Forms of Racial Discrimination
CRC	Convention on the Rights of the Child
CSPCA	International Convention on the Suppression and Punishment of the Crime of Apartheid
FAO	Food and Agriculture Organization of the United Nations
GAOR	General Assembly Official Records
GCC	Gulf Co-operation Council
IAEA	International Atomic Energy Agency
ICCPR	International Covenant on Civil and Political Rights
ICESCR	International Covenant on Economic, Social and Cultural Rights
ICJ	International Court of Justice
IHR	International Human Rights
ILO	International Labour Organization
LNTS	League of Nations -- Treaty Series (Société des Nations -- Receuil des Traités)
MINURSO	Mission des Nations Unies pour le réferendum en Sahara Occidental
NGO	Non-governmental organization
OAU	Organization of African Unity
OIC	Organization of the Islamic Conference
PICJ	Permanent International Court of Justice
PLO	Palestine Liberation Organization
UDHR	Universal Declaration of Human Rights
UIDHR	Universal Islamic Declaration of Human Rights
UNESCO	United Nations Educational, Scientific and Cultural Organization
UNIKOM	Unites Nations Iraq-Kuwait Observation Mission
UNSCOM	United Nations Special Commission
UNTS	United Nations -- Treaty Series
WHO	World Health Organization

Notes on language use and transcription

UN documents are usually quoted in their English or French original. In the case of Arabic originals, the Arabic text is given when available, in addition to the official English translation (in the few instances where this is not the case, a translation by the present author is provided). It is always indicated whether a text in a given language represents the original, an authentic/official version among several authentic/official versions, or merely an official translation. The same holds for occasional quotations from Hebrew, Amharic, and other languages. Those parts of the quotations that are especially relevant for the further argumentation are printed in italics. While transcriptions from Arabic and other languages are in alignment with accepted scholarly standards, as are transcriptions of names of Arab leaders (e.g., Ḥusayn, not *Hussein), names of Arab diplomats and officials at the United Nations are quoted according to these persons' own transcriptions of their names (e.g., Ali Mohamed Osman Yassin, not *ᶜAlī Muḥammad ᶜUṯmān Yāsīn) (see documents ST/SG/SER.A/273 ("Permanent Missions to the United Nations") and ST/OGS/SER.E/73 ("Telephone Directory" of the United Nations)). At the end of the appendix (analytical catalogue of data and sources), Arabic quotations that appear transcribed in this study are provided in their original script, i.e., untranscribed. References in European languages are consistently cited according to the format <<*author*>> <<year of publication[+index]>>: <<page number>>, e.g., *Lewis* 1993a: 99. Finally, a citation such as Qurʾān 9: 5 or *sūra* 9: 5 refers to *sūra* 9, *ʾāya* 5 of the Qurʾān.

Chapter One

Introduction

This study aims at investigating the important role that language plays as a medium of legal norms and cultural values as surfacing in documents in the United Nations system.[1] In this sense, this study is concerned with the interface of language and legal system with respect to the way of discussing the topics "war and peace" and "human rights".[2] More specifically, the focus will lie on diplomatic documents (bi- and multilateral treaties and correspondence) that simultaneously have official status ("authenticity") both in Arabic and in other languages, in order to determine to what extent textual differences are due to different legal and cultural concepts as opposed to mere linguistic factors.[3] In other words, the goal will be to investigate the role of language as a medium of cultural values, legal norms and concepts, and political motives. An especially important realm of application will be the vast field of human rights. For those Arab states which submit their periodic reports to human rights treaty bodies in Arabic, this boils down to the question as to whether certain statements that are comprehensible in the light of the history of Arabic Islamic legal and/or religious thought would be possible, or would make clear sense

---

[1] Some of the material adduced in this study has already been referred to in *Edzard* 1996 ("Stylistic elements in the use of Arabic as language in diplomacy: Recent developments in United Nations context", Die Welt des Islams 36/1 (1996), pp. 25ff) and *Edzard* 1997 ("Language as medium of legal norm: The topics "war and peace" and "human rights" in bi- and multilateral treaties with Arab states and organizations", in: *Edzard*, L./*Szyska*, C. (eds.) 1997. Encounters of Words and Texts. Intercultural Studies in Honor of Stefan Wild on the Occasion of His 60th Birthday, March 2, 1997, Presented by His Pupils in Bonn. Hildesheim, pp. 69ff).

[2] Cf., for instance, *Lewis* 1988 and *Mayer* 1991a/b. Extensive references will be given below in the relevant chapters.

[3] Relevant sources are: *LNTS*, *UNTS*, documents of the General Assembly (A/...) and the Security Council (S/...) of the United Nations, *Bowman/Harris* 1984, Bundesgesetzblatt II, *Davies* 1947, *Hurewitz* 1956, *Hurewitz* 1975/1979, *Mansoor* 1965, and *Rohn* 1984.

as such in English or French.[4] Not only is there a fundamental religious anchoring observable in documents originating in Arab or other Islamic countries; there is likewise a sense of history unparalleled in United Nations documents originating in other parts of the world. The investigation of the role of language as a window onto culture and religious background is especially relevant in the case of Arabic due to the interference of religion with law in most Islamic societies.[5]

This study aims at evaluating the question as to whether there is, synchronically speaking, substantial reference to the Islamic *šarīᶜa* in the realm of war and peace, or, put in another way, the question as to whether there is a contemporary "particular" Islamic Law of Nations.[6] In this context, both the Palestine conflict ("Middle East conflict") and the Iraq-Kuwait conflict will be investigated.

This study aims further at investigating and systematizing problems of interpretation that arise under circumstances of conflicting norms between human rights standards in international law and in the Islamic *šarīᶜa*. More specifically, problems will be pinpointed in the realms of personal statute law, the legal status of women, the laws of marriage, divorce, inheritance, freedom of opinion and religion, and penal law, where serious disparities can surface between the "Muslim" and the "Western" approach to international law. These problems arise in the periodic reports of states parties on the implementation of international human rights conventions, whether or not they have entered any formal reservations pointing to the Islamic *šarīᶜa*. Arguments that refer to the Islamic *šarīᶜa* can further be found in meetings with the committees (treaty bodies) in charge of the respective international human rights conventions, who scrutinize the reports and discuss them with representatives of the states parties.

Another research goal will be the investigation of what constitutes ethnic, linguistic and religious minorities in North Africa and the Middle East. This question is virulent, for instance, when it comes to

---

[4] For the history of Arabic as a language in diplomacy, cf. *Landau*, J. "Muᶜāhada", The Encyclopaedia of Islam (new edition), vol. 7: 250ff, *Ostrower* 1965, vol. 1: 240ff, *Bozeman* 1971: 50ff, as well as *Tabory* 1980: 11ff, 41ff, and 80ff.

[5] The present study will occasionally refer as well to the other two Semitic languages represented in the modern treaty collections, i.e., Hebrew and Amharic, when parallel texts in these languages are attested. However, English and Arabic are the two main languages of reference in this study. Looking at the Afroasiatic language family as a whole, Somali is represented as a Cushitic language in *UNTS*. No Berber, Chadic, or Omotic treaty texts or other diplomatic documents are officially available.

[6] This question is answered negatively, for instance, by *Fastenrath* (1991: 133n).

the ethnic and linguistic definition of the Berber/Amazigh population in North African countries and the remnants of Aramaic-speaking populations in the Eastern part of the Arab world, and plays a particular role in the respective diplomatic documents. In this context, special attention will be paid to terminological devices used to deny features of ethnic, linguistic and religious identity.

At the heart of this study is an application of Speech Act Theory to the analysis of the nature and consequences of textual differences between versions of one and the same document in several languages. Beyond that, Speech Act Theory will also be applied to intercultural misunderstanding as a result of the differing connotations that certain legal, political, and religious terms can bear, irrespective of the language used in the given context. The research will thus be conducive to a new lexicographical analysis of terms that have posed notorious problems in diplomatic documents.

Current misunderstandings regarding terminology associated with Islam make such a terminological analysis highly desirable. Prominent examples of problematic discourse-related issues include discussions on such concepts as Islamic fundamentalism and terms like *jihād*, *fatwā*, and others. It should be clear that neither a demonizing nor a downplaying of such problematic concepts is called for here.

Another important goal of this study will be to address the current problems associated with legal and cultural relativism in the wake of the "political correctness" debate.[7] While instances of legal and cultural "convergence" will be noted, this study will deliberately make no attempt to "synthesize" differing norms in international law on the one hand and in Islamic law (*šarī^c^a*) on the other. Rather, the author will adhere to strict universalism in the realms of "war and peace" and "human rights". Even though the picture of a monolithical *homo islamicus* does not make sense, it will be seen throughout this study that there is indeed such a thing as a "typical" Islamic perspective, at least in official diplomacy, and, moreover, a "clash of civilizations"[8] between the Western and the Islamic conceptualization of legal issues,

---

[7] For an analytical overview of related problems, cf. notably *Donoho* 1991.

[8] For the use of this term, cf. *Lewis* 1990b, *Huntington* 1993, *Tibi* 1995, and *Huntington* 1996. However, *Huntington*'s (1996: 254ff) concept of "the bloody borders of Islam" will not be adopted here.

especially in the realm of human rights.[9] While there are certainly a number of prominent progressive Muslim thinkers, such as Bassam Tibi, ᶜAlī ᶜAbdarrāziq, Ṣādiq al-ᶜAẓm, ᶜAbdallāh ʾAḥmad an-Naᶜīm, Muḥammad Šaḥrūr, and Naṣr Ḥāmid ʾAbū Zayd,[10] it is regrettable that their views, just as the views expressed by the *salafiya* reform movement,[11] have played no role whatsoever in Islamic diplomatic discourse. As this study is based in a strictly synchronic sense on a well-defined corpus of texts, namely modern diplomatic documents, "heretical" Islamic opinions as voiced by the authors cited above cannot be taken into consideration.

In the framework of this study, the discussion of whether or not it makes sense in the case of Islam to separate "religion", "state" and/or "civilization" appears to be a moot point, as diplomats from Islamic states have never argued in favor of such a distinction. More specifically, it does not make sense to speak of an "instrumentalization" of Islam in diplomatic context, as there has never been a perceivable distinction between religious and political goals in Islamic history.[12] As will be seen, diplomats of Islamic states argue quite openly and faithfully in this sense. Moreover, in the light of the overwhelming written and oral diplomatic evidence, the whole idea of a "Feindbild Islam" and/or "Orientalism" will be shown to be a mere mechanism of scholarly censorship which attempts to discredit even the most balanced (and self-reflecting) analysis of Islamic societies.

While it may be true that the Islamic *šarīᶜa* did contribute to a relative improvement in the human rights *status quo* in the seventh century A.D., this often cited argument can hardly justify human rights violations in the twentieth century that are explicitly or implicitly based on the Islamic *šarīᶜa*.[13]

Also, it is important to note that historical injustice on the part of Western civilization should not be used as a means of downplaying, if not denying human rights violations in contemporary non-Western

---

[9] In this context, the scope of this study, which is limited to official diplomatic documents, is crucial. Going beyond this scope, *Mayer* (1994: 402ff) arrives at a different perspective.

[10] Cf., for instance, *ᶜAbdarrāziq* 1972, *Tibi* 1980, *al-ᶜAẓm* 1981, *an-Naᶜīm* 1990, *Šaḥrūr* 1992, and *ʾAbū Zayd* 1994.

[11] Cf., for instance, *Hourani* 1983.

[12] This *dīn wa-dawla* principle is in sharp contrast to claims to the contrary, as proposed, for instance, in *Schulze* 1992.

[13] Cf., for instance, *Arzt* 1990: 209f.

civilizations.[14] All too often, human rights problems in Islamic countries have been discarded as a mere consequence of *divide-et-impera* politics and other machinations of former colonial régimes – a monocausal approach which will not be pursued in this study, especially as this would amount to denying the self-responsibility of Arab and other Islamic states.

The author of the present study is an Arabist/Semiticist and linguist by training, a factor which accounts for the emphasis on linguistic analysis and data as well as for the methodology used herein. Nevertheless, the analysis of legal concepts in international law play a paramount role in this study, given the nature of the material. Indeed, a large part of this study revolves around issues of "war and peace" and "human rights" in the light of the style used in the documents. Thus, the study aims at fulfilling two functions: first, that of a reference manual for legal scholars interested in the issues of "war and peace" and "human rights" in connection with Arab (and other Islamic) states; second, that of a reference manual for linguists and Arabists interested in the use of diplomatic Arabic. In this sense, the methodology of research is geared at constituting a contribution towards open intercultural communication and understanding. Also, the approach relies primarily on a legal and linguistic analysis of actual written and oral data as opposed to an approach – guided by cultural relativism – that aims *a priori* at proving the compatibility or the potential of mutual convergence between the precepts of international law and the Islamic *šarīᶜa*.[15] A final remark is in order here. While the author of this study is aware of recent developments in the realms of philosophy of law and philosophy of language, no attempt will be made to synthesize what has been hitherto discussed in these areas.[16] Rather, this study is result-driven, in the sense of presenting an analysis of conflicting norms in a well-defined corpus of texts.

---

[14] Cf. *Lewis* 1990a: 102: "That the myth has survived and been taken up enthusiastically in our time is due, I think, to another factor, to what might be called nostalgia for the white man's burden. The white man's burden in Kipling's sense – the Westerner's responsibility for the peoples over whom he ruled – has long since been cast off and seized by others. But there are those who still insist on maintaining it – this time as a burden not of power but of guilt, an insistence on responsibility for the world and its ills that is as arrogant and as unjustified as the claims of our imperial predecessors."

[15] Cf., for instance, *Boisard* 1979, *Boisard* 1980, and *Bielefeldt* 1992. Among pronounced exponents of progressive Islamic thought in the realm of human rights are Bassam *Tibi* and ᶜAbdallāh ᵓAḥmad *an-Naᶜīm*. A thorough analysis of the various positions of Muslim scholars and politicians on this issue is provided in *Mayer* 1991a: 11ff.

[16] Cf., for instance, *Carty* 1991 for an overview which draws attention to the approaches taken in the so-called theory of "critical legal studies".

Chapter Two

Basic legal and linguistic issues regarding Arabic and Islam

"The malicious secularism of the United Nations [i]s no longer a characteristic of all Member States." The Iranian diplomat *Khorasani*, as quoted in UN-doc. A/C.3/36/SR.29, p. 4.

A. Historical background: Middle East and North Africa

The Islamic conquests in Asia and Northern Africa have left a deep cultural and religious imprint in the conquered areas. Due to the continuing and even increasing impact of real or alleged historical circumstances on modern Arab political discourse,[1] it is useful to provide a synopsis as to how and where historical allusions (including religious formulae) are used in modern diplomatic documents and speeches.

Historical thinking is paramount in Arabic international documents to a degree unparalleled in documents in other languages used in the United Nations system.[2] Historical allusions to battles in early Islamic times were often made, for instance, during the Gulf War between Iran and Iraq. Terms such as *qādisīyat Ṣaddām* 'the "Qādisīya" of Ṣaddām [Ḥusayn]', which was used in the Gulf War between Iraq

---

[1] Cf., for instance, *Khadduri* 1955, *Lewis* 1988, *Pohl* 1988, *Mayer* 1991b: 195ff, and *Bedjaoui* 1992: 277ff.

[2] Cf. *Lewis* 1993: 117, in reply to statements to the contrary by Edward *Said*: "This insight would appear to be confirmed by Mr. Said's assertion, in a PBS debate in 1977, that the fourteen-centuries-old Islamic tradition and civilization are no more meaningful for the Arab world today than are seventh-century events in Europe for an understanding of present-day America. Experts in Iraq and Iran thought otherwise. Only a few years later, in their war propaganda against each other, both countries daily evoked events and personalities of the seventh century, in the sure knowledge that they would be understood. One does not quite see American contenders for power making a point by a rapid allusion to the Anglo-Saxon heptarchy, the rise of the Carolingians, or the war of the Lombards."

and Iran,[3] or the comparison of "Operation Desert Storm" with the Mongol invasion of Baghdad in 1258 illustrate this.[4] Both events are alluded to by the term *ʾumm al-maʿārik* 'mother of [all] the battles' in the following statement of the Iraqi Vice-President Ṭāhā Yāsīn Ramaḍān in the Jordanian newspaper *Ṣawt aš-šaʿb* on May 27, 1991:[5]

Item (1), Arabic original

Law ʾanna t-tārīḫa yuʿīdu nafsa-hū lan yakūna la-nā ġayru ḏālika l-mawqifi llaḏī ttaḫaḏnā-hu li-ʾanna l-ḥadīṯa ʿan ʾanna l-kuwayta juzʾun mina l-ʿirāqi lam yakun jadalan ʾaw ḫayālan bal qanāʿatan ... la-qad qaddamnā fī ʾummi l-maʿāriki t-taḍḥiyāti l-ġāliyata wa-lākin bi-juhūdin munaẓẓamatin wa-bi-ʾimkānīyātin mutawāḍiʿatin lakinna-hā muttaṣilatun, wa-ʿalay-nā ʾan naqṭifa ṯimāra hāḏihī l-maʿrakati fī l-maʿrakati l-qādimati wa-l-ʾasāsu llaḏī sanaʿtamidu ʿalay-hi huwa š-šaʿbu wa-min ḫilāli qiyādati-hī l-waṭanīya.

Item (1), official English translation

If history repeats itself, our position will remain unchanged; the statement that Kuwait is part of Iraq is neither controversial nor fictitious, but factual... During the mother of all battles, we made immense sacrifices. But thanks to well-organized efforts, with modest but constant resources, we will reap the fruits of that battle during the next battle, and for that we will rely on the people and on the national leaders.

Interestingly, the current (1998) German ambassador to the United Nations in New York, Tono Eitel, analyzed the Iraqi invasion of Kuwait in terms of the Arabic concept of *ġazwa* 'military attack':[6]

Lightning-fast surprise attacks on a neighbor under cover of night have a long tradition in Arabian history. The Ghazwa [...] was a veritable institution and in the early days of Islam was justifiable against any unbelieving neighbor, who, if not subjugated, was at least pillaged. The Iraqi attack on Kuwait in the night of 2 August 1990 had all the characteristics of a Ghazwa, in particular the subsequent plundering of everything from gold bars to hospital equipment. It differed, however, from a real Ghazwa, since it was not carried out against infidels.

Curiously, Iraq often makes reference to its early history in introductory passages of human rights documents. For instance, the discussion of Iraq's second report submitted to the Committee on Civil and Politi-

---

[3] Cf. *Barkho* 1987: 149 and *Lewis* 1988: 121f. The term refers to the defeat of the Zoroastrians at the battle of Qādisīya in the year 637 A.D.

[4] Cf. UN-doc. S/22452 (Letter dated 5 April 1991 from the Permanent Representative of Iraq to the United Nations [Abdul Amir A. Al-Anbari] addressed to the Secretary-General [Javier Perez de Cuellar]) (Arabic and English), pp. 2f.

[5] Cf. UN-doc A/45/1018 = S/22655 (Annex to the Letter dated 29 May 1991 from the Permanent Representative of Kuwait to the United Nations [Mohammad A. Abulhasan] addressed to the Secretary-General [Javier Perez de Cuellar]) (Arabic and English), pp. 1f and p. 1, respectively.

[6] *Eitel* 1992: 171.

cal Rights ("Human Rights Committee"), UN-doc. CCPR/C/37/Add.3 reaches as far back as the Codex Hammurabi, producing the following problematic statement:[7]

Item (2), English original

The law constituted the means by which society was organized and, as such, had to ensure a proper balance between the authority of the State and individual freedoms. Long ago, that had been the objective of the code of Hammurabi, the first written law known to man. That code formed part of the history of Iraq which, as everyone knew, had been the cradle of renowned civilizations. It could be said, therefore, that human rights had a very long history in Iraq.

Although slavery existed *de jure* in early Islam and still persists *de facto* in some Islamic countries, Jordan, for instance, deemed it appropriate to refer to early Islamic times in its first report on the implementation of the International Covenant on Civil and Political Rights, UN-doc. CCPR/C/1/Add.24, regarding article 8:[8]

Item (3), official English translation

Article 8 of the Covenant prohibits slavery and slave trade.

The prohibition contained in this article had already been proclaimed about 1,350 years ago by the Caliph Umar ibn al-Khattab, when he received a complaint from a Copt against Amr ibn al-Aas, Governor of Egypt. The Caliph wrote to the Governor saying: "Would you enslave free-born people?"

There are also examples of oral statements referring to early Arabic history that have had diplomatic repercussions. During a visit to a mosque in South Africa on May 10, 1994, Yāsir ʿArafāt[9] compared the Cairo Peace Accord ("Gaza-Jericho Accord") with the Treaty of Ḥudaybīya. This temporary truce agreement of 628 A.D. between the Muslim expedition led by Muḥammad and the tribe of Quraysh in Mecca lasted only until 630 A.D. "because a quarrel between allies of the contracting parties led to Muḥammad's victorious entry into

---

[7] Cf. UN-doc. CCPR/C/SR.744, p. 2. There are indeed commonalities between the Codex Hammurabi and modern Iraqi legislation. The amputation of an ear, for instance, is foreseen as penalty both in paragraph 205 of the Codex Hammurabi (cf., for instance, *Finet* 1973: 112) and in Revolution Command Council Resolution No. 115 of 25 August 1994 (cf. UN-doc. E/CN.4/1995/56, pp. 25ff, submitted by Special Rapporteur *van der Stoel*). In any event, the Codex Hammurabi could hardly be described as a prototypical human rights document.

[8] Cf. UN-doc. CCPR/C/1/Add.56 (Arabic and English), p. 10 in the English version (in this case, the Arabic original was not available at either the UN libraries or the Jordanian Mission).

[9] Interestingly, Yāsir ʿArafāt's former *nom de guerre*, *ʾAbū ʿAmmār* ('the father of ʿAmmār') is an allusion to the historic figure of *ʿAmmār ibn Yāsir* ('the son of Yāsir'), who was a military companion of Muḥammad (cf. *Lewis* 1993: 141).

Mecca".[10] The treaty is usually considered the Arabic source for the "ten year rule", i.e., the provision whereby peace with non-Muslims is defined as a temporary truce agreement. This comparison of ᶜArafāt's created considerable resentment on the part of the Israelis, resentment that was not voiced when the late Egyptian president ᵓAnwar as-Sādāt likened the Camp David Peace Accord to the Treaty of Ḥudaybīya.[11] For easy reference, here is the treaty of Ḥudaybīya in its Arabic original[12] and in an English translation:[13]

Item (4), Arabic original

Hāḏā mā ṣalaḥa ᶜalay-hi Muḥammadu bnu ᶜAbdi llāhi Suhayla bna ᶜAmr[w]in,

iṣṭalaḥā ᶜalā waḍᶜi l-ḥarbi ᶜani n-nāsi ᶜašra sinīna taᵓmanu fī-hinna n-nāsu wa-yakuffu baᶜḍu-hum min baᶜḍin,

ᶜalā ᵓanna-hū man ᵓatā Muḥammadan min Qurayšin bi-ġayri ᵓiḏni wālī-hi radda-hū ᶜalay-him,

wa-man jāᵓa Qurayšan mim-man maᶜa Muḥammadin lam yaruddū-hu ᶜalay-hi,

wa-ᵓinna bayna-nā ᶜaybatan makfūfatan,

wa-ᵓanna-hū lā ᵓislāla wa-la ᵓiġlāla,

wa-ᵓanna-hū man ᵓaḥabba ᵓan yadḫula fī ᶜaqdi Muḥammadin wa-ᶜahdi-hī daḫala fī-hi wa-man ᵓaḥabba ᵓan yadḫula fī ᶜaqdi Qurayšin wa-ᶜahdi-him daḫala fī-hi.

Item (4), English translation

This is what Muḥammad ibn ᶜAbdallāh has agreed upon peacefully with Suhayl ibn ᶜAmr.

They agreed peacefully to postpone war for a period of ten years.

People shall be secured and guaranteed [from attack] by each other.

If anyone from Qurayš wishes to join Muḥammad without the authorization of his *walī* ['protector'] he should be sent back.

If anyone of Muḥammad's followers wishes to join Qurayš, he will not be refused.

Unbecoming acts between each of us are prohibited;

---

[10] Cf. *Watt*, M. "Al-Ḥudaybīya", The Encyclopaedia of Islam (new edition), vol. 3: 539.

[11] Cf. *Rodan*, S. "Arafat implies agreement with Israel is only temporary", The Jerusalem Post, May 23, 1994 and *Haberman*, C. "Israel demands Arafat reaffirm peace accord", The New York Times, May 24, 1994.

[12] Cf. *Ibn Hišām/Wüstenfeld*, F. (ed.) [1858]. Kitāb sīrat rasūl allāh. Göttingen, vol. 2: 740.

[13] Cf. *Khadduri* 1955: 211f.

and there shall not be between us defection, nor treason.

Those [people] who want to join Muḥammad's alliance and his pact may do so; those who want to join Qurayš's alliance and its pact may do so.

B. Religious background: Judaism, Christianity, and Islam

It goes without saying that the three above-mentioned religions play a paramount role in various UN documents, both in the context of "war and peace" and in the context of "human rights". Many recent documents support this observation. A recent example regarding the Palestine conflict is the following:[14]

Item (5), English original

Jerusalem remains a central issue for the Palestinian people and for the Arab world and Islamic Ummah. Its holy places are of great value for Muslims, Christians, and Jews all over the world.

An appreciation of the history of religious conflicts is an equally important prerequisite for the understanding of contemporary clashes between differing cultural and legal norms in the Judeo-Christian and the Islamic traditions, as recent discussions in the wake of the "political correctness" discussion have amply shown; the impact of cultural and legal relativism has even affected the human rights debate in Middle Eastern Studies.[15] While Jews and Christians, as so-called *ʾahl al-kitāb* 'people of the book' [i.e., the Bible], have traditionally had a favorable status in the Islamic world, as compared to members of other religions and heretical sects (and certainly as compared to the status of non-Christian minorities in medieval Europe), considerable discrimination has existed nevertheless. Such discrimination persists up to the present, even though the contrary is often claimed on the diplomatic level and elsewhere. Reference to Islamic principles is routinely made when it comes to the discussion of the status of religious minorities in Middle Eastern and North African countries.[16]

The Arabic historical document which is most frequently cited by Arab diplomats in support of Islamic openness to peaceful interreligious dialogue, even though the text contains unfriendly references to

---

[14] UN-doc. A/49/288 (= UN-doc. S/1994/288) (Letter dated 29 July 1994 from the Permanent Observer for Palestine to the United Nations [Nasser al-Kidwa] addressed to the Secretary-General [Boutros Boutros-Ghali]), p. 2.

[15] Cf., for instance, *Lewis* 1993a: 130.

[16] Cf. below (chapter 6).

the Jews, is the treaty between the Caliph ᶜUmar ibn al-Ḫaṭṭāb and the Patriarch of Jerusalem which was reportedly concluded in the year 638 A.D. (15 A.H.):[17]

Item (6), Arabic original

Bi-smi llāhi r-raḥmāni r-raḥīmi

hāḏā mā ʾaᶜṭā ᶜAbdu llāhi ᶜUmaru ʾamīru l-muʾminīna ʾahla ʾĪliyāʾa mina l-ʾamani

ʾaᶜṭā-hum ʾamanan li-ʾanfusi-him wa-ʾamwāli-him wa-li-kanāʾisi-him wa-ṣulbāni-him wa-saqīmi-hā wa-barīʾi-hā wa-sāʾiri millati-hā

ʾanna-hū lā tuskanu kanāʾisu-hum wa-lā tuhdamu wa-lā yuntaqaṣu min-hā wa-lā min ḥayyizi-hā wa-lā min ṣalībi-him wa-lā min šayʾin min ʾamwāli-him

wa-lā yukrahūna ᶜalā dīni-him wa-lā yuḍārru ʾaḥadun min-hum

wa-lā yaskunu bi-ʾĪliyāʾa maᶜa-hum ʾaḥadun mina l-yahūdi

wa-ᶜalā ʾahli ʾĪliyāʾa ʾan yuᶜṭū l-jizyata ka-mā yuᶜṭī ʾahlu l-madāʾini

wa-ᶜalay-him ʾan yuḫrijū min-hā r-rūma wa-l-luṣūta

fa-man ḫaraja min-hum fa-ʾanna-hū ʾāminun ᶜalā nafsi-hī wa-māli-hī ḥattā yabluġū maʾmana-hum

wa-man ʾaqāma min-hum fa-huwa ʾāminun wa-ᶜalay-hi miṯlu mā ᶜalā ʾahli ʾĪliyāʾa mina l-jizyati

wa-man ʾaḥabba min ʾahli ʾĪliyāʾa ʾan yasīra bi-nafsi-hī wa-māli-hī maᶜa r-rūmi wa-yuḫallī biyaᶜa-hum wa-ṣuluba-hum fa-ʾanna-hum ʾāminūna ᶜalā ʾanfusi-him wa-ᶜalā biyaᶜi-him wa-ṣulubi-him ḥattā yabluġū maʾmana-hum

wa-man kāna bi-hā min ʾahli l-ʾarḍi qabla maqtali fulānin

fa-man šāʾa min-hum qaᶜada wa-ᶜalay-hi miṯlu mā ᶜalā ʾahli ʾĪliyāʾa mina l-jizyati

wa-man šāʾa sāra maᶜa r-rūmi

wa-man šāʾa rajaᶜa ʾilā ʾahli-hī fa-ʾanna-hū lā yuʾḫaḏu min-hum šayʾun ḥattā yuḥṣada ḥaṣādu-hum

wa-ᶜalā mā fī hāḏā l-kitābi ᶜahdu llāhi wa-ḏimmatu rasūli-hī wa-ḏimmatu l-ḫulafāʾi wa-ḏimmatu l-muʾminīna ʾiḏā ʾaᶜṭaw llaḏī ᶜalay-him mina l-jizyati

[17] For the closer circumstances underlying the conclusion of this treaty as well as the question of its authenticity, cf. *Busse* 1984. *Khadduri* (1955: 202) also adduces *sūra* 9: 7 of the Qurʾān as supporting evidence of peaceful Islamic intentions in this connection. For the contemporary relevance of the stipulations of this treaty with respect to Yemen, cf. *Klein-Franke* 1997: 183ff.

šahida ᶜalā ḏālika Ḫālidu bnu l-Walīdi wa-ᶜAmru bnu l-ᶜĀṣī wa-ᶜAbdu r-raḥmāni bnu ᶜAwfin wa-Muᶜāwiyatu bnu ᵓAbī Sufyān

wa-kataba [!] wa-ḥaḍara sanata 15.[18]

Item (6), English translation

In the Name of God, the Compassionate, the Merciful;

This is what ᶜAbdallāh ᶜUmar, Prince of the Believers has guaranteed to the people of ᵓĪliyāᵓ [Jerusalem];

He guaranteed their, i.e., ᵓĪliyāᵓ's poors', exempts' and other community's, lives, property, churches, and crosses;

Their churches will not be dwelt in [by foreigners], nor will they be destroyed or ruined in any part. Nor will their crosses or property [be destroyed];

They will not be persecuted for their religion, nor will they be molested;

Jews shall not be allowed to live with them in ᵓĪliyāᵓ;

The inhabitants of ᵓĪliyāᵓ shall pay the *jizya* as much as that of the inhabitants of the [other cities];

They shall require the Rūm [Byzantines] and the thieves to leave the city. If they leave, they shall be secured in their lives and property until they reach [their country].

Those [Byzantines] who prefer to stay, shall be given security and should accept the same obligations as those of the inhabitants of ᵓĪliyāᵓ concerning the *jizya;*

Those who prefer to go with the Rūm from among the inhabitants of ᵓĪliyāᵓ shall be secured in their lives and property, [provided] they leave their churches and crosses, and they shall be secured in their churches and crosses until they reach [their country];

Those who were in it [the city] from among the people of the land [farmers?], before the death of the *so-and-so*, shall be allowed, if they wish, to stay in the city and shall have the same obligations as those of the inhabitants of ᵓĪliyāᵓ concerning the *jizya;*

Those who prefer to leave with the Rūm, [may do so]; those who prefer to go to their people [their land], [may do so] until the time of their harvest;

This document is guaranteed by the assurance of Allāh, of His Apostle, of the Caliphs, and of the believers, if [the inhabitants] pay their duties of the *jizya;*

Witnesses are: Ḫālid ibn al-Walīd, ᶜAmr ibn al-ᶜĀṣ, ᶜAbdarraḥmān ibn ᶜAwf and Muᶜāwiya ibn ᵓAbī Sufyān.

It was signed in 15 A.H.[19]

---

[18] The Arabic original is found in *Ṭabarī / de Goeje* (ed.) [1893]. Tārīḫ ar-rusul wa-l-mulūk. Leiden, series 1, vol. 5: 2405f.

[19] English translations are found in *Khadduri* 1955: 214 and in *Friedmann* 1992: 191f.

As will be seen, an abundance of Islamic quotations can be found in modern Arabic diplomatic documents, especially in human rights contexts. Such quotations may be absent, however, in multilateral Arabic treaties to which Lebanon, a country with a sizeable Christian population, is a party, notably the Pact of the League of Arab States.[20]

C. Legal background: Islamic law

As will be seen throughout this study, Islamic law plays a more prominent role in the realm of human rights than in the realm of war and peace.[21] As is well known, religious aspects of the legal systems in Arab and other Islamic states are covered by the Arabic terms *šarīᶜa* and *fiqh*, whereas secular aspects are covered by the Arabic term *qānūn*.

Different systems of (international) law may have different political goals. With respect to external relations, traditional Islamic perspective partitions the world into three realms, *dār al-ᵓislām* 'realm ("house") of Islam', *dār aṣ-ṣulḥ* or *dār al-ᶜahd* 'realm ("house") of truce' (non-Islamic territory in the state of temporary truce), and *dār al-ḥarb* 'realm ("house") of war' (other territory). Nowadays, this tripartition is considered an anachronism. International relations in contemporary Islamic perspective are characterized by a certain sense of *realpolitik*; it would constitute an anachronism to project traditional principles of Islamic law[22] on all transactions in contemporary Arabic politics. Countries as Egypt can be cited as having a "mixed" system even on the *de jure* level,[23] and the *modus vivendi* with respect to diplomacy in other moderate Arab systems coincides more or less with modern Western perspectives. In the words of Majid Khadduri, "it is worth noting the extent to which the countries of the Middle East – and in particular the successor states of the Ottoman Empire – have adapted themselves to the predominantly Western legal concepts and

---

[20] Egypt, Iraq, Transjordan, Lebanon, Saudi Arabia, Syria, Yemen. Pact of the League of Arab States. Signed at Cairo, on 22 March 1945, *UNTS*, vol. 70 (1950), pp. 237ff.

[21] For an introductory overview, cf., for instance, *Schacht* 1964 and *Dilger* 1990. For extensive references, cf. *Al-Zwaini/Peters* 1994.

[22] For a "classical" source, cf. *as-Saraḫsī* [1971/1972]. A comprehensive list of historical references is found in *Pohl* 1988. For a comparative analysis, cf., e.g., *Bānāja* 1985.

[23] Cf. *Pohl* 1988. For an overview of modern legal systems in the Arab states, cf. *Redden*, K. (ed.) 1990. Modern Legal Systems Cyclopedia, vol. 5/5A (Middle East) and vol. 6/6A (Africa). For an overview of the realm of civil law, cf. *Krüger* 1987.

procedures of modern International Law insofar as their external relations are concerned".[24]

Nevertheless, Arab and other Islamic states have tended increasingly to invoke Islamic concepts, as expressed by Qurʾānic verses and the *sunna* (regulations based on deeds and sayings of Muḥammad), when the interpretation of international human rights conventions is at issue. While local constitutions are often based structurally on European models, they are rigged with reservations pointing to the Islamic *šarīʿa* as a central source of law. In this context, it can even be argued that the idea of a "Universal Islamic Declaration of Human Rights" is a contradiction in terms, even within the Islamic world, inasmuch as Islamic norms cannot be said to be universal.[25] The following excerpt from the verbatim record of a statement by a former Iranian ambassador to the UN, Khorasani, regarding the drafting of the "Declaration on the Elimination of All Forms of Intolerance and of Discrimination Based on Religion or Belief" in the Third Committee, is an example in which the logic of argumentation fundamentally differs from a "Western" perspective on International Law, in that a "secularist" approach is pinned against a "religious" one:[26]

Item (7), English original

The United Nations was a secular body, and the Universal Declaration of Human Rights was a secular instrument which permitted the vapid fabrications of Zionism and Western and Eastern imperialism to break the united front of the followers of divine faiths. [...]

Apart from the racist and expansionist organization of international Zionism, which had brought infamy to the faith of Moses and was the foremost enemy of peace, there were national organizations such as the Mossad, the Mafia, the CIA, and the KGB, which took advantage of the vagueness and ambiguity of the concept of religion in the International Covenant on Civil and Political Rights and which could, if need be produce new pseudo-religious attitudes.

However, a fact that could no longer be ignored was that the increasing religious awareness among the hundreds of millions of Muslims and other followers of divine faiths, thanks to the Islamic revolution, had become a determining factor in international affairs. The malicious secularism of the United Nations was no longer a characteristic of all Member States.

Muslims were receptive to knowledge and reason. Because of their refusal to compromise on their principles, some called them fanatics or extremists and labelled them with a variety of other names. But names were unimportant. In the

---

[24] Cf. *Khadduri* 1972: 133.

[25] Cf. *Kühnhardt* 1987: 188 and *Forstner* 1993: 92.

[26] UN-doc. A/C.3/36/SR.29, pp. 4ff. An extensive quotation (including the epigraph to the present chapter) is provided here, as this document features many typical and even stereotypical phrases of polemical Islamic discourse.

Islamic Republic of Iran, committed Muslims were the most favoured of God, and their patience, endurance and sacrifice, under their great leader and spiritual father Imam Khomeini, had brought unity, independence, contentment and pious and honest administration. They did not ask for toleration: what mattered between religions was respect. Believing that secular bodies were not qualified to deal with religious matters, they respectfully requested that such bodies not attempt it, since their efforts were out of place. In any case, if the results of such efforts were contrary to Islamic laws, they would be precluded under section 1; article 4, of the Constitution from being practiced in Iran.

There were contradictions in the International Covenant on Civil and Political Rights. In article 18, for example, paragraph 1 recognized freedom of religion, but paragraph 2, which precluded coercion that would impair freedom to adopt a religion of his choice, could never apply to Muslims, who were not permitted to adopt another religion. Article 18 would permit Muslims to practice Islamic law, which included criminal law, but article 6 did not permit the death penalty. A legal or any other code which caused anomalies was dangerous. The only solution was to recognize the right of all persons, including Muslims, to practice their religion and not be coerced. It was essential to give clear definitions of fundamental concepts, such as religion, freedom, justice, peace -- and man. To some, man was a kind of intelligent monkey, but Muslims believed that he was the vicegerent of God. Those two definitions opened the way to conflicting bills of rights, legal codes and scopes of action. On the one hand, it was recognized that all members of the human family were equal, while on the other, some nations were allowed to veto any decision. And all the time, lip service was paid to the International Covenants. [...]

Secularism and materialism were destructive. Religious and moral principles must be revived, and the United Nations should recognize that as its most important mission.

As will be seen throughout this study, there is no special and systematic inner-Islamic international law, as far as the realm of war and peace is concerned,[27] although, historically speaking, there was indeed an Islamic concept of a Law of Nations. However, there has definitely been a great deal of Islamic discourse on this subject in recent times, especially in documents concerning the Iraq-Kuwait conflict. Religious allusions and quotations are a cornerstone of argumentation when dealing with international conflict, especially in conflicts with "the West" and less so in inner-Arab or inner-Islamic conflicts. A typi-

---

[27] Cf. *Fastenrath* 1991: 132f: "Die islamischen Staaten haben bisher nicht versucht, ihre Glaubensgrundsätze – etwa diejenigen über den "Heiligen Krieg" – in das universelle Völkerrecht einzubringen; auch ein partikuläres islamisches Völkerrecht hat sich bis jetzt noch nicht gebildet." ("Until now, the Islamic states have not attempted to incorporate their religious dogmas – notably those regarding the "holy war" – into the universal Law of Nations; nor has there emerged a particular Islamic Law of Nations.") There are, however, exceptions, such as references to the Islamic Law of Nations in the course of the discussion of the Western Sahara case in 1975 (cf. *Mayer* 1991b: 213f, where the following citations are provided: Western Sahara Advisory Opinion, I.C.J. Pleadings 1982, 4: 172-176, 357, 368, 371-372, 489; 5: 292-299, 304-305, 368-370).

cal example of religious Islamic overtones occurs in the following excerpt from a Libyan letter in connection with the Lockerbie incident:[28]

Item (8), Arabic original

Wa-ḥawla ʾišārati ʾiʿlāni d-duwali t̲-t̲alāt̲i ʾilā qaḍīyati l-ḥujjāji l-lībīyīna wa-waṣfi safari-him ʾilā l-ʾarḍi l-muqaddasati bi-ʾanna-hū ntihākun li-l-jazāʾāti l-mafrūḍati ʿalā l-jamāhīrīyati l-ʿuẓmā, nawaddu ʾan nukarrira mā sabaqa ʾan ʾaḫṭarnā bi-hī raʾīsa lajnati l-jazāʾāti wa-huwa ʾanna l-jamāhīrīyata lam wa-lan [!] tantahika tilka l-jazāʾāti, ʾil-lā ʾanna qaḍiyata mumārasati l-lībīyīna li-mašāʿiri-himi d-dīnīyati qaḍīyatun muḫtalifatun, fa-hiya, fī l-maqāmi l-ʾawwali, mumārasatun li-mašāʿira dīnīyatin lā taḫḍaʿu li-ʾid̲nin min ʾaḥadin, lā majlisi l-ʾamni wa-lā l-ʿālami bi-rummati-hī, *fa-hiya qaḍīyatu "lā ṭāʿata li-maḫlūqin fī maʿṣiyati l-ḫāliqi"*, wa-ʿalay-him ʾan yudrikū bi-kulli wuḍūḥin ʾanna š-šaʿba l-lībīya sa-yumārisu šaʿāʾira-hū d-dīnīyata bi-kulli ḥurrīyatin wa-lan tat̲niya-hū ʿan d̲ālika qūwatun fī l-ʾarḍi ḥattā yarit̲a llāhu l-ʾarḍa wa-man ʿalay-hi.

Item (8), official English translation

With regard to the reference contained in the tripartite declaration to the case of Libyan pilgrims and the description of their airflight to the holy land as a violation of the sanctions imposed on the Great Jamahiriya, we should like to reiterate what we have stated to the Chairman of the Committee on sanctions, namely that the Jamahiriya has not and will not violate those sanctions; however, the issue of Libyans' performance of their religious rites is a different matter, for this is, primarily, a question of the performance of religious rights, which is not subject to authorization from anyone, whether it be the Security Council or the world as a whole. *This is a matter governed by the principle that "an act of obedience on the part of a creature ceases to be obedience if it entails disobeying the Creator"*. They must understand quite clearly that the Libyan people will perform its religious rites in all freedom and will not be deterred from that by any force on earth until such time as God inherits the earth and all who are upon it.

Recently, Iraq has violated the prohibition of flights imposed by the United Nations with similar arguments, under comparable circumstances of a flight of pilgrims to Mecca.

---

[28] UN-doc. S/1995/633 (Letter dated 31 July 1995 from the Permanent Representative of the Libyan Arab Jamahiriya to the United Nations [Mohamed Azwai] addressed to the Secretary-General [Boutros Boutros-Ghali]) (Arabic and English), p. 2. For the *ḥadīt̲* quotation (*lā ṭāʿata li-maḫlūqin fī maʿṣiyati l-ḫāliq* 'an act of obedience on the part of a creature ceases to be obedience if it entails disobeying the Creator'), cf. *Wensinck* [1962], vol. 4: 42 and 254.

Reference is frequently made, furthermore, to the role of the Islamic *ʾumma*, i.e., the political and spiritual community of Islamic nations, in international conflict resolution, as in the following document:[29]

Item (9), English original

I have the honour to quote below the text of appeal made by the Heads of State and Government of Bangladesh, Brunei Darussalam, Indonesia, Malaysia, Maldives and Pakistan addressed to President Saddam Hossein [!] urging withdrawal of Iraqi troops from Kuwait:

"We, the Heads of State and Government of Bangladesh, Brunei Darussalam, Indonesia, Malaysia, Maldives and Pakistan have been following with grave concern the rapid and unprecedented escalation of tension in the Gulf region and its critical implications for the world, in particular the Islamic Ummah. [...]

At this difficult moment in our history, we call upon President Saddam Hossain [sic!] to withdraw Iraqi troops from Kuwait in compliance with relevant Security Council Resolutions so that the legitimate Government of Kuwait is restored under the leadership of His Highness Shaikh Jaber Al-Ahmed Al-Jaber Al-Sabah. We commit ourselves to contribute in every way possible to efforts at peacefully settling any outstanding contentious issues between Iraq and Kuwait that may underlie the dispute.

We earnestly hope that in the true Islamic spirit and for the unity and solidarity of the Ummah our call will receive a positive response from President Saddam Hossain [sic!]."

I have the further honour to inform you that the President of Bangladesh took the initiative to consult the above Heads of State and Government for the issuance of the appeal.

I should be grateful if the message is circulated as a document of the Security Council.

D. Linguistic background: Arabic

I. General observations

The fourth cornerstone of historical understanding in the context of the present project is an analysis of the semantic development of Arabic terms that carry legal and/or religious connotations.[30] Gene-

[29] UN-doc. S/21884 (Letter dated 17 October 1990 from the Permanent Representative of Bangladesh to the United Nations [A. Mohiuddin] addressed to the Secretary General [Javier Perez de Cuellar]). Another example of such discourse, referring to a peaceful settlement of the civil war in Yemen, is found in UN-doc. S/1994/763 (Letter dated 13 June 1994 from the Minister of Foreign Affairs of Saudi Arabia [Saud Al-Faisal] addressed to the Secretary-General [Boutros Boutros-Ghali], Annex to the Letter dated 27 June 1994 from the Permanent Representative of Saudi Arabia to the United Nations [Gaafar M. Allagani] addressed to the Secretary-General [Boutros Boutros-Ghali]) (Arabic and English), pp. 2f.

rally speaking, the history of the Arabic language is marked by a high degree of conservatism, again largely due to religious reasons. Modern diplomatic Arabic, of course, represents the same official style, called *fuṣḥā* that in grammar and lexicon derives *grosso modo* from the classical Arabic language as represented, for instance, in the Qur'ān.[31] The precise description of linguistic innovations that have occurred is therefore all the more important.

As a result of the mentioned factors, Arabic has yet to come to grips with the tensions between its rooting in the Islamic tradition on the one hand, and the interference and borrowings from English- and French-coined linguistic patterns, on the other.[32] Special attention must be paid in this context to regional differences in the Arab world.

II. Arabic as a modern language of diplomacy

Although it became an official language of the United Nations only in 1973, Arabic has a long history as a language of diplomacy in its own right, a circumstance which has allowed for the independent semantic development of cultural and legal terms.[33] Hence, the precise rendition of such terms in European languages is a non-trivial task.[34] The converse holds true as well. Moreover, many technically and politically innovative terms and concepts are still resist translation into Arabic, a problem which has proved especially thorny in matters concerning the Law of the Sea.[35] Another difficulty is the use of religious metaphors and diplomatic euphemisms in Arabic letters addressed to the Secretary General of the United Nations and to the Security Council. Moreover, as pointed out above, there are numerous allusions to early Islamic history, especially in the vast output of Iraqi letters

---

[30] Cf. *Rebhan*, 1986, *Ayalon* 1987, and *Lewis* 1988.

[31] Cf., for instance, *Hary* 1992: 29ff for a discussion of related issues.

[32] Cf. notably *Monteil* 1960, *Issawi* 1967, *Stetkevych* 1970, *Lewis* 1974b, *Blau* 1981, *Wild* 1982b, *Rebhan* 1986, *Ayalon* 1987, and *Gully* 1993.

[33] Cf. *Ostrower* 1965, vol. 1: 240ff, *Bozeman* 1971: 50ff as well as *Tabory* 1980: 11ff, 41ff, and 80ff.

[34] Cf. *Szalay/Abu-Hilal/Strohl/Mason/Goodison* 1978, *Lewis* 1993a: 61ff, *Barkho* 1987, *Emery* 1989, and *Carter* 1993.

[35] Cf. *Nelson* 1986. For a synopsis of drafts of the respective texts in the six official languages, cf. UN-doc. A/CONF.62/DC/WP.2. For an overview of terminological problems, cf. UN-doc. ST/CS/SER.F/297/Rev.2 (Law of the Sea: List of Terms Relating to the Law of the Sea).

to the United Nations.[36] As will be shown, many written and oral statements that originate in Arabic could hardly have been made as such in English or French.[37]

The issues addressed in this study are by no means only of a theoretical nature, but have also been addressed by diplomats as a practical matter. An interesting example is the correspondence betwen the French and British High Commissioners surrounding the customs treaty between Iraq and Syria/Lebanon of 1925, in which philological problems of translation were discussed.[38]

Arabic in fact has quite a record as a modern language in diplomacy.[39] In the *League of Nations Treaty Series* (*LNTS*), forty treaties (plus nineteen legal follow-ups, such as exchanges of notes, etc.) are found in which Arabic is the or one of the official languages. In its successor series, the *United Nations Treaty Series* (*UNTS*), more than one thousand such treaties have been published to date, and the number is steadily increasing.[40] Moreover, there are many national treaty collections where Arabic treaty texts are published.[41] The German *Bundesgesetzblatt,* part II, for instance, lists twelve treaties involving a published Arabic text (since 1970 the Arabic versions have been

---

[36] An example is UN-doc. S/22452 (Letter dated 5 April 1991 from the Permanent Representative of Iraq to the United Nations [Abdul Amir A. Al-Anbari] addressed to the Secretary-General [Javier Perez de Cuellar]) (Arabic and English), p. 2, where "Operation Desert Storm" is likened to the Mongol invasion and destruction of Baghdad in 1258 A.D.

[37] A striking example is a diplomatic poem hailing Yemeni reunification by the current ambassador of Qatar to the United Nations, Al-Ni'mah, contained in UN-doc. S/1994/651 (Letter dated 1 June 1994 from the Permanent Representative of Qatar to the United Nations [Hassan Ali Hussain Al-Ni'mah] addressed to the President of the Security Council [at that time: Salim Bin Mohammed Al-Khussaiby]) (Arabic and English), pp. 3f. Cf. also below.

[38] Irak et Syrie et Liban. Convention douanière du 16 janvier 1925, et notes portant amendement au texte arabe de la convention. Beyrouth, 31 janvier, Bagdad, 2 mai, et Beyrouth, 9 juin 1925, *LNTS*, vol. 49 (1926), pp. 9ff.

[39] For brief sketches of Arabic as a language of diplomacy, cf. *Ostrower* 1965, vol. 1: 240ff, *Bozeman* 1971: 50ff, *Tabory* 1980: 11ff, 41ff, and 80ff, and *Didaoui* 1989, vol. 2: 625ff. For an overview concerning the use of all of the six languages in the United Nations system, cf. *Paqué* 1980.

[40] Interestingly, some of these documents are submitted in manuscript form and then reproduced as facsimiles in the treaty collections. Cf., for instance, Morocco's reservations to the Vienna Convention on the Law of Treaties, submitted in a calligraphic Maghrebi ductus and reproduced as such in *UNTS*, vol. 1155 (1980), pp. 499f.

[41] For a comprehensive overview of sources cf. *Landau*, J. "Muʿāhada", The Encyclopaedia of Islam (new edition), vol. 7: 250ff, *Bowman/Harris* 1984, and *Rohn* 1984. Among practical collections are *Davies* 1947, *Hurewitz* 1956, *Khalil* 1962, *Mansoor* 1965, *Hurewitz* 1975 and 1979. For formal aspects of diplomatic documents, cf. *Björkman*, W. "Diplomatic", The Encyclopaedia of Islam (new edition), vol. 2: 301 ff.

published separately).[42] Treaties that may be subject to possible further arbitration are deposited with the United Nations in accordance with article 102 of the Charter of the United Nations and then appear with a time lag of approximately eight years in *UNTS*.[43]

Arabic was included among the official and working languages of the General Assembly of the United Nations by way of resolution no. 3190 (XXVIII) ("Inclusion of Arabic among the official and the working languages of the General Assembly and its Main Committees") of the same body on 18 December 1973.[44]

Item (10), English original

The General Assembly,

Recognizing the significant role of the Arabic language in preserving and disseminating the civilization of man and his culture,

Recognizing further that Arabic is the language of nineteen Members of the United Nations and is a working language in such specialized agencies as the United Nations Educational, Scientific and Cultural Organization, the Food and Agriculture Organization of the United Nations, the World Health Organization and the International Labour Organization, as well as an official and working language of the Organization of African Unity,

Aware of the need to achieve greater international co-operation and to promote harmonization of the actions of nations as envisaged in the Charter of the United Nations,

Noting with appreciation the assurances of the Arab States Members of the United Nations that they will meet collectively the costs of implementing the present resolution during the first three years,

Decides to include Arabic among the official and the working languages of the General Assembly and its Main Committes and to amend accordingly the relevant provisions of the rules of procedures of the Assembly.

Since that date, documents submitted to the United Nations in Arabic have "official" status and non-Arabic documents of the United Nations have routinely been translated into Arabic. The same holds for numerous sub-organizations of the United Nations. In addition, interpretation services from and into Arabic are routinely offered in the United Nations system and its subsidiary organizations.[45]

---

[42] For details, cf. *Hilf* 1973: 13ff.

[43] *Status quo* as in 1997. For recent developments regarding the publication of treaties in the United Nations system, cf. *Tabory* 1982.

[44] Cf. General Assembly Official Records, 28th session, resolutions, vol. 1, suppl. no. 30 (UN-doc. A/9030), pp. 123f.

[45] For a precise overview of language use in the United Nations system and its subsidiary organizations, cf. *Tabory* 1980: 238f and 251ff. Cf. also UN-doc. A/32/237, Annex A.

III. Types of Arabic documents in the UN system

1. *Overview*

Generally speaking, there are four categories of documents that are relevant in the context of the present study. First bi-, pluri- and multilateral treaties;[46] second, diplomatic correspondence (including "annexes", which often constitute the bulk of the given document); third, "reports" (periodic reports by states members submitted to international human rights conventions and reports on certain human rights issues by "special rapporteurs"); and fourth, oral diplomatic contributions (mostly in human rights contexts). Occasional reference will also be made to documents belonging to a further category "other".

2. *Bi- and multilateral treaties*

Bilateral treaties are usually negotiated in English and French. Thereupon, they are translated into the native languages of the contracting parties, except for agreements of minor importance.[47] In recent times, though not historically, one has usually had recourse to English or French as a neutral language ("terms of reference"). The Treaty of Peace between Israel and Egypt, for instance, is "authentic", i.e., "official" in Hebrew, Arabic, and English, the English version providing the legally prevailing and binding "terms of reference".[48] Still, "native" versions are mutually checked by the contracting parties in order to eliminate any misunderstandings. Treaties between states which use the same language may be official just in that language. The 1963 treaty between Kuwait and Iraq, for instance, regarding the mutual recognition of boundaries, is official just in

[46] "Plurilateral" normally refers to treaties which are concluded by a limited number of contracting parties (greater than two); "multilateral" normally refers to treaties to which all states are invited to become members (such as international human rights conventions).

[47] A historical note: the first known Middle Eastern peace treaty, between Ram(es)ses II and Ḫattušili II (1271 B.C.), is transmitted in Egyptian and Hittite, each version being a translation of the respective (unknown) original in the other language. Cf. *Roeder* 1919, *Langdon/Gardiner* 1920, and *Edel* 1997.

[48] Israel and Egypt. Treaty of Peace (with annexes and maps). Signed at Washington on 26 March 1979, article 5/2, *UNTS*, vol. 1136, pp. 100ff.

Arabic.[49] All treaties deposited in accordance with article 102 of the United Nations Charter appear also in English and French, if these languages are not already authentic languages of a given treaty. As an example, here are the Arabic and English versions of the preamble to the Treaty of Peace between Egypt and Israel of 1979:[50]

Item (11), Arabic

ʾInna ḥukūmata dawlati ʾisrāʾīla wa-ḥukūmata jumhūrīyati miṣra l-ʿarabīyati

qtināʿan min-humā bi-ḍ-ḍarūrati l-māssati li-ʾiqāmati salāmin ʿādilin wa-šāmilin wa-dāʾimin fī š-šarqi l-ʾawsaṭi wafqan li-qarāray majlisi l-ʾamni 242 wa-338

ʾiḏ tuʾakkidāni min jadīdini ltizāma-humā bi-"ʾiṭāri s-salāmi fī š-šarqi l-ʾawsaṭi l-muttafaqi ʿalay-hi fī kāmb dāfīd", al-muʾarraḫi fī 17 sabtambir 1978

wa-ʾiḏ tulāḥiẓāni ʾanna l-ʾiṭāra l-mušāra ʿalay-hi ʾinna-mā quṣida bi-hī ʾan yakūna ʾasāsan li-s-salāmi, laysa bayna ʾisrāʾīla wa-miṣra fa-ḥasb, bal ʾayḍan bayna ʾisrāʾīla wa-ʾayyi min jirāni-hā l-ʿarabi kulli fī-mā yaḫuṣṣu-hū mimman yakūnu ʿalā stiʿdādi li-t-tafāwuḍi min ʾajli s-salāmi maʿa-hā ʿalā hāḏā l-ʾasāsi

wa-raġbatan min-humā fī ʾinhāʾi ḥālati l-ḥarbi bayna-humā wa-ʾiqāmati salāmin tastaṭīʿu fī-hi kullu dawlatin fī l-minṭaqati ʾan taʿīša fī ʾamnin

wa-qtināʿan min-humā bi-ʾanna ʿaqda muʿāhadati salāmin bayna ʾisrāʾīla wa-miṣra yuʿtabaru ḫuṭwatan hāmmatan fī ṭarīqi s-salāmi š-šāmili fī l-minṭaqati wa-t-tawaṣṣuli ʾilā taswiyatin li-n-nizāʿi l-ʿarabīyi l-ʾisrāʾīlīyi bi-kāffati nawāḥī-hi

wa-ʾiḏ tadʿuwāni l-ʾaṭrāfa l-ʿarabīyata l-ʾuḫrā fī n-nizāʿi ʾilā l-ištirāki fī ʿamalīyati s-salāmi maʿa ʾisrāʾīla ʿalā ʾasāsi mabādiʾi ʾiṭāri s-salāmi l-mušāri ʾilay-hā ʾānifan wa-stiršādan bi-hā

wa-ʾiḏ tarġabāni ʾayḍan fī ʾinmāʾi l-ʿalāqāti l-waddīyati wa-t-taʿāwuni bayna-humā wafqan li-miṯāqi l-ʾumami l-muttaḥidati wa-mabādiʾi l-qānūni l-duwalīyi llatī taḥkumu l-ʿalāqāti d-duwalīyata waqta s-salāmi

qadi ttafaqā ʿalā l-ʾaḥkāmi t-tāliyati bi-muqtaḍā mumārasati-himā l-ḥurrati li-siyādati-himā min ʾajli tanfīḏi l-ʾiṭāri l-ḫāṣṣi bi-ʿaqdi muʿāhadati s-salāmi bayna ʾisrāʾīla wa-miṣr.

---

[49] Iraq and Kuwait. Agreed Minutes regarding the restoration of friendly relations, recognition and related matters. Signed at Baghdad, on 4 October 1963, *UNTS*, vol. 485 (1964), pp. 322ff.

[50] Israel and Egypt. Treaty of Peace (with annexes and maps). Signed at Washington on 26 March 1979, *UNTS*, vol. 1136 (1979), pp. 110f and p. 116, respectively.

Item (11), English

The Government of the Arab Republic of Egypt and the Government of the State of Israel,

Convinced of the urgent necessity of the establishment of a just, comprehensive and lasting peace in the Middle East in accordance with Security Council resolutions 242 and 338;

Reaffirming their adherence to the "Framework for Peace in the Middle East Agreed at Camp David", dated September 17, 1978;

Noting that the aforementioned Framework as appropriate is intended to constitute a basis for peace not only between Egypt and Israel but also between Israel and each of its other Arab neighbors which is prepared to negotiate peace with it on this basis;

Desiring to bring to an end the state of war between them and to establish a peace in which every state in the region can live in security;

Convinced that the conclusion of a Treaty of Peace between Egypt and Israel is an important step in the search for comprehensive peace in the area and for the attainment of the settlement of the Arab-Israeli conflict in all its aspects;

Inviting the other Arab parties to this dispute to join the peace process with Israel guided by and based on the principles of the aforementioned Framework;

Desiring as well to develop friendly relations and cooperation between themselves in accordance with the United Nations Charter and the principles of international law governing international relations in times of peace;

Agree to the following provisions in the free exercise of their sovereignty, in order to implement the "Framework for the Conclusion of a Peace Treaty Between Egypt and Israel".

In pluri- and multilateral treaties, the languages agreed upon by the contracting parties are usually equally binding. The Charter of the Islamic Conference, for instance, is equally authoritative in Arabic, English, and French.[51] The Charter of the Organization of African Unity is equally authoritative in Amharic, Arabic, English, and French.[52] International Conventions tend to be equally authoritative in all of the six official languages of the United Nations (Arabic, Chinese, English, French, Russian, and Spanish), as in the case of the Convention on the Elimination of All Forms of Discrimination against Women.[53] The wording of these conventions is carefully scrutinized in drafting commissions, in which Arab and (other Islamic) representa-

---

[51] Multilateral. Charter of the Islamic Conference. Adopted by the Third Islamic Conference of Foreign Ministers at Djidda, on 4 March 1972, *UNTS*, vol. 914 (1974), pp. 103ff.

[52] Multilateral. Charter of the Organization of African Unity. Done at Addis Ababa, on 25 May 1963, *UNTS*, vol. 479 (1963), pp. 40ff.

[53] Multilateral. Convention on the Elimination of All Forms of Discrimination against Women. Adopted by the General Assembly of the United Nations on 18 December 1979, *LNTS*, vol. 1249 (1981), pp. 13ff.

tives often try to tone down statements that might be contrary to Islamic precepts. Again, treaties between states having the same language may be official in just that language, as in the case of the Pact of the League of Arab States or the Charter of the Co-operation Council for the Arab States of the Gulf, which are official just in Arabic.[54] Here is an excerpt from the preamble to the Pact of the League of Arab States:[55]

Item (12), Arabic original

ʾInna ḥaḍrata ṣāḥibi l-faḫāmati raʾīsa l-jumhūrīyati s-sūrīyati,

wa-ḥaḍrata ṣāḥibi s-sumūwi l-malakīyi ʾamīra šarqi l-ʾurdunni,

wa-ḥaḍrata ṣāḥibi l-jalālati malika l-ʿirāqi,

wa-ḥaḍrata ṣāḥibi l-jalālati malika l-mamlakati l-ʿarabīyati s-saʿūdīyati,

wa-ḥaḍrata ṣāḥibi l-faḫāmati raʾīsa l-jumhūrīyati l-lubnānīyati,

wa-ḥaḍrata ṣāḥibi l-jalālati malika miṣra,

wa-ḥaḍrata ṣāḥibi l-jalālati malika l-yamani,

taṯbītan li-l-ʿalāqāti l-waṯīqati wa-r-rawābiṭi l-ʿadīdati llatī tarbuṭu bayna d-duwali l-ʿarabīyati,

wa-ḥirṣan ʿalā daʿmi hāḏihī r-rawābiṭi wa-tawṭīdi-hā ʿalā ʾasāsi ḥtirāmi stiqlāli tilka d-duwali wa-siyādati-hā,

wa-tawjīhan li-juhūdi-hā ʾilā mā fī-hi ḫayru l-bilādi l-ʿarabīyati qāṭibatan wa-ṣalāḥi ʾaḥwāli-hā wa-taʾmīni mustaqbali-hā wa-taḥqīqi ʾamānī-hā wa-ʾāmāli-hā,

wa-stijābatan li-r-raʾyi l-ʿarabīyi l-ʿāmmi fī jamīʿi l-ʾaqṭāri l-ʿarabīyati,

qadi ttafaqū ʿalā ʿaqdi mīṯāqin li-hāḏihī l-ġāyati [...]

Item (12), official English translation

His Excellency the President of the Syrian Republic,

His Royal Highness the Emir of Transjordan,

His Majesty the King of Iraq,

---

[54] Egypt, Iraq, Transjordan, Lebanon, Saudi Arabia, Syria, Yemen. Pact of the League of Arab States. Signed at Cairo, on 22 March 1945, *UNTS*, vol. 70 (1950), pp. 237ff; Bahrain, Kuwait, Oman, Qatar, Saudi Arabia, and United Arab Emirates: Charter of the Co-operation Council for the Arab States of the Gulf (with Rules of procedures of the Supreme Council and of the Commission for Settlement of Disputes). Concluded at Abu Dhabi on 25 May 1981, *UNTS*, vol. 1288 (1982), pp. 131ff.

[55] *UNTS*, vol. 70 (1950), p. 247 and p. 248, respectively. For a list of Arabic honorifics, cf. below (appendix).

His Majesty the King of Saudi-Arabia,

His Excellency the President of the Lebanese Republic,

His Majesty the King of Egypt,

His Majesty the King of Yemen,

With a view to strengthen the close relations and numerous ties which bind the Arab States,

And out of concern for cementing and reinforcing of these bonds on the basis of respect for the independence and sovereignty of these States,

And in order to direct their efforts toward the welfare of all the Arab States their common weal, the guarantee of their future and the realization of their aspirations,

And in response to Arab public opinion in all the Arab countries,

Have agreed to conclude a pact to this effect ...

3. *Diplomatic correspondence*

Besides the already mentioned bi- and pluri-/multilateral treaties, there are the following types of diplomatic correspondence:[56]

1. Letter (*risāla*), a communication between heads of states, e.g., letters of credence for ambassadors, or, in the context of the present study, correspondence addressed to the President of the Security Council or to the Secretary General of the United Nations.

2. Exchange of notes (*tabādul al-muḏakkirāt*), a proceeding in the course of the implementation of details of a contract which need not be ratified anymore.

3. Note verbale (*muḏakkira šafawīya*), a form of correspondence between embassies and governments which calls for acknowledgment in writing.

4. Aide-mémoire (*mufakkira*), a form of "reminder" of the contents of a conversation.

5. Non-paper (as of now, there is no Arabic equivalent for this term), an informal agreement, reminiscent of a "gentlemen's agreement" (*ittifāqīyat al-ʾašrāf*).

---

[56] Cf. *Satow* 1957: 57ff. Probably the most famous Arabic diplomatic correspondence was the (originally secret) McMahon-Ḥusayn correspondence, which took place between July 14, 1915, and March 10, 1916. Cf. Great Britain, *Parliamentary Papers*, 1939, Misc., no. 3, Cmd. 5957 and *Hurewitz* 1979, vol. 2: 46ff. Cf. also below (chapter four).

The largest group of United Nations documents originating in Arabic are letters by Arab heads of state, foreign ministers, and diplomats (ambassadors and chargés d'affaires) addressed to the Secretary-General of the United Nations or the president of the Security Council. Messages by heads of state, foreign ministers etc. are usually attached to short introductory notes by their United Nations ambassadors as "annexes", which may, however, constitute the bulk of the given document. All letters that appear as official United Nations documents are translated into all of the six official languages of the United Nations.

Correspondence may also take place between international organizations, e.g., between the League of Arab States and the United Nations. The following is an example of subtype (1) above, taken from the correspondence on the Lockerbie incident:[57]

Item (13), Arabic original

Fī ᵓiṭāri stimrāri jāmiᶜati d-duwali l-ᶜarabīyati fī badli juhūdi-hā buġyata ᵓījādi taswiyatin silmīyatin li-l-ᵓazmati l-lībīyati maᶜa kullin mina l-wilāyāti l-muttaḥidati wa-barīṭāniyā wa-faransā, wa-ᵓilḥāqan bi-risālat-ī la-kum bi-tārīḫi 3/4/94 bi-ḫuṣūṣi qarāri majlisi jāmiᶜati d-duwali l-ᶜarabīyati bi-hāḏā š-šaᵓni wa-l-muqtaraḥi llaḏī taḍammana-hā hāḏā l-qarāru ḫāṣṣatan fī-mā yataᶜallaqu "bi-ᵓijrāᵓi muḥākamatin ᶜādilatin li-l-muštabahi fī-himā min qibali quḍātin iskutlandīyīna wafqa l-qānūni l-iskutlandīyi, wa-fī maqarri maḥkamati ᶜadli d-duwalīyati bi-lā hāy [La Haye], wa-ḥatta majlisi l-ᵓamni ᶜalā ᵓaḫḏi hāḏā l-iqtirāḥi l-jāddi wa-l-jadīdi bi-ᶜayni l-iᶜtibāri, li-l-baḥṯi ᶜan ḥallin silmīyin manᶜan li-ᵓayyi taṣᶜīdin fī l-mawqifi min šaᵓni-hī ziyādata t-tawatturi fī l-minṭaqa".

Wa-fī ḍawᵓi l-mawqifi l-lībīyi l-multazimi bi-hāḏā l-qarāri wa-mā ᵓabdathu l-jamāhīrīyatu l-lībīyatu min murūnatin wa-ᵓījābīyatin kabīratin fī t-taᶜāmuli maᶜa hāḏihī l-ᵓazmati buġyata t-tawaṣṣuli ᵓilā taswiyatin silmīyatin la-hā.

ᵓArjū min-kumu t-takarruma bi-ᶜarḍi hāḏā l-muqtaraḥi l-ᶜarabīyi ᶜalā majlisi l-ᵓamni bi-š-šakli llaḏī tartaᵓawna-hū wa-kull-ī ṯiqatun ᵓanna-kum satuwāṣilūna badla l-juhūdi min ᵓajli t-tawaṣṣuli li-ḥallin silmīyin li-hāḏihī l-ᵓazma.

Item (13), official English translation

In the context of the continuing efforts of the League of Arab States to seek a peaceful settlement to the crisis between the Libyan Arab Jamahiriya and the United States, the United Kingdom and France;

---

[57] Cf. UN-doc. S/1994/928 (Letter dated 28 July 1994 from the Secretary-General of the League of Arab States [Ahmed Esmat Abdel Meguid] addressed to the Secretary-General [Boutros Boutros-Ghali]) (Arabic and English), p. 1.

Further to my letter of 3 April 1994 concerning the resolution adopted by the Council of the League on the matter and the proposal made in the resolution, in particular, "that the two suspects should be judged equitably by Scottish judges in conformitiy with Scottish law, and that their trial should take place at the seat of the International Court of Justice at The Hague, and to urge the Security Council to take this new and constructive proposal into consideration with a view to arriving at a peaceful settlement and avoiding any escalation which might exacerbate tension in the region";

And in light of Libya's attitude of compliance with the resolution and of the flexibility and great responsiveness shown by the Libyan Jamahiriya in its handling of the crisis in a desire for a peaceful settlement;

I request you to be so kind as to present this inter-Arab proposal to the Security Council in whatever form you deem appropriate. I am fully confident that you will continue your efforts to reach a peaceful solution to this crisis.

Exchanges of notes (2) and notes verbales (3) follow the English and French coined models quite faithfully. No Arabic aides-mémoire (4) or non-papers (5) are officially available. As an example, here is an excerpt of an exchange of notes (2):[58]

Item (14), English/Arabic

The Chief, Special United States Diplomatic Mission of the Kingdom of the Yemen [William A. Eddy], to the Deputy Minister of Foreign Affairs [Abdul Karim Mutahhar]

Sana'a, May 4, 1946

English original: Excellency: I have the honor to make the following statement of my Government's understanding of the agreement reached through conversations held at Sana'a April 14 to May 4 by representatives of the Government of the United States of America and the Government of the Kingdom of the Yemen with reference to diplomatic and consular representation, juridical protection, commerce and navigation as hereafter defined. [...]

English: Article 1

The United States of America and the Kingdom of the Yemen will exchange diplomatic representatives and consular officers at a date which shall be fixed by mutual agreement between the two Governments. [...]

English original: If the above provisions are acceptable to the Government of the Kingdom of the Yemen this note and the reply signifying assent thereto shall, if agreeable to that Government, be regarded as constituting an agreement between the two Governments which shall become effective on the date of such acceptance.

Accept, Excellency, the assurances of my highest consideration.

The Yemen Deputy Minister of Foreign Affairs [Abdul Karim Mutahhar] to the Chief, Special United States Diplomatic Mission of the Kingdom of the Yemen [William A. Eddy]

---

[58] Exchange of Notes between the United States of America and the Kingdom of the Yemen Constituting an Agreement Relating to Friendship and Commerce. Sana'a, 4 May 1946, *UNTS*, vol. 4 (1947), pp. 165ff. The Arabic version of the agreement is embedded in the Arabic response by the Yemeni deputy foreign minister.

Sana'a, May 4, 1946

Arabic original: L-ī š-šarafu ʾan ʾufīda saʿādata-kum bi-stilām-ī li-ḫiṭābi-kumu l-muʾarraḫi fī 4 māyū 1946 al-muwāfiqi 3 jamādā ṯ-ṯāniyati 1365 wa-llaḏī naṣṣu-hū ka-mā yalī:

Official English translation: I have the honor to acknowledge receipt of your Excellency's letter dated May 4, 1946, corresponding to Jamada-al-Thaniya 3, 1365, the text of which is as follows:

Official Arabic translation: L-ī š-šarafu ʾan ʾubayyina fahma ḥukūmat-ī li-l-ittifāqi llaḏī tamma baʿda muḥādaṯātin jarat muʾaḫḫaran fī ṣanʿāʾa yawma 14 ʾabrīla ʾilā 4 māyū 1946 bayna mumaṯṯilī ḥukūmati l-wilāyāti l-muttaḥidati l-ʾamrīkīyati wa-bayna ḥukūmati mamlakati l-yamani bi-šaʾni t-tamṯīli s-siyāsīyi wa-l-qunṣulīyi wa-ṣ-ṣiyānati l-qaḍāʾīyati wa-t-tijārīyati wa-l-milāḥati ka-mā hiya muwaḍḍaḥatun ʾadnā-hu. [...]

Arabic: Al-māddatu l-ʾūlā

Sa-tatabādalu l-wilāyātu l-muttaḥidatu l-ʾamrīkīyatu wa-mamlakatu l-yamani l-mumaṯṯilīna d-diblūmāsīyīna wa-l-qunṣulīyīna wa-ḏālika fī t-tārīḫi llaḏī sa-yuʿayyanu bi-l-ittifāqi bayna l-ḥukūmatayn. [...]

Arabic original: Wa-ʾinn-ī bi-n-niyābati ʿan ḥukūmati l-yamani ʾufīdu-kum bi-muwāfaqati ḥukūmat-ī ʿalā n-nuṣūṣi l-maḏkūrati fī hāḏihī l-ittifāqīyati wa-llatī tuʿtabaru sāriyata l-mafʿūli min tārīḫi hāḏā t-tawqīʿ.

Official English translation: On behalf of the Government of Yemen, I declare my Government's adherence to the provisions stated in this Agreement which is considered efffective on the date of signature.

To round up the presentation of types of diplomatic correspondence, here is an example of a note verbale (3), which features an interesting allusion to "the usurped rights of the Arab nation in Palestine" (*[a]l-ḥuqūq[u] l-muġtaṣabat[u] li-l-ʾummati l-ʿarabīyati fī filasṭīn*):[59]

Item (15), Arabic original

Tuhdī l-mumaṯṯilīyatu d-dāʾimatu li-l-ʿirāqi taḥīyāti-hā ʾilā l-ʾamānati l-ʿāmmati li-l-ʾumami l-muttaḥidati wa-tawaddu ʾan tušīra ʾilā l-waṯīqati A/45/916 al-muʾarraḫati fī 8 kānūna ṯ-ṯānī/yanāyir 1991 allatī taḍammanat risālata l-mumaṯṯili d-dāʾimi li-miṣra llatī yaʿtariḍu fī-hā ʿalā muḏakkarati wafdi l-ʿirāqi A/45/891 wa-Add.1 ka-mā yuʿlinu fī-hā taḥaffuẓa n-niẓāmi l-miṣrīyi ʿalā ʾawrāqi tafwīḍi l-wafdi l-ʿirāqī.

ʾInna-nā ʾiḏ narfiḍu muḏakkarata l-wafdi l-miṣrīyi nušīru ʾilā ʾanna hāḏā l-wafda lam yatajarraʾ ʿalā t-taḥaffuẓi ʿalā ʾawrāqi tafwīḍi wafdi l-kiyāni ṣ-ṣahyūnīyi l-ʿunṣurī. Ka-mā ʾanna-hū tamādā fī mawqifi-hī l-istislāmīyi ʾilā darajati taṣwīti-hī li-ṣāliḥi l-ʾijrāʾi n-nurwījīyi llaḏī ḥāla dūna ttiḫāḏi ʾayyi

[59] UN-doc. A/45/944 (Note verbale dated 24 January 1991 from the Permanent Mission of Iraq to the United Nations addressed to the Secretariat) (Arabic and English).

ʾijrāʾin ʿalā mašrūʿi t-taʿdīli l-ʿarabīyi llaḏī ṭuriḥa fī d-dawrati s-sābiʿati li-l-jamʿīyati l-ʿāmmati, mim-mā ʾulḥiqa ʾafdaḥu l-ʾaḍrāri bi-mawqifi l-majmūʿati l-ʿarabīyati fī hāḏā ṣ-ṣadadi bi-šiklin ḫāṣṣin wa-bi-l-qaḍīyati l-filasṭīnīyati bi-šiklin ʿāmm.

ʾInna wafda-nā yuʾakkidu ʾanna qarāra l-waḥdati l-indimājīyati llaḏī ʾaʿāda l-kuwayta ʾilā waṭani-hā l-ʾummi l-ʿirāqi fī ṯāmini min ʾāb/ʾaġusṭus 1990 qad karrasa l-ʿadālata wa-š-šarʿīyata wa-ʾaʿāda l-ḥaqqa l-muġtaṣaba li-š-šaʿbi l-ʿirāqīyi, ka-mā ʾanna-hū yušakkilu ḫuṭwatan ʿalā ṭarīqi ʾiʿādati l-ḥuqūqi l-muġtaṣabati li-l-ʾummati l-ʿarabīyati fī filasṭīn.

Narjū ʾan tunšara hāḏihī r-risālatu ka-waṯīqatun min waṯāʾiqi l-jamʿīyati l-ʿāmmati fī ʾiṭāri l-bandi 3 min jadwali l-ʾaʿmāl.

Item (15), official English translation

The Permanent Mission of Iraq presents its compliments to the Secretariat of the United Nations and has the honour to refer to document A/45/916 of 8 January 1991 containing a letter from the Permanent Representative of Egypt in which he protests against the notes of the delegation of Iraq contained in documents A/45/891 and Add.1 and registers the reservation of the Egyptian régime with respect to the credentials of the Iraqi delegation.

In rejecting the letter of the Egyptian delegation, we should like to point out that this delegation did not venture to express a reservation with regard to the credentials of the delegation of the racist Zionist entity. It has, moreover, persisted in its capitulationist position to the extent of voting in favour of the Norwegian motion which prevented any action being taken on the Arab draft amendment submitted to the General Assembly at its previous session, thereby causing the gravest harm to the position adopted by the Arab group on this matter, in particular, and to the Palestinian cause, in general.

Our delegation affirms that the decision made on the merger that restored Kuwait to its motherland, Iraq, on 8 August 1990 advanced justice and legitimacy and restored a usurped right to the Iraqi people, just as it constitutes a step on the way to the restoration of the usurped rights of the Arab nation in Palestine.

We request you to have this letter circulated as a document of the General Assembly under agenda item 3.

4. *Periodic reports*

States that become parties to international human rights conventions have to submit reports at certain intervals on their domestic implementation of the human rights precepts at issue. Such reports, which often are presented in Arabic,[60] are then discussed by com-

[60] This is in fact the default case. Only the Maghreb states Algeria, Morocco, and Tunisia submit their periodic reports (as well as other UN documents) in French. Relatively few periodic reports by Arab states have been submitted in English (cf. below (appendix)).

mittees composed of international lawyers, who question delegations from states parties and comment on the relationship between international human rights standards and the domestic situation in the particular country.

The following is an excerpt of a report of submitted by Yemen to the Committee on Civil and Political Rights ("Human Rights Committee"), featuring many typical traits of Islamic discourse such as copious quotation from the Qur'ān and the *sunna*, including the important Islamic concept of collective rights and responsibilities:[61]

Item (16), Arabic original

Yamliku l-yamanu tārīḫan ḥaḍārīyan ᶜarīqan yamtaddu ᶜabra l-ʾajyāli wa-l-ʾazmāni jussidat ḫilāla-hū l-kaṯīru mina l-ʾaᶜmāli l-ʾinsānīyati wa-l-ḥaḍārīyati wa-llatī lā zālat maᶜālimu-hā šāhidatan ᶜalā ḏālika ḥattā l-yawm.

ʾInna l-ʾislāma bi-n-nisbati li-š-šaᶜbi l-yamanīyi kāna wa-mā zāla ʾasāsa takwīni-hī l-fikrīyi wa-r-rūḥīyi, fa-huwa bi-mabādiʾi-hī wa-qiyami-hī l-ʾaḫlāqīyati llatī tarassaḫat ladā l-ʾinsāni l-yamanīyi munḏu ʾakṯara min 14 qarnan mina z-zamani jaᶜalat-hu yudriku ᶜan yaqīnin ʾanna llāha subḥāna-hū wa-taᶜālā karrama l-ʾinsāna wa-faḍḍala-hū ᶜalā jamīᶜi maḫlūqāti-hī: ḥayṯu qāla fī muḥkami ʾāyāti-hī *"wa-la-qad karramnā banī ʾādama wa-ḥamalnā-hum fī l-barri wa-l-baḥri wa-razaqnā-hum mina ṭ-ṭayyibāti wa-faḍḍalnā-hum ᶜalā kaṯīrin mim-man ḫalaqnā tafḍīlan"*.[62]

ʾInna hāḏihī n-naẓrata l-ʾislāmīyata li-l-ʾinsāni tatamayyizu bi-š-šumūli, fa-l-ʾislāmu lā yaᶜnī bi-fardin dūna ʾāḫara fa-l-kullu sawāsiya *"fa-lā faḍla li-ᶜarabīyin ᶜalā ᶜajamīyin ʾil-lā bi-t-taqwā"* (ḥadīṯun nabawī).[63] Wa-l-ʾislāmu yarᶜā l-farda ka-mā yarᶜā l-jamāᶜata kulla-hā; fa-ḥayātu-hū wa-karāmatu-hū wa-ḥurrīyatu-hū wa-ʾamnu-hū wa-ḥuqūqu-hū tusāwī fī ʾahammīyati-hā ḥayāta wa-ḥurrīyata wa-ʾamna wa-ḥuqūqa l-mujtamaᶜi kulli-hī. Wa-qad qāla taᶜālā *"wa-man qatala nafsan bi-ġayri nafsin ʾaw fasādin fī l-ʾarḍi fa-ka-ʾanna-mā qatala n-nāsa jamīᶜan"*.[64] Wa-inṭilāqan min hāḏihī l-maᶜānī l-karīmati wa-l-mafāhīmi li-qīmati l-ʾinsāni wa-ḥuqūqi-hī kāna jihādu wa-niḍālu l-yamanīyīna ṭawāla l-marāḥili l-māḍiyati li-stiᶜādati l-makānati t-tārīḫīyati wa-l-ḥaḍārīyati li-l-yaman. Wa-kāna nitāja kifāḥi wa-niḍāli l-yamanīyīna ᶜabra z-zamāni wa-l-makāni taḥqīqu l-waḥdati l-yamanīyati fī 22 ʾīyār/māyū 1990. Wa-kāna ḏālika stijābatan mawḍūᶜīyatan li-ẓurūfi l-ᶜaṣri wa-simāti-hī l-ᶜāmmati wa-ḫaṣāʾiṣi-hī l-bārizati llatī tuʾakkidu ᶜalā naḥwin jalīyini r-raġbata l-

---

[61] UN-doc. CCPR/C/82/Add.1 (Arabic and English), p. 3.

[62] This quotation is found in the Qur'ān 17: 70.

[63] This *ḥadīṯ* quotation is found in *Ibn Ḥanbal*, Musnad [no date], vol. 5: 411 (cf. *Wensinck* [1969], vol. 7: 300).

[64] This quotation is found in the Qur'ān 5: 32.

mutazāyidata wa-l-ḥaṯīṯata ladā muḫtalifi l-ʾumami wa-š-šuᶜūbi fī takwīni l-waḥdāti s-siyāsīyati wa-l-iqtiṣādīyati l-kubrā ᶜalā ʾususi l-maṣāliḥi l-muštarikati wa-t-takāmuli l-ᶜilmīyi l-wāsiᶜi, wa-tawfīqan bayna maṣāliḥi l-jamāᶜati l-ʾinsānīyati wa-maṣāliḥi l-ʾafrād. Wa-ʾaṣbaḥati l-waḥdatu l-yamanīyatu hiya silaḥa š-šaᶜbi l-yamanīyi li-duḫūli l-ᶜaṣri l-qādimi wa-t-tajārubi maᶜa ẓ-ẓurūfi r-rāhinati llatī yaᶜīšu-hā l-ᶜālam.

Item (16), official English translation

Yemen has a time-honoured history of civilization, typified by numerous human and cultural achievements, the traces of which can still be seen today.

Islam has always formed the basis of the intellectual and spiritual development of the Yemeni people; the principles and moral values of Islam, instilled over 14 centuries ago, made them positively aware that Almighty God exalted man and preferred him over all the creatures, for God said in His Holy Book: *"We have bestowed blessings on the sons of Adam and guided them by land and sea. We have provided them with good things and exalted them above many of Our creatures."*

This Islamic view of mankind is comprehensive; in Islam, all individuals are treated with the same concern, since everyone is equal. According to the Apostle of God: *"No distinction shall be made between an Arab and a non-Arab, except in terms of their piety."* Islam provides the same protection for both the individual and the community as a whole; the individual's life, freedom, dignity, security and rights are as equally important as those of society as a whole. In the words of God: *"Whoever kills a human being, except as a punishment for murder or other wicked crimes, shall be looked upon as though he has killed all mankind."* These noble ideas and concepts of the worth and rights of the human person formed the basis of the past efforts and struggles of the Yemeni people to restore Yemen's position in history and civilization, the outcome of which was the achievement of Yemeni unification on 22 May 1990. This was an objective response to the circumstances of the age and its general and more outstanding features, which clearly highlighted the growing and eager desire of various nations and peoples to form large political and economic unions based on common interests, broad intellectual complementarity and a reconciliation of the individual and collective interests of mankind. Yemeni unification is now the armour of the Yemeni people as they enter the coming age and respond to the present world situation.

5. Oral contributions

In the context of this study, the following three kinds of oral contributions (as found in the written documentation) are most important: first, discussions in the course of drafting international human rights conventions;[65] second, summary records of discussions of the reports that are presented to the treaty bodies by states parties; and third, the concluding observations of the treaty bodies on these reports and discussions. However, only the first type of statement is recorded in Arabic, while summary records and concluding observations are issued

[65] Examples are provided below (chapter five).

only in English or French. While the recommendations contained in concluding observations are not legally binding on the states involved, they nevertheless have considerable impact in the formation of opinion.

IV. Linguistic features of diplomatic Arabic

1. Syntactic features

Though diplomatic Arabic is highly standardized, its syntactical features still deserve attention.[66] Diplomatic Arabic exhibits many typical features of Modern Standard Arabic, such as the double-headed *ʾiḍāfa*,[67] as found, for instance, in the following example:[68]

Item (17), Arabic original

Wa-ʾaḫīran ʾarjū ʾan taṯiqū bi-ʾanna bilād-ī sawfa lan tataraddada fī l-istifāḍati min *ʾimkānīyāti wa-ḫayrāti l-ʾumami l-muttaḥidati* bi-ṣifatin ʿāmmatin, [...]

Item (17), official English translation

Lastly, I should like to assure you that my country will not hesitate, if necessary, to take advantage of *the capacities and competence of the United Nations* in general, [...]

Another modern feature is the unorthodox use of tense and aspect markers, as found, for instance, in the following example involving past *lam* and future *lan*:[69]

Item (18), Arabic original

Nawaddu ʾan nukarrira mā sabaqa ʾan ʾaḫṭarnā bi-hī raʾīsa lajnati l-jazāʾāti wa-huwa ʾanna l-jamāhīrīyata *lam wa-lan* tantahika tilka l-jazāʾāti, [...]

---

[66] For general syntactical features as found in Arabic legal texts, cf. *Emery* 1989 and *Aziz* 1993.

[67] For this phenomenon, cf. *Wild* 1982b: 54 and *Gully* 1993: 23ff.

[68] Cf. UN-doc. S/1994/870 (Letter dated 24 July 1994 from the Minister for Foreign Affairs of the Republic of Yemen [Mohamed Salem Basendwah] addressed to the Secretary-General [Boutros Boutros-Ghali], Annex to the Letter dated 25 July 1994 from the Permanent Representative of Yemen to the United Nations [Abdalla S. Al-Ashtal] addressed to the Secretary-General [Boutros Boutros-Ghali]) (Arabic and English), p. 3.

[69] UN-doc. S/1995/633 (Letter dated 31 July 1995 from the Permanent Representative of the Libyan Arab Jamahiriya to the United Nations [Mohamed Azwai] addressed to the Secretary-General [Boutros Boutros-Ghali]) (Arabic and English), p. 2.

Item (18), official English translation

We should like to reiterate what we stated to the Chairman of the Committee on sanctions namely, that the Jamahiriya *has not, and will not,* violate those sanctions, [...]

The Arabic equivalent to the *whereas*-clauses in the preambles to treaties and conventions are *ʾiḏ*-clauses and clauses introduced by adverbial accusatives.[70]

Diplomatic Arabic exhibits a high degree of nominalization, a circumstance that has recently been investigated critically by the Egyptian delegation to the United Nations. A typical example of this phenomenon is the Arabic wording of the concluding phrase in diplomatic letters addressed to the Security Council or the Secretary-General of the United Nations, as seen, for instance, in the following document:[71]

Item (19), Arabic original

Sa-ʾakūnu mumtannan law tafaḍḍaltum bi-*taʾmīni tawziʿi hāḏihī r-risālati* [...] ka-waṯīqatin rasmīyatin min waṯāʾiqi majlisi l-ʾamn.

Item (19), official English translation

I should be grateful if you would *have this letter [...] circulated* as a document of the Security Council.

2. *Lexical features*

The lexicon is among the most prominent features of diplomatic Arabic.[72] Broadly speaking, diplomatic Arabic has succeeded well in adapting itself to the innovations in political and technical terminology required in United Nations documents. The former Arabic term for the United States, *ʾitāzūnīyā* (phonetically "États-Unis") has long

---

[70] Cf. the examples above in the preamble to the Egyptian-Israeli peace treaty.

[71] UN-doc. S/23102 (Letter dated 30 September 1991 from the Permanent Representative of Iraq to the United Nations [Abdul Amir A. Al-Anbari] addressed to the Secretary-General [Javier Perez de Cuellar]).

[72] For terminological problems in international law, cf. *Weisgerber* 1961, *Reuter* 1970 *Pitamić* 1971, and *Podlech* 1976. For general terminological problems in modern Arabic, cf. *Monteil* 1960, *Issawi* 1967, *Wild* 1969, *Stetkevych* 1970, *Blau* 1981, and *Carter* 1993. For terminological problems as applying to Arabic legal texts, cf. *Lewis* 1974b, *Lewis* 1980, *Rebhan* 1986, *Barkho* 1987, *Ayalon* 1987, and *Lewis* 1988. Among dictionaries of modern political and diplomatic Arabic are *Lewis* 1956, *Fawq al-ʿĀda* 1974, and *ʿAbdallāh* 1982. A dictionary of modern diplomatic Hebrew is *Marwick* 1980.

since become *al-wilāyāt al-muttaḥida* via *al-ʾīyālāt al-muttaḥida*.[73] The term for 'states' in the sense of "Länder" is sometimes also rendered as *ʾaqṭār*.[74] Differences in the Arabic rendering of an English political term can depend on geographical as well as on fine semantic differences, as in the case of the triplet *quṭrī/qawmī/waṭanī* 'national'. Often, synonymous parallel terms are in use, as in the case of *qūwa ẓāhira/ ẓurūf ẓāhira* 'force majeure' and *raff qārrī/raṣīf qārrī/musaṭṭaḥ qārrī* 'continental shelf'. Some terms, such as 'case law', still pose problems: while there has arisen a consensus to use the gloss *ijtihād qaḍāʾī*, some translators and interpreters use unacceptable glosses such as *qānūn al-ḥāla*.[75] The translation of Arabic terms such as *fidāʾī* 'kamikaze'[76] and *ʾirhābī* 'terrorist' may clash with the translator's own ideological position. A historically interesting example of mistranslation occurred in the McMahon-Ḥusayn correspondence. The English term *men-of-war* (a metaphor for 'battleships') is rendered in the Arabic version as *rijāl al-ḥarb*, where the metaphor is not overtly intelligible. The exact Arabic context, which does not appear in the English editions of the correspondence, is:[77]

Item (20), Arabic version

Ṯumma yajibu ʾan lā tutᶜibū ʾanfusa-kum bi-ʾirsāli ṭ-ṭayyārāti ʾaw *rijāli l-ḥarbi*, li-ʾilqāʾi l-manāšīri, wa-ʾiḏāᶜati š-šāʾiᶜāti, ka-mā kuntum tafᶜalūna min qablu, li-ʾanna l-qaḍīyata qad qurrirati l-ʾān.

Item (20), English version

You should not bother to send war planes or *battleships* for the sake of dropping leaflets or broadcasting rumors, as you used to do, because a decision on the issue has been reached by now.

---

[73] Cf. *Didaoui* 1989, vol. 2: 633 and 689.

[74] This observation is due to Dr. Aref *Hajjaj* [personal communication]. Cf. also the preamble to the Pact of the League of Arab States above.

[75] This observation is due to Mahmud *Suqi* [personal communication].

[76] Cf. *Tabory* 1980: 89f for a diplomatic quarrel between Bahrain and Israel about the use of the term *fidāʾī* (UN-doc. A/C.1/PV.2016).

[77] This observation is due to Professor Stefan *Wild*. The Arabic text is reproduced in *al-ʾAḥmad* 1985: 91. For several references to these texts and to the problem as to which language version derives from which, cf. *Wagner* 1971: 107, n. 3 and *Lapidoth/Hirsch* (eds.) 1992: 2ff.

3. *Stylistic features*

Further interesting features of diplomatic Arabic include the resorting to historical literary forms, such as certain forms of poetry.[78] An especially interesting example is the following poem by a former ambassador of Qatar to the United Nations, which was part of a planned statement at the Security Council on June 1, 1994. Its function is to hail Arab understanding in general and Yemeni unity in particular:[79]

Item (21), Arabic original

Man mubliġu l-kawni ʾanna l-ʾamra muʾtamin(un)
  Tabqā wa-taslamu fī ʾawṭāni-nā l-yaman(u)
Dāru l-ḥaḍārati wa-ḏuẖru l-ᶜarabi mutlad-ī
  Tāha l-wujūdu bi-hā wa-stabšara z-zaman(u)
Yā dārata l-majdi wa-l-ʾaḏwāʾi min yaman(in)
  Qad hazza-nī fī darā-ki š-šawqu wa-š-šajan(u)
Ḥamaltu hamma-ki ʾīṯāran ᶜalā kubr(in)
  Wa-l-wajdu yalẓā ka-mā talẓā bi-ki l-miḥan(u)
Nafḥu š-šamāli ʾiḏā naddā bi-ṣayyibi-hī
  Wāfā l-janūba bi-mā yuhmī wa-yaẖtazin(u)
Ṣanᶜāʾu ḥāḍiratu t-tārīẖi ġāliyat-ī
  Wa-jannatu l-ẖuldi fī ʾalṭāfi-hā ᶜadan(u)
Kiltā-humā fī suwaydāʾ-ī wa-fī badan-ī
  Tanzilāni humā l-ī r-ruḥu wa-l-badan(u)
ᶜAynā-humā fī ʾasārīr-ī wa-ʾaẖyilat-ī
  Yaṭūfu fī-hā l-hawā wa-suhdu wa-l-wasan(u)
Nāma l-ẖālīyūna ʾil-lā muqlatun sahirat
  Fa-mā l-yamānīyu ʾil-lā sāhiru l-faṭin(u)
Ṭību l-yamānīyi fī ʾīmāḍi bāriqi-hī
  Yuhmī samāḥan ka-mā tuhmī l-ḥayā l-muzan(u)
Wa-yastaḍīʾu bi-nūrin ġibba ġurbati-hī
  Fa-mā l-yamānīyu ʾil-lā l-mājidu ẓ-ẓaᶜan(u)
Mā-ḏā naqūlu bi-tārīẖin yunāšidu-nā
  ʾAn narᶜawiya fa-kafā-nā l-buʾsu wa-l-ḥuzun(u)
Ḥulmu š-šuᶜūbi ʾiḏā mā ndāḥa ᶜan ġabaš(in)

[78] For references to examples of Arabic political poetry, cf. *Lewis* 1988: 122. Other examples of Arabic political poetry include the Qaṣīda by Maḥmūd *Darwīš*, Madīḥ aẓ-ẓill al-ᶜālī, which was recited at a conference of the PLO in Algiers [this was kindly pointed out to the author by Professor Stefan *Wild*]. It is also noteworthy that one of the most famous modern Arab poets, Nizār *Qabbānī*, started out as a professional diplomat.

[79] UN-doc. S/1994/651 (Annex to the Letter dated 1 June 1994 from the Permanent Representative of Qatar to the United Nations [Hassan Ali Hussain Al-Ni'mah] addressed to the President of the Security Council [at that time: Salim Bin Mohammed Al-Khussaiby]) (Arabic and English), pp. 3f and p. 3, respectively.

Fa-l-fajru ʾātin bi-hī l-ʾīḍāḥu wa-l-ʿalin(u)
ʾIn-nī ʾatūqu ʾilā l-ʾahlayni fī yaman(in)
Laysat tamziqu-hū lʾaḍġānu wa-l-fitan(u)
Bāqin ʿalā d-dahri yarqā li-l-ʿulā yamanan
Muwaḥḥadan yatasāmī bi-smi-hī l-waṭan(u)

Šukran la-kum sayyid-ī r-raʾīsu ʿalā luṭfi-kum wa-ḥusni stimāʿi-kum wa-s-salāmu ʿalay-kum.

Item (21), official English translation

Who will tell the world that all is well
And that Yemen survives and is safe and sound among our lands?
Home of civilizations, treasure of the Arabs from time immemorial,
The pride of creation and the delight of time.
O Yemen, abode of greatness and a royal race,
In your shelter I tremble with nostalgia and grief.
I chose to espouse your mighty cause in spite of the difficulty,
And the passion flames with the conflagration of your tribulations.
When the northern breeze brings rainy clouds,
It gives the south flowing water in abundant supply.
My precious San'a, historic metropolis,
And, amid the graces of paradise, Aden,
Both are in my heart and in my body,
Abiding in my spiritual and my physical being.
Both are in my mind and in my imagination,
Where yearning, sleeplessness and slumber range.
The carefree slept, but one eye was open.
The Yemeni is ever wakeful and alert.
The Yemeni's goodness in a lightning flash
Flows with magnanimity as the clouds pour with rain,
And he seeks guidance from a light after an absence.
The Yemeni is ever noble, ever moving onwards.
What shall we say to a history that calls on us
To take heed for we have had sufficient woe and grief?
The dream of the peoples when it emerges from the darkness -
With the dawn comes enlightenment and disclosure.
I wish for the two groups in Yemen
That they may not be torn apart by hatred and dissension,
But, surviving for all time, may rise to the heights
As a united Yemen to the greater glory of the Arab homeland.

Thank you, Mr. President.

The same author also composed a poem recently which he presented during a meeting of the Arab ambassadors to the United Nations (the "Arab group"), in which he argued for a second term for Secretary-General Boutros Boutros-Ghali.[80]

[80] As this was a closed meeting, the relevant UN document was not accessible to the author. The poem itself was published, however, in the Arab newspaper Al-Ḥayāt of September 14, 1996. Cf. *Darġām*, R. 1996. "Al-majmūʿa al-ʿarabīya fī l-ʾumam al-muttaḥida taḥtafī bi-Ġālī muʾayyidatan ʾiʿādat intiḫābi-hī", Al-Ḥayāt, September 14, 1996, p. 7.

4. *Pragmatic features*

Euphemistic terminology and discourse is a necessity in diplomacy. The degree of politeness and the means of circumlocution, however, may differ from language to language, as is apparent, for instance, in letters of recommendation.[81] With respect to Arabic, this is an entirely new area of research and deserves close observation. It has been alleged, for instance, that such difficulties may have played a role in the misunderstandings that arose in talks between Ṣaddām Ḥusayn and the last American ambassador in Iraq, April Glaspie, about "border corrections" between Iraq and Kuwait, a term which could have been misunderstood by the Iraqi side as an implicit approval of military attack on Kuwait.

While euphemistic style is a universal feature of diplomatic language,[82] certain elements of euphemistic and metaphorical language are specific to Arabic. In the Gulf War between Iraq and Iran, the term *ʾaḥdāf baḥrīya* 'naval targets' was the common euphemism for attacked supertankers in the Persian Gulf. When foreigners were being held hostage in Iraq prior to "Operation Desert Storm", this detention was officially labeled *istiḍāfa* 'invitation to hospitality'.[83] Sometimes, a somewhat pompous phrase has to be narrowed down in an accurate translation, as in the case of *al-ʾinjāzātu llatī taḥaqqaqat fī ẓilli qiyādati ḥukūmati l-ḥizbi wa-ṯ-ṯawra*, literally 'the achievements carried out under the leadership of the Government of the Party and Revolution', i.e., 'the Iraqi government's achievements'.[84] A historical example of euphemistic language was the Ottoman term *waqāʾiʿ ḫayrīya* 'beneficiary events', as used for a massacre committed by janizary armies.[85]

---

[81] Cf. below (chapter three).

[82] Cf. *Dolph* 1988. In United Nations contexts and elsewhere, euphemisms in the realms of "war and peace" and "human rights" have included such terms as "armed conflict" for *war* and "moderate physical pressure" for *torture*.

[83] Cf. UN-doc. S/21651 (Letter dated 19 August 1990 from the Permanent Representative of Iraq to the United Nations [Abdul Amir A. Al-Anbari] addressed to the Secretary-General [Javier Perez de Cuellar]) (Arabic and English), p. 3.

[84] Cf. *Barkho* 1987: 145.

[85] This observation was kindly pointed out to the author by Professor Stefan *Wild*.

5. *Islamic formulae*

A large inventory of quotations from the Qurʾān and the Islamic traditions (*sunna*) regularly appears in legal context, either literally or metaphorically, and may cause considerable difficulties for translators and interpreters as well as for legal scholars and diplomats who have to deal with these documents.[86] Generally speaking, such quotations are more frequent in the realm of human rights than in the realm of war and peace. The function of the quotations is twofold: they can either be used to show an assumed equality between the Islamic and the Western perspective on international (human rights) law, or they can be used to show an assumed superiority of the Islamic perspective.

Though Arabic-language treaties between Arab (and/or other Islamic) states more or less adhere to the formal international requirements for such documents, the *basmala*[87] is often, but by no means always, used to introduce bi- and multilateral treaties between Arab states as well as Arabic diplomatic letters. The already-mentioned Charter of the Islamic Conference features the *basmala* at the beginning of its preamble, whereas the more secular Pact of the League of Arab States does not. Inner-Arab and inner-Islamic treaties with "emotional" content and character, as exemplified in the phrase *ʾuḫūwa ʿarabīya* 'Arab brotherhood',[88] tend to start out with the *basmala*, but not treaties with more prosaic content like the avoidance of double taxation or establishment of air traffic, to name just two frequent subjects in bilateral treaties. As an example, here is an excerpt of a preamble to a treaty with "emotional" character:[89]

---

[86] Such Islamic formulae can occur, of course, in almost any context. Cf. *Piamenta* 1979 for the impact of Islamic formulae on various aspects of everyday life.

[87] *Basmala* is an acronym of the Islamic formula *bi-smi llāhi r-raḥmāni r-raḥīm* 'in the name of God, the Merciful, the Compassionate', which opens all *sūras* but one in the Qurʾān and which is used by traditionally oriented Muslims to introduce almost any written or oral statement. For the different pragmatic functions of the *basmala*, cf. *Piamenta* 1979: 32ff and *Wild* 1994.

[88] Cf., for instance, Arabie Saoudienne et Irak. Traité de fraternité arabe et d'alliance. Signé à Bagdad, le 2 avril 1936, *LNTS*, vol. 174 (1937); Iraq and Transjordan. Treaty of Brotherhood and Alliance. Signed at Baghdad, on 14 April 1947, *UNTS*, vol. 23 (1948/49). Such treaties may also contain references to such concepts as *wadd ʾaḫawī* 'fraternal unity', *tamassuk bi-rābiṭat al-ʿurūba* 'tenacity to the Arab bond' and *ʾahdāf ʿarabīya ʿulyā* 'high Arab aims' (cf., for instance, Kuwait and Iraq. Agreed Minutes regarding the restoration of friendly relations, recognition and related matters. Signed at Baghdad, on 4 October 1963, *UNTS*, vol. 485 (1964), pp. 324f and p. 326).

[89] Arabie Saoudienne et Irak. Traité de fraternité arabe et d'alliance. Signé à Bagdad, le 2 avril 1936, *LNTS*, vol. 174 (1937), p. 136 and p. 132.

Item (22), Arabic original

Bi-smi llāhi r-raḥmāni r-raḥīmi,

ḥaḍratu ṣāḥibi l-jalālati maliku l-ʿirāqi,

ḥaḍratu ṣāḥibi l-jalālati maliku l-mamlakati l-ʿarabīyati s-saʿūdīyati,

bināʾan ʿalā r-rawābiṭi l-ʾislāmīyati wa-l-waḥdati l-qawmīyati llatī tajmaʿu-humā wa-buġyata l-muḥāfaẓati ʿalā salāmati bilādi-himā wa-bināʾan ʿalā mā taqtaḍī-hi l-ḥājatu l-māssatu li-t-taʿāwuni fī-mā bayna-humā wa-t-tafāhumi fī š-šuʾūni llatī tahummu maṣlaḥata mamlakatay-himā fa-qadi ttafaqā ʿalā ʿaqdi muʿāhadati ʾuḫūwatin ʿarabīyatin wa-taḥālufin wa-ʿayyanā ʿan-humā li-hāḏā l-ġaraḍi mandūbayni mufāwwaḍayn: [...]

Wa-baʿda ʾan tabādalā waṯāʾiqa tafwīḍi-himā fa-wajadā-hā muṭābiqatan li-l-ʾuṣūli taḥālafā wa-taʿāhadā ʿalā l-mawāddi l-ʾātiya. [...]

Item (22), official English translation

In the name of God the Merciful the Compassionate,

His Majesty the King of Iraq and

His Majesty the King of Saudi Arabia,

In view of the ties of the Islamic faith and of racial unity which unite them; desirous of safeguarding the integrity of their territories; and having regard to the necessity which they feel for mutual co-operation and understanding in regard to matters affecting the interests of their Kingdoms;

Have agreed to conclude a Treaty of Arab Brotherhood and Alliance, and for this purpose have appointed as their Plenipotentiaries: [...]

Who, having reciprocally communicated their full powers found in due form, have entered into an Alliance and have concluded the following Treaty. [...]

Many Arabic letters and oral statements in United Nations context, while formally adhering to international standards, exhibit a vast use of Qurʾānic quotations and other Islamic formulae. It has been shown that such formulae often have a demarcating function in addition to conveying their overt religious message. This is clearly the case, for instance, in the following quotation, which concludes with the formula *wa-llāhu ʾakbar* 'and God is great':[90]

---

[90] UN-doc. S/24118 (Statement by the head of the Iraqi delegation, Mr. Tariq Aziz, Deputy Prime Minister, at the Conference on Environment and Development, Brazil (3-14 June 1992), Annex to the Letter dated 18 June 1992 from the Permanent Representative of Iraq to the United Nations [Abdul Amir A. Al-Anbari] addressed to the Secretary-General [Javier Perez de Cuellar]) (Arabic and English), p. 7 and p. 6, respectively. Following *Wild* 1994: 305f, in which the demarcating function of the *basmala* is dealt with, *wa-llāhu ʾakbar* could be labeled a concluding signal in this context. Ironically, Ṭāriq ʿAzīz is a Christian himself but must, of course, stick to Islamic discourse in his official functions.

Item (23), Arabic original

Hāḏihī hiya risālatu-nā ʾilā l-muʾtamari wa-naʾmulu ʾan tajida ṣ-ṣadā l-maṭlūba bi-l-ittijāhi llaḏī yuḥaqqiqu l-ʿadālata wa-yansajimu maʿa l-ʾahdāfi l-ʾinsānīyati li-hāḏā l-muʾtamar.

Wa-llāhu ʾakbar.

Item (23), official English translation

This is our message to the Conference. We hope that it will find the desired echo along the lines that will achieve justice and accord with the humanitarian goals of the Conference.

God is great.

Many more examples of the use of religious formulae can be found in Iraqi and Kuwaiti diplomatic documents (cf. also below). Here is a further example, which, again, refers to the idea of the Arab and Islamic *ʾumma*:[91]

Item (24), Arabic original

Wa-llāha nasʾalu ʾan yuḫalliṣa l-ʾummata l-ʿarabīyata wa-l-ʾislāmīyata min šurūri hāḏā n-niẓāmi l-ʾāṯimi llaḏī rtakaba mina l-jarāʾimi fī ḥaqqi š-šaʿbi l-ʿirāqīyi wa-š-šaʿbi l-kuwaytīyi bal wa-l-ʾummati l-ʿarabīyati mā lā yumkinu ḥaṣru-hū wa-lā taṣawwuru-hū, ʾinna-hū samīʿun mujīb.

Wa-sa-ʾakūnu mumtannan law tafaḍḍaltum bi-tawzīʿi hāḏihī r-risālati ka-waṯīqatin min waṯāʾiqi majlisi l-ʾamn.

Item (24), official English translation

We pray that God will rid the Arab and Islamic community of the evil represented by this wicked [Iraqi] régime, which has committed crimes that can neither be counted nor imagined against the Iraqi people, the Kuwaiti people and even the Arab community as a whole. God is all-hearing and answers prayers.

I should be grateful if you would have this letter circulated as a document of the Security Council.

Interestingly, the United Nations Congress on Public International Law, 13-17 March 1995,[92] following the opening statement of the Legal Counsel, started out with a presentation by the deputy foreign minister of the Islamic Republic of Iran, Javad Zarif, in which he made use of the *basmala* as well.

---

[91] UN-doc. S/21566 (Letter dated 20 August 1990 from the Chargé d'affaires a.i. of Kuwait to the United Nations [Mohammad Saad Al Sallal] addressed to the Secretary-General [Javier Perez de Cuellar]) (Arabic and English), p. 2; the concluding phrase *ʾinna-hū samīʿun mujīb* is not found as such in the Qurʾān.

[92] For the program of that conference, cf. UN-doc. A/CONF.176/1*.

E. Summary of Chapter Two

This overview shows clearly that modern diplomatic Arabic style is deeply rooted in the Arab Islamic tradition, both stylistically and spiritually. Quite apart from religious aspects, the Moroccan philosopher Mohamed Aziz Lahbabi attributes strong importance to what he considers to be significant influence of Arabic written prose style on diplomatic Arabic in general – observations which, if made by any "Western" scholar, would immediately expose him or her to the reproach of "Orientalism", i.e., scholarship that is allegedly culturally biased. Specifically, Lahbabi cites the following three characteristics:[93] *at-tarāfud wa-ᶜadam at-tadqīq fī stiᶜmāl al-madlūlāt at-taqrībīya* 'purposeless synonymy and the imprecise usage of approximative significancies', *aṣ-ṣināᶜa al-lafẓīya al-jawfāʾ wa-s-sajᶜ al-muṣṭanaᶜ* 'pompous word artificiality and mannered assonance in prose style' and *al-ḥašw* 'redundancy'. It will be seen in the following chapter that this characterization can be more appropriately replaced by an analysis in terms of Speech Act Theory. In fact, features such as "synonymy", "word artificiality", and "redundancy" in a given language may not automatically be equated to redundancy or triviality of content, but rather are typically to be attributed to cultural/religious connotations, both historical and contemporary.

---

[93] Quoted according to *Didaoui* 1989, vol. 2: 631 and 687.

Chapter Three

The theory of interpretation

"La difficulté dont il s'agit aurait été écartée si, comme il arrive souvent dans les traités avec les peuples barbares dont la langue est mal connue et peut prêter à des ambiguïtés dont ces peuples seraient tentés d'abuser, on avait dit que, en cas de divergence, le texte dans la langue de l'Etat civilisé ferait seul foi." *Despagnet*, F. 1897. "Le conflit entre l'Italie et l'Abyssinie", Revue générale de droit international public 4, p. 29.

A. Legal and linguistic interpretation

In this chapter, the theoretical groundwork will be laid for exploring the hypothesis that different legal norms in international law, as reflected in a "Western" and an Islamic perspective, may be contingent upon and mirrored by the languages used in the respective documents. More specifically, the question will be addressed as to what extent language constitutes the medium for the "intensional" meaning of the Arabic text of diplomatic letters, "declarations of principles", armistice and peace treaties, and other instruments, as well as of International Human Rights conventions and of texts expressing the reservations of Arab states to the said conventions. Here, following Fastenrath (1993), "intensional" will be used as an umbrella term for legal, political, and cultural/religious connotations that can be observed in the Arabic versions of the said documents. The term "extensional" then will refer to the grammatical (syntactical and lexical) surface of the texts or, from a slightly different perspective, to the "list" of occurrences of a given lexical item or syntactic structure .[1]

[1] The present use of this pair of terms somewhat transcends, but nevertheless is in the same general spirit as, the classical definition in first order logic, as laid out in the following quotation (cf. *Fastenrath* 1993: 312): "Extensional definitions involve the listing of all objects to which a word may refer. Intensional definitions clarify the characteristics common to all objects to which a word may refer, and distinguish them from other objects." The classic example proposed by the philosophers Gottlob Frege and Bertrand Russell was the pair of terms *morning star* and *evening star*. Both terms have the same

The theory of interpretation used herein will rely both on the traditional methods of treaty interpretation[2] and on the theoretical tools offered by Speech Act Theory. Two issues are crucial in this respect: analysis of the nature and consequences of the textual differences between multiple versions of one and the same document in several languages (among which is Arabic) on the one hand, and intercultural misunderstanding resulting from conflicting norms in the wake of different connotations of certain legal, political, and cultural/religious terms, which need not be specific to the languages used, on the other.

After discussion of theoretical considerations and illustration with sample texts, the theory will then be applied in subsequent chapters to more complex issues representing case studies in the domains of "war and peace" and "human rights". Among other subjects, the Iraqi concepts of "law", "truth", "peace", and "justice" as well as the general Islamic concept of "equality" will be scrutinized in the light of the theoretical tools developed, and a number of general conclusions will be drawn. The method of interpretation will draw heavily on an application of Speech Act Theory to international law developed by Nicholas Onuf and Ulrich Fastenrath.

As will be shown below, cultural and legal concepts in the areas of "war and peace" and "human rights" are far from being congruent, when legal documents of Arab and other Islamic states[3] are compared with legal documents issued by Western democratic systems, even if the terminology used in the respective documents may be similar. This circumstance demands a closer look at the theoretical tools used for analysis. In the present context, "analysis" is understood here simply as the insightful laying open of the hermeneutic problems involved. It does not automatically entail neat patent solutions as a kind of argumentative panacea. It is not even claimed that all the ambiguities cited in this study actually have engendered disputes that need to be formally and theoretically settled, as there may be pragmatic solutions to the issues at hand on a case-by-case basis. Rather, the goal is to develop a systematization and methodology for the solution of potential problems of diplomatic misunderstanding.

"extension", i.e., the planet Venus; however, the "intension" of those terms differs, as there exist clearly different connotations depending on which term is used. Cf. *Frege* 1892a/b and *Russell* 1905.

[2] For an overview and the relevant references, cf. *Verdross/Simma* 1984: 490ff and *Fastenrath* 1991: 176ff.

[3] For a careful definition of "Islamic state", cf., for instance, *Arzt* 1990: 203.

B. The Vienna Convention on the Law of Treaties

The Vienna Convention on the Law of Treaties, articles 31 through 33, provides a set of rules and guidelines for the interpretation of unilingual and multilingual treaties.[4] These rules and guidelines pertain to the investigation of a given legal text from four perspectives: grammatical (i.e., by looking at its grammatical meaning), systematic (by looking at comparable legal issues within the same legal system), historical (by looking at comparable legal issues in texts of the past), and teleological (by looking at the object and purpose of the text).[5] Article 33/3, i.e., the assumption of equal meanings of related terms in different languages, is a focal point of the present investigation, as is article 33/4 of the Convention, which takes into account the goals ("object and purpose") of a treaty, i.e., its teleological sense. Article 33 of the Convention, in a nutshell, deals with problems of legal interpretation in their linguistic context. In a sense, this approach is the mirror image of an analysis along the lines of Speech Act Theory: the latter looks at linguistic issues in their legal and religious setting and thus can fruitfully precede analysis along the lines of the Convention.[6] For easy reference, here are articles 31 through 33 of the Convention.

---

[4] Cf. *Hardy* 1961, *Makarov* 1968, *Germer* 1970, *Mössner* 1972, *Rudolf* 1972, *Hilf* 1973, *Tabory* 1980, *Rosenne* 1983, *Nelson* 1986, and *Kuner* 1991. These studies investigate problems of interpretation in cases of linguistic conflict in legal documents that are "authentic" in more than one language, the focus, however, not necessarily being on underlying cultural, ideological, and/or religious differences. Cf. also *Lewis* 1993b, a monograph on the Soviet-United Arab Republic Treaty of 27 May 1971.

[5] Further guidelines that were not adopted in the Vienna Convention on the Law of Treaties, and which play no role in the framework of the present study, include the principles *contra proferentem, in dubio mitius*, "effet utile" (*ut res magis valeat quam pereat*), "conformity with International Law" and the "*implied powers*-rule" (cf. *Verdross/Simma* 1984: 493ff).

[6] According to *Tabory* (1980: 177), the analytical process can be divided into the following steps:

- Understanding the treaty on the basis of any one authentic text, assumed to express the meaning common to all the authentic texts (Art. 33(3));

- Comparison of the authentic texts (Art. 33(4)) in an effort to find their common meaning;

- [Application of] Art. 31;

- [Application of] Art. 32 (only supplementary to Art. 31);

- Reconciliation of texts and object and purpose.

Item (25), English

Article 31. General rule of interpretation

1. A treaty shall be interpreted in good faith in accordance with the ordinary meaning to be given to the terms of the treaty in their context and in the light of its object and purpose.

2. The context for the purpose of the interpretation of a treaty shall comprise, in addition to the text, including its preamble and annexes:

(a) any agreement relating to the treaty which was made between all the parties in connexion with the conclusion of the treaty;

(b) any instrument which was made by one or more parties in connexion with the conclusion of the treaty and accepted by the other parties as an instrument related to the treaty.

3. There shall be taken into account, together with the context:

(a) any subsequent agreement between the parties regarding the interpretation of the treaty or the application of its provisions;

(b) any subsequent practice in the application of the treaty which establishes the agreement of the parties regarding its interpretation;

(c) any relevant rules of international law applicable in the relations between the parties.

4. A special meaning shall be given to a term if it is established that the parties so intended.

Article 32. Supplementary means of interpretation

Recourse may be had to supplementary means of interpretation, including the preparatory work of the treaty and the circumstances of its conclusion, in order to confirm the meaning resulting from the application of article 31, or to determine the meaning when the interpretation according to article 31:

(a) leaves the meaning ambiguous or obscure; or

(b) leads to a result which is manifestly absurd or unreasonable.

Article 33. Interpretation of treaties authenticated in two or more languages

1. When a treaty has been authenticated in two or more languages, the text is equally authoritative in each language, unless the treaty provides or the parties agree that, in case of divergence, a particular text shall prevail.

2. A version of the treaty in a language other than one of those in which the text was authenticated shall be considered an authentic text only if the treaty so provides or the parties so agree.

3. The terms of the treaty are presumed to have the same meaning in each authentic text.

4. Except where a particular text prevails in accordance with paragraph 1, when a comparison of the authentic texts discloses a difference of meaning which the application of articles 31 and 32 does not remove, the meaning which best reconciles the texts, having regard to the object and purpose of the treaty, shall be adopted.

C. Speech Act Theory

Speech Act Theory, as developed in the two seminal works by Austin (1962) and Searle (1969), captures the different strata of explicit and implicit information that accompany a given utterance.[7] Austin (1962) distinguished five levels ("acts") in the course of such an utterance: the "phonetic act" (reflecting the phonetic surface of the utterance), the "phatic act" (reflecting the grammatical and lexical structure of the utterance), the "rhetic act" (reflecting a predication on a certain subject), the "perlocutive act" (reflecting a performative function of the utterance) and the "illocutive act" (reflecting an intended result of the utterance).[8] Searle (1969) subsumed Austin's levels of "phonetic act" and "phatic act" under the heading "locution" (act of utterance), and adopted Austin's level of "rhetic act" as "proposition" (propositional act). This proposition then is divided into two aspects: a reference to the "world" (i.e., a universe of persons and things) and a predication about this world. Searle's notions of "perlocutive act" and "illocutive act" correspond precisely to Austin's.[9]

In the framework of the present study, it makes sense to apply "Speech Act Theory" to written "utterances" as well, a stratum for which the levels listed above hold equally, with obvious changes for the exception of the "phonetic act" and the "phatic act".

Speech Act Theory then will be understood here as a way of formally accounting for the fact that written or oral statements function on two planes: the "locutionary" plane which represents the linguistic surface of the statement and the "illocutionary" plane, which accounts for semantic features (including those relating to special terminology) and pragmatic features (including those relating to discourse structure) behind this surface. The locutionary and the illocutionary planes exist for each "speaker", i.e., each participating negotiator, contracting party, etc. The two planes exist likewise for the author of a diplomatic message and its receiver, who may be of different cultural and religious backgrounds. Misunderstandings can then be described to arise

---

[7] The term *Sprechakt* 'speech act' was originally coined by the German linguist Karl *Bühler* in 1934. For a summary analysis, cf. *Lyons* 1977, vol. 2: 725ff, *Bußmann* 1982: 497ff, and *Schneider* 1992. A very technical approach is pursued in *Ulkan* 1992.

[8] Nowadays, discourse analysts generally use "phatic" for the non-information-conveying aspect of communication (e.g., "social bonding").

[9] *Fastenrath* (1993: 309) applies the terms "locutionary" and "illocutionary" to the content and to the accompanying functions of a statement (e.g., order or warning), respectively.

as a consequence of a combination of differences between the "speakers" on the locutionary and illocutionary planes.

In terms of philosophy of language, legal texts and oral political statements then have an extension or denotation (grammatical-lexical surface, corresponding to the philosophical *de dicto* stratum) and an intension or connotation (cultural-religious background, underlying legal concepts, political motives, corresponding to the philosophical *de re* stratum) from the perspective of each "speaker". In the following, "extension" will be understood as the basis of the locutionary act, and "intension" will be understood as the basis of the illocutionary act.

Speech Act Theory provides a theoretical framework that allows for possible different intensions of one and the same surface statement.[10] Onuf (1985) has extended this distinction to the realm of legal interpretation, identifying extension (the textual surface) with legal proposition, and intension (underlying cultural/religious connotations and/or political motives) with legal norm. Schematically:

extension	intension
|	|
(per-)locutive act	illocutive act
|	|
legal proposition	legal norm

In the following table, this scheme is expanded to capture the different aspects of extensionality and intensionality from the standpoint of a "Western" and an "Arab"/"Islamic" contracting party:[11]

[10] Cf. *Weil* 1983, *Habermas* 1985, *Onuf* 1985, *Fastenrath* 1991: 68ff, and *Fastenrath* 1993.

[11] The arrangement and sequence of the items in this chart is inspired by *Fastenrath* 1991: 167-187.

Table 1

Traditional methods of interpretation and Speech Act Theory

```
                  "Western" contracting party   "Arab"/"Islamic" contracting party
                                            |        |
                           bi-/multilateral treaty / legal document
                                    |                       |
          | --- European term --- |            | --- Arabic term --- |
          |                       |            |                     |
European language    International Law in   Arabic               International Law in
|                    "Western" perspective  |                    Islamic perspective
|                    |                      |                    |
semantics            grammatical sense      semantics            grammatical sense
pragmatics           systematic sense       pragmatics           systematic sense
discourse structure  historical sense       discourse structure  historical sense
special terminology  teleological sense     special terminology  teleological sense
|                    |                      |                    |
extension–intension  |                      extension–intension  |
|                    |                      |                    |
Speech Act Theory    Vienna Convention      Speech Act Theory    Vienna Convention
               |     on the Law of          |                    on the Law of
               |     Treaties (1969)        |                    Treaties (1969)
               |     |                      |                    |
        "Western" perspective           "Arab"/"Islamic" perspective
```

With respect to the notions of extensionality and intensionality from two (or more) perspectives, the following picture can be drafted:

	"speaker A"-perspective	**"speaker B"-perspective**
EXTENSION:	extension (A)	extension (B)
INTENSION:	intension (A)	intension (B)

While the Vienna Convention on the Law of Treaties sets a framework of interpretation based on grammatical, systematic, historical, and teleological deliberations, Speech Act Theory provides a theoretical basis for understanding the circumstance that different legal concepts may be concealed behind one and the same statement even in the same language.

Interestingly, a group of American psychologists adopted a comparable approach in their *U.S.-Arabic Communication Lexicon of Cultural Meanings*, in which they contrast the associations which Americans have to certain terms with those held by Jordanians and Egyptians. Specifically, the subjects are the following: "country image", "self image", "family", "marriage", "love", "friendship", "society", "nation"/"government", and "freedom". *Grosso modo*, collectivist interpretations are shown to stand in contrast to individualist ones, e.g., in the case of *ištirākīya* vs. *socialism*.[12] The authors summarized their findings as follows:[13]

Success in intercultural communication settings depends on our ability to recognize that people with a different cultural background have different priorities and different meanings. Thus, for instance, an American can be expected to communicate more effectively with an Arab if the American has some understanding of issues and predispositions which are dominant in the Arab's mind rather than merely focusing on topics which are salient solely in the American frame of reference. More importantly, in addressing those subjects of particular importance to the Arab, the American must be aware of the special meaning the topics may have. In other words, in order to relate to their interest, the communication should focus on those elements of the Arab's subjective understanding which are particularly salient.

The example *par excellence* of this issue is the term *Zionism*, whose European original and Hebrew rendering *tsionut* simply refer to the legitimate claim to a Jewish homeland, whereas the Arabic cognate *ṣahyūnīya* has adopted the intensionality of "anti-Arab racism and imperialism" as surfacing in the term for Israel, *al-kiyān aṣ-sahyūnī [al-ʿunṣurī]* 'the [racist] Zionist entity'.[14] By the same token, the Arabic term *ʾarāḍin muḥtalla* 'occupied territories' appears to be restricted to territory occupied by Israel as opposed to territory occupied by other (Arab) states.

In more general terms, the issues discussed here also have to do with the phenomenon of "faux amis" in linguistics, i.e., the circumstance that certain homophones or literally translated terms or phrases may have totally different meanings or connotations in different languages or even different areas of the same language.[15] In his memoirs, Churchill mentions the phrase *to table a paper* as an example which has contradictory meanings in British and American English and which once caused a misunderstanding between British and American chiefs of staff: in British English, the phrase means 'to put something

---

[12] Even within European languages, the meaning of this term ranges from "social-democratic" (as in the French *Parti Socialiste*) to "communist" (as in the former *Sozialistische Einheitspartei Deutschlands*).

[13] Cf. *Szalay / Abu-Hilal / Strohl / Mason / Goodison* 1978: 1.

[14] Cf., for instance, *Lewis* 1993: 185 and *Edzard* 1996: 42ff. With reference to material such as the *Brōtōkōlāt ḥukamāʾ Ṣahyūn* (the Arabic translation of the forged pamphlet *Die Protokolle der Weisen von Zion*), the Egyptian linguist El-Said *Badawi* of the American University in Cairo characterizes the term *ṣahyūnī* in contemporary Arabic as a mere anti-Semitic fighting word [personal communication]. Hopefully, such differences will be ironed out in the course of the ongoing peace process in the Middle East.

[15] For a systematic treatment of this issue, cf. the references provided in *Bußmann* 1983: 138f.

on the agenda', in contrast to the American English meaning 'to close a matter'.[16]

With respect to international relations, Huntington gives an incisive analysis of the relativism inherent in seemingly "elementary" terms such as "good" and "bad":[17]

It should be noted that, at least in the United States, terminological confusion exists with respect to relations between countries. "Good" relations are thought to be friendly, cooperative relations; "bad" relations are hostile, antagonistic relations. This usage conflates two very different dimensions: friendliness vs. hostility and desirability vs. undesirability. It reflects the peculiarly American assumption that harmony in international relations is always good and conflict always bad. The identification of good relations with friendly relations, however, is valid only if conflict is never desirable. Most Americans think that it was "good" that the Bush administration made U.S. relations with Iraq bad by going to war over Kuwait. To avoid the confusion over whether "good" means desirable or harmonious and "bad" undesirable or hostile, I will use "good" and "bad" only to mean desirable and undesirable. Interestingly, if perplexingly, Americans endorse competition in American society between opinions, groups, parties, branches of government, businesses. Why Americans believe that conflict is good within their own society and yet bad between societies is a fascinating question which, to the best of my knowledge, no one has seriously studied.

As already pointed out in the introduction, it is "better" in the perspective of this study to openly address differences in perspectives on international law than to downplay them.

D. A typology of diplomatic misunderstanding

I. General considerations

In the following, a typology of differences will be developed which will be applied in later chapters to the topics "war and peace" and "human rights". The typology does not formally take into account the question whether differences are intentional, i.e., due to deliberate distortions or mistranslations, or unintentional, i.e., due to well-nigh unavoidable cultural misunderstandings.

Legal concepts reflected by certain terms may have different connotations in different languages, even if carefully translated, or matching terms may be missing altogether in one of the languages.

---

[16] Cf. *Watzlawick* 1978: 75.

[17] Cf. *Huntington* 1996: 221.

Here is an illustration. In the "Exchange of Letters between the PLO and the Government of the State of Israel" which accompanies the "Agreement on the Gaza Strip and the Jericho Area" of 4 May 1994, a passage is found whose Arabic version does not (and cannot) reflect the semantic shades of difference between "Chairman" and "President". The passage runs as follows:[18]

Item (26), English

When *Chairman Arafat* enters the Gaza Strip and the Jericho Area, he will use the title *"Chairman (Ra'ees in Arabic) of the Palestinian Authority"* or *"Chairman of the PLO"*, and will not use the title *"President of Palestine"*.

Item (26), Arabic

Yastaḫdimu *r-ra'īsu ᶜArafāt*, ᶜinda duḫūli-hī qiṭāᶜa ġazzata wa-minṭaqata 'arīḥā, laqaba *"ra'īsu s-sulṭati l-filasṭīnīyati"* 'aw *"ra'īsu munaẓẓamati t-taḥrīri l-filasṭīnīyati"*, wa-lā yastaḫdimu laqaba *"ra'īsu filasṭīn"*.

In the Arabic version of this passage the shades of difference between *Chairman* and *President* cannot be reflected; rather, there is only the one term *ra'īs*, which covers both degrees of prestige. Based on this circumstance, the current "Observer for Palestine" to the United Nations, Nasser al-Kidwa, regularly refers to "President ᶜArafāt" in meetings of the "Committee on the Inalienable Rights of the Palestinian People".

Certain technical legal terms of the Islamic *šarīᶜa*, such as *ḥadd* and *qiyās*, resist direct translation altogether and therefore are retained as such in English translations of Arabic UN documents. Conversely, English terms and phrases, such as *due process of law*, do not seem to be readily available in Arabic and therefore occasionally appear untranslated in Arabic UN-documents.[19] Such cases then pose no problem for Speech Act Theory, as both the extensional and the intensional level are in congruence.

The extension of a given text can differ grammatically, lexically, and as a result of addition/omission. The intension of a given text can differ in terms of culture (religion, ideology, legal system) or otherwise, independently of whether or not the extension coincides.

[18] UN-doc. A/49/180 = S/1994/727 (Agreement on the Gaza Strip and the Jericho Area. Cairo, 4 May 1994) (Arabic and English), p. 207 and p. 195, respectively.

[19] Cf. the translator's note in UN-doc. S/22629 (Comments of the Permanent Representative of Iraq, Dr. Abdul Amir A. Al-Anbari, on Security Council resolution 692 of 20 May 1991) (Arabic and English), p. 3 of the English translation.

Problems of interpretation can even persist when the extension and intension of a given statement are more or less congruent.

Misunderstandings can thus be classified as the outcome of one of the following four scenarios:

II. The extension coincides, the intension differs

In a democratic political system, the term *peaceful coexistence* denotes a peaceful state of mutual tolerance, whereas in a Marxist dictatorship the same term may serve as a euphemism for a military offensive. Similarly, the Islamic term *jihād* has a defensive connotation ("intension") for some Shiite scholars (reminiscent of the euphemistic use of the term *peaceful coexistence* in Marxist theory), whereas it has an offensive connotation ("intension") for most Sunnite scholars.[20] Literally, i.e., on the "extensional" level, the term *jihād* just means "effort", but on the "intensional" level it clearly amounts to "(holy) war", as proven by the activities of groups with names like *al-jihād al-ʾislāmī*. The Arabic word *Havarie* in German (ultimately from Arabic *ᶜawār* 'defect') tends to denote a maritime accident in Germany and an auto accident in Austria. In the Mavrommatis Palestine concessions case, the English term *control* turned out to be semantically more restricted than its French counterpart *contrôle*.[21] The same holds for the term *svjazy* in the Russian version of the Quadripartite Agreement on Berlin of 1971, which for the Russian side implied only the notion of "travel connections", as opposed to the English term "ties", which further implied the idea of "social and political ties".[22] A further prominent example of such a scenario is a passage in the recent German-Czech declaration signed by Helmut Kohl and Vaclav Klaus on January 21, 1997, in Prague. Here, the German term *Vertreibung* 'expulsion' is paralleled in the Czech text by the term *vyhánění* 'expulsion', which has the connotation of "pushing on cattle" rather than "expelling people" – unlike the more closely corresponding Czech term

---

[20] For a concise analysis of this point (with further references), cf. *Ende* 1996: 24ff. In addition to military and religious usages of this term (*al-jihād fī sabīl allāh* 'the "effort" on the path of God'), the term *jihād* has also been applied in secular context to economic endeavors in Tunisia.

[21] Cf. *Pitamić* 1971 and *Verdross/Simma* 1984: 501.

[22] Cf. *Schiedermair* 1975: 89ff and *Doeker/Melsheimer/Schröder* 1973: 59. The relevance of this document for the present study was kindly pointed out to the author by Wolfgang *Dik* of the German Foreign Office.

vyhnání 'expulsion', which was avoided in the document for obvious political reasons.[23]

III. The extension differs, the intension coincides

The terms *Near East* and *Middle East* denote – at least in common American usage – the same geographical region, but at different times: *Near East* can refer to ancient or modern times, *Middle East* to modern times only.[24] Likewise, the terms *Arabian Gulf* and *Persian Gulf* denote the same area geographically, only with different political connotations.[25] In the peace accord between Israel and Egypt, the term *Gulf of Aqaba* (in Arabic: *ḫalīj al-ᶜaqaba*) was under discussion in the Hebrew text of the agreement. Israel had to replace its term *mifrats 'eilat* 'Gulf of Eilat' by *mifrats 'aqaba ('eilat)*, so that the following texts became official:[26]

Item (27), Hebrew

Ha-tsᵊdadim ro'im bᵊ-meitsar tiran u-vᵊ-*mifrats 'aqaba ('eilat)* nᵊtivei mayim bein-lᵊ'umiyim ha-pᵊtuchim lᵊ-khol ha-'ummot lᵊ-chofesh shayit vᵊ-tayis bilti mufra' u-bilti nitan lᵊ-hatlaya. Ha-tsᵊdadim yikhvᵊdu kol 'echad 'et zᵊkhut zulat-o lᵊ-shayit u-lᵊ-tayis lᵊ-shem gisha lᵊ-khol 'achat min ha-'aratsot derekh meitsar tiran u-*mifrats 'aqaba ('eilat)*.

Item (27), Arabic

Yaᶜtabiru ṭ-ṭarafāni ᵓanna madīqa tīrāna wa-*ḫalīja l-ᶜaqabati* mina l-mamarrati l-māᵓīyati d-duwalīyati l-maftūḥati li-kāffati d-duwali dūna ᶜāᵓiqin ᵓaw ᵓiqāfin li-ḥurrīyati l-milāḥati ᵓawi l-ᶜubūri l-jawwī. Kamā yaḥtarimu ṭ-ṭarafāni ḥaqqa

---

[23] *Filip*, O. "Wenn man "odsun" und "vyhnání" kreuzt, kommt "vyháněni" heraus. Der Streit um Abschiebung und Vertreibung, die philologischen Finessen und ihre glorreiche Auflösung in der deutsch-tschechischen Erklärung", Frankfurter Allgemeine Zeitung, December 24, 1996.

[24] The potential misunderstanding here apparently caused the former American vice president Dan Quayle to say: "The global function of the Middle East is that it keeps the Near East and the Far East from encroaching on each other."

[25] Originally, these terms were used by the respective sides in the sense of a waterway viewed from their own perspective, not in accordance with misguided national pride. Hence the Arabs used the term *al-ḫalīj al-fārisī* 'the Persian Gulf', just as the Persians had no problem referring to a certain waterway as *šaṭṭ al-ᶜarab*. On this issue, cf. *Kaikobad* 1980.

[26] Israel and Egypt. Treaty of Peace (with annexes and maps). Signed at Washington on 26 March 1979, authoritative in Arabic, English and Hebrew, the English version being binding, article 5/2, *UNTS*, vol. 1136 (1979), pp. 105, 113, and 118, respectively. For a monograph on this article, cf. *Lapidoth* 1983.

kulli min-humā fī l-milāḥati wa-l-ᶜubūri l-jawwīyi min wa-ʾilā ʾarāḍi-hī ᶜabra madīqi tīrāna wa-*ḫalīji l-ᶜaqaba*.

Item (27), English

The Parties consider the Strait of Tiran and *the Gulf of Aqaba* to be international waterways open to all nations for unimpeded and non-suspendable freedom of navigation and overflight. The Parties will respect each other's right to navigation and overflight for access to either country through the Strait of Tiran and *the Gulf of Aqaba*.

Similar problems exist with respect to territory which is claimed by both the Israelis and the Palestinians. Recently, the quarter in the outskirts of Jerusalem which is called Har Homa by the Israelis and Jabal ʾAbū Ġunaym by the Palestinians came under dispute due to Israeli settlement activities, a circumstance which has had negative impact on the ongoing peace process.

IV. The extension differs, the intension differs

The example *par excellence* in this context is resolution 242 of the Security Council, which features both extensional and intensional differences.[27] To say the least, the question as to whether an intensional difference is recognized in this case clearly depends on the political viewpoint of the given commentator. The crux concerns the phrase *(the) territories*. While the French and Spanish versions make use of the definite article and the English version does not, this opposition is nonexistent in the Chinese and Russian versions, as these languages have no definite article at all.[28] It is surprising that the (unofficial) Arabic translation is based on the English and not on the French version, with respect to the (in)definiteness of "territories", this having engendered considerable dismay on the part of contemporary Arab officials. Summarizing, one winds up with three types of statements regarding the definiteness of "territories":

---

[27] Cf. *Lapidoth* 1976, *Valdès* 1977, *Lord Caradon* et al. 1981: 22 and 31ff, *Schaefer* 1981: 229ff, *Bailey* 1985, Institute for Palestine Studies (ed.) 1988, vol. 1: 143, *Boyle* 1989, and *Rosenne*, in: *Moore* (ed.) 1974-1991, vol. 2: 906ff.

[28] Resolution No. 242, first principle (Security Council: Resolution No. 242 (1967) of 22 November 1967), authoritative in Chinese, English, French, Russian, Spanish. The transcription from Russian follows *Rosenne*, in: *Moore* (ed.) 1974-1991, vol. 2: 906; the transcription from Chinese is courtesy of the United Nations, Department of Public Information.

(i) versions marked definite:

Item (28), French

Retrait des forces armées israéliennes *des territoires* occupés lors du récent conflit.

Item (28), Spanish

Retiro de las fuerzas armadas israelís *de los territorios* que ocuparon durante el reciente conflicto.

(ii) version marked indefinite:

Item (28), English

Withdrawal of Israeli armed forces *from territories* occupied in the recent conflict.

Item (28), Arabic

Saḥbu l-qūwāti l-musallaḥati l-ʾisrāʾīlīyati *min ʾarāḍini* ḥtallat-hā fī n-nizāʿi l-ʾaḫīr.

(iii) versions unmarked with respect to definiteness/indefiniteness:

Item (28), Chinese

Yisieli jundui cheli qi yu zuijin chongtu suo zhanling *zhi lingtu*.

Item (28), Russian

Vyvod izrailskikh voruzhennikh *sil s territorii*, okkupirovannykh vo vremya n'edavn'ego konflikta.

The following remark by Shabtai Rosenne illustrates to what extent linguistic deliberations can be used to underline a political point: "The upshot was at the time a general understanding that, in the same way that the English and Russian languages can get by without use of the definite (or indefinite) article, the genius of the French and Spanish languages requires use of definite articles to a degree which a non-Latinist may find excessive or misleading, or at least confusing."[29] This argument is problematic in light of the fact that the "sponsors" of the resolution, notably the United Kingdom and the United States, resisted and would have vetoed an inclusion of "the", let alone "all (the)" in front of "territories".

Another notorious example is article 17 of the Treaty of Wəçale ("Uccialli") of 1889 between Italy and Ethiopia,[30] which features an extensional and intensional difference due to the euphemistic use of

---

[29] Cf. *Rosenne*, in: *Moore* (ed.) 1974-1991, vol. 2: 909.

[30] Cf. *Work* 1935 and *Rubenson* 1964. Facsimiles of the Italian and Amharic texts can be found in *Rubenson* 1964: 65ff.

the verbal form *consente* 'agrees' in the Italian text as opposed to the more literal use of the Amharic verbal form *yᵊčalaččᵊwal* 'shall have the option' in the Amharic text.

Item (29), Italian

Sua Maestà il Re dei Re d'Etiopia *consente* di servirsi del Governo di Sua Maestà il Re d'Italia per tutte le trattazioni di affari che avesse con altre Potenze o Governi.

Item (29), Amharic

Yä-ʾityop̣p̣ᵊya nᵊgusä nägäst kä-ʾawroppa nägästat l-ämm-ifallᵊgu-t gudday hullu bä-ʾiṭalya mängᵊst ʾaggažᵊnnät mällalak *yᵊčalaččᵊwal*.[31]

Historically, the problem of textual difference in this case was exacerbated by the lack of prestige of the "non-Western" language, as shown by the the following quotation, which directly pertains to this article (and which was mentioned above as the epigraph to this chapter): "La difficulté dont il s'agit aurait été écartée si, comme il arrive souvent dans les traités avec les peuples barbares dont la langue est mal connue et peut prêter à des ambiguïtés dont ces peuples seraient tentés d'abuser, on avait dit que, en cas de divergence, le texte dans la langue de l'Etat civilisé ferait seul foi."[32]

V. The extension coincides, the intension coincides partially

The trickiest case may lie in a scenario where hermeneutical difficulties persist in spite of congruent extensionality and intensionality. Such a scenario can arise, for instance, when the euphemistic usage of certain terms is apparent in one language but not necessarily in the other. For example, a very positive German letter of recommendation may only convey a "somewhat above average" level to an American reader in a literal English translation. Thus, the euphemistic use of the phrase *agrees to be guided* in the following example is more ob-

---

[31] A literal translation of the Amharic text is: "The King of Kings of Ethiopia shall have the option of communicating with the assistance of the Italian government regarding all affairs which he wants [to conduct] with the kings of Europe." The verbal form *yᵊčalaččᵊwal* derives from the root *čalä* (compound imperfect with an object suffix of the 3rd ps. pl.).

[32] Cf. *Despagnet* 1897: 29.

vious in the English text than in the corresponding phrase *yuwāfiqu ... ᶜalā ʾan yastadilla* in the Arabic version.[33]

Item (30), English

Without prejudice to the provisions of Articles XVII and XVIII of this Treaty, *His Majesty the King of Iraq agrees to be guided* by the advice of His Britannic Majesty tendered through the High Commissioner on all important matters affecting the international and financial obligations and interests of His Britannic Majesty for the whole period of this Treaty. His Majesty the King of Iraq will fully consult the High Commissioner on what is conducive to a sound financial and fiscal policy and will ensure the stability and good organization of the finances of the Iraq Government so long as that Government is under financial obligations to the Government of His Britannic Majesty.

Item (30), Arabic

Yuwāfiqu jalālatu maliki l-ᶜirāqi wa-ḏālika min ġayri misāsin bi-nuṣūṣi l-māddayni 17 wa-18 min hāḏihī l-muᶜāhadati *ᶜalā ʾan yastadilla* bi-mā yuqaddimu-hū jalālatu maliki barīṭāniyata mina l-mašwarati -- bi-wāsiṭati l-muᶜtamadi s-sāmī -- fī jamīᶜi š-šuʾūni l-muhimmati llatī tamassu bi-taᶜahhudāti wa-maṣāliḥi jalālati maliki barīṭāniyata d-duwalīyati wa-l-mālīyati wa-ḏālika ṭūla muddati hāḏihī l-muᶜāhada. Wa-yastašīru jalālatu maliki l-ᶜirāqi l-muᶜtamada s-sāmiya l-istišārata t-tāmmata fī mā yuʾaddī ʾilā siyāsatin mālīyatin wa-naqdīyatin salīmatin wa-yuʾamminu ṯabāta wa-ḥusna niẓāmi mālīyāti ḥukūmati l-ᶜirāqi mā dāmat tilka l-ḥukūmatu madwīnatan li-ḥukūmati jalālati maliki barīṭāniya.

E. Summary of Chapter Three

Speech Act Theory cannot and is not intended to replace the approach of the Vienna Convention on the Law of Treaties in dealing with the problems of contradiction in parallel authentic texts. Rather, its merits lie in providing a precise theoretical framework which can account for both the reasons and the potential purposes underlying those semantic differences associated with differing legal norms ("intensionality"), as reflected in problems related to terminology and discourse-structure. In this sense, it represents a linguistic complement to the four traditional legal methods of treaty interpretation.

---

[33] Grande Bretagne et Iraq. Traité d'alliance, avec protocole, signés à Bagdad, les 10 octobre 1922 et 30 avril 1923 respectivement, *LNTS*, vol. 35 (1925), p. 15 and p. 26, respectively.

Chapter Four

Application of the theory of interpretation to the realm of war and peace

"The term used in international documents as they affected us so far is the state of belligerency and the end of the state of belligerency. I think both in Arabic and in Hebrew our people do not have such a term. But we have accomplished and what we are committed to is the end of the state of war between Jordan and Israel." King *Ḥusayn* of Jordan on the occasion of the "Washington Declaration" between Israel and Jordan, July 25, 1994, as quoted in The New York Times of July 26, 1994.

A. Overview of problems

I. Basic considerations

In the following, two major topics in international relations and international law will be discussed in terms of the theoretical tools developed. These topics are the Palestine conflict ("Middle East conflict") and the Iraq-Kuwait conflict. Even though there is no clear-cut separation of perspectives (e.g., "Arab"/"Islamic" vs. "Western") in either case, there is still sufficient, if not abundant, material in United Nations documents that supports such a basic dichotomy of perspectives. This chapter is topic oriented and does not necessary follow the taxonomic sequence of types of misunderstandings listed in the previous chapter. Throughout the chapter, corresponding Arabic and English terms in the realm of war and peace with potentially different connotations will be scrutinized in different contexts and textual environments.[1]

[1] For relevant monographs applying to Arabic, especially with respect to terminological innovation in the realms of law, culture, and technology, cf. *Lewis* 1956, *Monteil* 1960, *Mansoor* 1965, *Wild* 1969, *Stetkevych* 1970, *Fawq al-ʿĀda* 1974, *Blau* 1981, *ʿAbdallāh* 1982, *Wild* 1982b, *Rebhan* 1986, *Ayalon* 1987, and *Gully* 1993.

Two further preliminary remarks are in order here. First, there may be a considerable discrepancy between the legal norms in "Western"-influenced constitutions of Arabic and other Islamic states, on the one hand, and the actually observable reality in terms of legislation, judicial system, and exercise of executive power on the other. Second, and conversely, there may be a considerable discrepancy between the official *šarīᶜa*-influenced politics of an Islamic state and the unofficial, pragmatic *realpolitik* actually exercised. Thus, even parties which are engaged in an open diplomatic feud due to antagonistic legal, cultural, and/or religious systems may cooperate *backstage* on certain issues. Iran, for instance, cooperated with the Holy See on a number of issues during the last Population Conference in Cairo, just as it has cooperated with Israel in numerous cases in spite of much official diplomatic venom.

II. The Islamic concept of *jihād*

A crucial point in historical and contemporary context is the definition of the concept of *jihād*. Again, it should be pointed out that this term, both historically and synchronically speaking, has primarily had an aggressive connotation, as appears clearly from the two crucial quotations to that effect in the Qurʾān:[2]

Item (31), Arabic original

Fa-ʾiḏā nsalaḫa l-ʾašhuru l-ḥurumu fa-qtulū l-mušrikīna ḥayṯu wajadtumū-hum wa-ḫuḏū-hum wa-ḥṣurū-hum wa-qᶜudū la-hum kulla marṣadin fa-ʾin tābū wa-ʾaqāmū ṣ-ṣalāta wa-ʾātū z-zakāta fa-ḫallū sabīla-hum ʾinna llāha ġafūrun raḥīm.

Item (31), English translation

When the sacred months have slipped away, slay the polytheists wherever ye find them, seize them, beset them, lie in ambush for them everywhere; if they repent, and establish the prayer and pay the *zakāt*, then set them free; for Allah is forgiving, compassionate.

Item (32), Arabic original

Qātilū llaḏīna lā yuʾmunūna bi-llāhi wa-lā bi-l-yawmi l-ʾāḫiri wa-lā yuḥarrimūna mā ḥarrama llāhu wa-rasūlu-hū wa-lā yadīnūna dīna l-ḥaqqi mina llaḏīna ʾūtū l-kitāba ḥattā yuᶜṭū l-jizyata ᶜan yadin wa-hum ṣāġirūn.

---

[2] Qurʾān 9: 5 and 29 (translations from *Bell* 1937, vol. 1: 174 and 177). Cf. also *an-Naᶜim* 1987b: 325f, *Lewis* 1988: 73f and 145ff, *Pohl* 1988: 65ff, *Mayer* 1991b: 208f, and above (chapter three).

Item (32), English translation

Fight against those who do not believe in Allah nor in the Last Day, and [those who] do not make forbidden what Allah and his messenger have made forbidden, and [those who] do not practice the religion of truth, [out of those] who have been given the Book [i.e., Christians and Jews], until they pay the *jizya* off-hand, being subdued.

In terms of the extension and intension of the term *jihād*, Werner Ende provides an interesting definition of the Islamic concept of "defense":[3]

Allgemeines Ziel dieses Handelns [*jihād*] ist die Verteidigung des Islams, wobei diese Verteidigung auch die Expansion seines Machtbereichs über die ganze Menschheit einschließen kann bzw. in letzter Konsequenz einschließen muß. Insofern ist, wie zahllose Abhandlungen muslimischer Juristen und Theologen zeigen, mit Dschihad in erster Linie bewaffneter Kampf gemeint.

Of course, the concept of *jihād* has in modern times also been invoked in a defensive way, notably in the course of the Palestine conflict ("Middle East conflict").[4] In terms of the typology of diplomatic misunderstanding established above, *jihād* then represents a case of an overlapping extension and a differing intension when viewed from a Muslim and a non-Muslim perspective.

III. Islam and terrorism

Another important issue in this context is whether and/or how Islam is to be connected with acts of terrorism. In the literature, it is repeatedly stated that "mainstream Islam", whatever that may be, does not support terrorism.[5] However, the problem remains that "mainstream Islam" usually does not distance itself from violent actions, even if these actions are not explicitly condoned. Thus, ᶜAbdallāh ᵓAḥmad an-Naᶜīm writes quite appropriately, regarding the Rushdie affair:[6]

Khomeini does not speak for all Shiᶜa Muslims of the world, let alone the Sunni Muslims, who are by far the vast majority of Muslims today. Nevertheless, since

---

3 *Ende* 1996: 24f ("The general goal of this course of action [*jihād*] is the defense of Islam. This defense can and ultimately must include the expansion of the hegemony of Islam to humanity as a whole. Thus, *jihād* denotes first of all armed struggle, as numerous treatises of Muslim jurists and theologians have shown."). Cf. also above (chapter three).

4 Cf. *Mayer* 1991b: 215ff.

5 Cf., for instance, the balanced views expressed in *an-Naᶜīm* 1988 and *Mayer* 1991b: 218f.

6 Cf. *an-Naᶜīm* 1990: 183.

the vast majority of Muslims have failed to condemn Khomeini's action, they are to be taken as acquiescing to it.

There have undeniably been certain journalistic and scholarly double standards in the discussion of what constitutes "terrorism", particularly in the Palestine conflict ("Middle East conflict"). Noam Chomsky once made this point during a lecture (in Frankfurt a.M. on April 26, 1986) with regard to the one-sided use of the terms "terrorism" and "retaliation" in the mass media. In terms of the typology of diplomatic misunderstanding established above, *terrorism* and *retaliation* then represent a case of a differing extension and a differing intension when viewed from an Israeli and an Arab perspective.

IV. Contemporary conflicts in the Arab world

If we attempt to look beyond the Palestine conflict and the Iraq-Kuwait conflict, we find that there is little available treaty material on other contemporary inner-Arab and Arab/non-Arab conflicts. Some such conflicts have ended unresolved, in a kind of political and diplomatic *cul-de-sac*, notably the crisis in the Western Sahara.[7] In numerous other cases, the solution is still pending, as in many border conflicts between Arab states, or the recent conflict between Yemen and Eritrea.[8] Still, the solution of many border conflicts between Arab states is still pending. By and large, the same holds for many other conflicts in the Muslim world, such as the Kurdish crisis or the East Timor crisis.[9] In the following, a couple of relevant examples are analyzed in terms of their extension and intension.

Concerning the Iran-Iraq war, no documents are available concerning the cease-fire of August 8, 1988. The excessive diplomatic correspondence in the aftermath of this war borders on *Realsatire* in the wording of its counteraccusations; what is "attack on" for one side of the conflict is usually "liberation of" for the other side. A recent

---

[7] Cf. *Chappez* 1976, *Franck* 1976, *Prévost* 1976, *Riedel* 1976, *Shaw* 1978, *Oeter* 1986, and *Tabouillot* 1989.

[8] The accord of May 21, 1996, aiming at a peaceful settlement of this conflict is reproduced in UN-doc. S/1996/447.

[9] For the Kurdish crisis, cf. below (chapter six). For the East Timor crisis, cf. *Chinkin* 1993 and *Maffei* 1993.

example of such discourse exhibiting different intensions of *terms of the cease-fire* is the following:[10]

Item (33), Arabic original

Binā'an ᶜalā tawjīhātin min ḥukūmat-ī, wa-bi-l-'išārati 'ilā risālati l-mumaṯṯili d-dā'imi li-jumhūrīyati 'īrāna l-'islāmīyati l-mu'arraḫati fī 17 ḥazīrāna/ yūniyā 1994 (al-waṯīqatu S/1994/726), nawaddu 'an nūḍiḥa 'anna mā warada fī-hā ᶜan ḥālati ntihākatin mazᶜūmatin min jānibi l-ᶜirāqi li-*waqfi 'iṭlāqi n-nāri* bayna l-baladayni wa-'aḥkāmi minṭaqati l-ᶜazli mahdu ddāᶜātin da'aba n-niẓāmu l-'īrānīyu ᶜalā ḫtilāqi-hā buġyata ḫalqi 'ajwā'i tawatturin lā mubarrira la-hā.

Item (33), official English translation

On instructions from my Government and with reference to the letter dated 17 June 1994 from the Permanent Representative of the Islamic Republic of Iran to the United Nations addressed to you (S/1994/726), we should like to state that the references it contains to alleged violations by Iraq of the terms of *the cease-fire* and the provisions governing the area of separation between the two countries are pure inventions that the Iranian regime has persisted in fabricating with a view to creating an unwarranted climate of tension.

The letters addressed by Yemeni politicians to the Security Council in the context of the Yemeni civil war of 1994 feature many examples of problematic language use in this context. Terms such as "cease-fire" are rendered by expressions as different as *waqf[u] 'iṭlāqi n-nār* 'stopping of firing'[11] and *intihā'[u] ḥalati l-qitāl* 'ending of the state of combat'.[12] In the following letter, quoting an "authoritative source", the notion of who attacked whom is in fact totally distorted, as it were ultimately the troops of (the former) North Yemen, who crushed the troops of the South. Thus, a different underlying intension of "cease-fire" is produced:[13]

Item (34), Arabic original

'Inna-nā fī l-waqti llaḏī nu'akkidu fī-hi stimrāra ltizāmi qūwāti-nā l-musallaḥati bi-*waqfi 'iṭlāqi n-nāri* nuḥmilu l-mutamarridīna l-ḫārijīna ᶜalā š-šarᶜīyati mas'ūlīyata rafḍi-him li-hāḏihī l-mubādarati wa-ntihāki-him li-l-marrati s-sādisati li-muḥāwalāti taṯbīti *waqfi 'iṭlāqi n-nāri* wa-ḍ-ḍarba bi-ᶜurḍi

[10] UN-doc. S/1994/869 (Letter dated 25 July 1994 from the Permanent Representative of Iraq to the United Nations [Nizar Hamdoon], addressed to the Secretary-General [Boutros Boutros-Ghali]) (Arabic and English), p. 1.

[11] Cf., for instance, UN-doc. S/1994/804 (Arabic), p. 2.

[12] Cf., for instance, UN-doc. S/1994/870 (Arabic), p. 2.

[13] UN-doc. S/1994/761 (Letter dated 27 June 1994 from the Permanent Representative of Yemen to the United Nations [Abdalla S. Al-Ashtal], addressed to the Secretary-General [Boutros Boutros-Ghali] (Arabic and English), p. 2.

l-ḥāʾiṭi bi-kulli n-nidāʾāti wa-l-masāʿī wa-l-muḥāwalāti l-mabḏūlati min ʾajli taṯbīti *waqfi ʾiṭlāqi n-nār.*

Item (34), official English translation

We reaffirm that our armed forces continue to comply with *the cease-fire agreement*, and we wish at the same time to stress that it is solely the insurrectionary outlaws who have rejected the initiative described above and for the sixth consecutive time thwarted efforts to consolidate *the cease-fire agreement*, completely ignoring the appeals made and the efforts and steps taken to that end.

The point of these examples is definitely not to single out any specific countries; conflicts, especially border conflicts, surface almost everywhere in the Arab world. Other examples of mutually polemical rhetoric that invite an analysis in terms of Speech Act Theory include numerous letters concerning the conflict between Egypt and Sudan on the Halaib region. Here is a sample excerpt from such a letter:[14]

Item (35), official English translation

I have the honour to refer to the letter dated 10 July 1995 addressed to you by the Minister of Foreign Affairs of Egypt concerning Egypt's aggression against the Sudanese province of Halaib (S/1995/559, Annex) and to the allegations, accusations and slander regarding so-called established facts and historical reality adduced in it. The letter contains many contradictions, lacks objectivity and avoids giving a direct reply to the two letters from Sudan to which it refers. Likewise, it is clear that the author of the letter has a tendency to provocative rhetoric and to repeat allegations that the Egyptian government continues to make against the Sudan; these allegations have no factual basis and their only purpose is to rally neighbouring States in the region to the Egyptian cause.

V. The diplomatic use of the term "Zionism"

The problem of "Zionism" is relevant not only for the Palestine conflict (to be treated below), but for conflicts in the Arab world in general.[15] One of the most notorious examples of a congruent extension and a differing intension is the traditional Arabic political term for Israel, *al-kiyān aṣ-ṣahyūnī* 'the Zionist element/entity', as is found

---

[14] UN-doc. S/1995/587 (Letter dated 17 July 1995 from the Minister for Foreign Affairs of the Sudan addressed to the President of the Security Council, Annex to the Letter dated 17 July 1995 from the Permanent Representative of the Sudan to the United Nations [Ali Mohamed Osman Yassin] addressed to the President of the Security Council) (Arabic and English), pp. 2ff. The Arabic original of this letter was not available to the author.

[15] Cf. *Dinstein* 1987 and the other contributions in the Israel Yearbook on Human Rights 17 (1987) which emanated from the "International legal conference on anti-Semitism, anti-Zionism and the United Nations", held at the New York University School of Law on April 13-15, 1986. For an overview of the development of perspectives on the term *Zionism* from a Palestinian perspective, cf. *Wild* 1993.

frequently in letters and recorded statements in United Nations context. The use of the term *ṣahyūnī* 'Zionist' in (mainly Iraqi) Arabic international documents is indeed noteworthy. In a way, it evokes General Assembly resolution 3379 (XXX) of November 10, 1975, which – inter alia – "*[d]etermines* that Zionism is a form of racism and racial discrimination".[16] Hence, Israel as a whole is often referred to as *al-kiyān aṣ-ṣahyūnī* 'the Zionist entity'[17] or even as *al-kiyān aṣ-ṣahyūnī al-ᶜunṣurī* 'the racist Zionist entity',[18] Israeli diplomats are labeled *wafd al-kiyān aṣ-ṣahyūnī al-ᶜunṣurī* 'the delegation of the racist Zionist entity',[19] Western armies are dubbed *al-qūwāt al-ʾamrīkīya al-ʾaṭlasīya aṣ-ṣahyūnīya* 'the United States-NATO-Zionist forces',[20] American politicians are called *ad-dawāʾir al-ʾamrīkīya aṣ-sahyūnīya* 'the United States and Zionist circles',[21] and Western politics are *al-muḫaṭṭaṭāt al-ʾimbīrīyalīya aṣ-ṣahyūnīya* 'the imperialist Zionist schemes',[22] to give just a few examples.

Here are a number of quotations, that pick up on the use of the term *ṣahyūnī* in broader context. The first example refers to the context of "the ninth anniversary of Israel's military aggression against Iraqi nuclear installations devoted to peaceful purposes":[23]

Item (36), Arabic original

Wa-min hāḏā l-munṭaliqi waḥdi-hī jāʾa taḥḏīru s-sayyidi r-raʾīsi Ṣaddām Ḥusayn fī l-ʾawwali min nisān/ʾabrīl al-māḍī bi-ʾanna l-ᶜirāqa sa-yastaᶜmilu ḥaqqa-hū fī d-difāᶜi š-šarᶜīyi li-r-raddi ᶜalā ʾayyi ᶜudwānin yutaᶜarraḍu la-hū min qabli *l-kiyāni ṣ-ṣahyūnī*.

Item (36), official English translation

It was on this premise alone that President Saddam Hussein's warning of 1 April last was made that Iraq would exercise its legitimate right to self-defence in response to any aggression launched against it by *the Zionist entity*.

---

[16] This resolution was reversed, however, by means of resolution A/RES/46/86 of December 16, 1991.

[17] Cf., for instance, UN-doc. S/21348 (7 June 1990) (Arabic and English), p. 3.

[18] Cf., for instance, UN-doc. A/45/944 (29 January 1991) (Arabic and English), p. 1.

[19] Cf., for instance, UN-doc. A/45/944 (29 January 1991) (Arabic and English), p. 1.

[20] Cf., for instance, UN-doc. S/22203 (6 February 1991) (Arabic and English), p. 1.

[21] Cf., for instance, UN-doc. S/23102 (1 October 1991) (Arabic and English), p. 2.

[22] Cf., for instance, UN-doc. S/22728 (20 June 1991) (Arabic and English), p. 2.

[23] UN-doc. S/21348 (Letter dated 7 June 1990 from the Permanent Representative of Iraq to the United Nations [Abdul Amir A. Al-Anbari] addressed to the Secretary-General [Javier Perez de Cuellar]) (Arabic and English), p. 3.

The second example, referring to yet another crushing of the Kurds in northern Iraq, is an excerpt from a statement issued by the Iraqi "Revolution Command Council":[24]

Item (37), Arabic original

Bi-smi llāhi r-raḥmāni r-raḥīmi,

Naḥmadu llāha subḥāna-hū wa-taᶜālā fī hāḏā š-šahri l-fāḍili ᵓiḏ nuᶜlinu li-ᵓabnāᵓi šaᶜbi l-ᶜirāqi l-ᶜaẓīmi nabaᵓa l-qaḍāᵓi t-tāmmi ᶜalā ᵓaᶜmāli l-fitnati wa-t-taḫrībi wa-š-šaġabi fī kulli muduni l-ᶜirāq. [...]

Wa-lam yakun min qabīli ṣ-ṣudfati ᵓan tanṭaliqa hāḏihī l-ᵓaᶜmālu š-šāᵓinatu llatī hiya laysat min ᵓaḫlāqi l-ᶜirāqīyīna wa-min taqālīdi niḍāli-himi l-waṭanīyi ḫilāla *l-ᶜudwāni l-ᵓamrīkīyi l-ᵓaṭlasīyi ṣ-ṣahyūnīyi* ᶜalā l-ᶜirāq. [...]

ᵓInna bilāda-nā llatī taᶜarraḍat ᵓilā *l-ᶜudwāni l-ᵓimbirīyalīyi l-ᵓaṭlasīyi ṣ-ṣahyūnīyi* taᶜarraḍat ᵓilā ġazwin ᵓāḫara mušābihin li-ġazwi hūlākū li-baġdāda ᶜāma 1258.

Item (37), official English translation

In the Name of God, the Merciful, the Compassionate,

We praise God Almighty in this pre-eminent month as we announce to the mighty people of Iraq the news that a complete end has been put to acts of sedition, sabotage and strife in all the towns of Iraq. [...]

It was no coincidence that these disgraceful acts, which are not consonant with the ethics of Iraqis or the traditions of their national struggle, should occur during the *United States-NATO-Zionist aggression* against Iraq. [...]

Our country, which was subjected to *imperialist NATO-Zionist aggression*, was subjected to an attack like that of Hulagu on Baghdad in 1258. [...]

The use of the term *ṣahyūnī* 'Zionist' is by no means restricted to Israel, as shown by the frequent oral labeling of Iran as *niẓām ṣahyūnī* 'Zionist régime' by Iraqi diplomats; Iraqi sources even coined the neologism *ṣahyūḫumaynīya* 'Zio-Khomeinism' as a term for Iranian politics.[25] In the following Kuwaiti quotation, the situation of occupied Kuwait is likened to the situation of the territories occupied by Israel:[26]

---

[24] UN-doc. S/22452 (Annex to the Letter dated 5 April 1991 from the Permanent Representative of Iraq to the United Nations [Abdul Amir A. Al-Anbari] addressed to the Secretary-General [Javier Perez de Cuellar]) (Arabic and English), pp. 2f.

[25] This observation was kindly pointed out to the author by Professor Stefan *Wild*.

[26] UN-doc. S/21505 (Statement issued on 12 August 1990 by the Council of Ministers of Kuwait, Annex to the Letter dated 13 August 1990 from the Permanent Representative of Kuwait to the United Nations [Mohammad A. Abulhasan] addressed to the Secretary-General [Javier Perez de Cuellar]) (Arabic and English), pp. 2f.

Item (38), Arabic original

Iᶜtarafa l-ᶜirāqu fī bayāni-hī l-ʾaḫīri bi-ʾanna ḥtilāla-hū li-dawlati l-kuwayti yumāṯilu ḥtilāla ʾisrāʾīla li-baᶜḍi l-ʾarāḍī l-ᶜarabīyati wa-huwa bi-ḏālika kašafa ᶜan nafsi-hī bi-ᶜtibāri-hī yalᶜabu nafsa d-dawri llaḏī yumārisu-hū *l-kiyānu ṣ-ṣahyūnīyu* fī l-minṭaqati -l-ᶜarabīya. [...]

Item (38), official English translation

In its most recent statement, Iraq has acknowledged that its occupation of the State of Kuwait resembles Israel's occupation of Arab territories, and it has thereby revealed itself as playing the same role as that of *the Zionist entity* in the Arab region. [...]

"Zionist" activities, independently of any Israeli context, can also constitute one of a long list of reasons for the death penalty in Iraq, as apparent from the following regulation:[27]

Item (39), Arabic original

ʾAmma l-jarāʾima l-māssata bi-ʾamni d-dawlati d-dāḫilīyi wa-llatī ᶜuqūbatu-hā l-ʾiᶜdāmu fa-hiya: [...]

(i) man jannada ʾaw zawwaja *mabādiʾa ṣahyūnīyatan* bi-mā fī ḏālika l-māsōnīyatu ʾawi ntasaba ʾilā *muʾassasāti-hā* (al-māddatu 201);

Item (39), official English translation

The following are offences prejudicial to the internal security of the State for which the death penalty is imposed: [...]

(i) Any person who propagates *Zionist* or Masonic *principles* or who joins or advocates membership of *Zionist* or Masonic *institutions* (art. 201);

Even in academic context, the term *ṣahyūnī* 'Zionist' is sometimes used in a polemical fashion.[28]

B. The Palestine conflict ("Middle East conflict")

I. Overview of general discourse problems

It is quite understandable that the Palestine conflict (often referred to in a *totum-pro-parte* sense as simply the "Middle East conflict") has played a major role in legal and political studies.[29] However, as a re-

---

[27] UN-doc. CCPR/C/37/Add.3 (Arabic and English), p. 29 and pp. 29f, respectively.

[28] Cf. *ʾAbū Luġud* 1974: 5ff, where the term *sayṭara ṣahyūnīya* 'Zionist domination' characterizes the faculty composition of Near Eastern Studies departments in the USA.

[29] For an overview of relevant historical documents, cf. *Moore* (ed.) 1974-1981 and *Laqueur/Rubin* (eds.) 1984. An extensive collection of pertinent UN documents as well as

sult of conflicting interests involving different "lobbies" of journalists and scholars, the legal and political discussion of the Palestine conflict has been characterized by a considerable degree of double standards and one-sidedness on the part of the journalistic and scholarly mainstream.[30] Noam Chomsky in particular has pointed out problems and double standards regarding the use of the term "rejectionism", i.e., the quite different positions taken vis-à-vis the denial of the right of self-determination of the Israeli and the Palestinian people, respectively, in the American mass media.[31]

On the other hand, while Israel has routinely been characterized by media and academia in other parts of the world as the intransigent "aggressor" in the region, a number of historical and contemporary factors have often been overlooked – factors that should matter, especially from a German perspective. First, Syria, Lebanon, and Palestine were basically a Judeo-Christian area before the Islamic conquests. Second, it was unfortunate in retrospect that the Palestinians and other Arabs did not accept the 1947 United Nations partition plan.[32] Third, the West Bank and the Gaza Strip were Jordanian and Egyptian territory, respectively, before 1967 and nobody referred to these territories as *ʾarāḍin muḥtalla* 'occupied territories' prior to that date. Fourth, the Jews did not have access to *their* holy sites before 1967 (mainly the Wailing Wall, the sole remaining part of the Temple). Fifth, Israel, whatever has undeniably occurred in terms of human rights violations at the expense of the Palestinians, fares comparatively well as compared to any of the surrounding states. And sixth, Israel *did* finally engage in a negotiating process, however slow and difficult, with the subdued Palestinians – unlike other states in the region like Syria or Morocco, which have shown little intention, if any, of peacefully settling their conflicts of interest with the Lebanese and the Ṣaḥrāwī population, respectively, not to mention Turkey, Indonesia, and other Islamic states that are much less criticized than Israel, in spite of their far worse human rights record. In terms of Speech Act Theory this is particularly interesting inasmuch as the very same kind of actions, e.g., the military unification of Jerusalem in 1967, that are described with terms such as "Zionist", imperialist",

---

of bibliographical resources is provided in UN-doc. ST/LIB/SER.B/22/Add.1 (Palestine Question. A select bibliography, 1976-1993). Cf. also the contributions and the overview of documents in *Volle/Weidenfeld* (eds.) 1997.

[30] For an analysis of this problem, cf. *Crawford* 1990: 307f.

[31] Cf. *Chomsky* 1983 and *Chomsky* 1987: 371ff.

[32] GA res. 181 (II) of 29 November 1947. Cf. *Hurewitz* 1956, vol. 2: 281ff.

etc. when committed by Israel, are not criticized (i.e., are not labelled negatively) when they are committed by Muslims.[33] Thus, the historical conquest of Jerusalem under the Caliph ᶜUmar ibn al-Ḫaṭṭāb is nowhere in the literature described as an aggressive act; on the contrary, the "benevolence" of the Caliph in his dealings with the Christians of the city is the subject of ample praise.[34]

It was already mentioned above (chapter two) that Yāsir ᶜArafāt's comparison of the Oslo agreements with the Treaty of Ḥudaybīya created considerable resentment on the Israeli side, resentment that was not voiced when the late Egyptian president ᵓAnwar as-Sādāt likened the Camp David Peace Accord to the Treaty of Ḥudaybīya.[35] Assuming that ᶜArafāt had fundamentally different connotations in mind than Sādāt when citing the treaty, this would constitute the classic example of an overlapping extension and a contradictory intension. Recently, a former president of the International Court of Justice, Mohammed Bedjaoui, clearly supported a reading different from the Israeli interpretation of ᶜArafāt's remark, a reading that does not question peaceful intentions on the part of a politician who would cite this treaty.[36]

In the following sections, a number of crucial documents in the history of the Palestine conflict ("Middle East conflict") will be

---

[33] On double standards regarding the political, journalistic, and academic treatment of such problems, cf. *Dinstein* 1987: 18: "Moreover, a double standard, which is so characteristic of the General Assembly, develops. Israel is condemned for acts that are not perceived as blameworthy when committed by other States." Cf. also the statement of the former German ambassador to the United Nations, Rüdiger *von Wechmar*, regarding the appropriateness of German involvement in a peaceful solution of the Palestine conflict ("Middle East conflict"), reproduced in UN-doc. A/PV.2291. *Lewis* (1995: 58) remarks quite appropriately: "My impression is that if there is a solution of the Arab-Israeli conflict, so that it no longer arouses the interest of the outside world, the outside world will forget about the Middle East and will care no more about its conflicts than it does about the problems and conflicts of Inner Africa, except of course to the extent that they affect vital interests like oil, as long as that remains a vital interest. But within the region, a solution would release interest and energy and attention, and make it possible to work for a better understanding of the other problems, and perhaps even ultimately for their solution."

[34] Regarding the sources for this event, cf. above (chapter two).

[35] Cf. *Rodan*, S. "Arafat implies agreement with Israel is only temporary", The Jerusalem Post, May 23, 1994, and *Haberman*, C. "Israel demands Arafat reaffirm peace accord", The New York Times, May 24, 1994.

[36] "Fundamentally, therefore, Islam regards war as *pis-aller*. Citing the attitude of the Prophet Muhammad during the Hodaibiya [sic!] expedition, Sheikh Mohammed Draz has written: 'In the eyes of Islam, an international agreement which is somewhat disadvantageous for Muslims but is likely to avoid bloodshed is better than a bloody victory for the just cause.'" *Bedjaoui*, in: *Dekker & Post* (eds.) 1992: 283.

picked out and analyzed in terms of their relevance for Speech Act Theory.

II. The McMahon-Ḥusayn correspondence (1915/1916)

The problems involved in interpreting the McMahon-Ḥusayn correspondence (1915/1916) in the 1920s and 1930s can profit an analysis in terms of Speech Act Theory, as the question as to whether or not Palestine should be included in the territories claimed for Arab independence, was artfully obscured in the correspondence by the British High Commissioner McMahon.[37] The term *wilāya* in the Arabic original of the correspondence is unsystematically rendered in the English version as 'district', 'vilayet', 'sanjak', or 'province' throughout the correspondence, thus causing problems for interpretation. The following two excerpts illustrate this:[38]

Item (40), Arabic

ʾInna *wilāyatay* marsīna wa-ʾiskandarūnata wa-ʾajzāʾan min bilādi š-šāmi l-wāqiʿata fī l-jihati l-ġarbīyati li-*wilāyati* dimašqi š-šāmi wa-ḥimsa wa-ḥamāha wa-ḥalaba lā yumkinu ʾan yuqāla ʾinna-hā ʿarabīyatun maḥḍatun wa-ʿalay-hi yajibu ʾan tustaṯnā mina l-ḥudūdi l-maṭlūba.

Item (40), English

The two *districts* of Mersina and Alexandretta and portions lying to the west of the *districts* of Damascus, Homs, Hama and Aleppo cannot be said to be purely Arab, and should be excluded from the limits demanded.[39]

Item (41), Arabic

ʾAmma min ḫuṣūṣi *wilāyatay* baġdāda wa-l-baṣrati fa-ʾinna l-ʿaraba taʿtarifu ʾanna markaza wa-maṣāliḥa barīṭāniyata l-ʿuẓmā l-muwaṭṭadata hunāka tastalzimu ttiḫāḏa tadābīra ʾidārīyatin maḫṣūṣatin li-wiqāyati hāḏihī l-ʾaqālīmi mina l-iʿtidāʾi l-ʾajnabīyi wa-ziyādati ḫayri sukkāni-hā wa-ḥimāyati maṣāliḥi-nā l-iqtiṣādīyati l-mutabādala.

---

[37] Cf. *Kedourie* 1976.

[38] For several references regarding these texts and the problem as to which language version derives from which, cf. *Wagner* 1971: 107, n. 3 and *Lapidoth/Hirsch* (eds.) 1992: 2ff. The problems concerning the term *wilāya* are discussed in H.M. Stationary Office (ed.) 1939. Report of a Committee set up to consider Certain Correspondence between Sir Henry McMahon [His Majesty's High Commissioner in Egypt] and The Sharif of Mecca in 1915 and 1916. London.

[39] McMahon-Ḥusayn correspondence (14 July 1915 - 10 March 1916), 4th letter, 4th paragraph (after compliments), Arabic and English versions.

Item (41), English

With regards to the *vilayets* of Bagdad and Basra, the Arabs will recognise that the established position and interests of Great Britain necessitate special administrative arrangements in order to secure these territories from foreign aggression, to promote the welfare of the local populations, and to safeguard our mutual economic interests.[40]

In response, Ḥusayn observed in letter number 5 that "the two *vilayets* of Aleppo and Beirut and their sea coasts are purely Arab *vilayets*, and there is no difference between a Moslem and a Christian Arab; they are both descendants of one forefather",[41] a statement, which, in turn, led McMahon to observe in letter number 6 that "[w]ith regard to the *vilayets* of Aleppo and Beirut, the Government of Great Britain have fully understood and taken careful note of your observations, but, as the interests of our ally, France, are involved in them both, the question will require careful consideration".[42] Thus, the term *wilāyatun ᶜarabīyatun maḥḍa* 'purely Arab *vilayet*' represents another example of an overlapping extension and a differing intension when viewed from a European colonial and an Arab perspective. The Letter from Sir Henry McMahon Concerning the "McMahon Pledge" to "The Times" of July 23, 1937 best illustrates the problem in question and is therefore reproduced here in full:[43]

Item (42), English original

Many references have been made in the Palestine Royal Commission Report and in the course of recent debates in both Houses of Parliament to the "McMahon Pledge", especially to that portion of the pledge which concerns Palestine and of which one interpretation has been claimed by the Jews and another by the Arabs.

It has been suggested to me that continued silence on the part of the giver of that pledge may itself be misunderstood.

I feel, therefore, called upon to make some statement on the subject, but I will confine myself in doing so to the point now at issue –, i.e., whether that portion of Syria now known as Palestine was or was not intended to be included in the territories in which the independence of the Arabs was guaranteed in my pledge.

I feel it my duty to state, and I do so definitely and emphatically, that it was not intended by me in giving this pledge to King Hussein to include Palestine in the area in which Arab independence was promised.

---

40 McMahon-Ḥusayn correspondence (14 July 1915 - 10 March 1916), 4th letter, 11th paragraph (after compliments), Arabic and English versions.

41 The Arabic original runs as follows: wa-ʾamma *wilāyatay* ḥalaba wa-bayrūta wa-sawāḥila-humā fa-hiya *wilāyātun ᶜarabīyatun maḥḍatun* wa-lā farqa bayna l-ᶜarabīyi l-masīḥīyi wa-l-muslimi fa-ʾinna-humā ʾabnāʾa jaddin wāḥid.

42 Cf. *Hurewitz* 1956, vol. 2: 13.

43 Cf. *Lapidoth/Hirsch* (eds.) 1992: 19.

I also had every reason to believe at the time that the fact that Palestine was not included in my pledge was well understood by King Hussein.

Thus, analysis of a crucial term in the McMahon-Ḥusayn correspondence amply demonstrates the benefits of Speech Act Theory.

III. The Armistice Agreements of 1949 between Israel and its neighbors

In connection with the cease-fire agreements between Israel and its neighbors, the very term *cease-fire line,* with its possibly different connotations in different languages, has been the subject of discussion.[44] As in this instance the only authentic texts were in English, however, just as in the case of a later aborted agreement with Lebanon,[45] there is no direct connection to the topic under investigation here.

IV. The Camp David Peace Accord between Israel and Egypt

This treaty in its Article 1 features the term *[end of] the state of war* for the first time in the history of the Middle East conflict. The exact wording is:[46]

Item (43), English

The state of war between the Parties will be terminated and peace will be established between them upon the exchange of instruments of ratification of this Treaty.

Item (43), Arabic

Tantahī ḥālatu l-ḥarbi bayna ṭ-ṭarafayni wa-yuqāmu s-salāmu bayna-humā ᶜinda tabāduli waṯāʾiqi t-taṣdīqi ᶜalā hāḏihī l-muᶜāhada.

Item (43), Hebrew

Matsav ha-milchama bein ha-tsᵊdadim yaggia' lᵊ-qeits-o wᵊ-shalom yᵊkhuwwan beinei-hem 'im hachlafat mismᵊkhei ha-'ishrur shel choze ze.

It should be understood that the English, Arabic, and Hebrew terms *war, ḥarb,* and *milchama* do not entail different interpretations in this

---

[44] Cf. UN-doc. S/7930, referred to in correspondence between Under Secretary for Political Affairs A. Nesterenko and Secretary General U Thant (Boxes DAG-1/5.2.2.1 in the UN Archives). Cf. also *Rosenne* 1951: 46ff.

[45] The text of this agreement can be found, for instance, in The Jerusalem Post of May 17, 1983.

[46] Article 1 in its English, Arabic and Hebrew versions is found in *UNTS*, vol. 1136 (1979), pp. 116, 110, and 114, respectively.

case. Likewise, the terms *peace, salām,* and *shalom* may be assumed to be semantically congruent in this treaty.

V. The Oslo Accords between Israel and the PLO[47]

In the Declaration of Principles on Interim Self-Government Arrangements between Israel and the PLO ("Oslo I"), the English phrases *end to decades of conflict and confrontation* and *peaceful coexistence* are matched by the Arabic phrases *ḥadd[in] li-ᶜuqūdin mina l-muwājahati wa-n-nizāᶜi* and *taᶜāyuš[in] silmī[yin]*.[48] The Agreement on the Gaza Strip and the Jericho Area between Israel and the PLO ("Oslo II") features similar terms; the English phrase *just, lasting and comprehensive peace settlement,* which appears in both documents, is matched by the Arabic phrase *taswiya[tin] silmīya[tin] ᶜādila[tin] wa-dāʾima[tin] wa-šāmila[tin]*.[49] None of these phrases pose any problem for interpretation; the intensional overlap is almost perfect. In the light of the importance of these two treaties, here is the full text of the preamble of the "Declaration of Principles":

Item (44), English

The Government of the State of Israel and the PLO team (in the Jordanian-Palestinian delegation to the Middle East Peace Conference) (the "Palestinian Delegation"), representing the Palestinian people, agree that it is time to put an end to decades of confrontation and conflict, recognize their mutual legitimate and political rights, and strive to live in peaceful coexistence and mutual dignity and security and achieve *a just, lasting and comprehensive peace settlement* and historic reconciliation through the agreed political process.

Item (44), Arabic

ʾInna ḥukūmata ʾisrāʾīla wa-farīqa munaẓẓamati t-taḥrīri l-filasṭīnīyati (fī l-wafdi l-ʾurdunnīyi - l-filasṭīnīyi ladā muʾtamari s-salāmi fī š-šarqi l-ʾawsaṭi) ("al-wafdu l-filasṭīnīyu") yattafiqāni ʾanna l-waqta qad ḥāna li-waḍᶜi ḥaddin li-ᶜuqūdin mina l-muwājahati wa-n-nizāᶜi, wa-yaᶜtarifāni kullu min-humā bi-l-ḥuqūqi l-mašrūᶜati wa-s-sīyāsīyati li-l-ʾāḫari, wa-yasᶜāyāni ʾilā l-ḥayāti fī taᶜāyušin silmīyin wa-karāmatin wa-ʾamnin mutabādalayni, wa-ʾilā taḥqīqi *taswiyatin silmīyatin ᶜādilatin wa-dāʾimatin wa-šāmilatin,* wa-muṣālaḥatin tārīḫīyatin ᶜan ṭarīqi l-ᶜamalīyati s-sīyāsīyati l-muttafaqi ᶜalay-hā.

---

[47] For an overall legal assessment of the treaties between Israel and the PLO, cf. *Malanczuk* 1996: 488ff (with copious further references).

[48] UN-doc. A/48/486 = S/26560 (English and Arabic), p. 4.

[49] UN-doc. A/49/180 = S/1994/727 (English and Arabic), pp. 5 and 6, respectively.

VI. The Washington Declaration between Israel and Jordan

The epigraph of the present chapter is taken from an oral diplomatic address which highlights the circumstance that legal concepts are not necessarily overlapping in two different languages.

In the course of the meeting between King Ḥusayn of Jordan, Israeli Prime Minister Rabin, and American President Clinton on July 25, 1994, in Washington, King Ḥusayn made the following remark in an address:[50]

The term used in international documents as they affected us so far is the state of belligerency and the end of the state of belligerency. I think both in Arabic and in Hebrew our people do not have such a term. But we have accomplished and what we are committed to is the end of the state of war between Jordan and Israel.

According to a former Jordanian ambassador to the United Nations, Adnan Abu Odeh,[51] this remark reflects the circumstance that the slight legal difference between *war* and the somewhat stronger term *belligerency* cannot be captured in Arabic.[52] Conversely, the Arabic terms *ṣulḥ* ('transition from war to peace') and *salām* ('peace'), with contrasting military vs. psychological connotations, have no direct equivalents in English.[53] Historically, at least, the Arabic term *salām* had the connotation of "being at peace with oneself and the world" and cannot automatically be equated semantically with the cognate Hebrew term *shalom*.[54]

Paragraph (C) of the Washington Declaration between Jordan and Israel runs as follows:[55]

Item (45), English

The long conflict between the two states is now coming to an end. In this spirit, the state of belligerency between Jordan and Israel has been terminated.

Item (45), Arabic

ʾInna ṣ-ṣirāʿa ṭ-ṭawīla l-ʿamadi bayna d-dawlatayni ʾaṣbaḥa l-ʾāna fī nihāyatihī. Wa-bi-hāḏihī r-rūḥi ʾunhiyat ḥālatu l-ḥarbi bayna l-ʾurdunni wa-ʾisrāʾīl.

---

[50] The New York Times, July 26, 1994.

[51] Interview with the author on August 23, 1994.

[52] The English-Arabic dictionary Al-Mawrid gives the gloss 'ḥālat al-ištirāk al-fiʿlī fī l-ḥarb' for *state of belligerency*, i.e., "state of actual participation in war" as opposed to "state of war".

[53] Cf. *Lewis* 1988: 78ff.

[54] Cf. *Fikentscher* 1975-1977, vol. 1: 319ff.

[55] UN-doc. A/49/300 = S/1994/939 (English and Arabic), pp. 2 and 3, respectively.

Assuming that *belligerency* is stronger a term than *war*, the wording of the English text is surprising, insofar as there has been in fact a *de facto* peace between Israel and Jordan for quite some time. The Arabic text has instead *ḥālat[u] l-ḥarb* 'state of war'. In terms of Speech Act Theory, this case could be analyzed as an example of differing extension and overlapping intension.

VII. The Treaty of Peace between Israel and Jordan

For the sake of completeness, here are the last two "whereas-clauses" in the preamble to the Treaty of Peace between the State of Israel and the Hashemite Kingdom of Jordan of 26 October 1994; this time *state of belligerency* is rendered as *ḥālat[i] l-ʿadāʾ* (literally 'state of hostility, enmity'):[56]

Item (46), English

Bearing in mind that in their Washington Declaration of 25th July, 1994, they declared the termination of the state of belligerency between them;

Deciding to establish peace between them in accordance with this Treaty of Peace;

Item (46), Arabic

Wa-ʾiḏ taʾḫuḏāni bi-ʿayni l-iʿtibāri ʾanna-humā ʾaʿlanatā ntihāʾa ḥālati l-ʿadāʾi bayna-humā bi-mujībi ʾiʿlāni wašinṭūn al-muwaqqaʿi fī 25 tammūza 1994.

Wa-ʾiḏ tuqarrirāni ʾiqāmata salāmin bayna-humā bi-mujībi muʿāhadati s-salāmi hāḏihī.

VIII. The Protocol Concerning the Redeployment in Hebron

As of this writing, the Protocol Concerning the Redeployment in Hebron of January 17, 1997, represents the latest step in the Middle East peace process.[57] Just as in the previous documents, terms such as "every possible effort to prevent friction" or "relevant security provisions" pose no linguistic difficulties of interpretation. Here is paragraph 1 of the protocol:

---

[56] UN-doc. A/50/73 = S/1995/83 (27 January 1995) (English and Arabic), pp. 4 and 2, respectively.

[57] As of this writing, the Protocol has not yet been submitted as a UN document.

Item (47), English

In accordance with the provisions of the Interim Agreement and in particular of Article VII of Annex I to the Interim Agreement, both Parties have agreed on this Protocol for the implementation of the redeployment in Hebron.

Security Arrangements Regarding Redeployment in Hebron

1. Redeployment in Hebron

The redeployment of Israeli Military Forces in Hebron will be carried out in accordance with the Interim Agreement and this Protocol. This redeployment will be completed not later than ten days from the signing of this Protocol. During these ten days both sides will exert every possible effort to prevent friction and any action that would prevent the redeployment. This redeployment shall constitute full implementation of the provisions of the Interim Agreement with regard to the City of Hebron unless otherwise provided for in Article VII of Annex I to the Interim Agreement.

C. The Iraq-Kuwait crisis

I. Overview of general discourse problems

The Iraq-Kuwait crisis, which began on August 2, 1990, with Iraq's invasion of Kuwait, has produced hundreds of documents in United Nations context: Security Council resolutions, letters of Iraqi and Kuwaiti diplomats, reports of the Secretary-General, and other documents.[58] Iraq has never openly admitted its true rationale for invading Kuwait, which was its refusal and inability to pay back the enormous debts it owed to Kuwait as a result of the protracted war with Iran.[59] Instead, Iraq has consistently argued that the annexation of Kuwait served three purposes: first, the restoration of Kuwait to its "motherland" (in spite of the treaty between Kuwait and Iraq of 1963,[60] regarding the mutual recognition of boundaries); second, "the assistance provided [...] to the people of Kuwait, who have overthrown

---

[58] For a comprehensive overview of documents pertaining to the Iraq-Kuwait conflict, as well as a chronology of events, cf. *Lauterpacht* et al. (eds.) 1991 as well as *United Nations, Department of Public Information* (ed.) 1996. The United Nations and the Iraq-Kuwait Conflict 1990-1996. New York (= *Al-ʾUmam al-muttaḥida, ʾIḍārat šuʾūn al-ʾiʿlām* 1996. Al-ʾUmam al-muttaḥida wa-n-nizāʿ bayna l-ʿirāq wa-l-kuwayt 1990-1996. New York), pp. 139-164. For the background as well as the legal consequences of the conflict, cf., for instance, *Alston* 1992, *Eitel* 1992, *Kaikobad* 1992, *Gray* 1994, and *Mendelson / Hulton* 1994.

[59] For a concise analysis of this point, cf. *Eitel* 1992: 173f.

[60] Kuwait and Iraq. Agreed Minutes regarding the restoration of friendly relations, recognition and related matters. Signed at Baghdad, on 4 October 1963, *UNTS*, vol. 485 (1964), pp. 322ff.

the régime of the Sabah family";[61] and third, a preventive counter to "United States-NATO-Zionist"[62] hegemony in the Middle East. From the "Western" point of view, of course, and also from the point of view of the "Islamic *ʾumma*", the occupation of Kuwait represented nothing but an act of international aggression contrary to the precepts of international law. As to the question of whether human rights considerations played a role in the "Western" reaction to the Iraqi invasion of Kuwait, the following polar positions have been articulated:[63] "(1) the view that the [Second] Gulf War had nothing to do with world order and everything to do with assured access to cheap oil; and (2) the view that the resort to armed force to ensure Iraq's compliance with the decisions of the Security Council was aimed almost entirely at ensuring respect for the principles of the non-use of force in international relations and respect for the territorial integrity of states."

Regarding the outbreak of the Second Gulf War, it has been alleged that the use of terms such as "border corrections" in its different (euphemistic) connotations may have contributed to the diplomatic "misunderstanding" between Iraq and the USA. Thus, American ambassador April Glaspie's alleged (silent and/or implicit) approval of a "border correction" between Iraq and Kuwait could have been interpreted as (silent and/or implicit) approval of an Iraqi annexation of Kuwait, wholly or partially. Should there prove to be any substance to these allegations, this would constitute another example of an overlapping extension and a contradictory intension with respect to the term "border correction", in terms of the analytical approach pursued in this study.

---

[61] Cf. for instance, UN-doc. S/21494 (Arabic and English), p. 2, or the Iraqi statements in the Security Council, reproduced in UN-doc. S/PV.2932. Regarding this point, *Eitel* (1992: 171f) provides the following analysis: "Soon after, when it was clear that the claim that it [sc. the attack on Kuwait] was only a response to the call for help from the "Free Provisional Government of Kuwait" was no longer viable, Saddam Hussein forgot his origins in the laicizing *Ba'th* (Reawakening) [*baʿṯ* 'resurrection'] political movement. He slipped further and further into the traditional historical role of a Ghazi [*ġāzī* 's.o. executing a *ġazwa* 'military attack'], an Islamic fighter, acting to free the land from the grip of the non-believers, if necessary through a jihad [*jihād*]. This transition could be seen in the Iraqi polemic against the westernized rulers of Kuwait and could not be missed in the propaganda against Operation "Desert Storm", that is, against the presence of non-Moslem troops on the soil of the Arabian peninsula, which had been made sacred by the Prophet."

[62] For numerous quotations involving this term, cf. above (this chapter).

[63] *Alston* 1992b: 110.

The following representative quotation is instructive for an analysis in terms of Speech Act Theory, as it highlights the characteristic Iraqi "teleological" viewpoint with regard to the international actions regarding Iraq under chapter VII of the United Nations Charter in general and "Operation Desert Storm" in particular – actions that have been regularly referred to by Iraq as *al-ᶜudwān aṯ-ṯalāṯīnī al-ġāšim* 'the brutal thirty-power agression':[64]

Item (48), Arabic original

ʾInna hāḏā l-ᶜamala l-ᶜudwānīya juzʾun mina l-muʾāmarati l-ʾamrīkīyati l-ʾaṭlasīyati ṣ-ṣahyūnīyati li-l-haymanati wa-taṯbīti n-niẓāmi l-istiᶜmārīyi l-jadīdi fī minṭaqati š-šarqi l-ʾawsaṭ.

Item (48), official English translation

This aggression is part of the United States-NATO-Zionist plot aimed at establishing hegemony and a new imperialist order in the Middle East.

II. Crucial documents

The multiplicity of documents regarding the Iraq-Kuwait conflict can be broken down into the following categories:[65]

(a) Resolutions of the General Assembly

(b) Resolutions of the Security Council

(c) Statements by the President of the Security Council

(d) One letter from the President of the Security Council to Iraq

(e) Communications from Iraq

(f) Communications from Kuwait

(g) Reports and letters of the Secretary General to the Security Council concerning UNIKOM

(h) Other reports and letters of the Secretary-General to the Security Council

(i) Statements by the Secretary-General

(j) Correspondence of the Secretary-General

(k) Reports of humanitarian missions

(l) Reports and other documents of the IAEA Director General

---

[64] UN-doc. S/22204 (Letter dated 6 February 1991 from the Permanent Representative of Iraq to the United Nations [Abdul Amir A. Al-Anbari] addressed to the Secretary-General [Javier Perez de Cuellar]) (Arabic and English), p. 1.

[65] Cf. *United Nations, Department of Public Information* (ed.) 1990. The United Nations and the Iraq-Kuwait Conflict 1990-1996. New York, p. 155.

(m) Reports of the Executive Chairman of the United Nations Special Commission (UNSCOM)

(n) Decisions and reports of the United Nations Compensation Commission

(o) Reports and other documents of the Security Council Sanctions Committee

(p) Memoranda of Understanding

(q) Reports on the situation of human rights in Iraq

(r) Other documents

In the following, several of the most crucial of these documents will be highlighted as regards their relevance for an analysis in terms of Speech Act Theory.

The first document is an excerpt from an "initiative" announced by Ṣaddām Ḥusayn, proposing that Iraq would leave Kuwait if Israel left the occupied territories; it thereby demonstrates the "marketing" of the occupation of Kuwait by Iraq. In terms of Speech Act Theory, the document provides an interesting conception of "genuine climate of peace in the [Middle Eastern] region":[66]

Item (49), Arabic original

Bi-smi llāhi r-raḥmāni r-raḥīmi,

Musāhamatan min-nā fī ḫalqi ᵓajwāᵓi salāmin ḥaqīqīyin fī l-minṭaqati, wa-tashīlan li-waḍᶜi l-minṭaqati fī ḥālati stiqrārin, wa-kašfan li-zayfi ᵓamrīka wa-ḥalīfati-hā l-masḫi ᵓisrāᵓīla, wa-faḍḥan li-ᶜumalāᵓi-hā ṣ-ṣiġāri wa-jarāᵓimi-him ḍidda l-ᵓummati wa-tawkīdan li-l-ḥaqqi min mawqiᶜi l-iqtidāri l-muᵓmini bi-llāhi wa-š-šaᶜbi wa-l-ᵓummati qarrarnā ᵓan nataqaddama bi-l-mubādarati t-tāliya: [...]

ᵓIᶜdāda tartībāti nsiḥābin wafqa mabādiᵓa wāḥidatin li-nsiḥābi ᵓisrāᵓīla fawran wa-bi-lā šurūṭin mina l-ᵓarāḍī l-muḥtallati fī filasṭīna wa-sūriyā wa-lubnāna, wa-nsiḥābi sūriyā min lubnāna, wa-l-insiḥāba bayna l-ᶜirāqi wa-ᵓīrāna, wa-waḍᶜa tartībātin li-ḥālati l-kuwayti, wa-ᵓan tansaḥiba t-tartībātu l-ᶜaskarīyatu fī tawqītāti-hā wa-kullu mā yattaṣilu bi-hā min tartībātin siyāsīyatin, ᶜalā kulli l-ḥālāti wa-wafqa nafsi l-ᵓususi wa-l-mabādiᵓi, wa-l-munṭaliqāti l-muᶜtamidati, ᵓāḫidīna bi-naẓari l-iᶜtibāri l-ḥuqūqa t-tāriḫīyata li-l-ᶜirāqi fī ᵓarḍi-hī, wa-ḫtiyāra šaᶜbi l-kuwayti, wa-ᵓan takūna l-bidāyatu fī taṭbīqi l-barnāmiji li-mā huwa ᵓasbaqu li-l-iḥtilāli ᵓaw mā summiya ḥtilālan, mubtadiᵓīna bi-taṭbīqi kulli mā ṣadara min qarārātin li-majlisi l-ᵓamni wa-hayᵓati l-ᵓumami l-muttaḥidati li-kulli l-ḥālāti, wa-ha-ka-ḏā wuṣūlan ᵓilā ᵓaqrabi ḥālatin fī-hā, wa-ᵓan tuṭabbaqa nafsu l-ᵓijrāᵓātu llatī ttaḫaḏa-hā majlisu

[66] UN-doc. S/21494 (Annex to the Letter dated 12 August 1990 from the Permanent Representative of Iraq to the United Nations [Abdul Amir A. Al-Anbari] addressed to the Secretary-General [Javier Perez de Cuellar]) (Arabic and English), pp. 3f.

l-ʾamni ḥiyāla l-ʿirāqi, tujāha man lā yaltazimu bi-hāḏā t-tartībi ʾaw yatajāwabu maʿa-hū.

Wa-fī kulli ʾaḥwāli wa-ʿinda-mā lā tatajāwabu ʾamrīkā hiya wa-ḥulafāʾu-hā ṣ-ṣiġāru min ʿumalāʾi-hā maʿa mubādarati-nā hāḏihī, fa-ʾinna-nā sa-nuqāwimu bi-qūwatin, naḥnu wa-l-ḫayyirūna min ʾabnāʾi l-ʾummati l-ʿarabīyati wa-šaʿbi l-ʿirāqi l-ʿaẓīmi, nazaʿāti-hā š-šarīrata wa-muḫaṭṭaṭāti-hā l-ʿudwānīyata, wa-sa-nantaṣiru bi-ʿawni llāhi, wa-sa-yandamu l-ʾašrāru ʿalā faʿlati-him baʿda ʾan yuḫrajū madḥūrīna malʿūnīna mina l-minṭaqati yujrūna ʾaḏyāla l-ḫizyi wa-l-ʿār.

Wa-llāhu ʾakbaru wa-l-yaḫsaʾi l-ḫāsiʾūn.

Item (49), official English translation

In the Name of God, the Merciful, the Compassionate,

In order to facilitate the establishment of a genuine climate of peace in the region and restore stability, expose the deception by the United States of America and its despicable ally, Israel, and to denounce their lackeys and the crimes they have committed against the nation and to restore truth, we have decided, strengthened by our faith in God, in our people and in the nation, to take the following initiative: [...]

The elaboration, on the basis of the same principles, of provisions for the immediate and unconditional withdrawal of Israel from the occupied Arab territories in Palestine, Syria and Lebanon, as well as the withdrawal of Syria from Lebanon and the withdrawal of Iraq and Iran, and the formulation of provisions relating to the situation in Kuwait, on the understanding that military arrangements – which must be implemented according to a precise timetable – and all related political arrangements shall be made on the basis of the same grounds and the same principles and shall be applicable in all cases, and that the historic rights of Iraq to its territories and the choice of the people of Kuwait will be taken into account. As a first step, this plan must be applied initially to prior cases of occupation and to cases alleged as such, through the systematic implementation, first of all, of all Security Council and United Nations resolutions, until the most recent case is reached, all the while ensuring that those measures taken by the Security Council with respect to Iraq are applied to all who do not respect or comply with this arrangement.

In any event, if the United States and its allies and lackeys fail to respond positively to our initiative, we shall oppose their evil inclinations with force, assisted by the worthy sons of the Arab nation and the great Iraqi people, and we shall triumph with the help of God, causing the forces of evil, who will be routed and forced to leave the region defeated, vanquished, damned and humiliated, to regret their acts.

God is great and woe unto the vanquished.

Perhaps the most grotesque example of conflicting legal norms and historical revisionism is the following document, of which a large portion will be reproduced here, as it reflects, at least implicitly, the historical and contemporary rationales for Iraq's way of action. The document contains the other of the two "initiatives" announced by Ṣaddām Ḥusayn at the outset of the Iraqi occupation of Kuwait. The "initiative" itself essentially calls for an inner-Arab solution to the conflict and tries to justify the Iraqi taking of foreign hostages in Iraq (euphemistically labeled *istiḍāfa* 'invitation to hospitality') as a preventive measure, thus yielding another interesting example for the application of Speech Act Theory:[67]

Item (50), Arabic original

Bi-smi llāhi r-raḥmāni r-raḥīmi,

Risālatun maftūḥatun ʾilā ᶜawāʾili l-ʾajānibi llaḏīna qarrara mumaṯṯilū š-šaᶜbi l-muntaḫabīna [sic!] "l-majlisu l-waṭanīyu" stiḍāfata-hum fī l-ᶜirāqi ḥattā tanfarija l-ʾazmatu ... wa-min ḫilāli-him ʾuḫāṭibu l-ġarbīyīna bi-wajhin ᶜāmmin wa-l-ʾamrīkīyīna min-hum bi-wajhin ḫāṣṣin ...

ʾAyyu-hā s-sayyidātu wa-s-sādatu ... ʾayyu-hā l-ʾaṭfālu l-ʾaᶜizzāʾu ... ʾinna-nī ʾuᶜribu bi-ʾanna-kum tataʾallamūna li-ᶜadami s-samāḥi li-ḏawī-kum bi-s-safari ḫārija l-ᶜirāqi wa-ʾinna-nī maᶜa-kum ʾataʾallamu li-hāḏā, bal wa-ʾinna-nī ᶜalā yaqīnin tamāman bi-ʾanna raʾīsa wa-ʾaᶜḍāʾa l-majlisi l-waṭanīyi fī l-ᶜirāqi yataʾallamūna ʾayḍan, miṯla-mā huwa ḥālu kulli l-ᶜirāqīyīna wa-l-ᶜarabi, ḏālika li-ʾanna-nī ʾaᶜrifu ʾanna ʾaᶜḍāʾa l-majlisi l-waṭanīyi fī l-ᶜirāqi muʾminūna bi-llāhi, wa-muʾminūna bi-ḥuqūqi l-ʾinsāni li-ʾanna-hum kāfaḥū sinīna ṭawīlatan ḥattā yafūzū fī-mā hum fī-hi min ḥālin yaḥmadūna llāha ᶜalay-hi wa-ʾinna-hum yaᶜrifūna miṯla-mā ʾanā ʾaᶜrifu bi-ʾanna bilāda-hum qad ᶜallamati l-ʾinsānīyata ʾawwala ḥarfin wa-bi-ḏālika ᶜallamat-humu l-kitābata, wa-ʾinna bilāda-hum ᶜallamati l-ʾinsānīyata ʾawwala qānūnin sunna ᶜalā wajhi l-ʾarḍi ḏālika huwa qānūnu ḥammūrābī, llaḏī ruttiba fī-hi l-ḥuqūqu wa-l-wājibātu l-ʾinsānīyatu qabla ʾarbaᶜati ʾālāfin wa-ḫamsa-miʾati sanatin, wa-li-ḏālika fa-ʾinna-hum yaᶜrifūna bi-ʾanna lā qīmata li-s-saᶜādati fī bilādi-him ʾin lam tafhami l-ʾinsānīyatu kullu-hā ʾanna ʾayya ḥtijāzin li-ḥurrīyati ʾayyi ʾinsānin huwa ẓalmun li-l-ḥurrīyati fī jānibin min jawānibi-hā, wa-ʾinna-hum yuḥibbūna l-ʾinsāna mahmā takun jinsīyatu-hū wa-lawnu-hū wa-jinsu-hū, ḏālika li-ʾanna-hum yuḥibbūna llāha, wa-ʾinna llāha lā yufarriqu bayna ᶜibādi-hī ʾil-lā ᶜalā ʾasāsi darajati l-ʾimāni wa-muqtaḍayāti-hī.

Li-ḏālika fa-ʾinna ʾaᶜḍāʾa l-majlisi l-waṭanīyi yataʾallamūna miṯla-mā ʾantum tataʾallamūna, wa-naḥnu jamīᶜan ʾāsifūna li-llaḏī ḥaṣala wa-huwa laysa min ʾirādati-nā wa-ʾinna-mā huwa ʾasāsan nābiᶜun min fiᶜli ʾirādati ʾunāsin tajabbarū wa-ḫarajū ᶜan ʾirādati llāhi wa-taᶜālīmi-hī ʾanna l-masʾūla l-mubāšira ᶜan hāḏā bi-d-darajati l-ʾasāsi [sic!] humā l-ʾidāratu l-ʾamrīkīyatu wa-l-ʾidāratu l-ʾinkilīzīyatu ... kayfa ḏālika?

---

[67] UN-doc. S/21651 (Letter dated 19 August 1990 from the President of the Republic of Iraq [Ṣaddām Ḥusayn], Annex to the Letter dated 19 August 1990 from the Permanent Representative of Iraq to the United Nations [Abdul Amir A. Al-Anbari] addressed to the Secretary-General [Javier Perez de Cuellar]) (Arabic and English), pp. 3ff. Instances of "[sic!]" in the transcription of this document refer to obvious grammatical mistakes in the Arabic original.

Taᶜrifūna ᵓayyu-hā s-sayyidātu wa-s-sādatu ᵓanna l-ᶜirāqa qad ḫaraja min ḥarbin dāmat ṯamāniya sanawātin bayna-hū wa-bayna ᵓīrāna wa-taᶜrifūna ᵓanna tilka l-ḥarba llatī dāmat ṯamāniya sanawātin kānat bayna dawlatayni nafṭīyatayni, wa-ᵓinna-hā kānat ᵓayḍan ḍimna ḥuqūli nafṭi l-ḫalīji, wa-ᵓinna fī hāḏihī l-ḥarbi ṣādafa ᵓan daḫalati l-juyūšu l-ᶜirāqīyatu ᵓilā dāḫili ᵓīrāna, wa-ᵓan daḫalati l-juyūšu l-ᵓīrānīyatu ᵓilā dāḫili l-ᶜirāqi fa-li-mā-ḏā lam tatadaḫḫal ᵓamīrikā wa-barīṭāniyā wa-l-ᵓāḫarūna li-ᵓīqāfi-hā wa-li-mā-ḏā lam yuhaddidū man lam yaltazim bi-l-qarārāti llatī ᵓaṣdara-hā majlisu l-ᵓamni fī ḥīni-hī? *[ᵓInna-hum lam yafᶜalū ḏālika li-ᵓanna-hum qad ᵓashamū fī ᵓišᶜāli-hā wa-li-ᵓanna-hum hum wa-ḥulafāᵓu-humu l-mutaḫallifūna min ᵓamṯāli qārūni l-kuwayti wa-ᵓaᶜwānu-hū ᵓarādū la-hā ᵓan tastamirra wa-ᵓan lā tatawaqqafa ḥattā šāᵓa la-hā llāhu ᵓan tatawaqqafa, wa-ᶜinda-mā tawaqqafat sallaṭū ᶜalay-nā ᶜumalāᵓa-hum fī l-minṭaqati wa-fī muqaddimati-him qārūna l-kuwayti wa-zumrata-hū li-yuḥāribū šaᶜba l-ᶜirāqi bi-luqmati ᶜayši-hī wa-yaḥrimūna-hū bi-l-ḥarbi l-iqtiṣādīyati wa-bi-l-iᶜtidāᵓi ᶜalā ḥuqūli bitrūli-nā, min ᵓabsaṭa mā yalīqu bi-hī, wa-huwa šaᶜbu l-ḥaḍārāti wa-l-ᵓamjādi, ḥattā ᵓawṣalū qīmata dīnāri l-ᶜirāqi ᵓilā mā yaqrubu min 1 [dīnār] ᵓilā 54 filsin [sic!] min qīmati dīnāri l-kuwayti, maᶜa ᵓanna qīmata dīnāri l-ᶜirāqi kānat fī ᶜāmi 1980 ᵓaᶜlā min qīmati dīnāri l-kuwayti, ḥattā ᵓaṣbaḥa yataᶜaḏḏaru ᶜalay-nā tawfīru ḥalībin li-ᵓaṭfāli-nā wa-naḥnu bilādu mā bayna n-nahrayni, bilādu l-ḫayri wa-l-ᶜaṭāᵓi, wa-qad lā taᶜrifūna ᵓayyu-hā s-sādatu ᵓanna hāḏā l-balada llaḏī taᵓammara man nuṣṣibū ḥukkāman ᶜalay-hi [sic!] huwa juzᵓun mina l-ᶜirāqi ḥattā ᶜāmi 1913. Wa-ᵓanna l-ᶜirāqa lam yaᶜtarif bi-hī ka-dawlatin ḥattā s-sittīnāti min hāḏā l-qarni wa-ᵓanna raᵓīsa wuzarāᵓi l-ᶜirāqi ᵓaṣdara qarāran ᶜāma 1961 yaqḍī bi-ḍammi l-kuwayti ᵓilā l-ᶜirāqi wa-ᵓaᶜāda l-kuwayta ka-qaḍāᵓin murtabiṭin bi-l-baṣrati, wa-ᶜayyana šayḫa-hā qāᵓim-maqāman la-hā miṯla-mā kāna ᶜalay-hi ḥattā qiyāmi l-ḥarbi l-ᶜālamīyati l-ᵓūlā. Wa-ᵓanna l-majlisa l-istišārīya fī l-kuwayti qarrara marratayni fī ṯ-ṯalāṯīnāti l-waḥdata maᶜa l-ᶜirāqi ḥattā ḥulla bi-qarārin mina l-ᵓusrati l-ḥākimati ᵓāna-ḏā-ka, wa-ᵓanna raᵓīsa wuzarāᵓi l-ᶜirāqi Nūrī s-Saᶜīd ṭaraḥa ᶜalā ḥilfi baġdāda wa-bi-ḥuḍūri mumaṯṯili ᵓamīrikā fī ᶜami 1958 al-waḥdata maᶜa l-kuwayti ...

Fa-li-mā-ḏā yurīdu raᵓīsu l-wilāyāti l-muttaḥidati l-ᵓamīrikīyati wa-raᵓīsatu wuzarāᵓi barīṭāniyā tajwīᶜa šaᶜbi l-ᶜirāqi ḥattā l-mawti, ḫāba mā yafᶜalūna, wa-mā-ḏā ᶜamila šaᶜbu l-ᶜirāqi ġayra ᵓanna-hū waḥḥada nafsa-hū, wa-waḥḥada šaᵓna l-ᶜawāṭili llatī šaṭara-hā d-dahru bayna l-ᶜirāqi wa-l-kuwayti wa-dāfaᶜa ᶜan nafsi-hī wa-sāᶜada fī ḫalᶜi šayḫi l-kuwayti l-mutaḫallifi llaḏī lā hamma la-hū ġayru jamᶜi l-ᵓamwāli wa-n-nisāᵓi fa-li-mā-ḏā yafriḍūna l-ḥiṣāra ᶜalā l-ᶜirāqi li-yumītū l-ᵓaṭfāla r-ruḍḍaᶜa wa-š-šuyūḫa wa-kulla n-nāsi llaḏīna lā yatawaffara la-humu l-ġaḏāᵓu wa-d-dawāᵓu law ᵓanna llaḏī turīdu-hū l-ᵓidāratu l-ᵓamīrikīyatu wa-l-barīṭānīyatu yataḥaqqaq! Wa-li-mā-ḏā yaḥšidūna l-ᵓasāṭīla l-baḥrīyata wa-ᵓasrāba ṭ-ṭāᵓirāti wa-l-qūwāti l-barrīyata llatī yurīdūna bi-ktimāli ḥušūdi-hā l-hujūma ᶜalā l-ᶜirāq? ᵓInna-hum qālū bi-ᵓanna-hum jāᵓū ᵓilā hunā, wa-ᵓahānū ᵓarḍa l-ᶜarabi wa-muqaddasāti lmuslimīna bi-ḥtilāli-him li-ʾarḍi l-ḥijāzi wa-najda,]*[68] li-yudāfiʿū ʿani s-saʿūdīyati tujāha ḫaṭari l-ʿirāqi, wa-hum yakḏibūna li-ʾanna-hum yaʿrifūna ʾanna l-ʿirāqa lā yaʿtadī wa-ʾinna-mā yaḍribu ʿinda-mā yuʿtadā ʿalay-hi. Fa-ʾin lam yakun hunālika man qarrara ḍarba l-ʿirāqi fa-l-yanam muṭmaʾinnan hāniʾan fī nawmi-hī qarīra l-ʿayn ...

ʾAqūlu ʾayyatu-hā s-sayyidātu wa-ʾayyu-hā s-sādatu wa-yā ʾaḥibbāʾa llāhi wa-ʾaḥibbāʾ-ī l-ʾaṭfālu l-ʾaʿizzāʾu fī ʾūrūbbā wa-ʾamīrikā ... ʾinna waṭana-nā ka-mā huwa wāḍiḥun la-kum muhaddadun min ʾamīrikā wa- barīṭāniyā wa-man sa-yatawarraṭa maʿa-humā mina l-ḫāʾibīna l-ʾaḏillāʾi ... wa-ʾinna šaʿba-nā muʿraḍun li-ʾīḏāʾin šadīd. Wa-ʾiḏā mā ʾaqdama l-ḫāsiʾūna ʿalā l-ʿudwāni sa-tasquṭu l-kaṯīru min ruʾūsi l-ḥukkāmi ʿani l-ʾaktāfi, wa-sa-yamūtu nisāʾun wa-rijālun wa-ʾaṭfālun bi-ʿašarāti l-ʾulūfi mina l-jānibayni, [...]

Tarka mawḍūʿi l-kuwayti li-yuʿālija-hū l-ʿarabu ka-šaʾnin ʿarabīyin, miṯla-mā ḥaṣala fī kulli l-qaḍāyā l-mumāṯilati, ka-qaḍīyati ṣ-ṣaḥrāʾi fī maġribi l-waṭani l-ʿarabīyi bayna l-maġribi wa-ʾaṭrāfi l-qaḍīyati, wa-ka-qaḍīyati l-iḥtilāli s-sūrīyi li-lubnāna, wa-ġayri-hā mina l-qaḍāyā l-mumāṯila.

Hāḏihī hiya ʾayyatu-hā l-ʾaḫawātu wa-l-ʾiḫwatu wa-ʾayyu-hā l-ʾaṭfālu l-ʾaʿizzāʾu mubādaratu-nā wa-ʾinna-nī ʾasʾalu-kum hal fī-hā mā huwa muḫālifun li-l-qānūni d-duwalīyi ʾaw muʿādin li-l-ʾinsānīyati ʾaw munāqiḍun li-l-maṣāliḥi l-mašrūʿati li-l-ġarb?

Fa-ʾiḏā kāna l-jawābu ʾanna l-mubādarata ʿādilatun fa-l-nataʿāwun jamīʿan li-taḥqīqi-hā wa-bi-ḏālika yataḥaqqaqu s-salāmu li-l-jamīʿi wa-tataḥaqqaqu l-ḥurrīyatu wa-l-ḥayātu l-hāniʾatu li-l-jamīʿi, fa-hal sa-yasmaʿu llaḏī fī ʾuḏni-hī waqr ...?

Suʾālun muwajjahun ʾilā l-ʾidārati l-ʾamīrikīyati bi-wajhin ḫāṣṣin wa-bil-jawābi ṣ-ṣaḥīḥi ʿalay-hi yataḥaqqaqu l-kaṯīru mim-mā yaḫdimu l-ʾinsānīya.

Wa-s-salāmu ʿalay-kum wa-raḥmatu llāhi wa-barakātu-hū.

(Tawqīʿ) Ṣaddām Ḥusayn

19 ʾāb/ʾaġusṭus 1990

Item (50), official English translation

In the Name of God, the Merciful, The Compassionate,

An open letter to the families of foreigners whom the elected representatives of the people, the National Assembly, have decided to receive as guests in Iraq until the crisis is over; through them I address Westerners in general and United States nationals in particular.

Ladies and gentlemen, dear children: I know that you are feeling anguish because your relatives are not allowed to leave Iraq. Like you, I too am anguished about this, and indeed I am quite sure that the Chairman and members

[68] The portion in brackets of the Arabic original does not appear in the official English translation (cf. below).

of the National Assembly in Iraq also feel anguish, as do all Iraqis and Arabs. I say this because I know that members of the National Assembly in Iraq believe in God and in human rights, because for long years they fought for victory in their cause, praising God as they did so. They know just as I do, that their country gave mankind its first script and so taught them to write and that their country gave mankind the first law to be codified on the face of the Earth, namely, the Law of Hammurabi, which made provisions for human rights and obligations 4,500 years ago. They therefore know that happiness in their country can have no value unless all mankind recognizes that any restriction on the freedom of any human being represents a breach of some aspect of human freedom. They love their fellow men, whatever their nationality, colour or race. This is because they love God, who distinguishes between His servants only by the strength of their faith and its associated requirements.

So the members of the National Assembly feel anguish just as you do. We are all sorry for what happened, for something which has not arisen of our own volition but is basically caused by the deliberate actions of people who have acted arrogantly and gone against the will of God and his teachings. The persons who are directly and fundamentally responsible for this situation are the United States Administration and the British Administration. Why so?

You know, ladies and gentlemen, that Iraq has emerged from a war which lasted eight years between it and Iran. You know that the eight-year-long war was fought between two oil states and that it took place inside the Gulf oil fields. In that war, it happened that Iraqi troops entered Iran and that Iranian troops entered Iraq. So why did the United States, Britain and the others not intervene to halt them? Why did they not threaten those who failed to adhere to the resolutions adopted at that time by the Security Council? And yet they do so *[they did not do so because they had taken part in inflaming this war, and because they and their retarded allies like the *qārūn*[69] of Kuwait and his associates wanted it to continue and not to end until God decided it should do so. And when it ended, they appointed as rulers over us their agents in the region, and at their forefront the *qārūn* of Kuwait and his kin, so that they would fight the Iraqi people with hunger [literally: "with the mouthful of their livelihood/ bread"] and deprive them of their most elementary needs with economic warfare and attacks on our oil fields – the Iraqi people being the people who promulgated cultures and glorious ideas! And they finally made the value of the Iraqi dinar depreciate to only 54% of the value of the Kuwaiti dinar, although the value of the Iraqi dinar was higher than that of the Kuwaiti dinar in 1980, so that it became impossible for us to provide our children with milk – we being Mesopotamia, "the country of the best and the gift". And don't you know, gentlemen, that this country [i.e., Kuwait] which is ruled by people whom they [i.e., the "coalition"] appointed as governors over it, was part of Iraq until 1913; and that Iraq did not recognize it as an independent state until the sixties of this century; and that the Prime Minister of Iraq issued a resolution in 1961 in which the annexation of Kuwait to Iraq was declared and Kuwait was "brought home" as a district depending on Basra and a deputy governor was appointed, as was the case before the outbreak of World War I; and that the Advisory Council in Kuwait decided on unification with Iraq twice in the thirties until this was reversed by a decision of the ruling family at the time; and that the Prime Minister of Iraq, Nuri Said, suggested to [states parties of] the Baghdad pact the unification with Kuwait in 1958, in the presence of an American diplomat?

---

[69] A pejorative term in contemporary Arabic, originally designating a minister of the Pharaoh in ancient Egypt.

So why do the President of the United States and the British Prime Minister want to starve the Iraqi people to death – may they fail in what they are doing – and what has the Iraqi people done other than to unite itself, to unite the loose ends that time had parted between Iraq and Kuwait, to defend itself, and to help overthrow the retarded Sheikh of Kuwait to whom only the accumulation of women and money matters? So why do they impose a blockade on Iraq so as to cause suckling babies to die, old people, and everyone who has no reserves of food and medicine, should what the American and British administrations want materialize! And why do they deploy navy, air force, and army with whom they want to attack Iraq? They said that they had come here – whereby they vilified the land of the Arabs and the holy places of the Muslims in occupying the territory of al-Ḥijāz and Najd –]*[70] to defend Saudi Arabia against the danger represented by Iraq. They are lying because they know that Iraq will not attack and will only strike if it itself is attacked. If no one decides to strike against Iraq, then they may sleep soundly, peacefully and contentedly.

I tell you, ladies and gentlemen, dear people of God, my dear children in Europe and the United States, that our country -- as is clear to you -- is threatened by the United States and Britain and by those contemptible and futile elements who may become involved with them. Our people is being subjected to a terrible injustice. If these despicable elements should proceed to commit an act of aggression, many heads of rulers will fall from their shoulders and tens of thousands of women, men and children will die on both sides. [...]

The question of Kuwait should be left to the Arabs to be addressed as an Arab issue, as has been the case in all similar questions such as that of the Sahara, in the western part of the Arab world, between Morocco and the other parts of the dispute, the question of the Syrian occupation of Lebanon and other similar issues.

This, O brothers and sisters and dear children, is our initiative. I ask you whether there is anything in it which runs counter to international law, is anti-humanitarian or incompatible with the legitimate interests of the West?

If the response is that the initiative is fair, let us all cooperate to put it into practice. Peace, freedom and a contented life will thereby be assured for all. Will this message be heard by those who turn a deaf ear?

This question is directed in particular to the United States Administration. A positive response to it will ensure much that is of service to mankind.

Peace be upon you, the mercy of God and His blessings.

Saddam HUSSEIN

19 August 1990

A further example of comparable discourse is the following statement of a spokesman in the Iraqi Foreign Ministry, regarding sanctions pronounced against Iraq by the Security Council:[71]

---

[70] The English text in brackets, which does not appear in the official English translation, probably by oversight, was translated by the author.

[71] UN-doc. S/21790 (Annex to the Letter dated 19 September 1990 from the Permanent Representative of Iraq to the United Nations [Abdul Amir A. Al-Anbari] addressed to the Secretary-General [Javier Perez de Cuellar]) (Arabic and English), p. 2.

Item (51), Arabic original

Taᶜqīban ᶜalā qarāri majlisi l-ʾamni 666 fī 13 ʾaylūl/sabtambir [1990] ṣarraḥa nāṭiqun rasmīyun bi-smi wizārati l-ḫārijīyati bi-mā yalī: [...]

Fa-l-ʾijrāʾātu l-wāridatu fī hāḏā l-qarāri hiya ʾijrāʾātun muhīnatun li-šaᶜbin ʾabīyin yafḫaru bi-turāṯi-hī l-ʾinsānīyi wa-musāhamati-hī l-bārizati fī ḥaḍārati l-ʾinsān. Wa-ᶜalā hāʾulāʾi llaḏīna dafaᶜū bi-ttijāhi ʾiṣḏāri hāḏā l-qarāri ʾan yataḏakkarū bi-ʾanna bilāda mā bayna n-nahrayni kānat markazan li-t-tijārati wa-markazan li-l-ʾintāji ᶜinda-mā kāna ʾajdādu-hum yaᶜīšūna fī l-kuhūf. Li-ḏālika fa-ʾinna šaᶜba-nā l-mubdiʾa wa-l-muntija wa-l-wāṯiqa min nafsi-hī wa-l-muṣammina ᶜalā d-difāᶜi ᶜan ḥuqūqi-hī wa-siyādati-hī yarfuḍu bi-ʾibāʾin wiṣāyata l-qūwā l-kubrā ᶜalay-hi wa-sa-yuwāṣilu kifāḥa-hū l-ᶜādila wa-ẓ-ẓāfira muttakilan ᶜalā llāhi, wa-ᶜalā ʾirādati-hī ṣ-ṣulbati wa-ᶜalā ʾummati-hī l-ᶜarabīyati l-majīdati wa-ᶜalā l-ḫayyirīna wa-š-šurafāʾi fī l-ᶜālam.

Item (51), official English translation

Commenting on Security Council resolution 666 (1990) of 13 September 1990, an official spokesman for the Ministry of Foreign Affairs stated as follows: [...]

The arrangements set forth in this resolution are an insult to a lofty people which is proud of its humanitarian heritage and of its outstanding contribution to human civilization. Those who urged the adoption of the resolution should recall that the land of Mesopotamia was a centre of trade and a centre of production at a time when their ancestors were still living in caves. Our creative, fecund, and self-confident people, determined to defend its rights and its sovereignty, proudly rejects the tutelage of the great Powers. It will continue its just and triumphant struggle, placing its trust in God, in its firm will, in the glorious Arab nation to which it belongs and in men of good will and honour in the world.

An example which highlights the immense discourse gap between Iraq and the Security Council is the following document, in which the Iraqi Minister for Foreign Affairs [ʾAḥmad Ḥusayn] concedes in a most cumbersome way that Iraq has no choice but to accept the provisions of Security Council resolution 687 (1991):[72]

Item (52), Arabic original

Wa-ġayra ʾanna l-majlisa bi-qarāri-hī l-mujḥifi hāḏā, wa-bi-l-ʾuslūbi l-intiqāʾīyi llaḏī mārasa-hū ḍidda šaᶜbi l-ᶜirāqi ʾaṯbata l-ḥaqīqata llatī ʾakadnā ᶜalay-hā bi-stimrārin wa-hiya ʾanna l-majlisa qad taḥawwala ʾilā ʾadātin ṭayyiᶜatin fī yadi l-wilāyāti l-muttaḥidati li-tanfīḏi raġabāti-hā wa-siyāsāti-hā fī l-minṭaqati, wa-ʾanna l-hadafa l-ʾasāsīya min ḏālika huwa ḥimāyatu ᶜudwānīyati ʾisrāʾīla wa-siyāsati-hā t-tawassuᶜīyati bi-raġmi l-kalāmi llaḏī lā yaqtarinu bi-fiᶜlin ḥawla s-silmi wa-l-ᶜadālati fī š-šarqi l-ʾawsaṭi llaḏī ṣadara

[72] UN-doc. S/22456 (Identical Letters dated 6 April 1991 from the Minister for Foreign Affairs of the Republic of Iraq addressed respectively to the Secretary-General and to the President of the Security Council) (Arabic and English), pp. 6f and 7f, respectively. For a legal assessment of Security Council resolution 687 (1991) and its aftermath, cf. *Gray* 1994.

ᶜan hāḏā l-ᶜuḍwi ʾaw ḏālika min ʾaᶜḍāʾi l-majlisi llaḏīna ṣawwatū ᶜalā hāḏā l-qarār.

Wa-mina l-wāḍiḥi tamāman li-kulli š-šurafāʾi wa-l-munṣifīna fī l-ᶜālami ʾanna hāḏihī l-ʾijrāʾāti l-intiqāmīyata wa-l-jāʾirata llatī tuttaḫaḏu ḍidda l-ᶜirāqi laysat natījatan li-l-ʾaḥdāṯi llatī waqaᶜat fī 2 ʾāb/ʾaġusṭus 1990 wa-baᶜda-hā bal ʾinna s-sababa l-jawharīya llaḏī yumkinu warāʾa-hā huwa li-ʾanna l-ᶜirāqa lam yaqbal bi-l-waḍᶜi l-mujḥifi llaḏī furiḍa ᶜalā l-ʾummati l-ᶜarabīyati wa-duwali l-minṭaqati munḏu ᶜuqūdin ᶜadīdatin wa-llaḏī jaʾala min ʾisrāʾīla l-qūwata l-ᶜudwānīyata l-muhayminata bi-mā tamtaliku-hū min ʾaḥdaṯi wa-ʾaqwā l-ʾasliḥati t-taqlīdīyati wa-ʾasliḥati d-damāri š-šāmili wa-min-hā s-silāḥu n-nawawī. Wa-ʾinna hāḏihī l-ḥaqīqata tuʾakkidu mā bayyana-hū l-ᶜirāqu qabla ʾaḥdāṯi 2 ʾāb/ʾaġusṭus 1990 min ʾanna-hū yataᶜarraḍu ʾilā muʾāmaratin tastahdifu l-qaḍāʾa ᶜalā l-ʾimkānāti llatī waffara-hā min ʾajli ʾiqāmati tawāzunin ᶜādilin fī l-minṭaqati min šaʾni-hī ʾan yumahhida ṭ-ṭarīqa li-ʾiḥlāli s-silmi l-munṣifu wa-l-ᶜadālati fī-hā.

Wa-mina l-muʾsifi ʾanna duwalan lam taqṣid bi-l-ʾasāsi ʾan tušārika l-wilāyāti l-muttaḥidata wa-ʾisrāʾīla fī taḥqīqi hāḏihī l-ʾahdāfi qad ʾashamat rubba-mā min ġayri qaṣdin fī taḥqīqi min ḫilāli t-taṣwīti ᶜalā hāḏā l-qarāri l-jāʾir.

Wa-fī l-waqti llaḏī yusajjilu fī-hi l-ᶜirāqu hāḏihī l-mulāḥaẓāti l-mabdaʾīyata wa-l-qānūnīyata wa-š-šarᶜīyata li-yaḥuṯṯa ʾaṣḥāba ḍ-ḍamīri min ʾaᶜḍāʾi l-mujtamaᶜi d-duwalīyi wa-r-aʾyi l-ᶜāmmi l-ᶜālamīyi ᶜalā fahmi l-ḥaqīqati ka-mā hiya wa-l-intiṣāri li-l-ḥaqqi ka-mā yanbaġī, fa-ʾinna l-ᶜirāqa yajidu nafsa-hū ᶜalā ḫiyārin wāḥidin lā ġayra huwa l-qubūlu bi-hāḏā l-qarār.

ʾArjū taʾmīna tawzīᶜi hāḏihī r-risālati ka-waṯīqatin min waṯāʾiqi majlisi l-ʾamni, wa-tafaḍḍalū bi-qubūli wāfiri l-iḥtirām.

(Tawqīᶜ) ʾAḥmad Ḥusayn

Wazīr ḫārijīyati l-jumhūrīyati l-ᶜirāqīya

Item (52), official English translation

By adopting this unjust resolution and by this selective treatment of the Iraqi people, the Council has merely confirmed the fact that we have never ceased to emphasize, namely that the Council has become a puppet which the United States of America is manipulating in order to achieve its political designs in the region, the prime objective being to perpetuate Israel's policy of aggression and expansion, despite the empty words about peace and justice in the Middle East uttered by one or another of the Council members which voted for this resolution.

It could not be more clear to all men of honour and justice that these iniquitous and vengeful measures against Iraq are not a consequence of the events of 2 August 1990 and the subsequent period, for the essential motive underlying these measures stems from Iraq's rejection of the unjust situation imposed on the Arab nation and the countries of the region for decades, a situation which has enabled Israel, a belligerent Power heavily armed with the most modern and fearsome conventional weapons and with weapons of mass destruction, including nuclear weapons, to exercise hegemony in the region. This reality confirms what Iraq had stated before the events of 2 August 1990, namely that it was the target of a plot aimed at destroying the potential it had deployed with a view to arriving at a just balance in the region which would pave the way for the institution of justice and of a lasting peace.

It is unfortunate that states whose intention was not in any way to help the United States and Israel attain their objectives should involuntarily have contributed to their attainment by voting for this iniquitous resolution.

As Iraq makes its preliminary comments on the juridical and legal aspects of this resolution, so as to encourage men of conscience in the countries members of the international community and world public opinion to make an effort to understand the truth as it is and the need to ensure the triumph of justice, it has no choice but to accept this resolution.

I should be grateful if you would have this letter circulated as a document of the Security Council.

Ahmed HUSSEIN

Minister of Foreign Affairs for Iraq

The response of the President of the Security Council is noteworthy for its brevity and technicality, as it only replies to the legal essence of that letter, i.e., the acceptance of the said resolution:[73]

Item (53), English original

I have the honour to acknowledge receipt of your communication dated 6 April 1991 (S/22456).

You thereby transmit to me the letter addressed to me by the Minister for Foreign Affairs of Iraq, the penultimate paragraph of which contains official notification of the acceptance, irrevocable and without qualifying conditions, by Iraq of resolution 687 (1991), in accordance with paragraph 33 of that resolution.

Another Iraqi document which pertains to Security Council resolution 692 of May 20, 1991, juggles grotesquely with the terms "law" and "legality":[74]

Item (54), Arabic original

ʾInna l-majlisa bi-smi š-šarᶜīyati d-duwalīyati yuḫālifu jawhara hāḏihī š-šarᶜīyati wa-yaᶜūdu ʾilā širᶜati l-ġābi ḥayṯu takūnu l-qūwatu wa-laysa l-qānūnu hiya l-ḥākima l-muṭlaq. ʾInna jawhara š-šarᶜīyati sawāʾa fī l-qawānīni l-waṭanīyati ʾawi l-qānūni d-duwalīyi huwa laysa fī taṭbīqi l-qānūni faqaṭ wa-

[73] UN-doc. S/22485 (Letter dated 11 April 1991 from the President of the Security Council [Paul Noterdaeme] addressed to the Permanent Representative of Iraq), p. 1.

[74] UN-doc. S/22629 (Comments of the Permanent Representative of Iraq, Dr. Abdul Amir A. Al-Anbari, on Security Council resolution 692 of 20 May 1991, Annex to the Letter dated 20 May 1991 from the Permanent Representative of Iraq to the United Nations [Abdul Amir A. Al-Anbari] addressed to the Secretary-General [Javier Perez de Cuellar]) (Arabic and English), p. 3.

ʾinna-mā taṭbīqi-hī bi-ṣūratin salīmatin tuḥawwilu dūna ʾisāʾati stiʿmāli-hī wa-ḏālika murāʿātan li-mutaṭallabāti l-qānūn (Due Process of Law).

Item (54), official English translation

In the name of international legality, the [Security] Council is violating the very essence of that legality and returning to the law of the jungle, whereby force, rather than the law, rules supreme. Whether with respect to national or international law, the essence of legality does not lie simply in enforcing the law, but rather in enforcing it soundly in such a way as to prevent its misuse; this should be done by observing the "due process of the law".

An especially interesting quotation that exhibits (ab)use of technical language for political purposes and adduces inappropriate political comparisons is found in an interview with a former Iraqi Minister of Culture and Information, as cited in the following document:[75]

Item (55), Arabic original

Al-qūwā l-kubrā qad tuġayyiru l-jūġrāfiyā lākinna-hā lā tuġayyiru t-tārīḫa, wa-hāḏā l-kalāmu laysa ʿāṭifīyan, wa-l-ʾamṯilatu ʿalā ḏālika kaṯīratun, fa-l-qaḍīyatu l-filasṭīnīyatu maṯalan, mahmā kānat hunāka ḥulūlun juzʾīyatun, fa-hiya lā taʿnī ʾanna l-qaḍīyata l-filasṭīnīyata ntahat ʾasāsan, wa-ʾanna filasṭīna ntahat. Ka-ḏālika hunāka ʾamṯilatun, fa-ṣ-ṣīnu lam tansa juzura furmūzā, wa-ʾalmāniyā l-ġarbīyatu lam tansa ʾalmāniyā š-šarqīyata, wa-l-kuwaytu kānat juzʾan mina l-ʿirāq.

Item (55), official English translation

The major Powers may change geography, but they cannot change history. This is not an emotional observation; the examples are numerous. Take the Palestinian issue, for example. However many partial solutions there are, they do not mean an end to the issue or an end to Palestine is finished [sic!]. China did not forget Formosa. West Germany did not forget East Germany. And Kuwait was a part of Iraq.

Meanwhile, Iraq has reverted to a diplomatic style closer to international standards in acknowledging the independence of Kuwait by way of Revolution Command Council decision No. 200 of November 10, 1994:[76]

---

[75] UN-doc. S/26887 (Statement by the Iraqi Minister of Culture and Information [Hamad Youssef Hammadi], Annex to the Letter dated 16 December 1993 from the Permanent Representative of Kuwait to the United Nations [Mohammad A. Abulhasan] addressed to the President of the Security Council) (Arabic and English), p. 1.

[76] Cf. UN-doc. S/1994/1288 (Letter dated 12 November 1994 from the Minister for Foreign Affairs of Iraq [Mohammed Said Al-Sahaf] addressed to the Secretary-General [Boutros Boutros-Ghali], Annex to the Letter dated 13 November 1994 from the Permanent Representative of Iraq to the United Nations [Nizar Hamdoon] addressed to the Secretary-General [Boutros Boutros-Ghali]) (Arabic and English), p. 3. Revolution Command Council decision No. 200 is reproduced in this annex.

Item (56), Arabic original

Imtiṯālan li-qarāri majlisi l-ᵓamni t-tābiᶜi li-l-ᵓumami l-muttaḥidati raqmi 833 (1993) taᶜtarifu jumhūrīyatu l-ᶜirāqi bi-l-ḥudūdi d-duwalīyati bayna jumhūrīyati l-ᶜirāqi wa-dawlati l-kuwayti ka-mā rassamat-hā lajnatu l-ᵓumami l-muttaḥidati ti-tarsīmi l-ḥudūdi bayna l-ᶜirāqi wa-l-kuwayti l-mušakkalatu bi-mūjibi l-fiqrati (3) mina l-qarāri 687 (1991), wa-taḥtarimu ḥurmata l-ḥudūdi l-maḏkūra.

Item (56), official English translation

The Republic of Iraq, in compliance with the United Nations Security Council Resolution 833 (1993), recognizes the international boundary between the Republic of Iraq and the State of Kuwait as demarcated by the United Nations Iraq-Kuwait Boundary Demarcation Commission established in pursuance to paragraph 3 of resolution 687 (1991), and respects the inviolability of the said boundary.

D. The Iraqi concepts of "law", "truth", "peace", and "justice": a comparative analysis of the traditional methods of treaty interpretation and Speech Act Theory

I. Basic considerations

Just as was the case with the Arabic and Hebrew renditions of such terms as "cease-fire", "truce", and "peace" in the Arab-Israeli documents, there are no linguistic differences *per se* between the English and Arabic semantics of terms and phrases such as *širᶜa* 'law', *al-ḥaqīqa ka-mā hiya* 'the truth as it is', *aš-šarᶜīya ad-duwalīya* 'international legality', *as-silm wa-l-ᶜadāla fī š-šarq al-ᵓawsaṭ* 'peace and justice in the Middle East', *as-silm al-munṣif wa-l-ᶜadāla* 'lasting [literally: "just"] peace and justice', and other phrases, as appeared in the just cited documents. However, the connotations of these phrases on the Iraqi side differ fundamentally from the connotations a "Western" observer would have with these terms.

In the following, the four traditional methods of treaty interpretation (grammatical, systematic, historical, and teleological) as well as Speech Act Theory will be briefly applied to the arguments found in legal documents.

II. The traditional methods of treaty interpretation

From the perspective of grammatical and systematic interpretation, no arguments can be made in the Iraq-Kuwait context. From the perspective of historical interpretation, Iraq defines the terms *širᶜa* 'law', *ḥaqīqa* 'truth', *šarᶜīya duwalīya* 'international legality', *silm* 'peace', and *ᶜadāla* 'justice' as reflecting the claimed historical "unity" of Iraq and Kuwait. From the perspective of teleological interpretation, Iraq defines the listed terms with a view to attaining the state of *tawāzun ᶜādil* 'just balance' between Iraq/the Arab world and Israel.

III. Speech Act Theory

Speech Act Theory can be adduced in this context to account for the different usage of the terms *širᶜa* 'law', *ḥaqīqa* 'truth', *šarᶜīya duwalīya* 'international legality', *silm* 'peace', and *ᶜadāla* 'justice' by the two parties concerned, as a result of the strange blend of propaganda and distortion of facts found in the Iraqi documents. The different *Weltanschauungen* of the two parties involved – Iraq as an "Arab"/"Islamic" party on the one hand, and the "Western" party, i.e., mainly the United States, on the other – emerge all too clearly in this context.[77] In all fairness, it must be stated that the Iraqi perspective in these instances cannot be taken as a model of a general "Islamic" perspective, even though Iraq has regularly claimed to act in the interests of the Arab and Islamic *ʾumma* in general, and of the Palestinian people in particular.

The two theories of interpretation (i.e., the respective articles in the Vienna Convention on the Law of Treaties, on the one hand, and the tenets of Speech Act Theory on the other) and their implications for the analysis of conflicting ideas can be combined in a formal table, as already developed above (chapter three). Using the just mentioned example of *širᶜa* 'law', *ḥaqīqa* 'truth', *šarᶜīya duwalīya* 'international legality', *silm* 'peace', and *ᶜadāla* 'justice', the following picture emerges:

[77] Cf. again the methodology laid out in *Szalay/Abu-Hilal/Strohl/Mason/Goodison* 1978 and the typology of diplomatic misunderstanding laid out above (chapter three).

Table 2

Comparative analysis of the "Western" vs. Iraqi concepts of "law", "truth", "peace", and "justice"

```
      "Western" contracting party   "Arab"/"Islamic" contracting party
                                 |          |
                          treaty/legal document:
     Iraqi letters addressed to the Security Council or the Secretary General
                       |                                  |
                      law                               šir^ca
                     truth                              ḥaqīqa
             international legality              šar^cīya duwalīya
                     peace                               silm
           | ---   justice   --- |        | ---   ^cadāla   --- |
           |                     |        |                     |
European language    International Law in  Arabic             International Law in
|                    "Western" perspective |                  Islamic perspective
|                    |                     |                  |
semantics            grammatical sense     semantics          grammatical sense
pragmatics           systematic sense      pragmatics         systematic sense
discourse structure  historical sense      discourse structure historical sense
special terminology  teleological sense    special terminology teleological sense
|                    |                     |                  |
extension-intension  |                     extension-intension |
|                    |                     |                  |
Speech Act Theory    Vienna Convention     Speech Act Theory  Vienna Convention
                |    on the Law of                        |   on the Law of
                |    Treaties (1969)                      |   Treaties (1969)
                |    |                                    |   |
          "Western" perspective                     Iraqi perspective
```

E. Summary of Chapter Four

In the realm of "war and peace", no systematic references to the Islamic traditions in general or the Islamic concept of *jihād* in particular were found in official documents, although the Islamic concept of "war and peace" proved to play a certain role in the rhetorical ranting by a number of states. While many Iraqi and Iranian documents exhibit disregard of, if not outright contempt for international law, there is no direct religious motivation reflected in the language use as far as international transactions and agreements are concerned. Speech Act Theory proves a useful tool for capturing the different intensionalities of seemingly elementary terms such as *šir^{c}a* 'law', *ḥaqīqa* 'truth', *šar^{c}īya duwalīya* 'international legality', *silm* 'peace', and *^{c}adāla* 'justice' in diplomatic discourse between "Western" and "Arab"/"Islamic" parties.

Chapter Five

Application of the theory of interpretation to the realm of human rights

"[I]t [i]s difficult [...] to engage in a debate on the fulfilment of international legal obligations when one side declare[s] its right to opt out of them by recourse to a higher law dictated by forces on which the international community ha[s] no influence." Bruno *Simma*, as quoted in UN-doc. E/C.12/1994/SR.8, p. 5.

A. Overview of problems

I. Basic considerations

While the Islamic theory of war and peace nowadays plays a relatively minor role in international relations,[1] as was seen in the previous chapter, the Islamic approach to human rights issues continues to be a virulent issue.[2] In his book *Toward an Islamic Reformation,* a notable example of progressive Muslim thought, the Sudanese scholar ᶜAbdallāh ʾAḥmad an-Naᶜīm writes:[3]

It is difficult to provide detailed and conclusive documentation of human rights violations in many countries, especially in the Muslim world because of the lack of verifiable records. Moreover, it is much more difficult to link those violations, to the extent that they are documented, to the influence of *šarīᶜa*. Nevertheless, the ambivalence of Muslim countries in the field of human rights can be illustrated by comparing the content of the international human rights documents to which a particular Muslim country has subscribed and the *šarīᶜa* rules being enforced in that country as a matter of domestic law.

---

[1] Cf., for instance, *Khadduri* 1955, *Pohl* 1988, *Mayer* 1991b: 195ff, and *Bedjaoui* 1992: 277ff.

[2] Cf., for instance, *Noth* 1980: 415ff, *Dilger* 1981, *Abu-Sahlieh* 1985, *Mayer* 1987, *an-Naᶜīm* 1987b, *Arzt* 1990, *an-Naᶜīm* 1990, *Mayer* 1991a, *Bielefeldt* 1992, *Forstner* 1993: 49ff, and *Mayer* 1994.

[3] Cf. *an-Naᶜīm* 1990: 178.

Exactly this program will be pursued in what follows, with the focus on Arab states and Iran.[4]

In this context, the very term *šarīʿa* deserves clarification. Originally designating the path to a watering place ("source") for animals, *šarīʿa* soon came to mean "source" in a figurative sense, i.e., (source of) Islamic law in general, pertaining to both religious acts of worship (*ʿibādāt*) and other acts of social intercourse (*muʿāmalāt*). The Islamic *šarīʿa* comprises four "branches" (*ʾuṣūl al-fiqh* 'sources of legal theory'): (i) legal precepts found in the Qurʾān, (ii) sayings and deeds of the founder of Islam, Muḥammad (the so-called *sunna*), (iii) consensus of the Islamic scholars (the so-called *ʾijmāʿ*), and (iv) reasoning by analogy (the so-called *qiyās*).[5] A further source of law close to the Islamic *šarīʿa* is *ʿurf* 'customary law', which regulates matters such as blood feuds between Bedouins. An important term is *ijtihād* 'independent legal reasoning', which will be briefly discussed below.

Beyond this, there exist a number of "schools of thought" (*maḏāhib* 'methods') with respect to the interpretation of Islamic law, the four major Sunnite ones being the Ḥanafite, the Malikite, the Shafiʿite, and the Ḥanbalite; these have acquired different degrees of prestige in different Islamic countries.[6] In addition, there is the Shiʿite school, which dominates in Iran. Synchronically speaking, however, differences among these schools play only a minor role in the analysis of conflicts between legal norms of the Islamic *šarīʿa* and international law, as no school is *a priori* more liberal in all areas than the others.

As will be seen, the only "branches" of Islamic law that really matter in the argumentation found in the periodic reports submitted to international treaty bodies and in the discussions of these reports with the treaty bodies are the Qurʾān and the *sunna*.

Regarding conflicts between precepts of the Islamic *šarīʿa* and obligations under international law, three prominent cases can be cited, all involving the alleged "crimes" of apostasy and/or criticism of Islam: the execution of the Sudanese engineer Maḥmūd Muḥammad

---

4 Cf. also *Abu-Sahlieh* 1985 and *Arzt* 1990: 217ff.

5 For a "classical" source, cf. *Ibn Taymīya* [1971]. For a systematic introduction to Islamic private and public law, cf., for instance, *Schacht* 1964 and *Dilger* 1990.

6 For a systematic introduction to these four "branches", cf., for instance, *Schacht* 1964 and *Muranyi* 1987: 307ff. Cf. also *Arzt* 1990: 204.

Ṭāhā,[7] the *fatwā* against the writer Salman Rushdie,[8] and the dissolution of the marriage of the Egyptian professor of literature Naṣr Ḥāmid ʾAbū Zayd (with subsequent death threats).[9] While the first two cases are well documented, the third deserves attention as it involves a supposedly moderate state, Egypt.

On June 14, 1995, an Egyptian appeals court ruled that the marriage of ʾAbū Zayd was to be dissolved on the grounds that ʾAbū Zayd must be considered an apostate, and that a marriage between a Muslim woman and an apostate (i.e., a non-Muslim) was invalid. The background can be summarized as follows: ʾAbū Zayd expressed views in his writings on the interpretation of the Qurʾān that made him, so to speak, a Hans Küng of Islam. ʾAbū Zayd has always stressed, however, that his criticism does not infringe upon the basic teachings of Islam. According to the so-called *ḥisba*-principle, any Muslim can sue another Muslim for alleged "apostate" behavior, and ʾAbū Zayd has become subject and victim of this principle, although appeals are still pending before the Egyptian courts. Beyond the individual problems confronting ʾAbū Zayd and his wife, the case demonstrates the problems encountered when Islamic norms collide with principles of international law – to which Egypt is subject, as it has become a signatory party to international human rights conventions, reserving the right, however, to give precedence to the precepts of the Islamic *šarīʿa* in cases of conflicting norms.

While the discussion in this chapter will focus on Arab states, other Islamic states, notably Iran, will be taken into account as well to the extent that they have entered reservations to IHR conventions or that their periodic reports and the discussions thereof reveal such reservations. Moreover, the discussions of Iranian IHR reports by the treaty bodies exhibit discourse structures unprecedented in the history of summary records issued by the United Nations.

In this chapter, the topic of human rights will be discussed using the theoretical tools developed. In contrast to the previous chapter, here we find a more clearly profiled separation of perspectives ("Western" vs. "Arab"/"Islamic"); abundant material found in United Nations documents supports such a dichotomy of perspectives. Again, this chapter is topic oriented, and does not necessarily follow the taxono-

---

[7] Cf., for instance, *an-Naʿīm* 1987a: 1ff.

[8] Cf., for instance, *Mayer* 1991a: 180ff.

[9] For an update of the legal proceedings regarding this case, cf. *Bälz* 1997.

mic sequence of types of misunderstandings listed in chapter three. As regards the interface between legal and linguistic issues, its practical importance was apparent in as recent a context as the last Population Conference in Cairo. Here the Arabic translators are said to have had considerable difficulties with such "Western" terms and concepts as "reproductive rights", "empowerment of women", and "single-parent household". In this chapter, corresponding Arabic and English terms in the realm of human rights with potentially different connotations will be scrutinized in different contexts and textual environments.

The case of "reproductive rights" provides a good illustration of the question at hand. Whereas the English term primarily denotes women's rights to access to birth control and, ultimately, abortion, the proposed Arabic equivalent *ḥuqūq ʾinjābīya* ('rights to procreate/give birth') seems to convey the opposite intension to its English original, i.e., the right to have as many children as one wants, a right which is not granted, for instance, in China. Again, Speech Act Theory provides an elegant theoretical account for this scenario, involving a differing intension and an overlapping extension.[10]

Not only terms and phrases but also whole discourse units can be illuminated by an analysis with the tools of Speech Act Theory. An example is the statement (quoted at length in chapter two, section C) by a former Iranian ambassador to the UN, Khorasani, regarding the drafting of the "Declaration on the Elimination of All Forms of Intolerance and of Discrimination Based on Religion or Belief" are considered. In terms of Speech Act Theory, his statement is interesting insofar, as it defines legal codes as being contingent upon the intensionality of basic terms, such as *freedom, justice,* and *peace,* and derived terms, such as *secularism* and *religion*. The illocutionary function of statements like Khorasani's, i.e., their diplomatic purpose, is not easy to determine. This statement also illustrates the hermeneutical difficulties which the members of the committees (treaty bodies) can face in their discussions of the reports.[11]

---

[10] *Maddox,* B. "Population Conference Hits a Language Barrier", The Financial Times, September 6, 1994. For the term "reproductive rights", cf. UN-doc. A/CONF.171/13 (Arabic and English), p. 43. Cf. also UN-doc. ST/CS/SER.F/348 (Women's Issues: Terminology Bulletin No. 348).

[11] An outright clash between members of the Human Rights Committee and Iranian representatives occurred in the discussions of Iran's second report on its implementation of CCPR, UN-doc. CCPR/C/1/Add.58. Cf. the concluding observations in UN-doc. A/37/40, p. 74.

II. "Western" vs. "Islamic" approaches to the issue

One fundamental observation is in order here. Though some of the following quotations may show the respective countries in an unfavorable light, this should not obscure the fact that many other Arab and Islamic countries, which have not become parties to the conventions under discussion at all, fare even worse, as they have not even entered into a forum of discussion.

Arab states, notably Saudi Arabia, have exerted strong resistance *vis-à-vis* the Universal Declaration of Human Rights (UDHR) (of which there is no official Arabic version), and there are numerous examples of suggested amendments by Arab states that reflect legal *šarīʿa* background.[12] The preamble to the Charter of the Islamic Conference, for example, exhibits the ambivalent attitude of Islamic legislators towards the implementation of human rights.[13] Two adjacent paragraphs run as follows:

Item (57), Arabic

Wa-ʾiḏ yuqarrirūna l-ḥifāẓa ʿalā l-qiyami r-rūḥīyati wa-l-ʾaḫlāqīyati wa-l-ijtimāʿīyati wa-l-iqtiṣādīyati l-mawjūdati fi-l-ʾislāmi, wa-llatī taẓallu ʿāmilan mina l-ʿawāmili l-hāmmati li-taḥqīqi t-taqaddumi bayna ʾabnāʾi l-bašar;

Wa-yuʿīdūna t-taʾkīda bi-taqayyudi-him bi-mīṯāqi l-ʾumami l-muttaḥidati wa-ḥuqūqi l-ʾinsāni l-ʾasāsīyati llatī tuʿtabaru ʾaġrādu-hā wa-mabādiʾu-hā ʾasāsan li-taʿāwunin muṯmirin bayna jamīʿi š-šuʿūb. [...]

Item (57), English

Resolved to preserve Islamic spiritual, ethical, social and economic values, which will remain one of the important factors of achieving progress for mankind;

Reaffirming their commitment to the U.N. Charter and fundamental Human Rights, the purposes and principles of which provide the basis for fruitful cooperation amongst all people. [...]

The "Universal Islamic Declaration of Human Rights" (UIDHR) published by the London-based Islamic Council on September 19, 1981, features significant differences between the Arabic original and the English and French translations, to the effect that the translations can

---

[12] Examples include UN-docs. A/C.3/240, A/C.3/241, A/C.3/247 and A/C.3/247/Rev.1 (Saudi Arabia) as well as UN-doc. A/C.3/332 (Iraq), referring to the law of marriage, the freedom of religion, and civil rights. Saudi Arabia was the only Arab country to abstain in the final vote on the Universal Declaration of Human Rights.

[13] This observation is due to *Mayer* 1991a: 14. The English and Arabic texts are found in *UNTS*, vol. 914 (1974), pp. 111f and p. 109, respectively.

serve to camouflage objectionable phrases in the original.[14] As Ann Mayer has shown with regard to the Cairo Declaration on Human Rights in Islam of August 5, 1990, the lack of a guarantee of equality in rights and freedoms can be carefully hidden behind phrases such as "basic human dignity and basic obligations and responsibilities".[15]

In a draft document by the League of Arab States, the "Project of the Arab(ic) Human Rights Charter" (*mašrūᶜ al-mīṯāq al-ᶜarabī li-ḥuqūq al-ʾinsān*), the *šarīᶜa* is explicitly stressed as a source of human rights. Paragraph (2) of the preamble runs as follows:[16]

Item (58), Arabic original

Wa-taḥqīqan li-l-mabādiʾi l-ḫālidīyati llatī ʾarsat-hā š-šarīᶜatu l-ʾislāmīyatu wa-d-diyānātu s-samāwīyatu l-ʾuḫrā fī l-ʾuḫūwati wa-l-musāwāti bayna l-bašar.

Item (58), English translation

Implementing the eternal principles that the Islamic *šarīᶜa* and the other divine religions have established in terms of fraternity and equality among (hu)mankind.

Interestingly, reference to "racism and Zionism" is made in the preamble to and in paragraph (8b) of the same document:

Item (59), Arabic original

Wa-rafḍan li-*l-ᶜunṣurīyati wa-ṣ-ṣahyūnīyati* llatayni tušakkilāni ntihākan li-ḥuqūqi l-ʾinsāni wa-tahdīdan li-s-salāmi l-ᶜālamī; [...]

ʾInna *l-ᶜunṣurīyata wa-ṣ-ṣahyūnīyata* wa-l-iḥtilāla wa-s-sayṭarata l-ʾajnabīyata hiya taḥaddin li-l-karāmati l-ʾinsānīyati wa-ᶜāʾiqun ʾasāsīyun yaḥūlu dūna l-ḥuqūqi l-ʾasāsīyati li-š-šuᶜūbi wa-mina l-wājibi ʾidānatu jamīᶜi mumārasāti-hā wa-l-ᶜamalu ᶜalā ʾizālati-hā.

Item (59), English translation

Refuting racism and *Zionism* which constitute a violation of human rights and a threat to world peace; [...]

Racism, Zionism, occupation and foreign domination are a challenge to human dignity and a fundamental obstacle which interferes with the basic rights of the peoples; it is necessary to condemn all their implementations and to work towards their elimination.

---

[14] Cf. *Mayer* 1991a: 86ff, 104ff, 120ff, and 173ff.

[15] Cf. *Mayer* 1994: 329ff. Cf. also *Forstner* 1992: 52ff as well as UN-doc. A/CONF.157/PC/62/Add.18 for an English translation of the declaration.

[16] This document was kindly brought to the author's attention by Professor Stefan *Wild*. The draft is reproduced in *Nuᶜmān* [no date]: 57ff.

Many more quotations from different contexts illustrate the pervasiveness of the clash between IHR norms and certain precepts of the Islamic *šarīᶜa*, or rather the perceived superiority of "divine" law in an Islamic perspective. Indeed, "it [i]s difficult [...] to engage in a debate on the fulfilment of international legal obligations when one side declare[s] its right to opt out of them by recourse to a higher law dictated by forces on which the international community ha[s] no influence".[17]

Beyond its religious implications for human rights issues, Islam can also be explicitly adduced in support of a specifically Islamic political system, as in the following two excerpts from the discussions of Morocco's first and second reports on the implementation of the International Covenant on Civil and Political Rights, UN-docs. CCPR/C/10/Add.2 and CCPR/C/42/Add.10:[18]

Item (60), official English translation

With regard to political rights, Muslim public law had affirmed from the outset the fundamental principles of modern democracy through Choura, which involved direct consultation of the representatives of the Muslim community, and the Baia,[19] which was the act through which the head of the community was recognized by the representatives of the people as the spritual and temporal head of the nation. As a result, there was a direct legal and spiritual link of allegiance between the members of the community and the monarch.

Item (61), official English translation

Under Islamic law, Muslims pledged allegiance to their leader in return for his protection and guidance in achieving political, economic and social progress. The position of the monarchy in Morocco was thus incontestable, and no attempt had ever been made to dispute it.

One further quotation that highlights the importance, and indeed the superiority , of the Islamic *šarīᶜa* (from an Egyptian point of view) is contained in the introduction to Egypt's most recent report on its implementation of the International Covenant on Civil and Political Rights:[20]

---

[17] Bruno *Simma*, as quoted in UN-doc. E/C.12/1994/SR.8, p. 5 (epigraph to the present chapter).

[18] The quotations are from UN-doc. CCPR/C/SR.332, p. 2 and UN-doc. CCPR/C/SR.1032, p. 14. The French originals were not available to the author .

[19] The terms are *šūrā* 'political consultation' and *bayᶜa* 'commercial agreement'/'political agreement [to be ruled]'.

[20] UN-doc. CCPR/C/51/Add.7 (Arabic and English), pp. 10 and 9, respectively.

Item (62), Arabic original

Wa-qad jā'ati š-šarī'atu l-'islāmīyatu l-ġarrā'u bi-qiyamin wa-mabādi'a wa-'aḥkāmin tušakkilu niẓāman kāmilan wa-mutakāmilan yaḍmanu li-l-'insāni, 'ayya mā kānat 'aqīdatu-hu, ḥuqūqa-hū wa-ḥurrīyāti-hī fī kāffati l-majālāti s-siyāsīyati wa-l-ijtimā'īyati wa-l-iqtiṣādīyati wa-hiya l-ḥuqūqu wa-l-ḥurrīyātu llatī bi-kitābi llāhi (l-qur'āni l-karīmi) wa-s-sunnati n-nabawīyati š-šarīfati mundu ẓuhūri l-'islāmi mundu 'arba'ta'ašra qarnan wa-qabla 'an yu'arrifa l-'ālamu 'āna-dā-ka minhājan fikrīyan yunaẓẓimu hādihī l-ḥuqūqa wa-tilka l-ḥurrīyāti wafqan li-mā tas'ā 'ilay-hi l-'āna l-bašarīyatu jum'ā'.

Item (62), official English translation

The noble Islamic Shariah embodies values, principles and precepts that constitute a complete and integrated system which safeguards all the political, social and economic rights and freedoms of all persons, regardless of their religious beliefs. These are the rights and freedoms recognized in God's Holy Book (the Koran) and in the Traditions of His Prophet, which have been applied since the dawn of Islam fourteen centuries ago, before mankind had developed an ideological system for the regulation of these rights and freedoms in the manner to which it is now aspiring.

Note that Egypt here characterizes the *šarī'a* as "noble" (Arabic *ġarrā'*) as opposed to "ideological" (Arabic *fikrī*), a term which is reserved for the precepts of international law.

In its most recent report on the implementation of the Convention on the Elimination of all Forms of Discrimination against Women, Yemen invoked *sūra* 24: 33 of the Qur'ān, regarding article 6 of the convention, as supporting evidence against prostitution:[21]

Item (63), Arabic original

Wa-l-yasta'fifi lladīna lā yajidūna nikāḥan ḥattā yuġniya-humu llāhu min faḍli-hī wa-lladīna yabtaġūna l-kitāba mim-mā malakat 'aymānu-kum fa-kātibū-hum 'in 'alimtum fī-him ḫayran wa-'ātū-hum min māli llāhi lladī 'atā-kum wa-lā tukrihū fatayāti-kum 'alā l-biġā'i 'in 'aradna taḥaṣṣunan li-tabtaġū 'araḍa l-ḥayāti d-dunyā wa-man yukrih-hunna fa-'inna llāha min ba'di 'ikrāhi-hinna ġafūrun raḥīm.

Item (63), official English translation

Let those who find not the wherewithal for marriage keep themselves chaste, until God gives them means out of his grace. And if any of your slaves ask for a deed in writing (to enable them to earn their freedom for a certain sum), give them such a deed if ye know any good in them; yea, give them something yourselves out of the means which God has given to you. But force not your maids to prostitution when they desire chastity, in order that ye make a gain in the goods of this life. But if anyone compels them, yet, after such compulsion, is God Oft-Forgiving, Most Merciful (to them).

---

[21] UN-doc. CEDAW/C/YEM/3 (Arabic and English), pp. 12 and 15, respectively.

This brief synopsis makes it plausible that the Arabic term *ḥuqūq al-ʾinsān,* while a linguistically faithful rendition of *human rights,* has a religiously defined collective intensionality, not an individual one, as in the "Western" perception.[22]

B. The periodic reports submitted to international treaty bodies

I. Synopsis: accession of Islamic states to international human rights conventions and their reservations

In the following, we will consider the periodic reports of Arab Islamic states to international treaty bodies, the summary records of the discussions thereof, and the final considerations and observations of the treaty bodies. As the reports will be the starting point of discussion, "preliminary" material, such as statements by Arab or other Islamic diplomats in discussions on the drafting of the conventions will be taken into consideration only marginally.[23] It must be borne in mind, however, that the periodic reports are often far from being a faithful representation of the real circumstances in the respective countries. Moreover, the material is fairly heterogeneous. While there are extremely brief and non-informative reports (e.g., the early reports of Kuwait and Qatar on CERD[24]), there are also very comprehensive and informative reports (e.g., the most recent report of Tunisia on CEDAW, UN-doc. CEDAW/C/TUN/1-2). For this reason, the reports of Special Rapporteurs on IHR issues and the country reports of NGOs constitute indispensable supplementary information.[25] The summary records ex-

---

[22] Cf., for instance, *Mayer* 1991a: 63ff.

[23] As already pointed out, both the preliminary discussions to the Universal Declaration of Human Rights (GA res. 217 (III)) and the preliminary discussions in the third committee to CESCR (GA res. 2200 (XXI)), CCPR (GA res. 2200A(XXI)), CRC (GA res. 44/25), and CEDAW (GA res. 34/180) contain references to the Islamic *šarīʿa*. The same holds true for the Declaration on the Elimination of All Forms of Intolerance and of Discrimination Based on Religion or Belief (GA res. 35/55). No such references are found, however, in connection with the Declaration on the Rights of Persons Belonging to National or Ethnic, Religious and Linguistic Minorities (GA res. 47/135).

[24] Here and in the following, the abbreviations CESCR, CCPR, CRC, CEDAW, CERD, CAT, and CSPCA serve for both the respective conventions and the respective committees (treaty bodies).

[25] *Šarīʿa*-relevant reports by Special Rapporteurs have been issued mainly on the following countries and issues (for each topic the most recent report is cited): "Afghanistan", by Felix *Ermacora* (UN-doc. E/CN.4/1995/64); "Iran" by Reynaldo *Galindo Pohl* (UN-doc. E/CN.4/1995/55); "Iraq" by Max *van der Stoel* (UN-doc. E/CN.4/1995/56); "Religious

hibit a similarly heterogeneous image. Depending on the country involved, conflicting norms can be discussed in a relatively constructive or in an outright antagonistic way. An example of the first type is Tunisia, the most progressive Arab country with respect to the interpretation of Islamic law as regards the prohibition of polygamy, for instance. An example of the second type is Iran, the most disturbing country with respect to the interpretation and application of the Islamic *šarīʿa*.

The following table provides a synopsis of the current *status quo* of accession and ratification, restricted, however, to those conventions that are subject to periodic reports:[26] the International Covenant on Economic, Social and Cultural Rights (CESCR), the International Covenant on Civil and Political Rights (CCPR), the Convention on the Rights of the Child (CRC), the Convention on the Elimination of All Forms of Discrimination against Women (CEDAW), the International Convention on the Elimination of All Forms of Racial Discrimination (CERD), the Convention against Torture and other Cruel, Inhuman or Degrading Treatment or Punishment (CAT), and finally the International Convention on the Suppression and Punishment of the Crime of Apartheid (CSPCA):[27]

Intolerance" by Abdelfattah *Amor* (UN-doc. E/CN.4/1995/91 + Add.1); "Sudan" by Gáspár *Bíró* (UN-doc. E/CN.4/1995/58); "Traditional Practices" by Halima *Embarek Warzazi* (UN-doc. E/CN.4/Sub.2/1994/10); "Violence against Women" by Radhika *Coomaraswamy* (UN-doc. E/CN.4/Sub.2/1995/42). Important NGO contributions are, among others, the *Country Reports* of Amnesty International. Cf. also the *Country Reports* of the U.S. Department of State.

[26] For an overview of the work of the treaty bodies, cf. the contributions in *Alston* (ed.) 1992a.

[27] Cf. UN-doc. ST/HR/4/Rev. 14 and updated information, as available on the Internet (http://www.un.org/Depts/Treaty/collection/series/search.htm). Palestine (a member of the League of Arab States and of the Organization of the Islamic Conference) is not yet in a position to become a party to any of these conventions and therefore does not figure in the table. Neither do Kazakhstan and Bosnia and Hercegovina, which have only observer status with the Organization of the Islamic Conference. This holds *a fortiori* for the Muslim communities "Turkish Muslim Communitiy of Kibris" and "Moro National Liberation Front", as well as a number of other international and regional organizations, all of which also have mere observer status with the Organization of the Islamic Conference.

Table 3a

Accessions and reservations to international human rights conventions by members of the Organization of the Islamic Conference*

1. Members of the League of Arab States

State Party	CESCR	CCPR	CRC	CEDAW	CERD	CAT	CSPCA
Algeria	+R	++-R	+R	+R	+	+	+
Bahrain	-	---	+	-	+	-	+
Comoros	-	---	+	+	-	-	-
Djibouti	-	---	+R	-	-	-	-
Egypt	+R	+--R	+R	+R	+	+	+
Iraq	+	+--	+R	+R	+	-	+
Jordan	+	+--	+R	+R	+	+	+
Kuwait	+R	+--R	+R	+R	+	+	+
Lebanon	+	+--	+	+R	+	-	-
Libya	+	++-	+	+R	+	+	+
Mauritania	-	---	+R	-	+	-	+
Morocco	+	+--	+R	+R	+	+	-
Oman	-	---	+R	-	-	-	+
Qatar	-	---	+R	-	+	-	+
Saudi Arabia	-	---	+R	-	-	-	-
Somalia	+	++-	s	-	+	+	+
Sudan	+	++-	+	-	+	s	+
Syria	+	+--	+R	-	+	-	+
Tunisia	+	+--	+R	+R	+	+	+
Un. Ar. Emirates	-	---	+R	-	+	-	+
Yemen	+	+--	+	+	+R	+	+

* "+" indicates ratification;

"-" indicates non-ratification;

"R" refers to a reservation made by the respective state party in which precepts of the Islamic *šarīʿa* are placed above IHR principles either explicitly or implicitly (other kinds of reservations (such as reference to the non-recognition of Israel, or the non-recognition of the competence of the International Court of Justice) are deliberately omitted here);

"s" refers to a signature, not (yet) followed by ratification;

the second and third values in the column under CCPR refer to signature/ ratification of the two optional protocols to CCPR.

Table 3b

Accessions and reservations to international human rights conventions by members of the Organization of the Islamic Conference

2. Further (non-Arab) members

State Party	CESCR	CCPR	CRC	CEDAW	CERD	CAT	CSPCA
Afghanistan	+	+--	+R	s	+	+	+
Albania	+	+--	+	+	+	+	-
Azerbaijan	+	+--	+	+	+	+	-
Bangladesh	-	---	+R	+R	+	-	+
Benin	+	++-	+	+	s	+	+
Brunei	-	---	+R	-	-	-	-
Burkina Faso	-	---	+	+	+	-	+
Cameroon	+	++-	+	+	+	+	+
Chad	+	+--	+	-	+	+	+
Gabon	+	+--	+	+	+	s	+
Gambia	+	++-	+	+	+	s	+
Guinea	+	++-	+	+	+	+	+
Guinea-Bissau	-	---	+	+	-	-	-
Indonesia	-	---	+R	+	-	s	-
Iran	+	+--	+R	-	+	-	+
Kyrgyzstan	+	++-	+	+	-	-	-
Malaysia	-	---	+R	+R	-	-	-
Maldives	-	---	+R	+R	+	-	+
Mali	+	+--	+	+	+	-	+
Mozambique	-	+-+	+	+	+	-	+
Niger	+	++-	+	-	+	-	+
Nigeria	+	+--	+	+	+	s	+
Pakistan	-	---	+R	+R	+	-	+
Senegal	+	++-	+	+	+	+	+
Sierra Leone	+	+--	+	+	+	s	-
Tajikistan	-	---	+	+	+	+	-
Turkey	-	---	+	+R	s	+	-
Turkmenistan	+	+--	+	+	+	-	-
Uganda	+	+--	+	+	+	+	+

A statistical survey yields the following percentages of ratification, excluding signatures not followed by ratification, and ignoring reservations:

Table 4
Statistics of ratification

	CESCR	CCPR	CRC	CEDAW	CERD	CAT	CSPCA
League of Arab States	62%	62%	95%	52%	81%	43%	76%
Islamic Conference	65%	65%	98%	73%	78%	39%	69%

Disregarding any reservations, the statistics show clearly that CERD, CSCPA, and CRC have the highest rate of acceptance in the two groups of states, while CAT has the lowest, with CESCR, CCPR, and CEDAW somewhere in the middle.

II. The situation in the Arab states and in Iran

In the following, with the single exception of Iran, the discussion will be restricted to the League of Arab states, insofar as they have ratified or acceded to the conventions. The reason is simply that reference to the Islamic *šarīʿa* is most "systematic" in this group, with the two notable exceptions of Afghanistan and Iran, where the *šarīʿa* holds an even more paramount position – hence the inclusion of Iran. Many of the other (non-Arab) member states of the Islamic Conference have only begun to accede to IHR instruments, and in some cases, especially in African context, it is not clear whether certain regulations are due to Islamic influence or to native "customary law". Moreover, the discussion will be restricted to CESCR, CCPR, CRC, CEDAW, CERD, and CAT, as a systematic examination of the reports to and discussions of CSPCA has not yielded any conflicting norms, which was not to be expected in the first place.[28] The only *šarīʿa*-relevant reservations to CERD (article 5 (c) and 5 (d) (iv), (vi) and (vii)) have been entered by Yemen; nevertheless, conflicting views as to the role of the Islamic *šarīʿa* almost always surface in discussions of the

[28] Beyond this, it can be argued that CSPCA, which was not supported by the Western European states and the USA, is redundant (and – at least with respect to South Africa – now obsolete), its essential tenets already being included in the other IHR conventions.

reports to CERD.[29] While no formal reservations have been made with respect to CAT, one instance of conflicting norms is found in the discussion of the report of Afghanistan.[30] Most states that apply the *ḥudūd* penalties,[31] however, have not become signatory parties to CAT in the first place.

A synopsis of the periodic reports of Arab states parties as submitted to the respective treaty bodies and a list of the summary records where these reports are discussed by the committees in charge will be found in the appendix.[32] As will be seen, *šarīᶜa*-relevant deliberations often surface in reports and oral discussions even when formal reservations have not been entered.

In all fairness, it must be noted that the *šarīᶜa* is occasionally also adduced in support of IHR principles.[33] This is systematically the case with CERD as the *šarīᶜa* stresses that all human beings (of the same sex) are equal, irrespective of race – as long as their religious faith is equally good, i.e., as long as they are Muslims. An example is found in Yemen's report of 1993 on the implementation of the International Covenant on Civil and Political Rights:[34]

Item (64), Arabic original

ʾInna hāḏihī n-naẓrata l-ʾislāmīyata li-l-ʾinsāni tatamayyazu bi-š-šumūli; fa-l-ʾislāmu lā yaᶜnī bi-fardin dūna ʾāḫara fa-l-kullu sawāsiya "fa-lā faḍla li-ᶜarabīyin ᶜalā ᶜajamīyin ʾil-lā bi-t-taqwā".

Item (64), official English translation

This Islamic view of mankind is comprehensive; in Islam, all individuals are treated with the same concern, since everyone is equal. According to the words of the Apostle of God: "No distinction shall be made between an Arab and a non-Arab, except in terms of their piety."

---

29 Such differences can be seen, for instance, in the observations to the discussions of the eighth report of Sudan on its implementation of CERD, UN-doc. CERD/C/222/Add.1 and 2, regarding the practices of amputation and flogging (cf. UN-doc. A/48/18, p. 69).

30 Cf. UN-doc. CAT/C/SR.121, p. 6, referring to UN-doc. CAT/C/5/Add.31.

31 Fixed [corporal] punishment for certain crimes (cf. below).

32 Status as of May 1997. Not all signatory parties have yet submitted reports, and not all submitted reports have yet been discussed by the respective treaty bodies.

33 Cf., for instance, item (63) above.

34 UN-doc. CCPR/C/82/Add.1 (Arabic and English), p. 3. The *ḥadīṯ* quotation can be found in *Ibn Ḥanbal*, Musnad [no date], vol. 5: 411 (cf. *Wensinck* [1969], vol. 7: 300).

"Piety" (in Arabic *taqwā*) is, of course, the *shibboleth* that distinguishes Muslims as being "more equal than the others" in this respect, as "piety" is intensionally restricted to Islam.

Sometimes, statements even go so far as to claim that Islam would make IHR provisions *stricto sensu* superfluous, as Islam already regulates all the questions concerned.[35]

Here are some general observations relating to the ratification and implementation of IHR conventions by the relevant states, and to the overall human rights situation and role that the Islamic *šarīᶜa* plays in these states.[36] Personal statute law, family law, and the law of succession (inheritance) continue to be governed in all states by the *šarīᶜa*, even if they have failed to enter formal reservations to that effect. A notable exception is Tunisia, which completely outlaws polygamy. Differences persist, however, in the realms of penal law and the law of procedure. It must also be borne in mind that some *šarīᶜa* regulations do not affect the non-Muslim minorities in the respective countries.[37]

Algeria has ratified all of the conventions under discussion, albeit with general *šarīᶜa*-reservations on CESCR and CCPR and specific reservations on CRC and CEDAW. Egypt has likewise ratified all of the conventions, entering general *šarīᶜa*-reservations on CESCR and CCPR and specific reservations on CRC and CEDAW. Iraq has ratified all of the conventions with the exception of CAT; it has entered specific reservations on CRC and CEDAW. The gap between the *de jure* and *de facto* situations appears to be especially wide in the case of Iraq, as there are plenty of regulations in Iraqi law which draw on Islamic penal law, as well as other human rights violations. Like Algeria, Egypt, Libya, and Tunisia, Jordan has ratified all of the conventions under discussion, with specific reservations on CRC and CEDAW.

---

[35] Cf., for instance, UN-doc. CCPR/C/51/Add.7 (Arabic and English), pp. 10 and 9, respectively. In its second report on the implementation of CCPR, Libya claims that both the Qurʾān and the Libyan "Great Green Document on Human Rights in the Age of the Masses" already contain all the relevant provisions found in UDHR, CESCR and CCPR (cf. UN-doc. CCPR/C/28/Add.16 (Arabic and English), pp. 18 and 16, respectively).

[36] For an overview of the modern legal systems in the Arab states cf. *Redden*, K. (ed.) 1990. Modern Legal Systems Cyclopedia, vol. 5/5A (Middle East) and vol. 6/6A (Africa). Further useful sources of information are the *Country Reports* issued by the U.S. Department of State, as well as reports issued by NGOs, such as Amnesty International.

[37] Arab states, more precisely Bahrain, Mauritania, Oman, and Saudi Arabia, which have acceded to CRC (with reservations), but have not yet submitted any reports, are not listed here. The Comoros, Djibouti, and Somalia, which cannot be said to be "Arab" states proper, are not listed here either (only Somalia has thus far submitted reports: UN-docs. CERD/C/39 and CERD/C/88/Add.6).

While Kuwait has also ratified CRC and CEDAW, albeit with general *šarīᶜa*-reservations, it has so far only submitted reports to CERD and CSPCA. Women in Kuwait do not have the right to vote or to stand for election. In this respect and in others, Kuwait is among the most conservative Arab states. Lebanon, which has ratified CESCR, CCPR, CRC, and CERD without reservations, has had a considerable backlog in its submission of reports due to tremendous internal political difficulties. The role of the *šarīᶜa* in Lebanon is restricted to Islamic family law. Like Algeria, Egypt, Jordan, and Tunisia, Libya has ratified all the conventions under discussion, with specific reservations only on CEDAW. However, the Qurʾān with all its legal implications is a direct source of law (the "social code") in Libya, and there is a considerable gap between the *de jure* and the *de facto* situations. Morocco has ratified all conventions except CSPCA, albeit with reservations on CRC and CEDAW. Like most of the other Arab states, it has a "dual" legal system, comprising both a secular component and the *mudawwana*, an Islamic legal code relating to personal status, characterized by "dahirs".[38] Qatar has only ratified CRC (with reservations), CERD, and CSPCA and thus is among the most conservative Arab countries. Sudan has ratified all conventions under discussion except CEDAW and CAT. The different implementations of the conventions under several changing Sudanese governments make an accurate assessment of the human rights situation difficult; Sudan is notorious for its excessive application of the precepts of Islamic penal law. Syria has ratified all the conventions under discussion with the exception of CEDAW and CAT. Notwithstanding serious human rights problems, the application of the Islamic *šarīᶜa* in Syria is restricted to matters of personal status. There is a heavy backlog in the submission of Syria's periodic reports. Like Algeria, Egypt, Jordan, and Libya, Tunisia has ratified all of the conventions under discussion, not without some reservations on CRC and CEDAW. As reflected in its reports, Tunisia is clearly the most modern state when it comes to the interpretation of the Islamic *šarīᶜa*, which is restricted to the law of inheritance. Not surprisingly, Arab/Muslim members of IHR treaty bodies are very often from Tunisia. Just as Qatar, the United Arab Emirates have only ratified CRC (with reservations), CERD, and CSPCA, ranking it among the most conservative Arab states. The former South Yemen ratified CESCR, CCPR, CEDAW, CERD, CAT, and CSPCA; upon unification of Yemen on 22 May, 1990, the former Yemen Arab Republic, which had not previously been a party to any of

---

[38] This term (*ẓahīr* 'royal decree') is found exclusively in Moroccan documents.

the conventions under discussion, acceded to these IHR conventions and also to CRC.[39] Still, united Yemen belongs to the conservative group of Arab states. Iran, which is included here as a case study, has ratified IHR conventions before the so-called "Islamic revolution" in 1978, with the exception of CRC, CEDAW, CAT, and CSPCA, to the first and last of which it acceded later. Reports originating after the "Islamic revolution", as well as statements of Iranian diplomats in their discussions of the reports with the treaty bodies appear to have been largely made *mala fide* and confirm the impression that "[i]t is apparent that the authorities in Iran are using the religion as a pretext to abuse these [human] rights".[40]

III. The specific problems

1. *Types of reservations*

Reservations can either be explicitly or implicitly expressed in the respective instruments of ratification, or they can explicitly or implicitly surface in the reports submitted to the treaty bodies. Explicit reservations typically feature the words *šarīᶜa, Qurʾān*, and/or *sunna*; implicit reservations typically refer to "the family code" etc. There has been extensive scholarly discussion with respect to the formal and procedural aspects of reservations.[41] Here is a recent assessment on reservations, emanating from the work of CEDAW:[42]

Item (65), English original

The Vienna Convention on the Law of Treaties 1969 prohibits reservations which are incompatible with the object and purpose of a particular treaty. Article 28 (2) of the Convention on the Elimination of All Forms of Discrimination against Women reiterates the Vienna Convention and prohibits reservations which are incompatible with its own object and purpose. Despite the prohibition of such reservations, there is no explicit mechanism, beyond the mechanism of objections by other States parties, in the Vienna Convention or in the Convention on discrimination against women itself by which a reservation can be adjudged incompatible with the Convention, and the Convention does not spell out the consequences of an incompatible reservation or an objection to such

---

[39] Cf. UN-doc. ST/LEG/SER.E/13, p. 10.

[40] Cf. UN-doc. E/1995/22, p. 33.

[41] In addition to the references in *Verdross/Simma* 1984: 466ff, cf. *Gaja* 1987, vol. 1: 307ff, *Lijnzaad* 1995, and the contributions in *Gardner* 1997. Cf. also UN-doc. CEDAW/C/1997/4 and the Reports on the Law and Practice Relating to Reservations to Treaties by Alain *Pellet*, Special Rapporteur [IL], UN-doc. A/CN.4/470 + Corr.1-2 and UN-doc. A/CN.4/477 + Add.1 + Add.1/Corr.1 + 478 (Bibliography).

[42] UN-doc. CEDAW/C/1997/4, para. 13-14.

a reservation. This is in contrast to the International Convention on the Elimination of All Forms of Racial Discrimination which, in article 20, provides that a reservation shall be regarded as incompatible or inhibitive if objected to by two thirds of the other States parties to the Convention.

Although there is no formal external or internal mechanism to determine the compatibility of reservations to the Convention, responses to these reservations by States parties to the Convention, the international community generally and others suggest that a significant number of extant reservations are incompatible with the Convention's object and purpose and thus contrary to article 28 (2).

So far, relatively little attention has been paid to the wording and substance of the specific reservations dealt with. Reservations of Arab states to international human rights conventions (and other multilateral treaties) have traditionally comprised three factors:

(i) non-recognition of Israel;

(ii) non-recognition of the competence of the International Court of Justice insofar as the interpretation of the convention in question is concerned;

(iii) restriction of the validity of the convention in question to the extent that it is not in alignment with the Islamic *šarīᶜa*.

The first of these is now becoming obsolete, and the second is certainly not specific to Arab states. This chapter will thus deal solely with the third type of reservation, which goes to the heart of article 19 (c) of the Vienna Convention on the Law of Treaties, i.e., the question of whether or not a reservation is compatible with the object and purpose of the treaty. As this question can only be decided by the parties themselves, it is fair to observe that "[i]n practice it is possible, due to the number and the kind of reservations, to make an international agreement *de facto* not binding for one of its parties".[43]

Two quotations may serve to illustrate the point in question (the first refers to a declaration, the second to a treaty). During the 73rd meeting of the General Assembly on 25 November, 1981, the Iranian representative Mahallati Shirazi made the following statement with respect to the "Declaration on the Elimination of All Forms of Intolerance and of Discrimination Based on Religion or Belief":[44]

---

[43] *Osmañczyk* 1990: 747.

[44] UN-doc. A/36/PV.71, p. 1219, regarding the Declaration on the Elimination of All Forms of Intolerance and on Discrimination Based on Religion or Belief (A/RES/36/55, pp. 171ff).

Item (66), English original

I should like to express my delegation's reservation to the effect that we accept the draft resolution and the Declaration just adopted in so far as they are in total conformity with Islamic jurisprudency.

When (the Arab Republic of) Yemen acceded in 1989 to the "International Convention on the Elimination of All Forms of Racial Discrimination",[45] its president ᶜAlī ᶜAbdallāh Ṣāliḥ submitted the instrument of ratification with the following reservation to article 5 (c) and article 5 (d) (iv), (vi), and (vii) of the said Convention (the listed paragraphs include political rights such as the right to participate in elections and the right to be a civil servant, as well as civil rights such as the right to marriage, the right to inherit, and the right to freedom of thought, conscience, and religion):

Item (67), Arabic original

Wa-baᶜda ʾiqrāri-nā min majlisi š-šūrā fa-qad ʾaṣdarnā l-qānūna raqma (3) li-sanati 1989 A.D. bi-l-muwāfaqati ᶜalā nḍimāmi l-jumhūrīyati l-ᶜarabīyati l-yamanīyati ʾilā l-ittifāqīyati l-madkūrati maᶜa t-taḥaffuẓi ᶜalā mā jāʾa fī l-fiqrati (j) fī l-māddati l-ḫāmisati min-hā, wa-ᶜalā mā jāʾa fī l-bunūdi (4, 6, 7) mina l-māddati l-madkūrati l-ḫāmisa.[46]

Item (67), English translation

And after the ratification on the part of our State Council, we have passed the law #3 in 1989 to the effect that the Yemeni Arab Republic becomes subject to the Convention in question with reservation to article 5 (c) and (d) (iv), (vi), and (vii).

2. *Hidden precepts*

Often, the *de facto* situation in a given country cannot easily be established from the legal documents, as provisions may be hidden. Here is an example, regarding the non-right of women in Kuwait to take part in or stand for elections.[47] Article 29 of the Kuwaiti constitution guarantees that human beings are equal in their rights and duties,

---

[45] *UNTS*, vol. 660 (1969), pp. 195ff.

[46] Excerpt from the *waṯīqat taṣdīq* 'instrument of ratification' signed by the president of Yemen. The Arabic text was provided by courtesy of the UN Office of Legal Affairs, Treaty Section. This (still unpublished) document is referred to in UN-doc. ST/LEG/SER.E (1992), p. 111. The reservation subsequently met objections on the part of Belgium, Canada, Czechoslovakia, Denmark, Finland, France, Germany, Italy, Mexico, Netherlands, New Zealand, Norway, Sweden, and the United Kingdom to the effect that it was incompatible with the object and purpose of this Convention.

[47] Cf. *Abu-Sahlieh* 1985: 700.

irrespective of sex, national origin, language, and religion. Article 82 of the constitution specifies that, in order to be elected to the Kuwaiti parliament, one must meet the conditions of the electoral law for parliament. Finally, article 1 of the Kuwaiti electoral law for parliament specifies that voters must be male and that, in order to be elected, one must be on the voters' register.

When Kuwait acceded to the International Covenant on Civil and Political Rights on May 21, 1996, it formulated the following interpretative declarations and reservations:[48]

Item (68), official English translation

Interpretative declaration regarding article 2, paragraph 1, and article 3:

Although the Government of Kuwait endorses the worthy principles embodied in these two articles as consistent with the Kuwaiti Constitution in general and of its article 29 in particular, the rights to which the articles refer must be exercised within the limits set by Kuwaiti law.

Interpretative declaration regarding article 23:

The Government of Kuwait declares that the matters addressed by article 23 are governed by personal status law, which is based on Islamic law. Where the provisions of that article conflict with Kuwaiti law, Kuwait will apply its national law.

Reservation concerning article 25 (b):

The Government of Kuwait wishes to formulate a reservation with regard to article 25 (b). The provisions of this paragraph conflict with Kuwaiti electoral law, which restricts the right to stand and vote in elections to males. It further declares that the provisions of the article shall not apply to members of the armed forces or the police.

Discriminination can surface in the reports in a very subtle form. Concerning "preservation of identity", Egypt stipulated the following in its first report on CRC:[49]

Item (69), Arabic original

Wa-yulzamu kullu miṣrīyin bi-ḥamli l-biṭāqati š-šaḫṣīyati, wa-ᶜalay-hi ᵓan yuqaddima-hā ᶜinda ᵓayyi taᶜāmulin madanīyin ᵓaw jināᵓīyin, wa-kullu man lā yaḥmilu l-biṭāqata yujawwizu musāᵓalata-hū qānūnīyan.

Wa-qad naṣṣa qānūnu s-sijilli l-madanīyu ᶜalā taġyīri nawᶜīyati l-biṭāqati ᶜinda z-zawāji li-ḏ-ḏakari, fa-yajibu ᵓan yuġayyira l-biṭāqata š-šaḫṣīyata bi-biṭāqatin ᶜāᵓilīyatin, wa-yaṯbutu bi-hā smu z-zawjati wa-ᵓasmāᵓu l-ᵓawlād.

---

[48] Text from the treaty database of the UN Office of Legal Affairs. The Arabic original was not available to the author.

[49] UN-doc. CRC/C/3/Add.6 (Arabic and English), pp. 27 and 23, respectively.

Item (69), official English translation

It is compulsory for all Egyptian males to carry identity cards and to present them in all civil and criminal proceedings. A person failing to carry an identity card is liable to punishment.

The Civil Record Act stipulates that on marriage, males must exchange their identity cards for family cards showing names of wife and children.

The underlying problem here is that women in most Arab states cannot obtain identity cards, let alone passports, without the permission of their husband, a circumstance that greatly impedes their *de facto* equality.

3. List of conflicting norms between international law and the Islamic šarīᶜa

Putting aside indirect forms of discrimination, the following articles in the relevant IHR conventions under investigation are the most prone to a conflict of norms between international law and the Islamic *šarīᶜa*.

Table 5

Conflicting norms between international law and the Islamic *šarīᶜa*

CESCR:[50]	art. 2/2:	non-discrimination on grounds of sex and religion
	art. 3:	equality of men and women
	art. 10/1:	freedom in concluding marriage
CCPR:[51]	art. 2/1:	non-discrimination on grounds of sex and religion
	art. 3:	equal rights of women
	art. 7:	non-application of torture and cruel, inhuman, and degrading treatment or punishment
	art. 18/1-4:	freedom of thought, conscience, and religion
	art. 23/3:	freedom in concluding marriage

[50] Religious or gender-motivated discrimination can also surface in the application of art. 6 (right to work), art. 12 (right to health), art. 13 (right to education), and art. 15 (right to participate in cultural life). Cf. UN-doc. E/1995/22, p. 33.

[51] The case of art. 6 (right to life) poses difficulties of interpretation. In its second report on the implementation of CCPR, Libya openly admitted that there is a problem with the concept of retaliation in the Qurʾān: "Human life is safeguarded and held sacred by the members of the Jamahiri society. However, the social code (the Qurʾān) stipulates that: "In retaliation you have a safeguard for your lives"." See UN-doc. CCPR/C/28/Add.16 (Arabic and English), pp. 6 and 5, respectively. The Qurʾānic quotation is from *sūra* 2: 179.

CCPR:	art. 27:	respect of ethnic, religious, and linguistic minorities
CEDAW:[52]	art. 2:	equality of men and women
	art. 9/1:	nationality in context of marriage
	art. 9/2:	nationality of children
	art. 16:	precepts of family law
CRC:[53]	art. 2:	non-discrimination on grounds of sex and religion
	art. 14:	freedom of religion
	art. 21:	institution of adoption
CERD:	art. 5 (a):	equal treatment before tribunals
	art. 5 (d):	catalogue of civil rights (including marriage, inheritance, and freedom of thought, conscience, and religion)
CAT:[54]		the whole convention (depending on the definition of "torture and cruel, inhuman, and degrading treatment or punishment")

From an Islamic perspective, and taking a systematic approach, these issues can be subsumed under the following categories:

(i) personal status (Muslims vs. non-Muslims, men vs. women, free persons vs. slaves, freedom of religious exercise);

(ii) family law (prohibition of marriage between Muslim woman and non-Muslim man, polygamy up to four wives, complementary distribution of "rights" and "obligations", disciplination of wives(s), prohibition for a woman to leave the house, let alone to travel without her husband's permission, institution of dowry, asymmetry in divorce regulations, prohibition of adoption);

(iii) law of succession/inheritance (female descendents inherit only half as much as male descendents);

(iv) penal law (absolute prohibiton for Muslims to change religion: apostasy entails death sentence for men and life imprisonment for

[52] Most Islamic states would argue that the very definition of "discrimination" in art. 1 is culture-dependent, i.e., subject to differing intensionalities.

[53] Again, the definition of "child" in art. 1 is often subject to problematic regulations, e.g., with respect to the minimum age for participation in war.

[54] Just as with CCPR, art. 7, it can be argued that corporal punishment under Islamic law as well as the practice of female genital mutilation should be considered under this heading (cf. *Krawietz* 1991: 223ff and *Alston* (ed.) 1992a: 511n and 520n).

women, stoning for adultery, amputations for theft, whipping and flogging for use of alcohol, etc.);

(v) procedure (women's testimony is worth only half as much as men's testimony).

Finally, there are phenomena that were originally allowed by the Islamic *šarīᶜa,* but have since been abolished by the Islamic states, at least *de jure.* While these problems continue to play a role in the work of the treaty bodies, they cannot be said, synchronically speaking, to represent conflicting norms between international law and the Islamic *šarīᶜa.* Notable examples of this are:

(vi) slavery, as prohibited by CCPR, art. 8;[55]

(vii) imprisonment for the mere inability to fulfil a contractual obligation, as prohibited by CCPR, art. 11.

Also, while physical disciplination of wives, as allowed by the Islamic *šarīᶜa,*[56] could be a potential point of discussion, no reference to it has been found in the periodic reports or the discussions.

IV. Overview of the specific problems, as appearing in UN documents

In the following, a brief discussion of the specific problems appearing in the relevant human rights documents will be presented. As the human rights precepts in the various IHR conventions are partially overlapping, the following remarks are oriented to the list of topics presented above from the Islamic perspective. However, only those issues are taken into consideration where conflicts arise between norms of international law and norms of the Islamic *šarīᶜa.*

1. Personal statute law

a) Muslims vs. non-Muslims

While the Islamic states parties to the IHR conventions usually insist that there is no formal discrimination with respect to religious af-

---

[55] Statements to the contrary, i.e., claims that the *šarīᶜa* disallows slavery, are simply untrue. Cf., for instance, Morocco's second report on its implementation of CCPR, UN-doc. CCPR/C/42/Add.10, p. 11. For an overview of this question, cf. *Lewis* 1990a.

[56] Qurʾān 4: 34.

filiation, there are indeed many legal provisions that prove the contrary. These range from the precept that the president of the respective country must be a Muslim to the *de facto* exclusion of non-Muslims from certain professions. Regarding article 27 of CCPR (respect of ethnic, religious, and linguistic minorities), it should be noted that, while *de facto* discrimination exists, this discrimination need not necessarily be based on religion.[57] Historically, Islamic societies have accommodated Christian and Jewish minorities as *ḏimmīs*, i.e., free non-Muslim subjects.

b) Men vs. women

Except in the large realm of family relations (cf. below), where all the Arab states and Iran adhere to the precepts of the Islamic *šarīᶜa*, states parties to IHR conventions insist likewise that there is no formal discrimination against women in Islamic societies. Rather, it is often argued that laws are set up so as to correspond to women's "natural dispositions" (cf. below).[58]

c) Freedom of religion, thought, and conscience

States parties to the IHR conventions usually insist that there are no impediments to free exercise of religion.[59] The following excerpt from Jordan's first report to CCPR pinpoints the problem in question:[60]

Item (70), English original

Freedom of religion is observed within the limits of the Islamic Sharia. According to the Sharia, there is no coercion in religion, "La Ikraha Fil Deen".[61] However, the children of a moslem are always moslems according to the Sharia.

---

[57] Cf. below (chapter six). For matters of personal statute in the Arab world, cf. also *Dilger* 1990: 66ff and *Ebert* 1996.

[58] Cf., for instance, Morocco's third report on its implementation of CCPR, UN-doc. CCPR/C/76/Add.3, p. 7, where quotations from the Qurʾān (*sūra* 49: 13) and the *sunna* are given to support this claim. For *de facto* impediments regarding women's rights to participate in political life and in the workplace, cf. *Abu-Sahlieh* 1985: 698ff.

[59] For a comprehensive overview of this topic, cf. the report by *Odio Benito* 1989. Elimination of All Forms of Intolerance and Discrimination Based on Religion or Belief. Geneva/New York.

[60] UN-doc. CCPR/C/1/Add.55, p. 5.

[61] The Qurʾānic quotation *lā ʾikrāha fi d-dīn* '[there shall be] no coercion in religion' is found in *sūra* 2: 256.

A further useful example is one relevant article of the Convention on the Rights of the Child in its English and Arabic versions, where the third paragraph allows for *šarīᶜa*-based reservations:

Item (71), English

Article 14

1. States Parties shall respect the right of the child to freedom of thought, conscience and religion.

2. States Parties shall respect the rights and duties of the parents and, when applicable, legal guardians, to provide direction to the child in the exercise of his or her right in a manner consistent with the evolving capacities of the child.

3. Freedom to manifest one's religion or beliefs may be subject only to such limitations as are prescribed by law and as are necessary to protect public safety, order, health or morals, or the fundamental rights and freedoms of others.

Item (71), Arabic

Al-māddatu 14

1 - Taḥtarimu d-duwalu l-ʾaṭrāfu ḥaqqa ṭ-ṭifli fī ḥurrīyati l-fikri wa-l-wijdāni wa-d-dīn.

2 - Taḥtarimu d-duwalu l-ʾaṭrāfu ḥuqūqa wa-wājibāti l-wālidayni wa-kaḏālika, tabaᶜan li-l-ḥālati, l-ʾawṣiyāʾa l-qānūnīyīna ᶜalay-hi, fī tawjīhi ṭ-ṭifli fī mumārasati ḥaqqi-hī bi-ṭarīqatin tansajimu maᶜa qadarāti ṭ-ṭifli l-mutaṭawwira.

3 - Lā yajūzu ʾan yuḫḍaᶜa l-ʾijhāru bi-d-dīni ʾawi l-muᶜtaqadāti ʾil-lā li-l-quyūdi llatī yanaṣṣu ᶜalay-hā l-qānūnu wa-l-lāzimatu li-ḥimāyati s-salāmati l-ᶜāmmati ʾawi n-niẓāmi ʾawi ṣ-ṣaḥḥati ʾawi l-ʾādābi l-ᶜāmmati ʾawi l-ḥuqūqi wa-l-ḥurrīyāti l-ʾasāsīyati li-l-ʾāḫarīn.

While freedom of thought and conscience is acknowledged in theory by all states under discussion, there is an abundancy of clauses in the reports that constrain the exercise of these freedoms to "the limits of the [Islamic] law".

2. *Family law*

Due to the Islamic concept of "complementarity between men's and women's rights and duties" in family matters (cf. below), the supporting evidence regarding equality of women which the Arab and other Islamic states adduce in reports on the implementation of the IHR conventions is hardly convincing. Technically, marriage in the Islamic perspective is a "contract" subject to a number of regulations.

a) Prohibition of marriage between Muslim women and non-Muslim men

This regulation is in place in all of the states under discussion.[62] From an Islamic perspective, the reverse case poses no problem, as the children of a Muslim man are automatically Muslims. In such a case the restriction holds that the wife of a Muslim man must belong to one of the other "divinely revealed" religions, i.e., Judaism or Christianity, if she is not a Muslim herself.[63]

b) Lack of freedom in contracting marriage

In many Muslim countries, first marriages are usually arranged marriages. *De facto,* women often lack the freedom to have any input whatsoever in the marriage contract, as they are supposed to "silently accept" the marriage.[64] The following recent quotation pertains to articles 23 and 40 of the International Covenant on Civil and Political Rights, from the perspective of Yemen:[65]

Item (72), Arabic original

Yaštariṭu riḍā l-marʾati l-bikri sukūta-hā wa-riḍā ṯ-ṯayyibi nuṭqa-hā. [...]

Item (72), official English translation

The woman must give her consent [to marriage]. In the case of a virgin, this shall be signified by her silence and, in the case of a woman who is not a virgin, by her verbal assent. [...]

The phrase *riḍā l-marʾa[ti]* 'consent of the woman' represents another example of an overlapping extension and a differing intension from a traditional Muslim and a "Western" perspective.

c) Polygamy up to four wives

As already stated, Tunisia is at present the only Arab country that outlaws polygamy (*taʿaddud az-zawjāt* 'polygyny')[66]. The only other

---

62 For details, cf. *Abu-Sahlieh* 1985: 650ff.

63 Qurʾān 2: 221, 4: 141, and 60: 10.

64 For details, cf. *Abu-Sahlieh* 1985: 692ff and *Dilger* 1990: 71.

65 UN-doc. CCPR/C/82/Add.1 (Arabic and English), pp. 18ff and 20ff, respectively.

66 Qurʾān 4: 3. Cf. *Abu-Sahlieh* 1985: 695f and *Dilger* 1990: 71f.

Arab country to outlaw polygamy and allow bigamy only in very limited circumstances, such as sterility of the first wife and her explicit consent to a second wife for her husband, was former South Yemen.[67] The arguments given for upholding the practice of polygamy will be analyzed below. Some states make it a condition that the husband must prove his financial capacity to maintain several wives, and stipulate that the first wife must give her "consent" to further marriages of her husband. *De facto,* however, the first wife is hardly able to withhold her "consent"; and it is unclear what interest she could have in giving her "consent" to further marriages of her husband in the first place.

d) Complementary distribution of "rights" and "obligations"

The reservations to the Convention on the Elimination of All Forms of Discrimination against Women (CEDAW) best illustrate the problem in question.[68] For the sake of demonstrating the specific means by which Islamic jurists and diplomats interpret this Convention, here are the relevant articles in their English and Arabic versions :[69]

Item (73), English

Article 9

1. States Parties shall grant women equal rights with men to acquire, change or retain their nationality. They shall ensure in particular that neither marriage to an alien nor change of nationality by the husband during marriage shall automatically change the nationality of the wife, render her stateless or force upon her the nationality of her husband.

2. States Parties shall grant women equal rights with men with respect to the nationality of their children.[70]

Article 16

1. States Parties shall take all appropriate measures to eliminate discrimination against women in all matters relating to marriage and family relations and in particular shall ensure, on a basis of equality of men and women:

---

[67] Cf. UN-doc. CEDAW/C/13/Add.24 (Arabic and English), pp. 8ff and 7ff, respectively.

[68] For procedural and *šarīʿa*-related aspects of this question, cf. *Cook* 1990: 687ff and 702ff, *Clark* 1991: 284, 287ff, and 299ff, *Lijnzaad* 1995: 298ff, 307, and 320ff, *Chinkin* 1997, *Connors* 1997 as well as UN-doc. CEDAW/C/1997/4.

[69] Convention on the Elimination of All Forms of Discrimination against Women. Adopted by the General Assembly of the United Nations on 18 December 1979, *UNTS*, vol. 1249 (1981), pp. 13ff.

[70] *UNTS*, vol. 1249 (1981), p. 17.

(a) The same right to enter into marriage;

(b) The same right freely to choose a spouse and to enter into marriage only with their free will and consent;

(c) The same rights and responsibilities during marriage

(d) The same rights and responsibilities as parents, irrespective of their marital status, in matters relating to their children; in all cases the interests of the children shall be paramount;

(e) The same rights to decide freely and responsibly on the number and spacing of their children and to have access to the information, education and means to enable them to exercise these rights;

(f) The same rights and responsibilities with regard to guardianship, wardship, trusteeship, and adoption of children, or similar institutions where these concepts exist in national legislation; in all cases the interests of the children shall be paramount;

(g) The same personal rights as husband and wife, including the right to choose a family name, a profession and an occupation;

(h) The same rights for both spouses in respect of the ownership, acquisition, management, administration, enjoyment and disposition of property, whether free of charge or for a valuable consideration.

2. The betrothal and the marriage of a child shall have no legal effect, and all necessary action, including legislation, shall be taken to specify a minimum age for marriage and to make the registration of marriages in an official registry compulsory.[71]

Item (73), Arabic

Al-māddatu 9

1 - Tamnaḥu d-duwalu l-ʾaṭrafu l-marʾata ḥaqqan musāwiyan li-ḥaqqi r-rajuli fī ktisābi jinsīyati-hā ʾawi l-iḥtifāẓi bi-hā ʾaw taġyīri-hā. Wa-taḍmanu bi-wajhin ḫāṣṣin ʾal-lā yatarattaba ʿalā z-zawāji min ʾajnabīyin ʾaw taġyīri jinsīyati z-zawji ʾaṯnāʾa z-zawāji ʾan tataġayyara tilqāʾīyan jinsiyatu z-zawjati, ʾaw ʾan tuṣbiḥa bi-lā jinsīyatin ʾaw ʾan tufraḍa ʿalay-hā jinsīyatu z-zawj.

2 - Tamnaḥu d-duwalu l-ʾaṭrāfu l-marʾata ḥaqqan musāwiyan li-ḥaqqi r-rajuli fī-mā yataʿallaqu bi-jinsīyati ʾaṭfāli-hā.[72]

Al-māddatu 16

1 - Tattaḫiḏu d-duwalu l-ʾaṭrāfu jamīʿa t-tadābīri l-munāsibati li-l-qaḍāʾi ʿalā t-tamyīzi ḍidda l-marʾati fī kāffati l-ʾumūri l-mutaʿalliqati bi-z-zawāji wa-l-ʿalāqāti l-ʾusrīyati, wa-bi-wajhin ḫāṣṣin taḍmanu, ʿalā ʾasāsi tasāwī r-rajuli wa-l-marʾa:

(a) nafsa l-ḥaqqi fī ʿaqdi z-zawāj;

---

[71] *UNTS*, vol. 1249 (1981), p. 20.

[72] *UNTS*, vol. 1249 (1981), p. 43.

(b) nafsa l-ḥaqqi fī ḥurrīyati ḫtiyāri z-zawji, wa-fī ᶜadami ᶜaqdi z-zawāji ʾil-lā bi-riḍā-hā l-ḥurri l-kāmil;

(c) nafsa l-ḥuqūqi wa-l-masʾūlīyāti ʾaṯnaʾa z-zawāji wa-ᶜinda fasḫi-hī;

(d) nafsa l-ḥuqūqi wa-l-masʾūlīyāti ka-wālidatin, bi-ġaḍḍi n-naẓari ᶜan ḥālati-hā z-zawjīyati, fī l-ʾumūri l-mutaᶜalliqati bi-ʾaṭfāli-hā; wa-fī jamīᶜi l-ʾaḥwāli, takūnu maṣāliḥu l-ʾaṭfāli hiya r-rājiḥa;

(e) nafsa l-ḥuqūqi fī ʾan tuqarrira bi-ḥurrīyatin wa-bi-šuᶜūrin mina l-masʾūlīyāti ᶜadada ʾaṭfāli-hā wa-l-fitrata bayna ʾinjābi ṭiflin wa-ʾāḫara, wa-fī l-ḥuṣūli ᶜalā l-maᶜlūmāti wa-t-taṯqīfi wa-l-wasāʾili l-kafīlati bi-tamkīni-hā min mumārasati hāḏihī l-ḥuqūq;

(f) nafsa l-ḥuqūqi wa-l-masʾūlīyāti fī-mā yataᶜallaqu bi-l-wilāyati wa-l-qiwāmati wa-l-wiṣāyati ᶜalā l-ʾaṭfāli wa-tabannī-him ʾaw mā šibhu ḏālika mina l-ʾanẓimati l-muʾassasīyati l-ijtimāᶜīyati, ḥīna tūjadu hāḏihī l-mafāhīmu fī t-tašrīᶜi l-waṭanī; wa-fī jamīᶜi l-ʾaḥwāli takūnu maṣāliḥu l-ʾaṭfāli hiya r-rājiḥa;

(g) nafsa l-ḥuqūqi š-šaḫṣīyati li-z-zawji wa-z-zawjati, bi-mā fī ḏālika l-ḥaqqu fī ḫtiyāri l-laqabi, wa-l-mihnati, wa-l-ᶜamal;

(h) nafsa l-ḥuqūqi li-kilā z-zawjayni fī-mā yataᶜallaqu bi-milkīyati wa-ḥiyāzati l-mumtalakati, wa-l-ʾišrāfi ᶜalay-hā, wa-ʾidārati-hā, wa-t-tamattuᶜi bi-hā, wa-t-taṣarrufi fī-hā, sawāʾan bi-lā muqābilin ʾaw muqābili ᶜiwaḍi ḏī qīma.

2 - Lā yakūnu li-ḫuṭūbati ṭ-ṭifli ʾaw zawāji-hī ʾayyu ʾaṯarin qānūnīyin, wa-tattaḫiḏu jamīᶜa l-ʾijrāʾāti ḍ-ḍarūrīyati, bi-mā fī-hā t-tašrīᶜu, li-taḥdīdi sinnin ʾadnā li-z-zawāji wa-li-jaᶜli tasjīli z-zawāji fī sijillin rasmīyin ʾamran ʾilzāmīyan.[73]

A few linguistic observations are in order before turning to the reservations. While the English text attempts to be gender-neutral, the Arabic text constantly has women grammatically and semantically "marked", with the consequence that equality as a symmetrical relation is *a priori* rejected as a concept.[74] This is especially apparent in paragraph (b) of article 16 (*nafsa l-ḥaqqi fī ḥurrīyati ḫtiyāri z-zawji, wa-fī ᶜadami ᶜaqdi z-zawāji ʾil-lā bi-riḍā-hā l-ḥurri l-kāmil*). Furthermore, the phrase *to enter into marriage* is not accurately rendered by *ᶜaqd[i] z-zawāj[i]* ('contraction of marriage'), probably due to a possible sexual undertone that could arise in a too literal Arabic translation. As will be shown later, the main problem of interpretation is that the Arabic

[73] *UNTS*, vol. 1249 (1981), p. 39.

[74] There is, of course, no "gender-neutral" Arabic equivalent of English *spouse*; however, a "symmetrical" construction along the lines of English *he-or-she* constructions would pose no major stylistic problems.

terms *ḥuqūq* 'rights' and *masʾūlīyāt* 'responsibilities' in (c) are not used in a symmetrical, but rather in a complementary sense ("complementary intensionality"). Thus, the husband is entitled to his wife's obedience, while his wife is entitled to sustenance.[75]

The following reservations were submitted by Egypt with respect to articles 9 and 16 of the above convention:[76]

Item (74), Arabic original

At-taḥaffuẓāt:

At-taḥaffuẓu ʿalā naṣṣi l-fiqrati ṯ-ṯāniyati mina l-māddati (9) bi-šaʾni manḥi l-marʾati ḥaqqan mutasāwiyan li-ḥaqqi r-rajuli fī-mā yataʿallaqu bi-jinsīyati ʾaṭfāli-hā, bi-ʾan yakūna ḏālika dūna ʾiḫlālin bi-ktisābi ṭ-ṭifli n-nātiji li-jinsīyati ʾabī-hi, wa-ḏālika tafādiyan mini ktisābi-hī li-jinsīyatayni fī ḥālati ḫtilāfi jinsīyati l-ʾabawayni ttiqāʾa ʾaḍrārin bi-mustaqbali-hī, wa mina l-jalīli ʾanna ktisāba ṭ-ṭifli li-jinsīyati ʾabī-hi huwa ʾansabu l-ʾawḍāʿi la-hu wa-lā misāsa bi-mabdaʾi l-musāwāti bayna r-rajuli wa-l-marʾati ʾiḏi l-maʾlūfu muwāfaqatu l-marʾati fī ḥālati zawāji-hā man ʾajnabīyan ʿalā ntisābi ʾaṭfāli-himā li-jinsīyati l-ʾab.

At-taḥaffuẓu ʿalā naṣṣi l-māddati (16) bi-šaʾni tasāwī l-marʾati bi-r-rajuli fī kāffati l-ʾumūri l-mutaʿalliqati bi-z-zawāji wa-ʿalāqāti l-ʾusrati ʾaṯnāʾa z-zawāji wa-ʿaqdi fasḫi-hī bi-ʾan yakūna ḏālika dūna ʾiḫlālin bi-mā takfulu-hū š-šarīʿatu l-ʾislāmīyatu li-z-zawjati la-ḥuqūqun muqābilatun li-ḥuqūqi z-zawji bi-mā yuḥaqqaqu t-tawāzunu l-ʿādilu bayna-humā wa-ḏālika murāʿātan bi-mā taqūmu ʿalay-hi l-ʿalāqātu z-zawjīyatu fī miṣra min qudsīyatin mustamaddatin mina l-ʿaqāʾidi d-dīnīyati r-rāsiḫati llatī lā yajūzu l-ḫurūju ʿalay-hā, wa-ʿtibāran bi-ʾan min ʾahammi l-ʾususi llatī taqūmu ʿalay-hā hāḏihī l-ʿalāqātu t-taqābulu bayna l-ḥuqūqi wa-l-wājibāti ʿalā naḥwin mina t-takāmuli llaḏī yuḥaqqiqu l-musāwāta l-ḥaqīqīyata bayna z-zawjayni lā maẓāhira l-musāwāti š-šiklīyati llatī lā tuḥaqqiqu li-z-zawjati maṣlaḥatan nāfiʿatan mina z-zawāji bi-qadri mā tuṯaqqilu kāhila-hā mina l-quyūd. Ḏālika ʾanna ʾaḥkāma š-šarīʿati l-ʾislāmīyati tafriḍu ʿalā z-zawji ʾadāʾa l-mahri l-munāsibi li-z-zawjati wa-l-ʾinfāqa ʿalay-hā min māli-hī ʾinfāqan kāmilan ṯumma ʾadāʾa nafaqatin la-hā ʿinda ṭ-ṭalāqi fī ḥīni(n) taḥtafiẓu z-zawjatu bi-ḥuqūqi-hā ʿalā ʾamwāli-hā wa-lā taltazimu bi-l-ʾinfāqi min-hā ʿalā nafsi-hā wa-[li-]ḏālika qayyadati š-šarīʿatu ḥaqqa z-zawjati fī ṭ-ṭalāqi bi-ʾan ʾawjabat ʾan yakūna ḏālika bi-ḥukmi l-qaḍāʾi fī ḥīni(n) lam taḍaʿ miṯla hāḏā l-qaydi ʿalā z-zawj. [...][77]

[75] It goes without saying that this "complementary" distribution, beyond the formal inequity, is also factually unfounded, given the amount of work in support of their families performed by most Arab and other Muslim women.

[76] Egypt in this context also formulated a reservation with respect to article 29/1 of the convention, thus excluding the submission to mandatory arbitration.

[77] *UNTS*, vol. 1249 (1981), p. 124.

Item (74), official English translation

In respect of article 9

Reservation to the text of article 9, paragraph 2, concerning the granting to women of equal rights with respect to the nationality of their children, without prejudice to the acquisition by a child born of a marriage of the nationality of his father. This is in order to prevent a child's acquisition of two nationalities where his parents are of different nationalities, since this may be prejudicial to his future. It is clear that the child's acquisition of his father's nationality is the procedure most suitable for the child and that this does not infringe upon the principle of equality between men and women, since it is customary for a woman to agree, upon marrying an alien, that her children shall be of the father's nationality.

In respect of article 16

Reservation to the text of article 16 concerning the equality of men and women in all matters relating to marriage and family relations during the marriage and upon its dissolution, without prejudice to the Islamic Sharia's provisions whereby women are accorded rights equivalent to those of their spouses so as to ensure a just balance between them. This is out of respect for the sacrosanct nature of the firm religious beliefs which govern marital relations in Egypt and which may not be called in question and in view of the fact that one of the most important bases of these relations is an equivalency of rights and duties so as to ensure complementarity which guarantees true equality between the spouses. The provisions of the Sharia lay down that the husband shall pay bridal money to the wife and maintain her fully and shall also make a payment to her upon divorce, whereas the wife retains full rights over her property and is not obliged to spend anything on her keep. The Sharia therefore restricts the wife's rights to divorce by making it contingent on a judge's ruling, whereas no such restriction is laid down in the case of the husband. ...[78]

A crucial omission is found in the English and French translations of the reservation: the passage *lā maẓāhira l-musāwāti š-šiklīyati llatī lā tuḥaqqiqu li-z-zawjati maṣlaḥatan nāfiᶜatan mina z-zawāji bi-qadri mā tuṯaqqilu kāhila-hā mina l-quyūd* near the end of item (73) is missing in the English and French translations. An accurate translation of the missing part is found, however, in Egypt's initial report submitted under article 18 of the convention:[79]

Item (75), Arabic original

[...] lā maẓāhira l-musāwāti š-šiklīyati llatī lā tuḥaqqiqu li-z-zawjati maṣlaḥatan nāfiᶜatan mina z-zawāji bi-qadri mā tuṯaqqilu kāhila-hā mina l-quyūd.

---

[78] *UNTS*, vol. 1249 (1981), pp. 125f.

[79] UN-doc. CEDAW/C/5/Add.10 (Arabic and English), p. 3.

Item (75), official English translation

[...] rather than the manifestations of formal equality which do not give the wife any useful interest to be obtained from the husband so much as they burden her with restrictions.

The English translation of Arabic *jalīl* 'great, important' as "clear" in the final sentence of the reservation to article (9) slightly distorts the tenor of this problematic statement: "it is important that the child's acquisition of his father's nationality ..."

From an international legal perspective, the following comments have been made on these types of reservations:[80]

Item (76), English original

A large number of States parties have entered reservations to article 16, which guarantees equality between women and men in marriage and family life, either in part or in its entirety. Commentators have been particularly critical of these reservations, suggesting that they manifest rejection of the extension of human rights protection into the private sphere and entrench an inferior role for women in domestic life. Controversy surrounded the drafting of article 16 during the preparation of the Convention, with States attempting, even in the discussions in the Third Committee of the General Assembly, to amend the draft Convention to conform with their domestic law. Reservations and declarations to this article are diverse. A number are imprecise and offer no explanation. Others are explicit and explain why the State party has made the reservation. Some States parties, whose reservations are based on the Islamic *shariah*, argue that women are in fact advantaged by the domestic regime. For example, Iraq has indicated that its reservation is based on the view that the *shariah* accords women rights equivalent to those of their spouses so as to ensure a just balance between them. Similar, but more detailed, explanations, are offered by the reservations of Egypt and Morocco. Reservations to article 16 have attracted the particular concern of the Committee on the Elimination of Discrimination against Women which, in general recommendation 21, relating to equality in marriage and family relations, expressed alarm at the number and scope of reservations to article 16, particularly in those cases where the State party has also entered reservations with respect to article 2. The Committee has urged States parties to discourage any notions of inequality between women and men which are affirmed by law, or by religious or private law or custom, and has encouraged them to progress towards a stage where reservations to article 16 could be removed.

e) Prohibition against women leaving the house, or traveling without husband's permission

This provision, at least with respect to foreign travel, is a notorious problem in virtually all Arab states, as the permission of a male "tutor" is usually a formal prerequisite. The following recent example

---

[80] UN-doc. CEDAW/C/1997/4, para. 12.

pertains to articles 23 and 40 of the International Covenant on Civil and Political Rights, from the perspective of Yemen:[81]

Item (77), Arabic original

Li-z-zawji ʿalā z-zawjati ḥaqqu ṭ-ṭāʿati fī-mā yuḥaqqiqu maṣlaḥata l-ʾusrati wa-ʿalā l-ʾaḫaṣṣi fī-mā yalī:

(i) Al-intiqālu maʿa-hū ʾilā manzili z-zawjīyati mā lam takun qadi štaraṭat ʿalay-hi fī l-ʿaqdi l-biqāʾa fī manzili-hā ʾaw manzili ʾusrati-hā fa-yakūnu ʿalay-hā tamkīnu-hū mina s-sakani maʿa-hā wa-d-duḫūli ʿalay-hā.

(ii) Tamkīnu-hū min-hā ṣāliḥa-hū li-l-waṭʾi l-mašrūʿi fī ġayri ḥuḍūri ʾaḥad.

(iii) Imtiṯālu ʾamri-hī, wa-l-qiyāmu bi-ʿamali-hā fī bayti z-zawjīyati miṯla ġayri-hā.

(iv) ʿAdamu l-ḫurūji min manzili z-zawjīyati ʾil-lā bi-ʾiḏni-hī, wa-laysa li-z-zawji manʿu zawjati-hī mina l-ḫurūji li-ʿuḏrin šarʿīyin ʾaw mā jarā l-ʿurfu bi-miṯli-hī mim-mā laysa fī-hi qaydu l-ʾiḫlāli bi-š-šarafi wa-lā bi-wājibāti-hā naḥwa-hū, wa-ʿalā l-ʾaḫaṣṣi l-ḫurūju fī ʾiṣlāḥi māli-hā ʾaw ʾādāʾu waẓīfati-hā, wa-yuʿtabaru ʿuḏran šarʿīyan li-l-marʾati ḫidmatu wāliday-hā l-ʿājizayni wa-laysa la-humā man yaqūmu bi-ḫidmati-himā ʾaw ʾaḥadi-himā ġayru-hā.

Item (77), official English translation

A husband has a right to his wife's obedience in matters affecting the family's interests, particularly with regard to the following:

(i) She must move with him to the conjugal home, unless she stipulated in the contract that he must allow her to remain in her home or her family's home, in which case she must permit him to live with her and enjoy access to her;

(ii) She must permit him to have licit intercourse with her, in private, when she is in a state of ritual purity;

(iii) She must obey his orders and perform her work in the conjugal home, like other women;

(iv) She must not leave the conjugal home without his permission, although the husband has no right to prevent his wife from going out for a legally valid or generally acceptable reason which is not prejudicial to honour or to her duties towards him. In particular, she may get out to attend to her property interests or discharge her employment-related duties. If the woman wishes to assist her aged parents when there is no one else to take care of either or both of them, this shall be deemed to be a legally valid reason.

On March 30, 1995, the legal adviser of the Yemeni foreign ministry, Al-Hubaishi, commented on critical questions regarding these paragraphs during a meeting of the Human Rights Committee in New York:[82]

---

81 UN-doc. CCPR/C/82/Add.1 (Arabic and English), p. 20 and 19, respectively.

82 UN-doc. (Press Release) HR/CT/403, p. 2.

Item (78), English original

The provision that the wife might not leave the house without her spouse's permission was not a general rule. The wife could leave the house to visit her relatives or to go to market. In practice, the husband, too, could not leave the house without permission. Perhaps he might be denied food if he did.

Again, this remark, which conveys the appearance of implying *de facto* equality between the sexes, in fact highlights the difference on the intensional level in the perception of the concept of "equality". Beyond that, the remark exhibits a disquieting lack of respect for the the work of the Human Rights Committee.

f) Institution of dowry

The institution of dowry plays a role in family law insofar as it is usually adduced as a rationale for excusing the formally inequitable inheritance regulations (cf. below). Here is an example, taken from Morocco's first report on CCPR:[83]

Item (79), French original

Certes, en droit musulman, la femme ne reçoit en héritage que la moitié de la quote-part de son frère, mais la jurisprudence islamique a, depuis toujours, aisément expliqué cela par une exigence d'équité du fait que c'est sur l'homme que pèse l'obligation de donner, en mariage, la dot (qui devient propriété personelle et inaliénable de la femme), et que c'est lui qui assume toutes les charges d'entretien du ménage; de plus, la pension alimentaire, en cas de séparation ou de divorce, n'incombe qu'à lui.

g) Asymmetry in divorce regulations

Whereas a Muslim man can "repudiate" one or several of his wives without explanation by way of *ṭalāq* ('divorce'), a Muslim woman can only sue for divorce under very limited circumstances, such as long absence of her husband and/or total financial negligence.[84] The following quite unrealistic statement was made in the course of the discussion of Iraq's second report on its implementation of CCPR, UN-doc. CCPR/C/37/Add.3:[85]

---

[83] UN-doc. CCPR/C/10/Add.2, p. 15.

[84] Qurʾān 2: 229. Cf. *Abu-Sahlieh* 1985: 694f and *Dilger* 1990: 73f.

[85] UN-doc. CCPR/C/SR.748, p. 9.

Item (80), English original

The dissolution of the marriage through divorce was governed by laws which were based exclusively on the Islamic Shariah; the husband had the right to initiate the divorce, but he could also give that right to his wife when the marriage took place.

h) Prohibition of adoption

This is another point in the realm of family law where reservations of Arab and other Islamic states are particularly common.[86] Here are the English and Arabic versions of the relevant articles in the Convention on the Rights of the Child:[87]

Item (81), English

Article 20

1. A child temporarily or permanently deprived of his or her family environment, or in whose own best interests cannot be allowed to remain in that environment, shall be entitled to special protection and assistance provided by the State.

2. States Parties shall in accordance with their national laws ensure alternative care for such a child.

3. Such care could include, inter alia, foster placement, *kafalah* of Islamic law, adoption or, if necessary, placement in suitable institutions for the care of children. When considering solutions, due regard shall be paid to the desirability of continuity in a child's upbringing and to the child's ethnic, religious, cultural and linguistic background.

Article 21

States Parties that recognize and/or permit the system of adoption shall ensure that the best interests of the child shall be the paramount consideration and they shall:

(a) Ensure that the adoption of a child is authorized only by competent authorities who determine, in accordance with applicable law and procedures and on the basis of all pertinent and reliable information, that the adoption is permissible in view of the child's status concerning parents, relatives and legal guardians and that, if required, the persons concerned have given their informed consent to the adoption on the basis of such counselling as may be necessary;

(b) Recognize that inter-country adoption may be considered as an alternative means of the child's care, if the child cannot be placed in a foster or an adoptive family or cannot in any suitable manner be cared for in the child's country of origin;

---

[86] For details, cf. *Abu-Sahlieh* 1985: 665ff and *Dilger* 1990: 75.

[87] Convention on the Rights of the Child. Adopted by the General Assembly of the United Nations on 20 November 1989, UN-doc. A/RES/44/25; for the reservations, cf. UN-doc. ST/LEG/SER.E/11 (Multilateral Treaties Deposited with the Secretary-General).

(c) Ensure that the child concerned by inter-country adoption enjoys safeguards and standards equivalent to those existing in the case of national adoption;

(d) Take all appropriate measures to ensure that, in inter-country adoption, the placement does not result in improper financial gain for those involved in it;

(e) Promote, where appropriate, the objectives of the present article by concluding bilateral or multilateral arrangements or agreements, and endeavour, within this framework, to ensure that the placement of the child in another country is carried out by competent authorities or organs.[88]

Item (81), Arabic

Al-māddatu 20

1 - Li-ṭ-ṭifli l-maḥrūmi bi-ṣifatin muʾaqqatatin ʾaw dāʾimatin min bīʾati-hī l-ʿāʾilīyati ʾawi llaḏī lā yusmaḥu la-hū, ḥifāẓan ʿalā maṣāliḥi-hī l-fuḍlā, bi-l-biqāʾi fī tilka l-bīʾati, l-ḥaqqu fī ḥimāyatin wa-musāʿadatin ḫāṣṣatayni tuwaffiru-humā d-dawla.

2 - Taḍmanu d-duwalu l-ʾaṭrāfu wafqan li-qawānīni-hā l-waṭanīyati, riʿāyatan badīlatan li-miṯli hāḏā ṭ-ṭifl.

3 - Yumkinu ʾan tašmala hāḏihī r-riʿāyatu, fī jumlati ʾumūrini, l-ḥiḍānata, ʾawi l-kafālata l-wāridata fī l-qānūni l-ʾislāmīyi, ʾawi t-tabanniya, ʾaw, ʿinda ḍ-ḍarūrati, l-ʾiqāmata fī muʾassasatin munāsibatin li-riʿāyati l-ʾaṭfāl. Wa-ʿinda n-naẓari fī l-ḥulūli, yanbaġī ʾīlāʾu l-iʿtibāri l-wājibi li-stiṣwābi l-istimrārīyati fī tarbīyati ṭ-ṭifli wa-li-ḫalfīyati ṭ-ṭifli l-ʾiṯnīyati wa-d-dīnīyati wa-ṯ-ṯaqāfīyati wa-l-luġawīya.

Al-māddatu 21

Taḍmanu d-duwalu llatī tuqirru wa-/ʾaw tujīzu niẓāma t-tabannī ʾīlāʾa maṣāliḥi ṭ-ṭifli l-fuḍlā l-iʿtibāra l-ʾawwala wa-l-qiyāma bi-mā yalī:

(a) Taḍmanu ʾal-lā tuṣarriḥa bi-tabannī ṭ-ṭifli ʾil-lā s-sulṭatu l-muḫtaṣṣatu llatī tuḥaddidu, wafqan li-l-qawānīni wa-l-ʾijrāʾāti l-maʿmūli bi-hā wa-ʿalā ʾasāsi kulli l-maʿlūmāti ḏāti ṣ-ṣilati l-mawṯūqi bi-hā, ʾanna t-tabanniya jāʾizun naẓaran li-ḥālati ṭ-ṭifli fī-mā yataʿallaqu bi-l-wālidayni wa-l-ʾaqāribi, wa-l-ʾawṣiyāʾi l-qānūnīyīna wa-ʾanna l-ʾašḫāṣa l-maʿnīyīna, ʿinda l-iqtiḍāʾi, qad ʾaʿṭaw ʿan ʿilmi muwāfaqati-him ʿalā t-tabannī ʿalā ʾasāsi ḥuṣūli-him ʿalā mā qad yalzamu mina l-mašwara.

(b) Taʿtarifu bi-ʾanna t-tabanniya fī baladin ʾāḫara yumkinu ʿtibāru-hū wasīlatan badīlatan li-riʿāyati ṭ-ṭifli, ʾiḏā taʿaḏḏarat ʾiqāmatu ṭ-ṭifli ladā ʾusratin ḥāḍinatin ʾaw mutabanniyatin, ʾaw ʾiḏā taʿaḏḏarati l-ʿināyatu bi-hī bi-ʾayyi ṭarīqatin mulāʾimatin fī waṭani-hī.

(c) Taḍmanu, bi-n-nisbati li-t-tabannī fī baladin ʾāḫara, ʾan yastafīda ṭ-ṭiflu min ḍamānātin wa-maʿāyīra tuʿādilu tilka l-qāʾimata fī-mā yataʿallaqu bi-t-tabannī l-waṭanī.

---

[88] UN-doc. A/RES/44/25 (English), articles 20 and 21.

(d) Tattaḫiḏu jamīᶜa t-tadābīri l-munāsibati kay taḍmana, bi-n-nisbati li-t-tabannī fī baladin ᵓāḫara, ᵓanna ᶜamalīyata t-tabannī lā taᶜūdu ᶜalā ᵓūlāᵓika l-mušārikīna fī-hā bi-kasbin mālīyin ġayri mašrūᶜ.

(e) Tuᶜazzizu, ᶜinda l-iqtiḍāᵓi, ᵓahdāfa hāḏihī l-māddati bi-ᶜaqdi tartībātin ᵓawi ttifāqātin ṯunāᵓīyati ᵓaw mutaᶜaddidati l-ᵓaṭrāfi, wa-tasᶜā, fī hāḏā l-ᵓiṭāri, ᵓilā ḍamāni ᵓan yakūna tabannī ṭ-ṭifli fī baladin ᵓāḫara min ḫilāli s-sulṭāti ᵓawi l-hayᵓāti l-muḫtaṣṣa.[89]

Egypt submitted the following reservations with respect to this convention:[90]

Item (82), Arabic original

Iᶜtibāran li-ᵓanna š-šarīᶜata l-ᵓislāmīyata hiya maṣdarun ᵓasāsīyun min maṣādiri t-tašrīᶜi fī l-qānūni l-waḍᶜīyi l-miṣrīyi, wa-naẓaran li-ᵓanna hāḏihī š-šarīᶜata ᵓiḏ tuwajjibu tawfīra kāffati wasāᵓili li-l-ḥimāyati wa-r-riᶜāyati li-l-ᵓaṭfāli bi-ṭuruqin wa-wasāᵓila mutaᶜaddidatin -- laysa min bayna-hā niẓāmu t-tabannī l-mawjūdi fī baᶜḍi l-qawānīni l-waḍᶜīyati l-ᵓuḫrā -- fa-ᵓinna ḥukūmata jumhūrīyati miṣra l-ᶜarabīyati tataḥaffaẓu ᶜalā kāffati n-nuṣūṣi wa-l-ᵓaḥkāmi l-ḫāṣṣati bi-t-tabannī fī hāḏihī l-ittifāqīyati, ᶜalā wajhin ḫāṣṣin mā warada bi-šaᵓni t-tabannī fī l-māddatayni 20 wa-21 mina l-ittifāqīya.

Item (81), official English translation

Since the Islamic Shariah is one of the fundamental sources of legislation in Egyptian positive law, and because the Shariah, in enjoining the provision of every means of protection and care for children in numerous ways and means, does not include among those ways and means the system of adoption existing in certain other bodies of positive law, the government of the Arab Republic of Egypt expresses its reservation with respect to all the clauses and provisions relating to adoption in the said Convention, and in particular with respect to the provisions governing adoption in articles 20 and 21 of the Convention.[91]

The term *kafāla* 'sponsorship'/'tutelage'/'adoption' marks a major stumbling block for interpretation, as it differs from its "Western" counterpart in both extension and intension. *Kafāla* does not allow the child to be taken care of to change his or her religion. This is the underlying motive for the rejection of the "Western" concept of *tabannin* 'adoption', which does allow for such a procedure.

The reservations of Egypt as well as the following reservations of Jordan come as a surprise, however, in light of the accommodating nature of the resolution, as the convention is expressly worded so as to

---

[89] UN-doc. A/RES/44/25 (Arabic), articles 20 and 21.

[90] The Arabic text was provided by courtesy of the UN Office of Legal Affairs, Treaty Section.

[91] UN-doc. ST/LEG/SER.E/11, p. 190.

take into equal consideration the Islamic concept of *kafāla* and the "Western" concept of *tabannin* 'adoption'.

Jordan submitted the following reservation with respect to the convention:

Item (83), Arabic original

Baᶜda ʾani ṭṭalaᶜnā ᶜalā ttifāqīyati ḥuqūqi ṭ-ṭifli llatī ᶜtumidat min qabli l-jamᶜīyati l-ᶜāmmati li-l-ʾumami l-muttaḥidati fī l-ᶜišrīna min šahri tišrīna ṯānī [sic!] li-ᶜāmi ʾalfin wa-tisᶜamiʾatin wa-tisᶜatin wa-ṯamānīna milādīyatin, nuᶜlinu muwāfaqata-nā wa-taṣdīqa-nā ᶜalay-hā fī majmūᶜi-hā wa-tafṣīlāti-hā wa-nataᶜahhadu bi-ʾan naqūma bi-mā warada fī-hā wa-nulāhiẓu bunūda-hā wa-lan nasmaḥa bi-ʾiḏni llāhi bi-ʾiḫlālin bi-hā. Wa-ʾinna l-mamlakata l-ʾurdunnīyata l-hāšimīyata tubdī taḥaffuẓa-hā wa-taᶜtabiru nafsa-hā ġayra mulzamatin bi-mā warada fī l-mawāddi r-rābiᶜati ᶜašrata wa-l-ᶜišrīna wa-l-wāḥidati wa-l-ᶜišrīna mina l-ittifāqīyati wa-llatī tuᶜṭī ṭ-ṭifla l-ḥaqqa fī ḥurrīyati ḫtiyāri d-dīni, wa-l-bunūdi l-mutaᶜalliqati fī qaḍīyati t-tabannī li-muᶜāraḍati-hā li-ʾaḥkāmi š-šarīᶜati l-ʾislāmīyati s-samḥa.[92]

Item (83), official English translation

[After acceding to the Convention on the Rights of the Child which was adopted by the General Assembly of the United Nations on 20 November, 1989 (C.E.), we proclaim our agreement with and faithfulness to the Convention in its entirety and in its details, we commit ourselves to the implementation of its contents and to the consideration of its articles, and we will not – if God wills – permit its violation.] The Hashemite Kingdom of Jordan expresses its reservation and does not consider itself bound by articles 14, 20 and 21 of the Convention, which grant the child the right of freedom of choice of religion and concern the question of adoption, since they are at variance with the precepts of the tolerant Islamic Shariah.[93]

The concluding phrase *[a]š-šarīᶜat[u] l-ʾislāmīyat[u] s-samḥa* 'the tolerant Islamic Shariah' is a further example of an overlapping extension and a differing intension. Apparently the adjective *samḥ* 'generous, tolerant' does not convey to the Arab reader the somewhat inappropriate or unintentionally ironical character that it carries for the "Western" reader in the context of this reservation.

---

[92] The Arabic text was provided courtesy of the UN Office of Legal Affairs, Treaty Section.

[93] UN-doc. ST/LEG/SER.E/11, p. 192. The whole first sentence is omitted in the English translation of the reservation, possibly due to the fact that this sentence was considered a near-meaningless formal introduction. A translation of the missing part is provided here by the author.

3. *Law of succession*

Female descendents inherit only half as much as male descendents.[94] Also, non-Muslims may not inherit from Muslims.[95] The first provision is even upheld by Tunisia, otherwise the most liberal state in this respect, mainly for historical reasons. Here is an excerpt from Tunisia's extremely comprehensive report on CEDAW:[96]

Item (84), French original

En matière successorale, le Code du statut personnel s'inspire du régime successoral musulman pour déterminer la situation respective des héritiers mâles ou féminins.

Les dispositions coraniques relatives aux droits successoraux de la femme représentaient à l'époque du prophète une grande acquisition pour la femme. Ainsi, elle s'est vue dotée de droits "révolutionnaires" dans un contexte farouchement patriarcal. L'Islam n'a pas voulu brusquer les mentalités de son temps et la proclamation du droit de la femme à la succession, après avoir été elle-même objet successoral, a été suivie de la fixation de parts doubles aux héritiers mâles. Mais ce principe ne s'applique pas à la totalité des cas: ainsi, dans les mêmes conditions, le mari hérite d'une double quote-part que sa femme, le fils hérite du double de sa sœur; cependant, la mère et le père héritent des mêmes parts. Ces règles sont reprises dans le Code du statut personnel.

4. *Penal law*

a) Absolute prohibition against Muslims changing religion

In theory, apostasy from Islam (*ridda*) entails the death sentence for men and life imprisonment for women.[97] While people have been executed for apostasy, notably the engineer Maḥmūd Muḥammad Ṭāhā in Sudan,[98] states parties to CESCR and CCPR do not usually insist on the application of this penalty.[99]

---

[94] Qur'ān 4: 12f and 4: 176. For details, cf. *Abu-Sahlieh* 1985: 696f. Cf. also the issue of the institution of dowry (above).

[95] Qur'ān 4: 141. For details, cf. *Abu-Sahlieh* 1985: 658ff.

[96] UN-doc. CEDAW/C/TUN/1-2, p. 178.

[97] For details, cf. *Abu-Sahlieh* 1985: 638ff.

[98] Cf., for instance, *an-Naʿīm* 1987a: 1ff.

[99] On this issue, cf., for instance, UN-docs. CCPR/C/SR.499, 500, and 505 (Egypt) and UN-docs. CCPR/C/SR.361 and 362 (Jordan).

b) *Ḥudūd* sentences

The so-called *ḥudūd* sentences include stoning to death for adultery (*zināʾ*), amputation of the right hand and subsequently of the left foot for theft (*sariqa*), whipping and flogging for use of alcohol (*šurb al-ḫamr*), and other severe penalties for other "crimes" that are contrary to the Islamic *šarīʿa*.[100]

In the discussion of the report of Afghanistan on its implementation of the Convention against Torture and other Cruel, Inhuman or Degrading Treatment or Punishment, UN-doc. CAT/C/5/Add.31, the delegation of Afghanistan made *inter alia* the following statement, referring to the *ḥudūd* sentences:[101]

Item (85), English original

Since such penalties were specified by God it was not for human beings to show clemency for persons guilty of crimes for which those penalties were applicable.

Here is a chillingly clinical document, decree No. 109 (18 August 1994) of the Iraqi "Revolution Command Council", which is reproduced in the most recent report on the human rights situation in Iraq by Special Rapporteur van der Stoel:[102]

Item (86), official English translation

In the Name of God, the Merciful, the Compassionate,

Pursuant to the provisions of article 42, paragraph 1, of the Constitution, the Revolution Command Council has decreed as follows:

1. Every person legally punished by amputation of the hand for a crime punishable by amputation of the hand shall be tattooed with a cross between the eyebrows. Each intersecting line of the cross shall be 1 centimetre in length and 1 millimetre thick.

2. The tattoo shall be carried out in the same public hospital in which the amputation was performed.

3. The public hospital shall prepare the technical and medical requirements to facilitate the performance of the tattooing procedure.

4. This Decree shall enter into force from the date of its publication in the *Official Gazette* until further notice and shall apply retroactively to every person who has already been punished by amputation of the hand.

---

100 Qurʾān 24: 2 (*zināʾ*), 24: 4 (*qaḏf*), 5: 38 (*sariqa*), 5: 33 (*qaṭʿ aṭ-ṭarīq*), 2: 219, 5: 90f (*šurb al-ḫamr*). For details, cf. *Abu-Sahlieh* 1985: 683ff and *Dilger* 1990: 84ff. For the situation in Iran, cf. *Tellenbach* 1996.

101 UN-doc. CAT/C/SR.121, p. 6.

102 UN-doc. E/CN.4/1995/56, p. 26. The Arabic original was not available to the author.

Practices of corporal punishment are rarely openly admitted in the reports. One example, reminiscent of the optional *ta^{c}zīr* sentences, is found in Sudan's first report on its implementation of CRC, concerning the disciplining of minors:[103]

Item (87), Arabic original

(b) Al-jaldu ^{c}alā sabīli t-taʾdībi li-man balaġa l-^{c}āširata bi-mā lā yujāwizu ^{c}išrīna jalda;

Item (87), official English translation

(b) He shall be punished by whipping, with not more than 20 lashes, if he has reached the age of 10.

5. *Law of procedure*

Under the precepts of the Islamic *šarī^{c}a*, women's testimony is worth only half as much as men's testimony.[104] The following excerpt from the statement of an Egyptian representative during the discussion of Egypt's second report on its implementation of CEDAW, UN-doc. CEDAW/C/13/Add.2, provides an illustration:[105]

Item (88), English original

The treatment accorded by the courts was equal for men and women. Women could be witnesses, but the testimony of a woman was considered to have one half of the weight of that of a man. That was a matter governed by certain religious prescriptions, and it was currently under discussion in Islamic and secular jurisprudence.

C. The Islamic concept of "equality": a comparative analysis of the traditional methods of treaty interpretation and Speech Act Theory

I. Basic considerations

The distinction made by Egypt in its reservation to article 16 of CEDAW (cf. above) between *musāwā(t) ḥaqīqīya* 'true equality' vs. *musāwā(t) šiklīya* 'formal equality' calls for a closer look at these terms.[106] Here again is the full context: *wa-^{c}tibāran bi-ʾan min ʾahammi*

---

103 UN-doc. CRC/C/3/Add.3 (Arabic and English), p. 49 and p. 46, respectively.

104 Qurʾān 2: 282 and elsewhere. For details, cf. *Abu-Sahlieh* 1985: 697f.

105 UN-doc. CEDAW/C/SR.164, p. 13.

106 Cf. notably *Mayer* 1991a: 93ff.

l-ʾususi llatī taqūmu ʿalay-hā hāḏihī l-ʿalāqātu t-taqābulu bayna l-ḥuqūqi wa-l-wājibāti ʿalā naḥwin mina t-takāmuli llaḏī yuḥaqqiqu l-musāwāta l-ḥaqīqīyata bayna z-zawjayni lā maẓāhira l-musāwāti š-šiklīyati llatī lā tuḥaqqiqu li-z-zawjati maṣlaḥatan nāfiʿatan mina z-zawāji bi-qadri mā tuṯaqqilu kāhila-hā mina l-quyūd 'and in view of the fact that one of the most important bases of these relations is an equivalency of rights and duties so as to ensure complementarity which guarantees true equality between the spouses rather than the manifestations of formal equality which do not give the wife any useful interest to be obtained from the husband so much as they burden her with restrictions'. From the beginnings of Islam, the theoretical concept of equality has been violated by three practical distinctions of legal status: master/slave, man/woman, and Muslim/non-Muslim. While the first of these has been abolished, at least *de jure*, the latter two legal distinctions still persist even though the contrary is frequently claimed on the diplomatic level.

In the next two sections the four traditional methods of treaty interpretation as well as Speech Act Theory will be applied to the arguments found in legal documents regarding the personal status of women under Islamic law, notably the question of polygamy. Here is the basic Qurʾānic quotation regarding the issue of polygamy (*taʿaddud az-zawjāt*):[107]

Item (89), Arabic original

Wa-ʾin ḫiftum ʾal-lā tuqsiṭū fī l-yatāmā fa-nkiḥū mā ṭāba la-kum mina n-nisāʾi maṯnā wa-ṯulāṯa wa-rubāʿa fa-ʾin ḫiftum ʾal-lā taʿdilū fa-wāḥidatan ʾaw mā malakat ʾaymānu-kum ḏālika ʾadnā ʾal-lā taʿūlū.

Item (89), English translation

If ye fear that ye may not act with equity in regard to the orphans, marry such of the women as seem good to you, double or treble or fourfold – but if ye fear that ye may not be fair, then one (only) or what your right hands possess; that is more likely to secure that ye may not be partial.

II. The traditional methods of treaty interpretation

From the perspective of grammatical (and lexical) interpretation, it is important to note that the Arabic term *taʿaddud az-zawjāt* 'multitude of wives' culturally does not have the negative connotations of its English equivalent *polygamy* (viz. *polygyny*). Another problem is the exact meaning of the verb *nakaḥa* which, at least historically, means 'to sleep with' rather than 'to marry', though in this case the precepts

[107] Qurʾān 4: 3 (translation from *Bell* 1937, vol. 1: 69).

in the conditional clauses point to a more permanent junction between the spouses. These issues are nowhere raised in the reports.

From the perspective of systematic interpretation, reference is made by the Muslim side in this context to the four sources of legal interpretation, although Qur'ān and *sunna* are the two main *ʾuṣūl al-fiqh* referred to in the reports.

From the perspective of historical interpretation, reference is made here to the particular historical circumstances in the seventh century, when many men died in battle. This led to a numerical imbalance between men and women; polygamy, so it is argued, was a way to right the imbalance and thus create a relative improvement in the situation of women. The argument is summarized, for instance, as follows:[108]

Item (90), English original

With regard to polygamy, the representative of Egypt explained that it was retained in Islamic law with definite restrictions because, at the time the message of Islam was first introduced, women did not work and outnumbered men because of war casualties. Such a solution was the only way to provide women with financial resources and to preserve their dignity.

From the perspective of teleological interpretation, finally, the goal is to achieve a perfect "balance" between men's and women's rights and duties which would justify formal discrimination. This is a ubiquitous argument in the reports and discussions. Also, reference is often made to the circumstance that it is considered "inappropriate" for a woman to be "single". This argument is frequently raised by representatives of African Muslim countries.

III. Speech Act Theory

While the Vienna Convention on the Law of Treaties allows for handling the text additions/omissions and other shades of text differences between the Arabic and English versions,[109] Speech Act Theory can account for the usage of the terms *ḥaqīqīya* 'real' and *šiklīya* 'formal' in connection with the term *musāwā(t)* 'equality' as used by Egypt, relating the different usages to the respective "speakers", i.e., contracting parties, involved: whereas the extension of this term, i.e., its lexical meaning, is the same, the intension, i.e., its cultural/religious meaning, clearly differs. This is why a distinction is made by Egypt

---

108 UN-doc. A/39/45, p. 29, referring to UN-docs. CEDAW/C/SR.34 and 39.

109 Cf. the "algorithm" proposed in *Tabory* 1980: 177.

between *musāwā(t) ḥaqīqīya* 'true equality' vs. *musāwā(t) šiklīya* 'formal equality'. The different *Weltanschauungen* behind Egypt as an "Arab"/"Islamic" signatory party on the one hand, and the "Western" signatory parties on the other, become all too clear in this context.

As in the case of the differing concepts of "law", "truth", "peace", and "justice" (cf. chapter four), the two theories of interpretation (i.e., the respective articles in the Vienna Convention on the Law of Treaties on the one hand, and the tenets of Speech Act Theory on the other) and their implications for the analysis of conflicting ideas can be combined in the following table, as already developed above (chapter three). Using the just mentioned example, the following picture emerges:[110]

Table 6

Comparative analysis of the "Western" vs. Islamic concepts of "equality [between the sexes]"

"Western" contracting party		**"Arab"/"Islamic" contracting party**	
treaty/legal document: CEDAW			
--- *equality* ---		--- *musāwā(t)* ---	
European language	International Law in "Western" perspective	Arabic	International Law in Islamic perspective
semantics pragmatics discourse structure special terminology	grammatical sense systematic sense historical sense teleological sense	semantics pragmatics discourse structure special terminology	grammatical sense systematic sense historical sense teleological sense
extension–intension		extension–intension	
Speech Act Theory	Vienna Convention on the Law of Treaties (1969)	Speech Act Theory	Vienna Convention on the Law of Treaties (1969)
"Western" perspective (formal equality = real equality)		Egyptian/Islamic perspective (*musāwā(t) šiklīya ≠ musāwā(t) ḥaqīqīya*)	

110 In this example, formal equality has the same extension and intension in the "Western" and in the "Islamic" perspective, while true equality has a different intension in the "Islamic" perspective, as compared with the "Western" perspective (in the "Western" perspective, there is, synchronically speaking, no different concept of formal vs. true equality).

D. Evaluation of the arguments

I. The anachronistic nature of the arguments

The major problem surfacing in the reports and in the discussion with the treaty bodies is the anachronistic nature of the arguments. The often-made argument, for instance, that the Islamic *šarīᶜa* represented a relative improvement of women's rights in the seventh century A.D. is simply irrelevant at the end of the twentieth century, a time when the rationale for inequality in family law, the law of succession, and the law of procedure cannot be upheld under any circumstances. This holds *a fortiori* for Qurʾānic precepts of penal law.

II. Discrepancies within Islamic theory

There are a number of logical contradictions within the Islamic scriptures. More precisely, there are early *ʾāyāt* ('Qurʾānic verses', the elements of the *sūras*) that in Islamic jurisprudence are said to be abrogated (*mansūḫ*) by later, contradictory *ʾāyāt* that are called *nāsiḫ* ('abrogating').[111] Certain *ʾāyāt* may also be in contradiction to precepts found in the *sunna*. The Qurʾānic principle *lā ʾikrāha fī d-dīn* '[there shall be] no coercion in religion' (cf. above), for instance, is clearly relativized by statements of Muḥammad to the effect that every apostate must be killed.[112] These and other logical contradictions should preclude a too literal interpretation or observation of precepts laid down in the Qurʾān or in the *sunna*.

III. Discrepancies between Islamic theory and practice

There are likewise a number of discrepancies between Islamic theory and practice. An example is the prohibition against taking interest (*ribā*). This precept is occasionally upheld *de jure* in that interest is technically redefined as a "commission fee", etc.; but the

---

[111] Cf., for instance, *ʾAbū Salāmā* [no date]. An-nāsiḫ wa-l-mansūḫ, a text which appears as marginal gloss in *Nīsābūrī* [no date]. ʾAsbāb an-nuzūl. Numerous references for this subject can be found in *Burton* (ed.) 1987.

[112] For references, cf. *Khadduri* 1984: 238.

prohibition against taking interest has hardly ever been observed *de facto* in the Islamic world.[113]

IV. Comparable issues in other religions

Muslim (and also Christian) Palestinians understandably resent the notion that Israeli territorial claims are being based on Biblical clauses in the Old Testament. Irrespective of one's degree of religious faith and rooting in the Judeo-Christian tradition, statements in the Old Testament are simply irrelevant when it comes to the evaluation of legal and political claims of Israeli or Palestinian claims in 1997. As a corollary, there can be no "contemporary" application of Biblical precepts to the Palestine question.[114] By the same token, the Qurʾān and the *sunna* should not be invoked when it comes to the interpretation of legal and political problems in the IHR realm. In this light, the notion of a "contemporary" application of the Islamic *šarīᶜa* to IHR issues verges on a contradiction in terms. One could, of course, try to draw a distinction between time-specific laws ("type (1)") and timeless laws ("type (2)") in "divinely revealed" scriptures, and then argue that it does not constitute an anachronism if type (2) continues to be re-applied and re-interpreted over the centuries. The problem is that, routinely, reality outgrows law – often an allegedly timeless law becomes gradually more and more irrelevant over time, so that it becomes a subjective matter whether it "really" belongs to type (1) or type (2). While "Westerners" tend to consider precepts of the Islamic *šarīᶜa* to be of type (1), Muslims tend to see them as type (2).

V. Problem of maintenance of *status quo*

A major point of criticism is that in many Islamic societies, religion is abused as a pretext to undermine human rights standards and to

---

113 For an in-depth analysis of this issue, cf. *Krüger* 1987: 116ff, *Dilger* 1990: 80ff, *Amereller* 1995, and *Saeed* 1996. For the role of the so-called *ḥiyal* 'legal ruses (to circumvent the *šarīᶜa*)', cf. *Schacht* 1964: 78ff.

114 Cf. *Fastenrath* 1991: 132f: "So wird die Gründung von Siedlungen auf der West Bank mit biblischen Ansprüchen auf diese Gebiete gerechtfertigt, vgl. Ministerpräsident Begin in seiner Regierungserklärung vom 10. 06. 1977, die mit den Worten beginnt: "Das jüdische Volk hat ein ewiges historisches Anrecht auf Eretz Israel ..."." ("Thus, the founding of settlements on the West Bank is being justified by recourse to Biblical claims to these areas; cf. prime minister Begin's governmental declaration of June 10, 1977, which started out as follows: "The Jewish people has an eternal historical title to Eretz Israel ...".")

maintain an unfair *status quo*. This *status quo* can be narrowed down to three principles: (i) men have wide leeway in family matters, (ii) women are permanently subordinated, and (iii) men remain in control of politics and finances. Interestingly, Tunisian representatives, who otherwise advocate a progressive reading of the Islamic *šarīᶜa*, openly admit that altering the precepts of the Islamic law of succession might cause social unrest, as the *status quo* for males would deteriorate.

VI. Insistence on international human rights principles

Is must be pointed out that no cultural and legal relativism should be allowed for, once a country has ratified a given IHR convention, as no country is *forced* to join IHR conventions in the first place, even though failure to accept IHR conventions may give the country a bad international image. Hence, upon ratification of a given IHR convention, the respective state party should strictly adhere to its precepts, especially in those cases where no reservations have been made.[115]

VII. The Islamic concept of *ijtihād*

Finally, it is important to look at ways to reconcile precepts of the Islamic *šarīᶜa* and international law. One important resource in this context is the Islamic concept of *ijtihād*, i.e., the effort to advance legal interpretation over the course of time.

Liberal Muslims would indeed argue that the so-called *bāb al-ijtihād* 'the door of independent legal reasoning' (in the sense of Qurʾānic exegesis), which was "closed" in the tenth century A.D., should be opened again in modern times. In this spirit, it would appear to be possible in principle for the method of *ijtihād* to be exploited by Islamic governments to bridge the gap between precepts of the *šarīᶜa* and international law.[116] Notably the Australian Elizabeth Evatt, who has served both on CEDAW and CCPR, has submitted several proposals to this effect. For instance, in the course of the discussion of Iran's second

---

[115] Cf., for instance, the concluding observations on Morocco's first report on its implementation of CESCR, UN-doc. E/1990/5/Add.13, UN-doc. E/1995/22, p. 29.

[116] Cf. notably *Clark* 1991: 287ff, where a recommendation of CEDAW to this effect is mentioned.

periodic report on its implementation of CCPR, UN-doc. CCPR/C/28/ Add.15, she inquired as follows:[117]

Item (91), English original

Lastly, it would be interesting to learn whether a study of the law had been undertaken to determine the extent to which Islamic scriptures contained texts that could be more fully emphasized because they supported the universal principles of the covenant and whether the assistance of Islamic scholars in other countries, including human rights experts and women scholars of Islam, had been sought.

However, such suggestions and requests are usually sternly rejected by representatives of the League of Arab States and the Organization of the Islamic Conference, so that the Human Rights Commission of the United Nations has never been able to establish a task force to look into this issue.

It is noteworthy that liberal Muslim members of the IHR committees often try to pave the way toward a progressive interpretation of the *šarīᶜa*. An example is the question of adoption, on which the Tunisian member of CESCR, Grissa, commented as follows:[118]

Item (92), English original

[T]he *šarīᶜa* was 1,400 years old and civilization had progressed since its day. It was less serious to violate the *šarīᶜa* than to violate the rights of a child. The *šarīᶜa* should not be interpreted in an anti-humanistic sense.

The Egyptian member of CEDAW, Tallawy, has likewise suggested that some *šarīᶜa*-based reservations by Arab states could be withdrawn.[119]

Finally, a reconciliation could be envisaged such that the coexistence of civil and of religious procedures, a "dual system", especially in marriage law, would be allowed for. While Islamic states allow non-Muslims in this respect to follow their own rules, no "civil" Muslim marriage, let alone an interfaith marriage between a Muslim woman and a non-Muslim man, has thus far been possible in the Islamic world. In other realms, especially in penal law, no "reconciliation" seems to be possible or even desirable.

---

117 UN-doc. CCPR/C/SR.1231, p. 7.

118 UN-doc. E/C.12/1994/SR.10/Add.1, p. 4.

119 Cf., for instance, UN-doc. CEDAW/C/SR.164, p. 15, the discussion of Egypt's second report on its implementation of CEDAW, UN-doc. CEDAW/C/13/Add.2.

E. Summary of Chapter Five

In the realm of "Human Rights", the language used on a regular basis hints explicitly or implicitly at religiously grounded legal norms, thus setting up a clash with "Western" norms. Especially in the cases of CEDAW and CRC, it is difficult to see how the positions and reservations of Egypt, Jordan, and other Arab and Islamic signatory parties to the conventions can be reconciled with the object and purpose of these conventions. The problem has been summarized as follows, also with a view to motivating the states parties to reconsider their reservations:[120]

Item (93), English original

An important component of the Committee's dialogue with reserving States parties is a comparative discussion of States parties' approach to obligations in other human rights treaties that are similar to those in the Convention. Articles 2, 9, 15 and 16 of the Convention are subject to the largest number of far-reaching reservations, many of which may be defined as contrary to article 28 (2). A number of other human rights treaties elaborate obligations which are similar to articles 2, 9, 15 and 16. Articles 2 (1) and 3 of the International Covenant on Civil and Political Rights, articles 2 (2) and 3 of the International Covenant on Economic, Social and Cultural Rights, and article 2 of the Convention on the Rights of the Child create similar obligations to article 2 of the Convention on the Elimination of All Forms of Discrimination against Women. Articles 12, 14, 16 and 26 of the International Covenant on Civil and Political Rights create similar obligations to article 15 of the Convention. Again, similar obligations to article 16 of the Convention are to be found in article 23 of the International Covenant on Civil and Political Rights.

During its dialogue with individual States parties, the Committee on the Elimination of Discrimination against Women may wish to draw attention to the fact that a State party may have ratified the Convention with reservations, but at the same time, may have ratified other treaties, such as the Covenants, without reservations to articles 2 and 3 of those treaties. In the event the State party has ratified the Covenants with reservations, the Committee should be in a position to compare the reach of those reservations with the reservations to the Convention and suggest that inconsistencies be eliminated.

A sample comparison of reservations indicates that Algeria has not entered reservations to the Convention on the Rights of the Child, but has indicated, in regard to the International Covenant on Civil and Political Rights, that it reserves with regard to the rights and responsibility of spouses. The Bahamas, State party to both Covenants, reserved only with regard to article 2 of the Convention on the Rights of the Child. In this reservation it reserves the right to apply its own Constitution insofar as the conferment of citizenship on children is concerned. Bangladesh is not State party to either Covenant and filed no reservations to the non-discrimination provision on the Convention on the Rights of the Child, a position which appears to be inconsistent with its reservations relating to the Convention on discrimination against women. Belgium's reservations to this Convention are echoed in its reservations to the International Covenant on Civil

[120] UN-doc. CEDAW/C/1997/4, para. 31-34.

and Political Rights. Egypt, State party to both international covenants and the Convention on the Rights of the Child, has entered no reservations to the equality guarantees of these treaties, although, as pointed out earlier, it has reserved to articles 2, 9 (2) and 16 of the Convention on the Elimination of All Forms of Discrimination against Women. Iraq, similarly State party to the Covenants and the Convention on the Rights of the Child, entered no reservations to the equality provisions of these treaties, although maintaining substantial reservations to the Convention on the Elimination of All Forms of Discrimination against Women. Jordan, Libya, Morocco and Tunisia, also States parties to the Covenants and the Convention on the Rights of the Child, have not replicated their reservations to the Convention on the Elimination of All Forms of Discrimination against Women where these other treaties are concerned. In contrast, Malaysia and Maldives entered consistent reservations to that Convention and the Convention on the Rights of the Child.

The Committee on the Elimination of Discrimination against Women could enter into a fruitful discussion with States parties which maintain inconsistent reservations and should encourage the other treaty bodies to raise these issues also. The United Nations system, and especially the Division for the Advancement of Women, as the secretariat to the Committee, and non-governmental organizations, should also focus on these inconsistencies in their work with States parties.

As in the realm of "war and peace", Speech Act Theory helps to formally capture the different intensionalities of seemingly elementary terms in the realm of "human right", as in the case of *musāwā(t) ḥaqīqīya* 'true equality' vs. *musāwā(t) šiklīya* 'formal equality', in diplomatic discourse between "Western" and "Arab"/"Islamic" parties.

Chapter Six

Case study: application of the theory of interpretation to the definition of "ethnic, religious, and linguistic minorities" in UN documents

"The Government of Thailand states that the concept of minority is unknown in the country: "Although this word has a Thai translation from English for the purpose of communication with the outside world, it has no social and cultural connotation whatsoever."" *Capotorti*, F. 1991. Study on the Rights of Persons belonging to Ethnic, Religious, and Linguistic Minorities. Geneva/New York, p. 13.

A. Overview of problems

I. Basic considerations

Denominations of peoples may pose a serious problem when the ethnic, religious, and linguistic usages of a term leave room for contradictions in the wake of intercultural problems. This holds true especially for a number of conflicts in the Middle East and North Africa. Problems of discourse arising out of this issue, of both a legal and a linguistic nature, will be analyzed in this chapter in terms of Speech Act Theory, which offers an instrument for a solution of related problems of ambiguity and contradiction. The goal is, *inter alia*, to offer a formal anaysis of terminological devices that have been used to deny aspects of ethnic, religious, and/or linguistic identity in international legal documents. In this chapter, the subject will thus be the interface between the legal and the linguistic aspects of historical and contemporary conflicts between ethnic, religious, and linguistic minorities and the respective majorities in various countries of the Middle East, including North Africa.[1] The scope will be limited to the termi-

[1] There exists, of course, an extensive literature on "minority issues" in general and "minorities in the Middle East" in particular. A comprehensive legal overview is given in *Tomuschat* 1983, *Capotorti* 1991, and in the most recent report of the Secretary General of

nological surface of the respective conflicts, as observed in international legal documents. More specifically, the interference between the ethnic, religious, and linguistic aspects of certain terms will be treated, and the potential for intercultural misunderstanding that such terms may entail.[2] In doing so, particular attention will be paid to the political (ab-)use of certain terms with a view to denying or at least downplaying ethnic, religious, and linguistic features of identity. Generally speaking, a majority can display three kinds of attitudes vis-à-vis a minority: (i) outright denial of identity (e.g., Turkey vis-à-vis the Kurds); (ii) treatment as an inferior class (e.g., Iran vis-à-vis the Baha'is and members of other religions that are not "divinely revealed"); and (3) treatment as an equal class (e.g., the interaction of the various "cultural communities" in Belgium and Canada). Cases of the second type, are, of course, only rarely openly admitted in international legal documents. The theme of the chapter is inspired by article 27 of the International Covenant on Civil and Political Rights, in which the rights of ethnic, religious, and linguistic minorities are explicitly formulated for the first time in the framework of international law:

Item (94), English

In those States in which ethnic, religious or linguistic minorities exist, persons belonging to such minorities shall not be denied the right, in community with the other members of their group, to enjoy their own culture, to profess and to practice their own religion, or to use their own language.

This chapter is structured as follows: First, a theoretical framework for the analysis of such conflicts will be outlined. Then, a range of relevant data will be presented and some virulent issues will be outlined. This part will be supplemented by an overview of the mechanisms of international law in United Nations context, as applying to the issues in question. Finally, the theory will be applied to a number of case studies, with special emphasis on the Kurdish question.

---

the United Nations on the issue, UN-doc. E/CN.4/1996/88 (Rights of Persons Belonging to National or Ethnic, Religious and Linguistic Minorities). Cf. also the references provided in *Verdross/Simma* 1984: 837ff. For the Middle East, cf., for instance, *McLaurin* (ed.) 1976, *Hartmann* 1980, *Chabry/Chabry* 1984, *Olmert* 1986, *Esman/Rabinovich* (eds.) 1988, *Andrews* 1989, *Scheffler* 1990, *Nisan* 1991, and *Tapper* (ed.) 1992. A bibliography on "minorities in the Middle East" is provided in *Franz* 1978. An example of a major symposium on related issues is the *Conference on Ethnicity and Ethnic Identity in the Middle East*, organized in 1991 by the University of Utrecht.

[2] For an overview of the linguistic issues associated with names and toponyms in the Middle East, cf. *Wild* 1982a and *Schimmel* 1989.

II. Instruments of international law for the protection of minorities

The subject of "minority rights" is a relatively new topic in international law.[3] While it was mentioned in the draft of article 6 of the Wilson Declaration of 1919, it failed to be included by the League of Nations in the final version of that document. The same holds for the charter of the United Nations, as the topic appears only implicitly, namely in articles 13, 55, 62, and 76, all of which refer to the principle of non-discrimination. All the same, a resolution of the General Assembly was passed in 1948 (res. 217 C (III)) which was dedicated to the "fate of minorities". Minority rights also play an implicit role in the following documents: the Convention on the Prevention and Punishment of the Crime of Genocide of 1948, the ILO Convention no. 107 of 1957, which deals with "indigenous and tribal populations", the UNESCO Convention against Discrimination in Education of 1960, and the Convention on the Elimination of All Forms of Racial Discrimination (CERD) of 1965. Also important is article 14 of the European Convention for the Protection of Human Rights and Fundamental Freedoms, which was passed in 1950 by the Council of Europe. Also, there were already a number of clauses indirectly pertaining to minority rights in the Parisian suburb peace treaties.

Minority rights are explicitly mentioned for the first time in article 27 (quoted above) of the International Covenant on Civil and Political Rights, which was passed on December 16, 1966, by the General Assembly and which came into force on March 23, 1976.

Negotiations on this article proved to be extremely difficult, and its final version can be said to be "watered down" insofar as the phrases "in those states" as well as "shall not be denied the right" offer a diplomatic "way out". This is so for two reasons: first, states parties may argue that they do not belong to "those states", depending on how they choose to define "minority"; second, it is not clear whether "shall not be denied" calls for active support of minorities as opposed to mere tolerance.

Two resolutions of the General Assembly are dedicated fully to the topic in question: resolution 36/55 of 1981, entitled "Declaration on the Elimination of All Forms of Intolerance and of Discrimination Based on Religion or Belief", and resolution 47/135 of 1992, entitled "Declaration on the Rights of Persons Belonging to National or Ethnic, Reli-

---

[3] Cf. *Capotorti* 1991: 16ff.

gious, and Linguistic Minorities". In his comprehensive report on the issue, Capotorti defines "minority" as follows:[4]

A group numerically inferior to the rest of a population of a State, in a non-dominant position, whose members – being nationals of the State – possess ethnic, religious or linguistic characteristics differring from those of the rest of the population and show, if only implicitly, a sense of solidarity, directed towards preserving their culture, traditions, religion or language.

Generally speaking, there are two "philosophies" with respect to minority issues, which depend on such criteria as ethnic composition, the relationship between religion(s) and state, and the status of minority languages. In the United States, for instance, there is a tendency to grant minorities far-reaching rights including quotas and "affirmative action" programs. France, in contrast, argues that minority status (e.g., being of "Basque", "Breton", "Catalan", or "Occitan" descent) is a completely private affair and rather of scientific than of political importance.

Analogous problems of definition hold for the seemingly elementary term "people". Speech Act Theory most appropriately enables us to capture the following conflicting definitions of "people", which reflect a differing intension, while the extension is the same:[5]

In sources that state principles of public international law [...] it is established that "all peoples" have a right to self-determination. States that deny "peoples" this right would therefore seem to be in violation of international law. But there are many disagreements regarding what the term "peoples" entails and how "peoples" denied this right may seek redress. According to Third World countries and the socialist bloc, "peoples" engaged in national liberation struggles enjoy legal personality and are covered by international law. In contrast, the Western powers tend to support the view that international law only addresses conflicts between states.

III. The data and the issues

Various kinds of problems arise when we consider the question of ethnicities and ethnonyms. First, there may be an "objective" set of criteria which constitute the extensional meaning of a people "X". These criteria may be broken down into ethnic, religious, and linguistic features. Even within such an "objective" extensionality, however, there may be a number of different denominations in various countries for the same people "X". The "objective" set of criteria thus may be ac-

---

[4] Cf. *Capotorti* 1991: 96.

[5] Cf. *Mayer* 1991b: 210.

companied by a "subjective" set of criteria which constitute the intensional meaning of the people "X". The intensional meaning may encompass non-objective features, notably historical or mythological traits that the people "X" claim for themselves, but also prejudice-based pejorative and ridiculing terms by which other peoples refer to the people "X" or endeavour to deny their very identity of the people "X". Just as the "objective" criteria, the "subjective" criteria may also be of ethnic, religious, or linguistic nature.[6]

The scenario may be further complicated by the circumstance that these two categories, i.e., the two sets of features need not necessarily be distinct as history may produce a transition in a given term from a "subjective" towards an "objective" criterion. There are terms which originally had a pejorative or even racist connotation and have nevertheless become completely accepted by the respective populations. The term *Ethiopia*, for instance, etymologically derives from Greek *aiti-ops* 'burnt in the face', just as *Erythrea* (*Eritrea*) and *Sūdān* literally mean 'the red one' and 'the black ones', respectively, but this does not bother anybody in the region. By the same token, hardly any Arab is nowadays irritated by the original "Eurocentricity" of the term *aš-šarq al-ʾawsaṭ* 'the Middle East'. Even the terms *Slav* does not pose any problems, synchronically speaking, in spite of the sociological implications of its etymology ("slave").

In some instances, these transitions take place with a rapidity which may be hard for an outsider to follow. An example of this is the terminology for Americans of African descent. While Martin Luther King still referred to himself by the "racial" term *negro,* a term which is now taboo, later the terms *black, Afro-American* and finally *African American* emerged. Interestingly, members of a community sometimes refer to themselves by a term which they would consider offensive if used by an outsider. In this context, the term *Falasha* 'Ethiopian Jews' is noteworthy. While the term etymologically just means 'émigré',[7] members of that community take offense at this term and consider it to be discriminatory.[8]

Semantically neutral terms can take on a negative meaning over time. For instance, the term *Kanake,* whose Polynesian root simply means 'human being', has wound up as a racist "fighting word" in

---

[6] Cf. *Scheffler* 1990: 17ff for a political science perspective concerning such problems.

[7] Cf., for instance, *Leslau* 1987: 160. Incidentally, 'émigré' or 'free' is also the etymological meaning of the linguistic term *Geʿez* ("classical Ethiopic"). Cf. *Leslau* 1987: 175f.

[8] Ephraim *Isaac*, Institute of Semitic Studies, Princeton [personal communication].

German, primarily aimed at the Turkish population. Likewise, the German term *Zulu-Kaffer*, a pejorative term for black Africans, is a completely de-etymologized derivation from the Arabic term *kāfir* 'non-believer'.[9]

Pejorative terms can, of course, occur even within one and the same speech community. In Israeli Hebrew, for instance, there is the term *tshachtshach*, by which Sephardic Jews are sometimes taunted by their Ashkenazi fellows. An even worse example is the term *djukim* 'cockroaches', as is sometimes used by secular Jews for (ultra-)orthodox Jews.

Historically, certain terms have always denoted "the other".[10] The Greek term *barbaroi*, for instance, simply denoted "non-Greeks", just as the Hebrew term *goyim* (literally 'nations') has denoted "non-Jews", or the Bavarian term *(Sau-)Breissn* (literally '(pig-)Prussians') has denoted not only "Prussians" (i.e., in a Bavarian perspective, unpleasant Germans *par excellence*) but also non-Bavarians in general. In Arabic the term *ᶜajamī* / *ʾaᶜjamī* 'non-Arab' quite early took on the specialized meaning 'Persian', the latter being, so to speak, the 'non-Arab' *par excellence*.[11]

Sometimes there can be outright linguistic chaos in the usage of ethnic terms, a prominent example being the abundance of terms that non-Germans use in referring to Germans: *Germans, Allemands, Tedeschi, Nemec*, and so forth.[12]

Furthermore, a transition may take place from one category of criteria to another, e.g., from the religious category to the ethnic or to the linguistic one. The first type of transition can be said to hold for the Druze communities in the Middle East; the second holds, for instance, for Judeo-Arabic (cf. below). Conversely, an ethno-linguistic category

---

[9] *Dinstein* (1987: 18f), in connection with the terms *anti-Semitism* and *anti-Zionism*, recognizes that both directions of semantic development play a role in political discourse: "The problem with the political terminology is that the common phraseology is affected by changing fashions. A word that originally has a neutral or even laudatory connotation (such as "imperialist") is turned into a term of abuse, whereas an idiom that initially has a disreputable meaning (e.g., "Whig" [n. 7: [o]riginally, this was "[a] name applied to Scottish cattle rustlers and horse thieves"]) becomes perfectly legitimate."

[10] Cf. *Gruenwald* 1994 for a definition of the "other" as relating to different religious communities in the Middle East. For a comprehensive historical overview of the terms *ġarīb* and *ʾajnabī* ('foreign'), cf. *Rosenthal* 1997.

[11] Cf. *Lewis* 1988: 118.

[12] The etymology of the term *Nemec* is simply 'dumb'/'mute', i.e., someone who neither speaks nor understands Slavonic.

may turn into a religious one, as happened in the case of the Copts; this term (in both its European form and its Arabic form *qibṭī*) is derived from Greek *Aigyptos*, which in turn is a corruption of ancient Egyptian *ha-ka-ptah* 'temple of the god Ptah' [i.e., Memphis].[13]

What is more, an internal religious division may entail linguistic diversification. In history, this kind of transition took place in the fifth century A.D. when the East-Syrian "Nestorians" broke off from the West-Syrian "Jacobites" as a result of "christological" differences, thereby triggering a dialectal cleavage within Eastern Aramaic and ultimately the development of the two major dialect groups of Eastern Neo-Aramaic, which still persist today.[14]

As will be shown, the very terms "majority" and "minority" as subsets of the people "X" may be subject to the same formal division into extensional and intensional features.[15] Notably, it is not necessarily a disadvantage to belong to a "minority", as amply shown by the role of the Chinese throughout South-East Asia. There is, of course, also the technical difference between "relative" and "absolute" majority, which may lead to confusion. Sometimes the very concept of a "minority" is rejected, as seen in the following quotation (epigraph to the present chapter):[16]

The Government of Thailand states that the concept of minority is unknown in the country: "Although this word has a Thai translation from English for the purpose of communication with the outside world, it has no social and cultural connotation whatsoever."

Some countries, e.g., India, have argued that it does not make sense to speak of minorities in a multi-ethnic society:[17]

Item (95), English original

Commenting on the reference made by members to minorities in India, the representative insisted that ethnic minorities did not exist in India, since the country had no ethnic majority either; all the different tribes in India were not racial categories but had different religions, linguistic and cultural backgrounds.

---

[13] Cf., for instance, *Atiya*, A. "Ḳibṭ", The Encyclopaedia of Islam (new edition), vol. 5: 90ff.

[14] Cf., for instance, *Tsereteli* 1978: 11ff.

[15] Cf. *Capotorti* 1991: 5ff and UN-doc. E/CN.4/1987/WG.5/WP.1 (Compilation of Proposals Concerning the Definition of the Term "Minority"). Cf. also *D'Souza* 1991: 112 and 156, where a statement is cited to the effect that some blacks consider "minority" to be merely a code word for "nigger".

[16] Cf. *Capotorti* 1991: 13.

[17] Cf. UN-doc. A/39/40, p. 54.

The latter two quotations show that the adjectives "ethnic", "religious", and "linguistic" pose the same problems as the denominations of peoples. Quite naturally, terms such as "race",[18] "ethnicity", and "religion" are subject to differing intensionalities, just as one would assume. Judaism, Christianity, and Islam feature different and often conflicting combinations of aspects of ethnic and religious affiliation, as well as of political attitude. Suffice it to say that, in the context of international law, "religion" and/or "belief" has been broadly defined as "an explanation of the meaning of life and how to live accordingly", a definition that can embrace theistic, non-theistic, and atheistic beliefs.[19]

The very term "language" as well as denominations of languages and language families are likewise subject to different intensionalities. Turkey, for instance, has long denied the separate linguistic identity of the Kurdish language (cf. below)."Afro-Asiatic" as a term for the language family that used to be called "Hamito-Semitic" has a clearly different connotation for a political scientist as opposed to a linguist; the term "Semitic" itself is subject to similar problems.[20] The same holds for the term "dialect". Thus, one finds references both to "Berber dialects" and to "Berber languages" in the literature (on the term "Berber", cf. below). Due to religious reasons associated with the phenomenon of diglossia/polyglossia,[21] the term "dialect" often has a negative connotation (intension) for Arabs themselves, who will then refer dismissively to their dialects as mere "slang".

In the case of the Middle East, there is an abundance of clashes between ethnic, religious and linguistic usages of terms. The present-day community of the "Assyrians", for instance, sees itself as deriving from the Assyrians of ancient Mesopotamia, even though it is diffi-

---

[18] This term, which has largely been replaced by "ethnicity" anyway, will be avoided in this study, one of the reasons being that the author, as a German, does not feel comfortable with it. For a number of relevant historical Arabic documents pertaining to "race", cf. *Lewis* 1974, vol. 2: 209ff. Interestingly, "ethnic" has also been defined as an umbrella term for "that which pertains to or has common racial, cultural, religious or linguistic characteristics, [...] designating a racial or other group within a large system" (cf. *Kedourie* 1988: 25).

[19] Cf. *Odio Benito* 1989: 3f.

[20] On the origin and development of these terms, cf. *Sasse* 1981a and *Sasse* 1981b. The author has met several Arabs who seriously claimed that Arabs could not have "anti-Semitic" attitudes because they were "Semites" themselves. This is, of course, not to say that Arabs have *a priori* a higher propensity to anti-Semitism than non-Arabs. Cf. also *Lewis* 1986.

[21] For a discussion of these terms, cf. *Hary* 1992: 3ff.

cult to construe any direct genealogical or linguistic lineage in this case. A possible explanation may also be an etymological confusion of Arabic *as-suryānī* 'the Syrian/Aramaic person' with "Assyrian" in the sense of the aforementioned assumed ethnic affiliation.[22]

Ethnic, religious, and linguistic identity can be openly denied, as has happened in the case of the Kurds in Eastern Anatolia. Turkish officials as well and even scholars have referred to these people as *dag türkler* "mountain Turks" or even *kürt türkler* "Kurd-Turks", although these terms do not appear in international legal documents. Apparently, the term *kürtler* 'Kurds' was first used in Turkish for Kurds in Iraq in the wake of the Iraqi poison gas attack on the city Halabja in 1988, but has never been used for Kurds within Turkish territory. Technically, the Turkish side has based its anti-Kurdish discrimination on articles 37 through 44 of the Treaty of Lausanne of 1923, which refers only to "non-Muslim minorities", i.e., Greeks, Armenians, and Jews, but not to (Muslim) Kurds (cf. below).

Interestingly, the discussion of the "Semiticity" of modern Semitic languages, notably Israeli Hebrew and Neo-Aramaic languages/dialects, has not proceeded without the incursion of political considerations regarding linguistic "legitimacy", in addition to the purely linguistic criteria of genetic and typological relationship.[23]

Ethnic, religious, and linguistic aspects of a given term may be differentiated by morphological, phonological, or even orthographical means. Thus the English terms *Arab*, *Arabian*, and *Arabic* refer to the ethnical-political, the geographical, and the linguistic identity of the Arabs, respectively. For many speakers of German, the term *Araber* can refer either to persons or to horses from Arabia, depending on whether the stress lies on the first or the second syllable.[24] Even within Arab culture, the term *ᶜarab* may denote either a single social stratum in society, notably Bedouins, or the society as a whole, depending on the context. Likewise, the terms *Ethiopian* and *Ethiopic* de-

---

[22] When teaching Arabic at UC Berkeley in 1991, the author and a colleague explained the potential for terminological misunderstanding here to a student who referred to herself as an "Assyrian" from Iraq. Her reaction was to accuse the two of us of "academic genocide [!]". For the term "Assyrian", cf., for instance, *Tsereteli* 1978: 13f. For a list of acceptable scholarly terms for the dialects that make up Northeast Neo-Aramaic, cf. *Fox* 1994: 156.

[23] Cf. *Friedrich* 1962, *Wild* 1975b, *Rosén* 1977, *Blau* 1981, *Sasse* 1981b, and *Wexler* 1990 with different perspectives on this issue. An extensive comparative discussion of the issue is provided in *Kapeliuk* 1996.

[24] Cf. *Vennemann* 1986: 30f.

note the ethnic-political-geographical and the linguistic component of that region, respectively. Hence, it is important to observe this distinction in conversations, say, with Eritreans, to whom the linguistic umbrella term *Ethiopic* may be acceptable but not the political umbrella term *Ethiopian*. Finally, the German homophones *bay(e)risch* and *bairisch* 'Bavarian' denote the ethnic-political-geographical and the linguistic component of that region, respectively.

Denominations of languages often just follow the denomination of the corresponding people. This holds, for instance, for the speakers of the modern South Arabian languages.[25] Thus, *Jibbālī* 'a mountain person' (i.e., of the mountain area in Ẓufār, Oman) refers to both the population and the language of that area. Interestingly, the same holds true for the (Neo-Aramaic) term *Ṭūrōyō* for the language of the inhabitants of the Ṭūr ᶜAbdīn, which has exactly the same meaning.[26] Indeed, such an overlap of designations of people, region and language is almost the default case in Africa:[27]

> Eine besondere Schwierigkeit bei der Behandlung der sprachlichen Verhältnisse auf dem afrikanischen Kontinent birgt das Problem der Nomenklatur, d.h. der Bezeichnungen für Sprachen und Völker, Dialekte und Volksgruppen usw., bei denen in der Fachliteratur eine nicht unbeträchtliche Verwirrung herrscht. So gehen mitunter Eigenbezeichnungen für Sprecher und Sprache, Fremdbezeichnungen unterschiedlicher Herkunft, die teilweise von den Betroffenen zu Recht als diskriminierend empfunden werden, sowie Orts- und Gebietsnamen munter durcheinander.

Certain historical and/or contemporary terms may lend themselves to ambiguity. For the Syriac term *r[h]ūmāyā* one finds in the dictionary the meanings 'Roman' and 'Frank'/'Greek' (in the sense of a citizen of the Eastern Roman Empire).[28] Likewise, the old Arabic term *rūm* could refer to the Romans or the Byzantines ("Ost-Rom"). Nowadays, the

---

[25] Cf. *Johnstone* 1975: 2f. *Johnstone* also reports that some members of this group dislike the term *Śiḥrī* (also attested as *Śḥawri*, *Śḥeri*, etc.), which is used in older treatises on the modern South Arabian languages.

[26] Cf. *Jastrow* 1967: VIIIff.

[27] Cf. *Heine* et al. (eds.) 1981: 8 ("The proper designation of languages, peoples, dialects, population groups etc. on the African continent poses considerable problems, a fact clearly borne out by the considerable confusion to that effect in the literature. Often, there is an almost chaotic interference of terms that peoples use themselves for their language and ethnicity, terms that were assigned from different external sources, and toponyms designating places and areas. One has to understand that some of these external designations are considered to be of discriminating nature by the affected people.").

[28] Cf. *Payne Smith* 1903: 531.

Arabic term *rūm* is restricted to the Byzantines, whereas the Romans would be referred to by the term *rūmān*.

Country names – this not being the subject proper of this chapter – often pose the same range of difficulties as do denominations of peoples. Denial of identity, for instance, can surface linguistically in such grotesque terms as "The former Yugoslav Republic of Macedonia".[29]

As a final point, it is noteworthy that ethnic, religious, or linguistic affiliation need not automatically entail political solidarity with members of the same group in other states. Thus, the Shiᶜites in Southern Iraq, in spite of the discrimination against them, did not necessarily want to become Iranian citizens in the course of the Gulf war between Iraq and Iran from 1980 to 1988; the same holds *vice versa* for Sunnites in Iran. Also, reference to a given affiliation can be "practical" in some instances, but not in others, thus creating further confusion with respect to the usage of a given term.

IV. Linguistic strata

In connection with minority issues, the social stratification of languages and dialects plays a major role.[30] The following is a typology of such strata:[31]

(i) *indigenous language* 'the language of the people considered to be the original inhabitants of an area' [example: *t-amazigh-t* (Berber) languages in Northern Africa];

(ii) *lingua franca* 'a language which is used habitually by people whose mother tongues are different in order to facilitate communication between them' [examples: Hausa or Swahili in sub-Saharan Africa];

(iii) *mother or native tongue* 'the language which a person acquires in early years and which normally becomes his natural instrument of thought and communication';

(iv) *national language* 'the language of a political, social, and cultural entity';

---

[29] For a universal multilingual overview of country names, cf. the following UN manual: Country Names. Terminology Bulletin No. 345. Compendium of country names in Arabic, Chinese, English, French, Russian and Spanish listed in English alphabetical order.

[30] Cf., for instance, *Wild* 1975a for the role of language hierarchies in the formation of Middle Eastern states.

[31] Definitions are taken from the UNESCO report of 1953, The Use of Vernacular Languages in Education, p. 46. Cf. also *Capotorti* 1991: 75.

(v) *official language* 'a language used in the business of government – legislative, executive, and judicial';

(vi) *regional language* 'a language which is used as a medium of communication between peoples living within a certain area who have different mother tongues'.

While the distinction between languages is generally a relatively straightforward matter, the distinction between dialects poses more difficulties. Just as with languages, one specific dialect may have higher prestige than all the others, a circumstance that can greatly affect intercultural communication. A well-known example is the role of the Cairene dialect as a result of the impact of the Egyptian film industry. Dialects can be of a regional or of a sociological nature. Sociologically divided dialects can further be broken down into dialects divided by race/ethnicity and into dialects divided by religion. An example of the first division is the phenomenon of "Black English" ("Ebonics") in the United States; an example of the second is the phenomenon of "communal dialects", e.g., the Arabic dialects of the Muslim and Jewish communities in Baghdad.[32] In fact, Judeo-Arabic provides a parade example of a case where linguistic, religious, and sociological criteria interfere in a complicated way.[33] Ultimately, the distinction between languages on the one hand and dialects on the other may pose problems; clearly, there is no universal distinction between these two categories. In the case of the Neo-Aramaic languages, which are attested in several regions of the Middle East, one can present arguments for both aspects (i.e., "language" vs. "dialect"), especially as there is a lot of linguistic interference with neighboring languages, notably Turkish, Kurdish, and Persian.[34]

Above, it was argued that belonging to an ethnic or religious minority does not necessarily constitute a disadavantage (or *vice versa*). By the same token, belonging to a linguistic minority need not be disadvantageous under all circumstances. In the course of a conquest, for instance, it may be easier and more practical for the conqueror to adopt linguistic features of the conquered than to impose his own linguistic features, even though it is generally true that linguistic substratum and superstratum correspond to the conquered and the conqueror, respectively.

---

[32] Cf. *Blanc* 1964.

[33] Cf. *Hary* 1992 for an overview of related problems.

[34] Cf. *Chyet* 1995.

B. Problems in the discussions of the treaty bodies

The definition of "ethnic, religious, and linguistic minorities" is also a notorious problem in the discussions of the Human Rights Committee and the Committee on Economic, Social and Cultural Rights.[35] Examples are the problems faced by the Kurds, "Assyrians" (Christian Chaldaeans and Nestorians, Syrian-Orthodox Jacobites), Turkomans, and Shiite "Marsh-Arabs" in Iraq,[36] the problems faced by the Baha'i community in Iran,[37] by the Copts in Egypt, by the Christians in southern Sudan,[38] by the Ṣaḥrāwīs in the Western Sahara,[39] and by several minorities in Turkey (including the Aramaic-speaking inhabitants of the Ṭūr ᶜAbdīn region).[40] The intricacy of the situation is augmented by the interdigitation of the different component aspects that can constitute a "minority". This is apparent when it comes to the two aspects which constitutes the "Assyrian" community in Iraq. In this case, the local communities use the term *Assyrian* in both a linguistic and an ethnic sense, in obvious reference to the Assyrians in ancient Mesopotamia.

The case of "Berber" poses even more difficulties. Western scholars use the term, which derives historically from Greek *barbaroi*, in both a linguistic and an ethnic sense, and certainly without any negative connotations whatsoever. The Berbers themselves resent the term, however, and prefer the native term *amazigh* for the ethnic aspect and the circumfixed form *t-amazigh-t* for the linguistic aspect. In the course of the discussion of Algeria's first report to the Committee on Economic, Social and Cultural Rights, the Algerian ambassador stated repeatedly that the Algerians insist on the use of the term *Amazigh*

---

[35] For an overview of the work of the treaty bodies, cf. the contributions in *Alston* (ed.) 1992.

[36] Cf. the reports prepared by the Special Rapporteur Max *van der Stoel*, UN-docs. E/CN.4/1992/31 = UN-doc. S/23685/Add.1, pp. 31ff and E/CN.4/1995/56.

[37] Cf. the report prepared by Reynaldo *Galindo Pohl*, UN-doc. E/CN.4/1995/55.

[38] Cf. the report prepared by Gáspár *Bíró*, UN-doc. E/CN.4/1995/58.

[39] Cf. the report of the Secretary General, UN-doc. S/1997/160 of February 27, 1997, and the response thereto by the Security Council, UN-doc. S/PRST/1997/16, on the problems of definition regarding voter identification for a referendum in the Western Sahara.

[40] There are, of course, other Middle Eastern groups that have been referred to as "minorities" in political science contexts, such as the Alawites, the Armenians, the Baluchis, and the Maronites (cf., for instance, *Scheffler* 1990: 7), but these do not play a role in the said documents. By and large, the same holds for the remaining Jewish communities in Arab countries (for a historical perspective, cf. *Lewis* 1984).

and that the *Amazigh* do not constitute a "minority" in Algeria, as the Algerians, while historically having been conquered by Muslim armies, had not lost their "Amazigh" ethnicity ("amazighité").[41] Linguistically speaking, however, the many *Amazigh* languages and/or dialects have clearly been pushed back by the Arabic superstratum. It should also be noted that the term *t-amazigh-t*, as used by linguists, does not comprise all linguistic subgroups within the Berber family, and therefore is not an ideal umbrella term for the group as a whole.[42]

The Concluding Observations of the Human Rights Committee and the Committee on Economic, Social and Cultural Rights furnish ample evidence of terminological conflicts which can be readily analyzed in terms of Speech Act Theory. Before doing so, a few typical problem cases, as quoted in the concluding observations of the committees, will be cited. Iraq, for instance, makes minority rights contingent upon the following definition:[43]

Item (96), English original

Freedoms [of minorities] have to be compatible with the nationalist and progressive line of the revolution.

In a later report, with special reference to the Kurds, Iraq put forward a skillfully made argument whereby minority rights are rejected by claiming the "oneness" of the whole population, a strategy which amounts to making interethnic treaty agreements superfluous:[44]

Item (97), English original

Since Kurds were part and parcel of the Iraqi people, there could be no [treaty] agreements between different ethnic groups.

On the other hand, Iraq has regularly characterized the Kurds with such terms as *al-ᶜanāṣir al-kurdīya ġayru l-masᵓūla wa-ġayru n-niẓāmīya* 'the irresponsible irregular Kurdish elements', rather than simply as *al-ᵓakrād* 'Kurds'.[45]

---

[41] Cf. the report (UN-doc. E/1990/5/Add.22), the summary records of the respective discussions (UN-docs. E/C.12/1995/SR.46-48) and the concluding observations of the committee (UN-doc. E/1996/22, pp. 54ff).

[42] Cf. *Basset* 1952. A comprehensive overview of definitions of "ethnicity" is given in *Kratochwil* 1996.

[43] Cf. UN-doc. A/35/40, p. 29.

[44] Cf. UN-doc. A/42/40, p. 89.

[45] Cf. UN-doc. S/24311, p. 1.

As is well known, the Iranian régime has, in addition to discriminating against "recognized" religions, i.e., Christianity, Judaism, and Zoroastrianism, consistently denied the religious identity of the Baha'i community and has made them subject to all kinds of discrimination and harassment.[46] The minority rights of the Baha'is have been denied with arguments such as the following:[47]

Item (98), English original

According to Islam only Christianity and Judaism were revealed religions. Persons belonging to the latter two faiths could exercise their religion freely and publicly. The Baha'i faith did not qualify as such and was considered as a heretical sect of colonial origin.

As remarked above for the Kurds, minority rights can also be relativized via rhetorical manipulation of the concept of integration.[48] Thus, representatives of Egypt have stated the following:[49]

Item (99), English original

The application of article 27 of the Covenant [on Civil and Political Rights] to ethnic minorities in Egypt, such as the Nubians, was not a problem because they were an integral part of society.

Some countries deny the very existence of minorities. Lebanese diplomats, for instance, officially do not admit the existence of minorities, let alone the existence of internal tensions, in their country and rather attribute all internal political difficulties to Israel (though hardly ever to Syrian occupation or Iranian political influence).[50]

C. Case study: the Turkish-Kurdish conflict

In this section, we will examine the Turkish-Kurdish conflict as a problem in minority rights. While there are serious human rights violations at the expense of the Kurds in other countries, too, notably in Iraq and Iran, it is in Turkey that the situation is the most virulent in

---

[46] Cf., for instance, the contribution "Persecution of the Baha'is in Iran", ICJ Review, June 1985, pp. 8ff, UN-doc. A/48/40, pp. 5f, and *Menashri* 1988.

[47] Cf. UN-doc. A/46/40, p. 15.

[48] Examples include, in addition to the already-mentioned case of the Kurds, UN-doc. A/46/40, p. 59 (Morocco vis-à-vis the Western Sahara), UN-doc. A/47/40, p. 66 (Algeria vis-à-vis Berber/Amazigh culture), UN-doc. A/46/40 (Jordan vis-à-vis the Palestinians), and many more.

[49] Cf. UN-doc. A/39/40, p. 59.

[50] Cf. UN-doc. A/38/40, pp. 79ff, where major abuse of the term "genocide" is found, in reference to Israeli military actions.

terms of the problems addressed in this chapter.[51] The difference is partly illusory, however. The technically better *de jure* situation of the Kurds in other countries, where Kurdish "autonomous regions" exist, is often meaningless in view of the grave *de facto* situation, especially in Iraq. Here, for a start, is an overview of the population distribution:[52]

Table 7

Statistics of the Kurdish population

country	**number of Kurds**	**% of whole population**
Turkey	9.600.000	19%
Iran	5.000.000	10%
Iraq	3.900.000	23%
Syria	900.000	8%
Armenia/ Azerbaidjan/ Turkmenistan	300.000	no data given

An important step for the Kurdish right to self-determination was point 12 of the Wilson Declaration of 1918, which stipulated that "[nationalities] now under Turkish rule should be assured an undoubted security of life and an absolutely unmolested opportunity of autonomous development". The treaty of Sèvres in its articles 62 and 64 then called for the establishment of a Kurdish state. However, due to the stronger position of Turkey in subsequent years, no such call was present in the treaty of Lausanne of 1923. On the contrary, the wording of articles 38 through 40 implicitly excluded the Kurds from political rights, as they did not belong to those "non-Muslim minorities" to which political rights were to be granted. Later, in the treaty of Saadabad of 1937, Turkey, Iraq, and Iran agreed upon a common proceeding against the Kurds. Article 7 of that treaty referred to "armed bands and organizations which aim to overthrow established institutions", an implicit reference to the Kurds. Further relevant points in Turkish legislation which exclude any legal political activity on the part of the Kurds are article 3 of the constitution of 1982, paragraph

[51] For modern perspectives on the Turkish-Kurdish conflict cf., for instance, *Bozarslan* 1996, *Gürbey* 1996, *Olson* 1996, *Barkey/Fuller* 1997, and *Yalcin-Heckmann* 1997. For the situation in Iraq, cf., for instance, *Malanczuk* 1991.

[52] Cf. *Kreyenbroek/Sperl* (eds.) 1992: 32. For a precise statistical overview regarding other minorities in Turkey, cf. *Andrews* 1989.

125 of the penal code, and paragraph 8 of the Turkish law no. 3.713 (the so-called "anti-terror law"). Only in the most recent times has there been any development towards the recognition of a "Kurdish reality".

The line of argument that the Turkish government has pursued emerges "between the lines" from a comparison of the relevant passages from the Treaty of Sèvres and the Treaty of Lausanne:[53]

Item (100), English

Excerpts from the Treaty of Sèvres (August 10, 1920):

Article 62: A Commission sitting at Constantinople and composed of three members appointed by the British, French and Italian Governments respectively shall draft within six months from the coming into force of the present Treaty a scheme of local autonomy for the predominantly Kurdish areas lying east of the Euphrates, south of the southern boundary of Armenia as it may be hereafter determined, and north of the frontier of Turkey with Syria and Mesopotamia, as defined in Article 27, II. (2) and (3). If unanimity cannot be secured on any question, it will be referred by the members of the Commission to their respective Governments. The scheme shall contain full safeguards for the protection of the Assyro-Chaldeans and other racial and religious minorities within these areas, and with this object a Commission composed of British, French, Italian, Persian and Kurdish representatives shall visit the spot to examine and decide what rectifications, if any, should be made in the Turkish frontier, where, under the provisions of the present Treaty, that frontier coincides with that of Persia.

Article 64: If within one year from the coming into force of the present Treaty the Kurdish peoples within the areas defined in Artcle 62 shall address themselves to the Council of the League of Nations in such a manner as to show that a majority of the population of these areas desires independence from Turkey, and if the Council then considers that these peoples are capable of such independence and recommends that it should be granted to them, Turkey hereby agrees to execute such a recommendation, and to announce all rights and titles over these areas.

The detailed provisions for such renunciation will form the subject of a separate agreement between the Principal Allied Powers and Turkey.

If and when such renunciation takes place, no objection will be raised by the Principal Allied Powers to the voluntary adhesion to such an independent Kurdish State of the Kurds inhabiting that part of Kurdistan which has hitherto been included in the Mosul Vilayet.

Item (101), English

Excerpts from the Treaty of Lausanne (July 24, 1923):

Article 38: [...] All inhabitants of Turkey shall be entitled to free exercise, whether in public or in private, of any creed, religion or belief, the observance of which shall not be incompatible with public order and with good morals.

Non-Moslem minorities will enjoy full freedom of movement and of emigration, subject to the measures applied, on the whole or on part of the territory, to all

---

[53] Cf. *Hurewitz* 1956, II: 82 and 122f, respectively.

Turkish nationals, and which may be taken by the Turkish government for national defence, or for the maintenance of public order.

Article 39: Turkish nationals belonging to non-Moslem minorities will enjoy the same civil and political rights as Moslems. [...]

Article 40: Turkish nationals belonging to non-Moslem minorities shall enjoy the same treatment and security in law and in fact as other Turkish nationals. In particular, they shall have an equal right to establish, manage and control at their own expense, any charitable, religious and social institutions, any schools and other establishments for instruction and education, with the right to use their own language and to exercise their own religion freely therein.

The Kemalist concept of minorities has also left its imprint in Turkey's policy of implementing obligations under international law. Turkey has not signed, let alone ratified, either the International Covenant on Economic, Social and Cultural Rights (CESCR) or the International Covenant on Civil and Political Rights (CCPR). It has, however, signed the Convention on the Rights of the Child (CRC), the Convention on the Elimination of All Forms of Discrimination against Women (CEDAW), the International Convention on the Elimination of All Forms of Racial Discrimination (CERD), and the Convention against Torture and other Cruel, Inhuman or Degrading Treatment or Punishment (CAT) – whatever that may have meant in practice.[54] Consider now the following excerpt from the Convention on the Rights of the Child:

Item (102), English

Excerpts from CRC (September 2, 1990):

Article 17: States Parties recognize the important function performed by the mass media and shall ensure that the child has access to information and material from a diversity of national and international sources, especially those aimed at the promotion of his or her social, spiritual and moral well-being and physical and mental health. To this end, States parties shall: [...]

(b) Encourage international co-operation in the production, exchange and dissemination of such information and material from a diversity of cultural, national and international sources; [...]

(d) Encourage the mass media to have particular regard to the linguistic needs of the child who belongs to a minority group or who is indigenous; [...]

Article 29: States Parties agree that the education of the child shall be directed to: [...]

(c) The development of respect for the child's parents, his or her own cultural identity, language and values, for the national values of the country in which the child is living, the country from which he or she may originate, and for the civilizations different from his or her own;

---

[54] Cf. UN-doc. ST/HR/4/Rev.11, p. 10f.

(d) The preparation of the child for responsible life in a free society, in the spirit of understanding, peace, tolerance, equality of sexes, and friendship among all peoples, ethnic, national and religious groups and persons of indigenous origin; [...]

Article 30: In those States in which ethnic, religious or linguistic minorities or persons of indigenous origin exist, a child belonging to such a minority or who is indigenous shall not be denied the right, in community with other members of his or her group, to enjoy his or her own culture, to profess and practise his or her own religion, or to use his or her own language.

In its reservation entered in regard to the Convention on the Rights of the Child, Turkey implicitly excludes the Kurds, as they do not belong to "non-Muslim minorities" (as stipulated in the Treaty of Lausanne):[55]

Item (103), English original

Reservation of Turkey to CRC:

The Republic of Turkey reserves the right to interpret and apply the provisions of articles 17, 29 and 30 of the United Nations Convention on the Rights of the Child according to the letter and spirit of the Constitution of the Republic of Turkey and those of the Treaty of Lausanne of 24 July 1923.

Just as it has denied the ethnic identity of the Kurds, Turkey has likewise denied the linguistic identity of the Kurdish language. The so-called "sun language theory" (*günes dil teorisi*) – propagated by the Turkish scholar Harun Resit Tankut based on work by Ziya Gökalp (1867-1924) – claims that all languages, and hence also Kurdish, derive from the Turkish language. The problem here has been characterized in the following terms:[56]

Auf die Sprache bezogen, bewegt sich die offizielle Haltung der Türkei offensichtlich in einem Zirkelschluß. Wenn es denn wahr sein sollte, daß die in Anatolien gesprochenen kurdischen Dialekte eigentlich Türkisch sind, warum darf dann dieses "Türkisch" nicht amtlich geredet, in Schulen gelehrt oder im Fernsehen gesprochen werden? So wird man den Verdacht nicht los, eigentlich solle durch Wissenschaft nur die Nichtexistenz von Kurden bewiesen werden.

In sum, one can only concur with the following statement:[57]

---

[55] Cf. UN-doc. ST/LEG/SER. E/13, p. 199.

[56] Cf. *Lerch*, W. 1996. "Alle unter einer Sonne. Linguistik als Politik: Wie die Türkei das Kurdische verdrängt", Frankfurter Allgemeine Zeitung, April 2, 1996, p. 39 ("With respect to [the Kurdish] language, the official argumentation of Turkey is obviously circular. If the Kurdish dialects spoken in Anatolia were indeed "Turkish", why then is the use of this "Turkish" forbidden in the contexts of administration, school system, and television? Hence, one cannot get rid of the suspicion that science is [ab]used to prove the [alleged] non-existence of the Kurds.") For the background of the "sun language theory", cf. *Gökalp* 1920 and *Tankut* 1937.

[57] Cf. *Bring* 1992: 168f.

As a minimum, it can be claimed that the Kurds are entitled to (1) the right to autonomy in the form of a local administration in line with the League of Nations Declaration of 1925 and in analogy with Article 76 of the UN Charter; and (2) the right to pursue their culture, practice their own religion and speak their own language in accordance with Article 27 of the UN Convention on Human and Political Rights.

D. Analysis: application of Speech Act Theory

We turn now to a formal analysis of the most salient issues mentioned in terms of Speech Act Theory. As was outlined above (chapter three), Speech Act Theory provides a theoretical framework that accounts for the possible different intensions of a given statement, as used by two (or more) different parties ("speakers").[58] Here again is the list of the theoretically possible types of misunderstanding (as above, "extension" will be understood as the basis of the locutionary act, and "intension" will be understood as the basis of the illocutionary act):[59]

(i) the extension is the same, the intension differs;
(ii) the extension differs, the intension is the same;
(iii) both the extension and the intension differ.

For each of the two "speakers" in question, i.e., in the framework of the present chapter, the majority and the minority, or an outside party (international political observer, "Western" scholar) and the minority, a tabular matrix can be established which lays out the relevant ethnic, religious, and linguistic features from two clashing perspectives (of course, not all three of these categories need be relevant in a given case):

features	**"speaker A"-perspective**	**"speaker B"-perspective**
ethnic:	ethnic features (A)	ethnic features (B)
religious:	religious features (A)	religious features (B)
linguistic:	linguistic features (A)	linguistic features (B)

Drawing on such tabular layouts, we will attempt in this section to bring the potentially different perceptions of these features into line with the typology of scenarios (i) - (iii).

---

[58] Cf. again *Weil* 1983, *Habermas* 1985, *Onuf* 1985, *Fastenrath* 1991: 68ff, and *Fastenrath* 1993.

[59] A formal analysis in the sense of a logical and set-theoretical notation (as provided, for instance, in *Ulkan* 1992) is not intended here.

Scenario (i): the problems regarding the term "Assyrian" match scenario (i) (the extension is the same, the intension differs). In the following table, *both* columns refer to the notion "Assyrian", but from two very different perspectives (note that the circumstance that the "Assyrians" are called "Arameans" in a "Western" perspective does not entail any denial of identity here):[60]

Table 8

Comparative analysis of the concept "Assyrian"

features	**"Western" perspective**		**"Assyrian" perspective**
ethnic:	(ancient) Semites		"Assyrians"
religious:	---		Christians/Jews
linguistic:	Akkadian (Assyrian-Babylonian)		"Assyrian" (dialects of North Eastern Neo-Aramaic)
EXTENSION	Assyrians	=	"Assyrians"
INTENSION	a distinct people in anient Mesopotamia	≠	a distinct people in modern Turkey/Iraq/ Iran/Azerbaidjan

Scenario (ii): the problems regarding the terms *Berber* and *Amazigh*, as described for the Algerian situation, match scenario (ii) (the extension differs, the intension is the same). A similar tabular layout yields the following picture, with the two columns presenting different perspectives on the notion "Berber"/"Amazigh" (again, no denial of identity, be it from an Arab or a "Western" perspective, is involved here):[61]

---

[60] Here "Westerners" and neo-Arameans differ. For the former, there are two utterly different intensions of "Assyrian" (or perhaps a "Westerner" sees "Assyrian" *only* in the sense of "ancient Mesopotamian"). For the latter, who view ancient Assyrians and modern "Assyrians" as somehow essentially the same, presumably the ancient and the modern Assyrians have the same intension.

[61] Cf. again the statements of the Algerian ambassador to the United Nations in Geneva, as reproduced in UN-docs. E/C.12/1995/SR.46-48, which stipulate that the Berber/Amazigh perspective identifies the term "Amazigh" with "all Algerians". An analogue for the use of "Amazigh" for *all* Algerians is the use of "British" for "*all* inhabitants of the UK". "British" originally refers to the British Celts (Welsh) – an analogue to the Berbers. This observation was kindly pointed out to the author by Orin *Gensler*.

Table 9
Comparative analysis of the concept "Berber"/"Amazigh"

features	"Western" perspective		Amazigh perspective
ethnic:	Berber (a minority in Algeria)		Amazigh (all Algerians)
religious:	Muslims		Muslims
linguistic:	Berber		tamazight
EXTENSION	Berber	≠	Amazigh
INTENSION	people in Algeria	=	people in Algeria

Scenario (iii): the various dimensions of the Turkish-Kurdish conflict match scenario (iii) (both the extension and the intension differ). Here the tabular matrix yields the following picture, with the two columns referring to the notion "Kurd(ish)", but from two very different perspectives (note that, in this case, the "Western" perspective overlaps more or less with the Kurdish perspective):[62]

Table 10
Comparative analysis of the concept "Kurd(ish)"

features	Turkish perspective[63]		Kurdish perspective
ethnic:	Turks		Iranians (Indo-Europeans)
religious:	undefined (i.e., not belonging to non-Muslim minorities)		Muslims (plus some other religions)
linguistic:	Turkish "dialect"		Kurdish (Iranian language)
EXTENSION	"not non-Muslims"	≠	Kurds
INTENSION	not a distinct people in Turkey	≠	distinct people in Turkey (and elsewhere)

---

[62] In this case, Searle's use of "extension" (i.e., the set of individuals who are selected by a given description or predicate) yields a slightly dfferent analysis: The terms "minority which is not non-Muslim" and "Kurds" do pick out the same group of people (extensionality); but in Kurdish eyes this group has a separate identity (intensionality), while in Turkish eyes it has not.

[63] There are, of course, dissenting views. Cf. the contributions in *Olson* 1996.

E. Summary of Chapter Six

As was the case in the realms of "war and peace" and "human rights", language has likewise been shown to play an important role in matters regarding the rights viz. denied rights of ethnic, religious, and linguistic minorities, properly speaking a subfield of the "human rights" realm. Speech Act Theory proved to be a useful formalism for the analysis of terminological conflicts associated with the ethnic, religious, and linguistics aspects of a people "X". However, in this area terminological devices in the service of abuse of power appear to be more language-specific (and certainly independent of Arabic), as compared with the realms of "war and peace" and "human rights", where issues associated with multilingualism were shown to play a major role in problems of (mis)interpretation between the "Western" and the "Arab"/"Islamic" parties.

Chapter Seven

Conclusion

"Sprache dient der Verständigung. So fing es möglicherweise einmal an, doch die kulturelle Entwicklung ging weiter." *Dolph*, W. 1988. "Nicht so gemeint ... Die UNO-Sprache", Vereinte Nationen 6/1988, p. 178.

A. General observations

This study has been devoted to two major issues: first, the issue of legal and linguistic conflicts between coexisting authentic versions of international legal documents in different languages; second, the issue of Arabic as a medium of *šarīᶜa*-based legal norms in the realms of "war and peace" and "human rights", including issues related to ethnic, religious, and linguistic minorities in the Middle East. Generally speaking, the second issue proved to be more virulent than the first, as the specific problems regarding the first issue are much more prone to pragmatic solutions on a case-by-case basis than are the specific problems associated with the second.

B. Legal aspects

With respect to the second, more important issue, a number of observations can be made. Again, a differentiation is necessary between the realms of "war and peace" and "human rights". While *šarīᶜa*-based arguments were found to be relatively rare in the realm of "war and peace", they are abundant in the realm of "human rights".[1]

In this light, the present study has attempted to make a constructive contribution in drawing attention to suggestions as to how *some* precepts of the Islamic *šarīᶜa* could perhaps be reconciled with the standards of international human rights law, though such reconcilia-

---

[1] Cf. UN-doc. CEDAW/C/1997/4.

tion seems neither possible nor desirable in a number of cases.[2] In this context, the most important goal is to induce Arab and other Islamic states to mitigate their reservations to IHR conventions both in quantity and in quality. It is worth while once again to cite the Australian human rights expert Elizabeth Evatt, who inquired as follows, in concluding her criticism of Iran's report UN-doc. CCPR/C/28/Add.15 on a constructive note: "Lastly, it would be interesting to learn whether a study of the law had been undertaken to determine the extent to which Islamic scriptures contained texts that could be more fully emphasized because they supported the universal principles of the covenant and whether the assistance of Islamic scholars in other countries, including human rights experts and women scholars of Islam, had been sought."[3] This question indeed would appear to be of the utmost importance. It would be highly desirable if the work of progressive Muslim thinkers such as Bassam Tibi, ᶜAlī ᶜAbdarrāziq, Ṣādiq al-ᶜAẓm, ᶜAbdallāh ᵓAḥmad an-Naᶜīm, Muḥammad Šaḫrūr, and Naṣr Ḥāmid ᵓAbū Zayd were to be taken into consideration in modern Islamic diplomatic discourse.[4] Perhaps the most impressive statement along these lines from a Muslim perspective is the following:[5]

> It is my conviction as a Muslim that the public law of Shariᶜa does not represent the law of Islam which contemporary Muslims are supposed to implement in fulfillment of their religious obligation. I also strongly believe that the application of the public law of Shariᶜa today will be counterproductive and detrimental to Muslims and to Islam itself. [...] My trust in God leads me to believe that current efforts to implement the public law of Shariᶜa will fail because they are harmful to the best interests of Islam and the Muslims. These efforts will fail because the public law of Shariᶜa is fundamentally inconsistent with the realities of modern life. This is my firm conviction as a Muslim. My only concern is to avoid the human suffering which is likely to be caused by this doomed endeavor.

The investigation of the periodic reports that have been submitted to international treaty bodies during the first fifty sessions of the General Assembly justifies a moment of reflection on whether or not progress has been made in the implementation of IHR conventions in Islamic countries, more specifically in he Arab states and Iran.[6] While certain states, notably Tunisia, deserve praise for their cooperation

---

[2] Cf. notably *an-Naᶜīm* 1990: 182ff.

[3] Cf. UN-doc. CCPR/C/SR.1231, p. 7.

[4] Cf., for instance, *ᶜAbdarrāziq* 1972, *Tibi* 1980, *al-ᶜAẓm* 1981, *an-Naᶜīm* 1990, *Šaḫrūr* 1992, and *ᵓAbū Zayd* 1994.

[5] Cf. *an-Naᶜīm* 1990: 187.

[6] The IHR committees have been active now for more than twenty-five years, since CERD started the consideration of reports in 1970.

with the IHR committees, other states have hardly made any progress, even though their reports may have come gradually closer to the guidelines for preparing IHR reports. All in all, it appears that the precepts of the Islamic *šarīʿa* are unlikely to be reconciled at any time soon with IHR concepts. In this context, it must be repeated that most Islamic states show no willingness to even look into modern methods of Qurʾānic interpretation, but rather accede all too readily to fundamentalists' demands. Again, in the context of this study, it is irrelevant whether human rights violations are merely based on a conservative interpretation of the Islamic *šarīʿa* for purely religious reasons, or whether these violations occur as the result of abuse of Islamic principles for the sake of maintenance of power of political and/or religious élites in Islamic countries. The universality of human rights must be insisted on, and attempts at legal and cultural relativism firmly rejected. In the words of Kühnhardt:[7]

> Es können in der Tat keinerlei Belege erbracht werden, die bezeugen würden, die westliche Menschenrechtsphilosophie habe nicht das Universalitätsprinzip, sondern eine ethnozentrische Position verfochten. Menschenrechte mögen in der kolonialen Zeit den eingeborenen Völkern vorenthalten worden sein; in der Menschenrechtstheorie aber kann nur ein universaler Menschenrechtsbegriff nachgewiesen werden.

Even more to the point are Donoho's remarks in this context:[8]

> Relativism clearly has a tremendous capacity to serve as the rhetorical justification for repressive practices by ruling élites. The fact that relativism is most often supported by repressive régimes [...] is ample grounds for a healthy skepticism regarding vague claims of cultural and ideological necessity for deviations from the specific requirements of human rights norms.

With respect to the issue of legal and cultural relativism, the following observations can also be made regarding article 27 of the International Covenant on Civil and Political Rights. While in the Islamic world the historical situation of the *ḏimmī*s (though not the situation of heretical Islamic sects) may have been favorable as compared to that of minorities in, say, medieval Europe, the contemporary situation of ethnic, religious, and linguistic minorities in the Middle East leaves much room for improvement. In this context, tension between

---

[7] *Kühnhardt* 1987: 183 ("In fact, no evidence can be adduced which would argue that the Western philosophy of human rights has been used in support of an ethnocentric position rather than a principle of universality. It is true that indigenous peoples may have been deprived of human rights in colonial times. However, in the theory of human rights there is only evidence for a universal concept of human rights."). On the question of legal and cultural relativism as affecting Middle Eastern Studies in general, cf. also *Mayer* 1991a: 9ff, *Forstner* 1993: 50ff, and *Lewis* 1993a: 129ff.

[8] *Donoho* 1991: 380. Cf. also *Mayer* 1994: 389.

majorities and minorities or between minorities themselves should not be attributed in a monolithic way to *divide-et-impera* politics under the Ottoman empire or former colonial régimes, though such problems did indeed exist in certain cases.[9] Also, given the extent of the problems relating to ethnic, religious, and linguistic minorities throughout the Muslim world, it would appear wise for scholars concerned with the study of Islam to take into consideration problems ranging from the West Sahara to East Timor, in addition to their justified concern about the problems usually more narrowly subsumed under the heading "Middle East conflicts".

C. Linguistic aspects

With respect to the first major issue of this study, that of legal and linguistic conflicts, a number of observations can be made as well. First and foremost, certain features that are often discarded as typical "clichés" with respect to the Arabic language have proved still to be potent factors in modern Arabic diplomatic discourse.[10]

Especially the vast output of Iraqi diplomatic letters supports the observation that standards in the realms of "war and peace" and "human rights" are by no means universal but rather dependent on the respective party's political and cultural-religious background. The resultant difficulties in responding constructively to many of the cited statements and the logic behind them, both for the United Nations as an international organization and for legal scholars as individuals, are deep and obvious.

The quoted documents show clearly that modern diplomatic Arabic still reflects a remarkable degree of historical, cultural, and religious consciousness that has no parallel in the other official languages used in the United Nations system. It seems a fair assumption that many of the cited documents could not have originated in their actually attested form in another language. In this context, and with special regard to the cited Iraqi documents, it is important not to forget the serious factual background underlying statements that may seem merely amusing when read in a European translation. At the same time, it must be noted that Arabic has fully adapted – where appro-

---

[9] Cf., for instance, *Childs/Williams* 1997 for an analysis of the cultural aftermath of such tensions.

[10] For a "politically incorrect" study on this issue, cf., for instance, *Shouby* 1951.

priate – to French- and English-based lexical and stylistic patterns. A high percentage of Arabic documents concerning matters of diplomatic routine, of no significance for the present study, reveal hardly any Islamic background and could just as well be translations from English or French.

Summarizing, one can discern three scenarios and underlying motivations for the use of Arabic in diplomacy in general and in United Nations contexts in particular:

(i) bi- and multilateral treaties on any subject involving Arab states and organizations, as well as periodic reports submitted to treaty bodies, in which the use of Arabic as one language simply acknowledges the Arab contracting party/parties involved but has no cultural significance beyond that;

(ii) letters by Arab states and organizations addressed to the United Nations that exhibit specific elements of Islamic thought and/or national pride; in recent times, most of those letters have originated in Iraq, Kuwait, Libya, and Yemen; in the majority of the quoted cases, the use of Islamic formulae indicates a high degree of political polarization;

(iii) texts where cultural sensitivities mandate the use of the native language Arabic, rather than the mere adaption of an English or French version.[11]

D. Summary of Chapter Seven

The overall goal of this study has been to lay out a number of observations and considerations on the use of language in international documents. Nuances of difference between authentic Arabic texts and their English counterparts were discussed in the theoretical framework of Speech Act Theory, drawing on the provisions of the Vienna Convention on the Law of Treaties. The problem of different semantic shades in different language versions, exacerbated by different cultural and legal backgrounds, turned out to be still potent in the realms

---

[11] An example is the Report of the International Conference on Population and Development (Cairo, 5-13-September 1994) (UN-doc. A/CONF.171/13, p. 5), which states that "[t]he official language of the Programme of Action is English, with the exception of paragraph 8.25, which was negotiated in all six official languages of the United Nations." Paragraph 8.25 is part of the section dealing with "Women's health and safe motherhood" and is particularly intricate and sensitive in its terminology.

of "war and peace" and "human rights". In the light of the terminology and style used in the cited documents, the basic hypothesis of this study, to the effect that different attitudes vis-à-vis the legal norms of international law may be contingent upon and reflected by the languages used in the respective documents, is clearly confirmed. It should be understood, however, that none of the issues discussed is *a priori* necessarily specific to Arabic, even though the particular encounter between "Arab"/"Islamic" and "Western" cultural and/or religious concepts as reflected by their respective linguistic systems may be unique. In this context, it is important to avoid the pitfall of legal and cultural relativism that has emerged in recent times, especially in the discussion of "non-Western" human rights issues.[12]

All in all, the presence of Arabic as an official language in the United Nations system constitutes an important enrichment in a world that calls for intercultural communication and understanding. Furthermore, it is of indisputable importance to preserve multilingualism in international relations, language being the medium of legal norms and cultural values.[13]

It should be noted in conclusion that a formal analysis (here: Speech Act Theory) can offer a potential for a precise overview and insight which might not be attainable without the formalism involved, even if the formal representation may be redundant once the results have been laid out.[14] It is hoped that the approach presented here may prove to be a useful model of interpretation for multilingual international documents in general, especially in cases where it can provide an explanation for conflicting attitudes vis-à-vis the legal norms of international law.

---

[12] On this question as affecting Middle Eastern Studies, cf. *Mayer* 1991a: 9ff and *Lewis* 1993a: 119ff. It is interesting to note that the very word *istišrāq* 'Orientalism' ("Orientalistik"), which used simply to denote scholarly work dealing with parts of Asia and Northern Africa, has taken on a new intension of "[allegedly] culturally biased scholarship vis-à-vis the Middle East" in contemporary English under the impact of attacks on Western scholarship by cultural relativists. On this question, cf. *Lewis* 1993a: 99ff and *D'Souza* 1991.

[13] Cf. again *Ostrower* 1965, *Bozeman* 1971, *Hilf* 1973, and *Tabory* 1980.

[14] The same argument can be made in favor of the formal approach that Angelika *Neuwirth* (1980) pursued in her colometric analysis of the Qurʾānic syntax, based on the methodology established by Wolfgang *Richter* (1971). Also, it is the conviction of the author that a precise formalism has an esthetic value in itself, beyond its potential for fostering a perspicuous layout of complex data.

Appendix

Analytical catalogue of data and sources

A. Arabic terminology

I. Glossary of Arabic legal/religious and political terms[1]

ʾahl al-kitāb	people of the book (i.e., the Bible or the Qurʾān), i.e., Jews, Christians and Muslims
ʿaqīda	tenet of faith, doctrine
ʾāya, pl. *ʾāyāt*	"sign", Qurʾānic verse, the basic element of a *sūra*
basmala	acronym of the formula *bi-smi llāhi r-raḥmāni r-raḥīm* 'in the name of God the Merciful the Compassionate'
baʿṯ	(political) resurrection
bayʿa	commercial agreement; political agreement (to be ruled)
dār al-ḥarb	realm ("house") of war (non-Islamic territory in a state of war)
dār al-ʾislām	realm ("house") of Islam (Islamic territory)
dār aṣ-ṣulḥ / dār al-ʿahd	realm ("house") of truce (non-Islamic territory in a state of temporary truce)
ḏimmī	free non-Muslim subject (Jew or Christian) living in a Muslim country
dīn wa-dawla	[the unity of] religion and state
fatwā, pl. *fatāwā*	legal opinion of a *muftī*
fiqh	Islamic law (opinions and commentaries of Muslim jurists)
ġazwa	military expedition, attack
ḥaḍāna	nursing of a child

[1] Arabic terms are listed in the order of the English alphabet, irrespective of diacritical marks.

ḥadd, pl. *ḥudūd*	fixed (corporal) punishment for certain crimes
ḥadīṯ	narrative tradition (going back to Muḥammad)
ḫalīfa	Caliph; religious/political successor of Muḥammad
hijra	emigration of the Muḥammad from Mecca to Medina in the year 622 A.D. (= year zero in the Islamic calendar)
ḥīla, pl. *ḥiyal*	legal ruse (to circumvent the *šarīʿa*)
ḥisba	duty of every Muslim "to promote good and to prevent evil"
ʿibāda, pl. *ʿibādāt*	worship ritual, practice
ʾijmāʿ	consensus of Islamic scholars
ijtihād	"effort", the use of individual legal reasoning
ʾimām	prayer leader; Imam
ʾislām	"submission" (to the will of God); Islam
jihād	"effort", war (against "unbelievers")
jizya	tax to be paid by *ḏimmīs*
kafāla	(Islamic) tutelage of a child
mansūḫ	abrogated (applying to an *ʾāya*)
maṣlaḥa	benefit, interest [of the Islamic *ʾumma*]
muʿāmala, pl. *muʿāmalāt*	act of social intercourse
mudawwana	an Islamic legal code relating to personal status (in Morocco)
muftī	specialist in religious law, issuing *fatāwā*
murtadd	apostate (from Islam)
muslim	follower of Islam
nāsiḫ	abrogating (applying to an *ʾāya*)
qaḏf	false accusation of unlawful sexual intercourse
qānūn	norm, (secular) law (from Greek *kanon*)
qaṭʿ aṭ-ṭarīq	highway robbery
qiṣāṣ	retaliation ("talio")
qiyās	legal reasoning by analogy
qurʾān	"something to be recited", the Qurʾān

ribā	usury; (financial) interest
ridda	apostasy (from Islam)
salafīya	an Islamic reform movement in Egypt, founded by Muḥammad ʿAbduh
ṣalāt	prayer
šarīʿa	"watering place", the sacred law of Islam
sariqa	theft
sīra, pl. *siyar*	way of life; conduct (of political affairs with non-Muslims)
sunna	sayings and doings of Muḥammad
sūra, pl. *suwar*	*sūra*, basic element ("chapter") of the Qurʾān
šūrā	political consultation
šurb al-ḫamr	wine drinking
taʿaddud az-zawjāt	"multitude of wives", polygamy (polygyny)
tabannin	adoption
ṭalāq	repudiation (with subsequent divorce) of a wife
taqlīd	(legal) tradition
taʿzīr	discretionary (optional) punishment
ʾumma	political community of Islamic states
ʾuṣūl al-fiqh	sources of Islamic law
waqf, pl. *ʾawqāf*	religious endowment
ẓahīr	royal decree (in Morocco)
zakāt	almsgiving
zināʾ	unlawful sexual intercourse

II. Arabic honorifics

Arabic diplomatic style features a vast spectrum of honorifics, depending on the rank of the person addressed, all captured by the English "your excellency". The following is a list:[2]

[2] Cf. *Lewis* 1956: 67.

Arabic honorific	gloss	person addressd
jalāla	'greatness'	king ("Majesty")
dawla	'state'	prime minister (Egypt)
rif^c^a	'height'	holder of the "collar of Fu'ad I" (Egypt) (historical title)
sa^c^āda	'luck'	pasha (historical title)
sumūw	'highness'	(crown-)prince
^c^izza	'strength'	bey (historical title)
^c^iṣma	'purity'	wife of cabinet minister (Egypt)
ġibṭa	'happiness'	patriarch of Eastern churches ("beatitude")
faḫāma	'stateliness'	ambassador, prime minister (Iraq), president of the republic (Syria)
ma^c^ālī	'noble things'	(ex-)cabinet minister, ambassador

B. Arabic terminology sources

I. Specialized dictionaries and manuals

^c^Abdallāh, Ḥ. 1982. A Dictionary of International Relations & Conference Terminology (Arabic: Qāmūs muṣṭalaḥāt al-^c^alāqāt wa-l-mu'tamarāt ad-duwalīya). Beirut.

Didaoui, M./UNIDO (United Nations Industrial Development Organization) 1989. Dalīl al-mutarjim ma^c^a tarkīz ^c^alā manẓūmat al-'umam al-muttaḥida (Manual for Arabic Translators with Emphasis on the Usage in the United Nations System), 2 vols. Vienna.

Fawq al-^c^Āda, S. 1974. A Dictionary of Diplomacy and International Affairs (Arabic: Mu^c^jam ad-diblūmāsīya wa-š-šu'ūn ad-duwalīya). Beirut.

Hamui, M. 1949. Diplomatic Terms. English Arabic. Damascus.

Lewis, B. 1956. A Handbook of Diplomatic and Political Arabic. London.

II. List of UN terminology manuals

Administrative and Financial Terms: FAO (05)/T319, No. 23/Rev.2.

Agricultural Credit: FAO (05)/T319, No. 32.

Bananas: FAO (05)/T319, No. 24/Ar.

Classification and Definition of Forest Products: FAO (05)/F715, No. 32.

Climate Change: Glossary: [ST/GENEVA/]TERM/41.

Country Names: States Members of the United Nations, Members of the Specialized Agencies, or Parties to the Statute of the International Court of Justice: ST/CS/SER.F/345.

Crime Prevention and Control: ST/CS/SER.F/340.

Currency Units: ST/CS/SER.F/346.

Department of Administration and Management: ST/CS/SER.F/336.

Dictionary of International Relations, Arabic-French-English: News, Economics, Politics: UNST/GENEVA (018)/D4.

Disarmament: ST/CS/SER.F/310.

Disarmament: ST/CS/SER.F/335.

Disarmament: A List of Selected Terms: [ST/GENEVA/]TERM/MISC/66.

Earth Summit: UNCED (English-Arabic Glossary): [ST/GENEVA/]TERM/PROV/44.

Energy: New and Renewable Sources: Provisional List of Terms: ST/CS/SER.F/320.

Environment and Development: ST/CS/SER.F/344.

Fibres and Fibre Products: Terminology: FAO (05)/T319, No. 29/Ar.

Food Aid Projects Terminology: FAO (05)/T319, No. 37.

Glossary od Administrative and Financial Terms: [UNESCO/]COL-T/TERM/13-[UNESCO/] COL-83/WS/8

Glossary of Conference Terms: Arabic, English, French: UNESCO (016)/G564.

Glossary of Telecommunication Terms: English-Arabic-French-Spanish: ITU(018)/G5.

Human Rights: Legal, Social and Administrative Terms: [ST/GENEVA/] TERM/MISC/62.

Industrial Property Glossary: WIPO/815.

Law of the Sea: List of Terms Relating to the Law of the Sea: ST/CS/SER.F/297/Rev.2.

List of Disarmament and Related International Instruments: [ST/GENEVA] TERM/MISC/67.

List of International Non-Governmental Organizations Admitted to the Various Categories of Relations with UNESCO: [UNESCO/]COL-T/TERM/5/Rev.-[UNESCO/]COL.81/WS/8.

List of Terms for the World Conference on Cultural Policies: [UNESCO/]COL-82/WS/8/Rev.

Liste multilingue provisoire de termes d'informatique: [UNESCO/]COL-T/TERM/9-[UNESCO/]COL.79/WS/14.

Manual for Arabic translators with emphasis on the usage in the United Nations System: [UNIDO/]ID/352/Rev.1 (SPEC) + Add.1.

Manual for Arabic Translators: With Studies on Language and Theory of Translation: UNIDO/CS/SER.B/1.

Multilingual Dictionary of Narcotic Drugs and Psychotropic Substances under International Control: ST/NAR/1.

Multilingual Dictionary of Narcotic Drugs and Psychotropic Substances under International Control: Addendum 1: ST/NAR/1/Add.1.

Multimodal Transport and Containerization: [ST/GENEVA/]TERM/MISC/63.

Names of Countries and Their Capital Cities Including Adjectives of Nationality and Currency Units: FAO (05)/T319, No. 20/Rev.10.

Non-Governmental Organizations in Consultative Status with the Economic and Social Council: ST/CS/SER.F/331/Rev.1.

Office for Research and the Collection of Infomation: ST/CS/SER.F/337.

Organization and Structure of the FAO: FAO (05)/T319, No. 15/Rev.6.

Outer Space: Provisional List of Terms: ST/CS/SER.F/326.

Plants and Plant Products of Economic Importance: FAO (05)/T319, No. 30/Ar.

Politiques culturelles: [UNESCO/]COL-T/TERM/4-[UNESCO/]COL.77/WS/13.

Provisional Glossary of Terms Relating to HABITAT: ST/CS/SER.F/308.

Provisional List of Terms Used in the Shipping Industry: English-Arabic: [TD/]UNCTAD/SHIP/444.

Revised Provisional List of Educational Terms: [UNESCO/]COL/83/WS/12.

Rice Terminology: FAO (05)/T319, No. 26/Ar.

Science and Technology for Development: ST/CS/SER.F/315.

Some Fishery Terms: FAO (018)/F4.

Technical Terminology Employed in the Standardization of Geographical Names: ST/CS/SER.F/330/Rev.1.

Terminology of Technical and Vocational Education: UNESCO/IBE (018)/V6, Rev. ed.

Trade and Development Terminology: [ST/GENEVA/]TERM/PROV/41.

Trilingual Demographic Dictionary: Arabic-English-French, English-French-Arabic, French-English-Arabic: E/ESCWA/Pop/88/3.

Trilingual Dictionary: Statistical and Demographic Terms: UNCDC (02)/D4.

UNCTAD: Meetings and Titles: Glossary of Titles: [ST/GENEVA/]TERM/PROV/22/Rev.1.

The Unified Medical Dictionary: English-Arabic-French: WHO/EMRO (018)/M3, 3rd ed.

United Nations Conference on Desertification: Provisional English-Arabic List of Terms: [ST/GENEVA/]TERM/MISC/35.

Vocabulaire polyglotte du service postal international: UPU (02)/V872.

Vocabulary of Agricultural and Other Terms in Use by FAO: FAO (05)/T319, No. 21.

Women' Issues: ST/CS/SER.F/348.

WIPO Glossary of Terms of the Law of Copyright and Neighboring Rights: WIPO/819.

C. Sources for treaties and other diplomatic documents

Bowman, M./*Harris*, D. 1984. Multilateral Treaties. Index & Current Status, 2 vols. (and further fascicles). London.

Bundesgesetzblatt II.

Davies, H. 1947. Constitutions, Electoral Laws, Treaties of States in the Near and Middle East. Durham.

Hurewitz, J. 1956. Diplomacy in the Near and Middle East. A Documentary Record: 1914-1956, 2 vols. Princeton.

– 1975/1979. The Middle East and North Africa in World Politics. A Documentary Record, 2 vols. New Haven.

Mansoor, M. 1965. Legal and Documentary Arabic Reader (Arabic: Qirāʾāt mina l-ᶜarabīya al-qaḍāʾīya wa-l-waṯāʾiqīya). Leiden.

Rohn, P. 1984. World Treaty Index, 5 vols., 2nd edition. Santa Barbara.

Société des Nations. Recueil des traités et des engagements internationaux enrégistrés par le Secrétariat de la Société des Nations, vol. 1 (1920) - vol. 205 (1944-46). (:=*LNTS*).

United Nations. Treaty Series. Publication of Treaties and International Agreements Registered or Filed and Recorded with the Secretariat of the United Nations, vol. 1 (1946-47) - open. (:=*UNTS*).

D. List of quoted treaties and declarations

I. Bilateral treaties and declarations (in chronological order)

Trattato di amicizia e commercio tra il Regno d'Italia e l'Impero Etiopico, signed on 2 May 1889.[3]

Grande Bretagne et Iraq. Traité d'alliance, avec protocole, signés à Bagdad, les 10 octobre 1922 et 30 avril 1923 respectivement, *LNTS*, vol. 35 (1925), pp. 15ff.

Irak et Syrie et Liban. Convention douanière du 16 janvier 1925, et notes portant amendement au texte arabe de la convention. Beyrouth, 31 janvier, Bagdad, 2 mai, et Beyrouth, 9 juin 1925, *LNTS*, vol. 49 (1926), pp. 9ff.

---

[3] For references, cf. *Rubenson* 1964: 11.

Arabie Saoudienne et Irak. Traité de fraternité arabe et d'alliance. Signé à Bagdad, le 2 avril 1936, *LNTS*, vol. 174 (1937), pp. 131ff.

Exchange of Notes between the United States of America and the Kingdom of the Yemen Constituting an Agreement Relating to Friendship and Commerce. Sana'a, 4 May 1946, *UNTS*, vol. 4 (1947), pp. 165ff.

Iraq and Transjordan. Treaty of Brotherhood and Alliance. Signed at Baghdad, on 14 April 1947, *UNTS*, vol. 23 (1948/1949), pp. 147ff.

Iraq and Turkey. Pact of Mutual Co-operation (with exchange of letters). Signed at Baghdad, on 24 February 1955, *UNTS*, vol. 233 (1956), pp. 200ff.

Iraq and United Kingdom of Great Britain and Northern Ireland. Special Agreement (with exchange of notes). Signed at Baghdad, on 4 April 1955, *UNTS*, vol. 233 (1956), pp. 220ff.

Kuwait and Iraq. Agreed Minutes regarding the restoration of friendly relations, recognition and related matters. Signed at Baghdad, on 4 October 1963, *UNTS*, vol. 485 (1964), pp. 322ff.

Israel and Egypt. Treaty of Peace (with annexes and maps). Signed at Washington on 26 March 1979, *UNTS*, vol. 1136 (1979), pp. 100ff.

Declaration of Principles on Interim Self-Government Arrangements, signed at Washington, D.C., on 13 September 1993 by the Government of the State of Israel and the Palestine Liberation Organization and witnessed by the United States of America and the Russian Federation. UN-doc. A/48/486 = UN-doc. S/26560.

Agreement on the Gaza Strip and the Jericho Area. Cairo, 4 May 1994, UN-doc. A/49/180 = UN-doc. S/1994/727.

Washington Declaration, signed at Washington, D.C., on 25 July 1994 by the Governments of Jordan and Israel and witnessed by the United States of America. UN-doc. A/49/300 = UN-doc. S/1994/939.

Treaty of Peace between the State of Israel and the Hashemite Kingdon of Jordan. 26 October 1994. UN-doc. A/50/73 = UN-doc. S/1995/83.

Protocol Concerning the Redeployment in Hebron, Jerusalem, January 17, 1997 (not a UN-doc.).

Deutsch-Tschechische Erklärung über die gegenseitigen Beziehungen und deren künftige Entwicklung, signed on 21 January 1997, Bulletin [of the German Federal Government] No. 7, January 24, 1997.

2. Pluri- and multilateral treaties and declarations (in chronological order)

Tripartite (Sykes-Picot) Agreement on the Partition of the Ottoman Empire: Britain, France, and Russia. 26 April - 23 October 1916.[4]

---

[4] For references, cf. *Hurewitz* 1979, vol. 2: 60ff.

Tripartite (Sèvres) Agreement on Anatolia: The British Empire, France, and Italy. 10 August 1920.[5]

(Lausanne) Treaty of Peace with Turkey and Accompanying Straits Convention and Declaration on the Administration of Justice. 24 July 1923.[6]

Treaty of Nonagression (Saᶜdabad Treaty): Afghanistan, Iran, Iraq and Turkey. 8 July 1937, *LNTS*, vol. 190 (1938), pp. 21ff.

Pact of the League of Arab States. Signed at Cairo, on 22 March 1945, *UNTS*, vol. 70 (1950), pp. 237ff.

Convention on the Prevention and Punishment of the Crime of Genocide. Approved and proposed for signature and ratification or accession by General Assembly resolution 260 A (III) of 9 December 1948, *UNTS*, vol. 78 (1951), pp. 277ff.

Universal Declaration of Human Rights. Adopted and proclaimed by General Assembly resolution 217 A (III) of 10 December 1948.

Charter of the Organization of African Unity. Done at Addis Ababa, on 25 May 1963, *UNTS*, vol. 479 (1963), pp. 40ff.

International Convention on the Elimination of All Forms of Racial Discrimination (CERD). Adopted and opened for signature and ratification by General Assembly resolution 2106 A (XX) of 21 December 1965, *UNTS*, vol. 660 (1969), pp. 195ff.

International Covenant on Economic, Social and Cultural Rights (CESCR). Adopted and opened for signature, ratification and accession by General Assembly resolution 2200 A (XXI) of 16 December 1966, *UNTS*, vol. 993 (1975), pp. 3ff.

International Covenant on Civil and Political Rights (CCPR). Adopted and opened for signature, ratification and accession by General Assembly resolution 2200 A (XXI) of 16 December 1966, *UNTS*, vol. 999 (1976), pp. 171ff and vol. 1057 (1977), pp. 407ff.

Optional Protocol to the International Covenant on Civil and Political Rights. Adopted and opened for signature, ratification and accession by General Assembly resolution 2200 A (XXI) of 16 December 1966, *UNTS*, vol. 999 (1976), pp. 171ff.

Vienna Convention on the Law of Treaties. Concluded at Vienna on 23 May 1969, *UNTS*, vol. 1155 (1980), pp. 331ff.

Declaration on Principles of International Law concerning Friendly Relations and Co-operation among States in Accordance with the Charter of the United Nations. Adopted by General Assembly Resolution 2625 (XXV) of 24 October 1970.

France, Union of Soviet Socialist Republics, United Kingdom of Great Britain and Northern Ireland and United States of America. Quadripartite Agreement (with annexes, agreed minutes and exchange of notes). Done in the building formerly occupied by the Allied Control Council in the American Sector of Berlin on 3 September 1971, *UNTS*, vol. 880 (1973), pp. 130ff.

---

5 For references, cf. *Hurewitz* 1979, vol. 2: 225ff.

6 For references, cf. *Hurewitz* 1979, vol. 2: 325ff.

Charter of the Islamic Conference. Adopted by the Third Islamic Conference of Foreign Ministers at Djidda, on 4 March 1972, *UNTS*, vol. 914 (1974), pp. 103ff.

International Convention on the Suppression and Punishment of the Crime of Apartheid. Adopted and opened for signature and ratification by General Assembly resolution 3068 A (XXVIII) of 30 November 1973, *UNTS*, vol. 1015 (1976), pp. 243ff.

Convention on the Elimination of All Forms of Discrimination against Women. Adopted and opened for signature, ratification and accession by General Assembly resolution 34/180 of 18 December 1979, *UNTS*, vol. 1249 (1981), pp. 13ff.

Bahrain, Kuwait, Oman, Qatar, Saudi Arabia, and United Arab Emirates: Charter of the Co-operation Council for the Arab States of the Gulf (with Rules of procedures of the Supreme Council and of the Commission for Settlement of Disputes). Concluded at Abu Dhabi on 25 May 1981, *UNTS*, vol. 1288 (1982), pp. 131ff.

Declaration on the Elimination of All Forms of Intolerance and of Discrimination Based on Religion or Belief. Proclaimed by General Assembly resolution 36/55 of 25 Nevember 1981.

Convention against Torture and other Cruel, Inhuman or Degrading Treatment or Punishment (CAT). Adopted and opened for signature, ratification and accession by General Assembly resolution 39/46 of 10 December 1984, *UNTS*, vol. 1465 (1996), pp. 85ff.

Convention on the Rights of the Child. Adopted and opened for signature, ratification and accession by General Assembly resolution 44/25 of 20 November 1989.

Second Optional Protocol to the International Covenant on Civil and Political Rights, aiming at the abolition of the death penalty. Adopted and proclaimed by General Assembly resolution 44/128 of 15 December 1989.

Declaration on the Rights of Persons Belonging to National or Ethnic, Religious and Linguistic Minorities. Adopted by General Assembly Resolution 47/135 of 18 December 1992.

E. List of quoted UN documents

I. List of letters, resolutions, verbatim records, special reports, legal references, and other documents

UN-doc. A/32/237.

UN-doc. A/36/PV.71.

UN-doc. A/45/1018 = S/22655.

UN-doc. A/45/944.

UN-doc. A/45/1018 = S/22655.

UN-doc. A/48/486 = S/26560.

UN-doc. A/49/180 = S/1994/727.

UN-doc. A/49/288 = S/1994/903.

UN-doc. A/49/300 = S/1994/939.

UN-doc. A/50/73 = S/1995/83.

UN-doc. A/9030.

UN-doc. A/C.1/PV.2016.

UN-doc. A/C.3/240.

UN-doc. A/C.3/241.

UN-doc. A/C.3/247.

UN-doc. A/C.3/247/Rev.1.

UN-doc. A/C.3/332.

UN-doc. A/C.3/36/SR.29.

UN-doc. A/CN.4/470 + Corr.1-2.

UN-doc. A/CN.4/477 + Add.1 + Add.1/Corr.1.

UN-doc. A/CONF.62/DC/WP.2.

UN-doc. A/CONF.157/PC/62/Add.18.

UN-doc. A/CONF.171/13.

UN-doc. A/CONF.176/1*.

UN-doc. A/PV.2291.

UN-doc. A/RES/181 (II).

UN-doc. A/RES/217 (III).

UN-doc. A/RES/2200 (XXI).

UN-doc. A/RES/2200A(XXI).

UN-doc. A/RES/34/180.

UN-doc. A/RES/35/55.

UN-doc. A/RES/36/55.

UN-doc. A/RES/44/25.

UN-doc. A/RES/46/86.

UN-doc. A/RES/47/135.

UN-doc. CEDAW/C/1997/4.

UN-doc. E/CN.4/1987/WG.5/WP.1.

UN-doc. E/CN.4/1992/31 = S/23685/Add.1.

UN-doc. E/CN.4/1995/55.

UN-doc. E/CN.4/1995/56.

UN-doc. E/CN.4/1995/58.

UN-doc. E/CN.4/1995/64.

UN-doc. E/CN.4/1995/91 + Add.1.

UN-doc. E/CN.4/1996/88.

UN-doc. E/CN.4/Sub.2/1994/10.

UN-doc. E/CN.4/Sub.2/1995/42.

UN-doc. HR/CT/403.

UN-doc. S/7930.

UN-doc. S/21348.

UN-doc. S/21494.

UN-doc. S/21505.

UN-doc. S/21566.

UN-doc. S/21651.

UN-doc. S/21790.

UN-doc. S/21799.

UN-doc. S/21883.

UN-doc. S/21884.

UN-doc. S/22203.

UN-doc. S/22204.

UN-doc. S/22452.

UN-doc. S/22456.

UN-doc. S/22485.

UN-doc. S/22629.

UN-doc. S/22728.

UN-doc. S/23102.

UN-doc. S/24118.

UN-doc. S/34311.

UN-doc. S/26887.

UN-doc. S/1994/651.

UN-doc. S/1994/761.

UN-doc. S/1994/804.

UN-doc. S/1994/869.

UN-doc. S/1994/870.

UN-doc. S/1994/928.

UN-doc. S/1994/1288.

UN-doc. S/1995/633.

UN-doc. S/1996/447.

UN-doc. S/1997/160.

UN-doc. S/PRST/1997/16.

UN-doc. S/PV.2932.

UN-doc. ST/CS/SER.F/297/Rev.2.

UN-doc. ST/CS/SER.F/348.

UN-doc. ST/HR/4/Rev.8.

UN-doc. ST/HR/4/Rev.11.

UN-doc. ST/HR/4/Rev.14.

UN-doc. ST/LEG/SER. E.

UN-doc. ST/LEG/SER.E/11.

UN-doc. ST/LEG/SER.E/13.

UN-doc. ST/LIB/SER.B/22/Add.1.

UN-doc. ST/OGS/SER.E/73.

UN-doc. ST/SG/SER.A/273.

II. List of periodic reports by Arab states and Iran, summary records of discussions, and concluding observations

The list is to be read as follows: for instance, an element of the chart in the form

Reports (language)		Summary Records (date)		Observations
<<A>>	--->	<<SR.1 (...)>>		
<<B>>	--->	<<SR.2 (...)>>		
		<<SR.3 (...)>>	--->	<<C>>

means that the concluding observations on report "A", which was discussed in the meeting whose summary records appear as "SR.1", and on report "B", which was discussed in the meetings whose summary records appear as "SR.2" and "SR.3", are reproduced in "C".

Algeria

Reports (language)		Summary Records (date)		Observations
E/1990/5/Add.22 (F)	--->	E/C.12/1995/SR.46 (30-11-95)		
(arts. 1-15)		E/C.12/1995/SR.47 (01-12-95)		
		E/C.12/1995/SR.48 (01-12-95)	--->	E/1996/22

CCPR/C/62/Add.1 (F)	--->	CCPR/C/SR.1125 (25-03-92)		
		CCPR/C/SR.1128 (27-03-92)		
		CCPR/C/SR.1129 (27-03-92)	--->	A/47/40
CERD/C/R.50/Add.9 (F)	--->	CERD/C/SR.182 (01-04-74)	--->	A/29/18
CERD/C/R.77/Add.13 (F)				
CERD/C/R.98/Add.2 (F)	--->	CERD/C/SR.342 (02-08-77)		
		CERD/C/SR.343 (02-08-77)	--->	A/32/18
CERD/C/48/Add.3 (F)	--->	CERD/C/SR.444 (06-08-79)		
		CERD/C/SR.445 (07-08-79)	--->	A/34/18
CERD/C/75/Add.4 (F)	--->	CERD/C/SR.536 (10-08-81)		
		CERD/C/SR.537 (10-08-81)	--->	A/36/18
CERD/C/106/Add.4 (F)	--->	CERD/C/SR.653 (07-03-84)		
		CERD/C/SR.654 (07-03-84)	--->	A/39/18
CERD/C/131/Add.3 (F)	--->	CERD/C/SR.769 (17-03-86)		
		CERD/C/SR.770 (17-03-86)	--->	A/42/18
CERD/C/158/Add.2 (F)				
+ Add.6 (F)	--->	CERD/C/SR.841 (15-08-89)	--->	A/44/18
CERD/C/209/Add.4 (F)	--->	CERD/C/SR.962 (04-03-93)		
		CERD/C/SR.963 (04-03-93)		
		CERD/C/SR.983 (18-03-93)	--->	A/48/18
CAT/C/9/Add.5 (F)	--->	CAT/C/SR.79 (25-04-91)		
		CAT/C/SR.80 (25-04-91)	--->	A/46/46

Egypt

Reports (language)		Summary Records (date)		Observations
HRI/CORE/1/Add.19 (A)				
CCPR/C/26/Add.1/Rev.1	--->	CCPR/C/SR.499 (02-04-84)		
(A/E)		CCPR/C/SR.500 (02-04-84)		
		CCPR/C/SR.505 (05-04-84)	--->	A/39/40
CCPR/C/51/Add.7 (A)				
+ Corr.1 (A)	--->	CCPR/C/SR.1244 (19-07-93)		

		CCPR/C/SR.1245 (19-07-93)		
		CCPR/C/SR.1246 (20-07-93)		
		CCPR/C/SR.1247 (20-07-93)	--->	A/48/40
CRC/C/3/Add.6 (A)	--->	CRC/C/SR.66 (25-01-93)		
		CRC/C/SR.67 (25-01-93)		
		CRC/C/SR.68 (26-01-93)	--->	A/49/41
CEDAW/C/5/Add.10 (A)				
+ Amend. 1 (A)	--->	CEDAW/C/SR.34 (30-03-84)		
		CEDAW/C/SR.39 (03-04-84)	--->	A/39/45
CEDAW/C/13/Add.2 (A)				
+ Amend. 1 (A)	--->	CEDAW/C/SR.164 (31-01-90)		
		CEDAW/C/SR.165 (31-01-90)	--->	A/45/38
CERD/C/R.3/Add.34 (E)	--->	CERD/C/SR.49 (16-04-71)		
(together with Syria)		CERD/C/SR.50 (19-04-71)	--->	A/8418
CERD/C/R.30/Add.36 (E)	--->	CERD/C/SR.135 (27-04-73)		
		CERD/C/SR.136 (30-04-73)	--->	A/28/18
CERD/C/R.70/Add.15 (A)	--->	CERD/C/SR.202 (13-08-74)	--->	A/29/18
CERD/C/90/Add.29 (A)	--->	CERD/C/SR.345 (03-08-77)	--->	A/32/18
CERD/C/20/Add.11 (A)	--->	CERD/C/SR.395 (31-07-78)	--->	A/33/18
+ Add.24 (A)				
CERD/C/66/Add.4 (A)	--->	CERD/C/SR.472 (03-04-80)	--->	A/35/18
CERD/C/91/Add.15 (A)	--->	CERD/C/SR.584 (09-08-82)		
		CERD/C/SR.585 (09-08-82)	--->	A/37/18
CERD/C/149/Add.22 (A)				
CERD/C/172/Add.12 (A)	--->	CERD/C/SR.837 (11-08-89)	--->	A/44/18
CERD/C/226/Add.13 (A)	--->	CERD/C/SR.1048 (04-08-94)		
		CERD/C/SR.1049 (05-08-94)		
		CERD/C/SR.1065 (17-08-94)	--->	A/49/18
CAT/C/5/Add.23 (A)	--->	CAT/C/SR.14 (20-04-89)		
		CAT/C/SR.15 (20-04-89)	--->	A/44/46

CAT/C/17/Add.11 (A)	--->	CAT/C/SR.162 (12-11-93)		
		CAT/C/SR.163/Add.1 (12-11-93)		
		CAT/C/SR.170 (18-11-93)	--->	A/49/44

Iraq

Reports (language)		Summary Records (date)		Observations
E/1980/6/Add.14 (A)				
(arts. 10-12)	--->	E/1981/WG.1/SR.12 (23-04-81)	--->	E/1981/64
E/1982/3/Add.26 (A)	--->	E/1985/WG.1/SR.3 (23-04-85)		
(arts. 13-15)		E/1985/WG.1/SR.4 (24-04-85)	--->	E/1985/18
E/1984/6/Add.3 (A)				
+ Add.8 (A)	--->	E/1985/WG.1/SR.8 (30-04-85)		
(arts. 6-9)		E/1985/WG.1/SR.11 (02-05-85)	--->	E/1985/18
E/1986/4/Add.3 (A)	--->	E/1986/WG.1/SR.8 (23-04-86)		
(arts. 10-12)		E/1986/WG.1/SR.11 (25-04-86)	--->	E/1986/49
E/1990/7/Add.15 (A)	--->	E/C.12/1994/SR.11 (09-05-94)		
(arts. 13-15)		E/C.12/1994/SR.14 (10-05-94)	--->	E/1995/22
CCPR/C/1/Add.45 (E)	--->	CCPR/C/SR.199 (20-03-80)		
		CCPR/C/SR.200 (20-03-80)		
		CCPR/C/SR.203 (24-03-80)		
		CCPR/C/SR.204 (24-03-80)	--->	A/35/40
CCPR/C/37/Add.3 (A)	--->	CCPR/C/SR.744 (15-07-87)		
		CCPR/C/SR.745 (15-07-87)		
		CCPR/C/SR.746 (16-07-87)		
		CCPR/C/SR.747 (16-07-87)		
		CCPR/C/SR.748 (17-07-87)	--->	A/42/40
CCPR/C/64/Add.6 (A)	--->	CCPR/C/SR.1080 (18-07-91)		
		CCPR/C/SR.1081 (18-07-91)		
		CCPR/C/SR.1082 (19-07-91)	--->	A/46/40
		CCPR/C/SR.1106 (30-10-91)		
		CCPR/C/SR.1107 (30-10-91)		
		CCPR/C/SR.1108 (31-10-91)	--->	A/47/40

CEDAW/C/5/Add.66/	--->	CEDAW/C/SR.212 (20-01-94)		
Rev. 1 (A)		CEDAW/C/SR.213 (20-01-94)		
		CEDAW/C/SR.216 (22-01-94)	--->	A/48/38

CERD/C/R.25 (E)	--->	CERD/C/SR.68 (27-08-71)		
CERD/C/R.53/Add.1 (E)				
+ Corr.1(E)	--->	CERD/C/SR.182 (01-04-74)	--->	A/29/18
CERD/C/R.78/Add.1 (E)	--->	CERD/C/SR.275 (02-04-76)	--->	A/31/18
CERD/C/50/Add.1 (A)	--->	CERD/C/SR.458 (25-03-80)		
		CERD/C/SR.459 (26-03-80)	--->	A/35/18
CERD/C/76/Add.5 (A)	--->	CERD/C/SR.631 (14-07-81)		
		CERD/C/SR.632 (14-07-81)	--->	A/38/18
CERD/C/107/Add.2 (A)				
+ Add.6 (A)	--->	CERD/C/SR.683 (15-08-84)	--->	A/39/18
CERD/C/132/Add.2 (A)	--->	CERD/C/SR.765 (13-03-86)		
		CERD/C/SR.766 (13-03-86)		
		CERD/C/SR.767 (14-03-86)	--->	A/42/18
CERD/C/159/Add.2 (A)				
CERD/C/185/Add.2 (A)	--->	CERD/C/SR.917 (07-08-91)		
		CERD/C/SR.920 (08-08-91)		
		CERD/C/SR.921 (09-08-91)		
		CERD/C/SR.922 (09-08-91)	--->	A/46/18

Jordan

Reports (language)		Summary Records (date)		Observations
HRI/CORE/1/Add.18/Rev.1 (A)				
E/1982/3/Add.38/Rev.1 (A)				
(arts. 13-15)	--->	E/C.12/1990/SR.30 (28-11-90)		
		E/C.12/1990/SR.31 (28-11-90)		
		E/C.12/1990/SR.32 (29-11-90)	--->	E/1991/23
E/1984/6/Add.15 (A)	--->	E/C.12/1987/SR.6 (11-03-87)		
(arts. 6-9)		E/C.12/1987/SR.7 (12-03-87)		
		E/C.12/1987/SR.8 (12-03-87)	--->	E/1987/28

E/1986/3/Add.6 (A)				
(arts. 10-12)	--->	E/C.12/1987/SR.8 (12-03-87)	--->	E/1987/28
E/1989/5/Add.6 (A)	--->	pending	--->	pending
(arts. 6-15)				
CCPR/C/1/Add.24 (A)	--->	CCPR/C/SR.103 (01-08-78)	--->	A/33/40
CCPR/C/1/Add.55 (E)	--->	CCPR/C/SR.331 (29-10-81)		
		CCPR/C/SR.332 (29-10-81)	--->	A/37/40
CCPR/C/1/Add.56 (A)	--->	CCPR/C/SR.361 (13-07-82)		
		CCPR/C/SR.362 (13-07-82)	--->	no observ.
CCPR/C/46/Add.4 (A)	--->	CCPR/C/SR.1077 (17-07-91)		
		CCPR/C/SR.1078 (17-07-91)		
		CCPR/C/SR.1079 (18-07-91)	--->	A/46/40
CCPR/C/76/Add.1 (A)	--->	CCPR/C/SR.1321 (05-07-94)		
		CCPR/C/SR.1322 (05-07-94)		
		CCPR/C/SR.1323 (06-07-94)		
		CCPR/C/SR.1324 (06-07-94)	--->	A/49/40
CRC/C/8/Add.4 (A)	--->	CRC/C/SR.143 (13-04-94)		
		CRC/C/SR.144 (13-04-94)		
		CRC/C/SR.145 (14-04-94)	--->	A/51/41
CERD/C/R.75/Add.3 (E)	--->	CERD/C/SR.289 (13-04-76)	--->	A/31/18
CERD/C/R.97/Add.1 (E)	--->	CERD/C/SR.346 (04-08-77)		
		CERD/C/SR.347 (04-08-77)	--->	A/32/18
CERD/C/74/Add.2 (A)	--->	CERD/C/SR.565 (11-03-82)	--->	A/37/18
CERD/C/105/Add.3 (A)				
+ Add.6 (A)	--->	CERD/C/SR.685 (15-08-84)	--->	A/39/18
CERD/C/130/Add.3 (A)				
CERD/C/183/Add.1 (A)	--->	CERD/C/SR.864 (07-08-90)	--->	A/45/18
CAT/C/16/Add.5 (A)	--->	CAT/C/SR.218 (01-05-95)		
		CAT/C/SR.219 (01-05-95)	--->	A/50/44

Kuwait

Reports (language)		Summary Records (date)		Observations
CERD/C/R.3/Add.24 (E)				
+ Add.36 (E)	--->	CERD/C/SR.44 (14-04-71)		
		CERD/C/SR.47 (15-04-71)		
		CERD/C/SR.56 (22-04-71)		
CERD/C/R.30/Add.4 (E)	--->	CERD/C/SR.128 (24-04-73)	--->	A/28/18
CERD/C/R.70/Add.6 (E)	--->	CERD/C/SR.190 (05-04-74)	--->	A/29/18
CERD/C/R.90/Add.8 (E)	--->	CERD/C/SR.280 (07-04-76)	--->	A/31/18
CERD/C/20/Add.13 (E)				
+ Corr.1 (E)	--->	CERD/C/SR.396 (01-08-78)		
		CERD/C/SR.397 (01-08-78)	--->	A/33/18
CERD/C/66/Add.23 (A)	--->	CERD/C/SR.509 (30-03-81)	--->	A/36/18
CERD/C/91/Add.3 (A)	--->	CERD/C/SR.563 (10-03-82)	--->	A/37/18
CERD/C/118/Add.3 (A)	--->	CERD/C/SR.687 (17-08-84)	--->	A/39/18
CERD/C/149/Add.16 (A)	--->	CERD/C/SR.824 (08-08-88)	--->	A/43/18
CERD/C/226/Add.5 (A)	--->	CERD/C/SR.995 (09-08-93)		
		CERD/C/SR.996 (09-08-93)		
		CERD/C/SR.1008 (17-08-93)	--->	A/48/18

Lebanon

Reports (language)		Summary Records (date)		Observations
HRI/CORE/1/Add.27 (F)				
E/1990/5/Add.16 (F)	--->	E/C.12/1993/SR.14 (25-05-93)		
(arts. 6-15)		E/C.12/1993/SR.16 (26-05-93)		
		E/C.12/1993/SR.21 (28-05-93)	--->	E/1994/23
CCPR/C/1/Add.60 (F)	--->	CCPR/C/SR.442 (14-07-83)		
		CCPR/C/SR.443 (14-07-83)		
		CCPR/C/SR.444 (15-07-83)		
		CCPR/C/SR.446 (18-07-83)	--->	A/38/40

CRC/C/8/Add.23 (E)	--->	pending	--->	pending
CERD/C/R.33/Add.4 (E)	--->	CERD/C/SR.152 (10-08-73)		
		CERD/C/SR.238 (27-06-75)		
+ Add.13 (A/F)	--->	CERD/C/SR.255 (08-08-75)	--->	A/30/18
CERD/C/65/Add.4 (A/F)	--->	CERD/C/SR.516 (02-04-81)	--->	A/36/18
		CERD/C/SR.923 (12-08-91)	--->	A/46/18

Libyan Arab Jamahiriya

Reports (language)		Summary Records (date)		Observations
E/1982/3/Add.6 + Add.25 (A)				
(arts. 13-15)	--->	E/1983/WG.1/SR.16 (28-04-83)		
		E/1983/WG.1/SR.17 (29-04-83)	--->	E/1983/41
CCPR/C/1/Add.3 (A)				
+ Corr.1 (A)				
CCPR/C/1/Add.20 (A)	--->	CCPR/C/SR.51 (18-01-78)	--->	A/33/40
CCPR/C/28/Add.16 (A)	--->	CCPR/C/SR.1275 (26-10-93)		
		CCPR/C/SR.1276 (28-10-93)	--->	A/49/40
		CCPR/C/SR.1376 (28-10-94)		
		CCPR/C/SR.1377 (28-10-94)	--->	A/50/40
CEDAW/C/LIB/1 (A)				
+ Add.1 (A)	--->	CEDAW/C/SR.237 (19-01-94)		
		CEDAW/C/SR.240 (21-01-94)	--->	A/49/38
CERD/C/R.3/Add.30 (E)	--->	CERD/C/SR.47 (15-04-71)		
		CERD/C/SR.56 (22-04-71)		
CERD/C/R.30/Add.27 (E)	--->	CERD/C/SR.144 (04-05-73)	--->	A/28/18
CERD/C/R.70/Add.31 (A)	--->	CERD/C/SR.237 (11-06-75)	--->	A/30/18
CERD/C/R.90/Add.18 (F)	--->	CERD/C/SR.302 (06-08-76)	--->	A/31/18
CERD/C/20/Add.29 (A)	--->	CERD/C/SR.426 (06-04-79)		
		CERD/C/SR.427 (09-04-79)	--->	A/34/18
CERD/C/172/Add.2 (A)	--->	CERD/C/SR.852 (22-08-89)	--->	A/44/18

CAT/C/9/Add.7 (A)	--->	CAT/C/SR.93 (14-11-91)	--->	A/47/44
CAT/C/9/Add.12/				
Rev.1 (A)	--->	CAT/C/SR.130 (17-11-92)		
		CAT/C/SR.135 (19-11-92)		
		+ Add.2 (19-11-92)	--->	A/48/44
CAT/C/25/Add.3 (A)	--->	CAT/C/SR.201 (15-11-94)		
		CAT/C/SR.202 (15-11-94)		
		+ Add.2 (15-11-94)	--->	A/50/44

Morocco

Reports (language)		Summary Records (date)		Observations
HRI/CORE/1/Add.23 (F)				
E/1990/5/Add.13 (F)	--->	E/C.12/1994/SR.8 (05-05-94)		
(arts. 6-15)		E/C.12/1994/SR.9 (05-05-94)		
		E/C.12/1994/SR.10 (06-05-94)	--->	E/1995/22
CCPR/C/10/Add.2 (F)	--->	CCPR/C/SR.327 (27-10-81)		
		CCPR/C/SR.328 (27-10-81)		
		CCPR/C/SR.332 (29-10-81)	--->	A/37/40
CCPR/C/42/Add.10 (F)	--->	CCPR/C/SR.1032 (07-11-90)		
		CCPR/C/SR.1033 (07-11-90)		
		CCPR/C/SR.1034 (08-11-90)		
		CCPR/C/SR.1035 (08-11-90)	--->	A/46/40
		CCPR/C/SR.1094 (22-10-91)		
		CCPR/C/SR.1096 (23-10-91)	--->	no observ.
CCPR/C/76/Add.3 (F)				
+ Add.4 (F)	--->	CCPR/C/SR.1364 (20-10-94)		
		CCPR/C/SR.1365 (20-10-94)		
		CCPR/C/SR.1366 (21-10-94)	--->	A/50/40
CERD/C/R.33/Add.1 (F)	--->	CERD/C/SR.111 (17-08-72)		
		CERD/C/SR.112 (18-08-72)	--->	A/27/18
CERD/C/R.65/Add.1 (F)	--->	CERD/C/SR.188 (04-04-74)	--->	A/29/18

CERD/C/R.88/Add.6 (F)	--->	CERD/C/SR.327 (05-04-77)		
		CERD/C/SR.328 (05-04-77)	--->	A/32/18
CERD/C/18/Add.1 (F)	--->	CERD/C/SR.370 (24-03-78)	--->	A/33/18
CERD/C/65/Add.1 (F)	--->	CERD/C/SR.481 (06-08-80)	--->	A/35/18
CERD/C/90/Add.6 (F)	--->	CERD/C/SR.602 (09-03-83)		
		CERD/C/SR.603 (10-03-83)	--->	A/38/18
CERD/C/117/Add.1 (F)	--->	CERD/C/SR.718 (18-03-85)	--->	A/40/18
CERD/C/148/Add.2 (F)	--->	CERD/C/SR.822 (05-08-88)	--->	A/43/18
CERD/C/225/Add.1 (F)	--->	CERD/C/SR.1020 (04-03-94)		
		CERD/C/SR.1021 (04-03-94)		
		CERD/C/SR.1038 (17-03-94)	--->	A/49/18
CAT/C/24/Add.2 (F)	--->	CAT/C/SR.203 (16-11-94)		
		CAT/C/SR.204 (16-11-94)		
		+ Add.2 (16-11-94)	--->	A/50/44

Qatar

Reports (language)		Summary Records (date)		Observations
CERD/C/26 (F)	--->	CERD/C/SR.371 (27-04-78)	--->	A/33/18
CERD/C/46/Add.2 (A)	--->	CERD/C/SR.480 (05-08-80)	--->	A/35/18
CERD/C/73/Add.1 (A)	--->	CERD/C/SR.557 (05-03-82)	--->	A/37/18
CERD/C/104/Add.1 (A)	--->	CERD/C/SR.667 (16-03-84)	--->	A/39/18
CERD/C/156/Add.2 (A)				
CERD/C/182/Add.1 (A)	--->	CERD/C/SR.874 (14-08-90)	--->	A/45/18
CERD/C/207/Add.1 (A)	--->	CERD/C/SR.964 (05-03-93)		
		CERD/C/SR.983 (18-03-94)	--->	A/48/18

Sudan

Reports (language)		Summary Records (date)		Observations
CCPR/C/45/Add.3 (A)	--->	CCPR/C/SR.1065 (08-07-91)		
		CCPR/C/SR.1067 (10-07-91)	--->	A/46/40
CRC/C/3/Add.3 (A)	--->	CRC/C/SR.69 (26-01-93)		
		CRC/C/SR.70 (27-01-93)		

		CRC/C/SR.71 (27-01-93)	--->	A/49/41
CRC/C/3/Add.20 (A)	--->	CRC/C/SR.89 (29-09-93)		
		CRC/C/SR.90 (29-09-93)	--->	A/49/41
CERD/C/87/Add.1 (E)				
+ Corr.1 (E)	--->	CERD/C/SR.580 (05-08-82)		
		CERD/C/SR.581 (05-08-82)	--->	A/37/18
CERD/C/114/Add.1 (E)	--->	CERD/C/SR.680 (13-08-84)		
CERD/C/114/Add.1/				
Rev.1 (E)	--->	CERD/C/SR.784 (06-03-87)		
		CERD/C/SR.785 (06-03-87)	--->	A/42/18
CERD/C/222/Add.1 (E)	--->	CERD/C/SR.968 (09-03-93)		
		CERD/C/SR.970 (10-03-93)		
		CERD/C/SR.971 (10-03-93)		
		CERD/C/SR.983 (18-03-93)	--->	A/48/18
CERD/C/222/Add.2 (E)	--->	CERD/C/SR.1052 (08-08-94)		
		CERD/C/SR.1053 (09-08-94)		
		CERD/C/SR.1068 (18-08-94)	--->	A/49/18

Syrian Arab Republic

Reports (language)		Summary Records (date)		Observations
E/1978/8/Add.25 (A/F)				
+ Add.31 (A) (arts. 6-9)	--->	E/1983/WG.1/SR.2 (19-04-83)	--->	E/1983/41
E/1980/6/Add.9 (A/E)				
(arts. 10-12)	--->	E/1981/WG.1/SR.4 (15-04-81)	--->	E/1981/64
E/1990/6/Add.1 (A)	--->	E/C.12/1991/SR.7 (28-11-91)		
(arts. 6-15)		E/C.12/1991/SR.9 (29-11-91)		
		E/C.12/1991/SR.11 (02-12-91)	--->	E/1992/23
CCPR/C/1/Add.1/				
Rev.1 (E)	--->	CCPR/C/SR.26 (16-08-77)	--->	A/32/44
CCPR/C/1/Add.31 (E)	--->	CCPR/C/SR.158 (02-08-79)		
		CCPR/C/SR.160 (03-08-79)	--->	A/34/40

CERD/C/R.3/Add.38 (E)				
+ Add.43 (E)	--->	CERD/C/SR.50 (19-04-71)		
		CERD/C/SR.56 (22-04-71)		
		CERD/C/SR.57 (23-04-71)		
+ Add.49 (E)	--->	CERD/C/SR.66 (26-08-71)		
(together with Egypt)		CERD/C/SR.67 (27-08-71)		
		CERD/C/SR.70 (30-08-71)		
		CERD/C/SR.71 (31-08-71)		
		CERD/C/SR.79 (08-09-71)	--->	A/8418
CERD/C/R.30/Add.32 (E)	--->	CERD/C/SR.129 (24-04-73)		
		CERD/C/SR.131 (25-04-73)	--->	A/28/18
CERD/C/R.70/Add.19 (E)	--->	CERD/C/SR.206 (15-08-74)		
		CERD/C/SR.207 (16-08-74)		
		CERD/C/SR.215 (22-08-74)	--->	A/29/18
CERD/C/R.90/Add.23 (E)	--->	CERD/C/SR.323 (01-04-77)		
		CERD/C/SR.324 (01-04-77)	--->	A/32/18
CERD/C/20/Add.21 (E)	--->	CERD/C/SR.416 (30-03-79)	--->	A/34/18
CERD/C/66/Add.22 (E)				
+ Add.32 (E)	--->	CERD/C/SR.507 (27-03-81)		
		CERD/C/SR.508 (27-03-81)		
		CERD/C/SR.519 (06-04-81)		
		CERD/C/SR.520 (06-04-81)		
		CERD/C/SR.526 (09-04-81)	--->	A/36/18
CERD/C/91/Add.36 (E)	--->	CERD/C/SR.661 (13-03-84)		
		CERD/C/SR.662 (13-03-84)	--->	A/39/18
CERD/C/118/Add.32 (A)	--->	CERD/C/SR.817 (02-08-88)	--->	A/43/18
CERD/C/197/Add.6 (A)	--->	CERD/C/SR.932 (16-08-91)	--->	A/46/18

Tunisia

Reports (language)		Summary Records (date)		Observations
HRI/CORE/1/Add.46 (F)				
E/1978/8/Add.3 (F)	--->	E/1980/WG.1/SR.5 (15-04-80		
(arts. 6-9)		E/1980/WG.1/SR.6 (16-04-80)	--->	E/1980/60

E/1986/3/Add.9 (F)	--->	E/C.12/1987/SR.9 (10-02-89)	--->	E/1989/22
(arts. 10-12)				
CCPR/C/1/Add.7/				
Rev.1 (F)	--->	CCPR/C/SR.28 (19-08-77)		
		CCPR/C/SR.29 (22-08-77)	--->	A/32/44
CCPR/C/1/Add.41 (F)				
+ Add.61 (F)				
CCPR/C/28/Add.5/Rev.1	--->	CCPR/C/SR.712 (30-03-87)		
(F)		CCPR/C/SR.713 (30-03-87)		
		CCPR/C/SR.714 (31-03-87)		
		CCPR/C/SR.715 (31-03-87)	--->	A/42/40
CCPR/C/52/Add.5 (F)	--->	CCPR/C/SR.990 (16-07-90)		
		CCPR/C/SR.991 (16-07-90)		
		CCPR/C/SR.992 (17-07-90)	--->	A/45/40
CCPR/C/84/Add.1 (F)	--->	CCPR/C/SR.1360 (18-10-94)		
		CCPR/C/SR.1361 (18-10-94)		
		CCPR/C/SR.1362 (19-10-94)	--->	A/50/40
CRC/C/11/Add.2 (F)	--->	CRC/C/SR.225 (01-06-95)		
		CRC/C/SR.226 (02-06-95)		
		CRC/C/SR.227 (02-06-95)	--->	A/51/41
CEDAW/C/TUN/1-2 (F)	--->	CEDAW/C/SR.269 (23-01-95)		
		CEDAW/C/SR.273 (26-01-95)	--->	A/50/38
CERD/C/R.3/Add.50 (F)	--->	CERD/C/SR.62 (24-08-71)		
		CERD/C/SR.63 (25-08-71)		
CERD/C/R.30/Add.8 (F)				
+ Add.29 (F)	--->	CERD/C/SR.131 (25-04-73)	--->	A/28/18
CERD/C/R.90/Add.3 (F)	--->	CERD/C/SR.279 (06-04-76)	--->	A/31/18
CERD/C/20/Add.3 (F)	--->	CERD/C/SR.388 (26-07-78)	--->	A/33/18
CERD/C/66/Add.11 (F)	--->	CERD/C/SR.484 (07-08-80)		
		CERD/C/SR.485 (08-08-80)	--->	A/35/18

CERD/C/91/Add.28 (F)	--->	CERD/C/SR.610 (15-03-83)		
		CERD/C/SR.611 (16-03-83)	--->	A/38/18
CERD/C/118/Add.27 (F)	--->	CERD/C/SR.755 (06-03-86)		
		CERD/C/SR.756 (06-03-86)	--->	A/42/18
CERD/C/226/Add.10 (F)	--->	CERD/C/SR.1016 (02-03-94)		
		CERD/C/SR.1017 (02-03-94)		
		CERD/C/SR.1034 (15-03-94)	--->	A/49/18

CAT/C/7/Add.3 (F)	--->	CAT/C/SR.46 (25-04-90)		
		CAT/C/SR.47 (25-04-90)	--->	A/45/44

United Arab Emirates

Reports (language)		Summary Records (date)		Observations
CERD/C/R.75/Add.4 (A)	--->	CERD/C/SR.343 (02-08-77)		
		CERD/C/SR.344 (03-08-77)	--->	A/32/18
CERD/C/27 (A)	--->	CERD/C/SR.389 (26-07-78)		
		CERD/C/SR.390 (27-07-78)	--->	A/33/18
CERD/C/47/Add.2 (A)	--->	CERD/C/SR.460 (26-03-80)	--->	A/35/18
CERD/C/74/Add.1 (A)	--->	CERD/C/SR.552 (03-03-82)	--->	A/37/18
CERD/C/105/Add.2 (A)	--->	CERD/C/SR.664 (14-03-84)	--->	A/39/18
CERD/C/130/Add.1 (A)	--->	CERD/C/SR.824 (08-08-88)	--->	A/43/18
		CERD/C/SR.1028 (10-03-94)		
		CERD/C/SR.1037 (15-03-94)	--->	A/49/18

Yemen

Reports (language)		Summary Records (date)		Observations
E/1990/5/Add.2** (A) (arts. 1-15)	--->	pending	--->	pending
CCPR/C/50/Add.2** (A/E) + Corr.1** (A/E)	--->	CCPR/C/SR.927 (25-10-89)		
		CCPR/C/SR.932 (30-10-89)	--->	A/45/40
CCPR/C/82/Add.1 (A)	--->	CCPR/C/SR.1372 (26-10-94)		
		CCPR/C/SR.1373 (26-10-94)		

		CCPR/C/SR.1403 (30-03-95)		
		CCPR/C/SR.1404 (30-03-95)	--->	A/50/40
CRC/C/8/Add.20	--->	CRC/C/SR.261 (09-01-96)		
		CRC/C/SR.262 (09-01-96)		
		CRC/C/SR.263 (10-01-96)	--->	A/51/41
CEDAW/C/5/Add.61** (E)				
CEDAW/C/13/Add.24 ** (A)				
+ Amend. 1** (E)				
CEDAW/C/YEM/3 (A)	--->	CEDAW/C/SR.225 (29-01-93)		
		CEDAW/C/SR.228 (02-02-93)	--->	A/48/38
CERD/C/R.50/Add.12** (E)				
	--->	CERD/C/SR.210 (19-08-74)	--->	A/29/18
CERD/C/R.77/Add.12** (E)				
	--->	CERD/C/SR.328 (05-04-77)	--->	A/32/18
CERD/C/48/Add.7** (A)	--->	CERD/C/SR.461 (27-03-80)		
		CERD/C/SR.462 (27-03-80)	--->	A/35/18
CERD/C/106/Add.6** (A)	--->	CERD/C/SR.657 (09-03-84)	--->	A/39/18
CERD/C/158/Add.10** (A)				
CERD/C/209/Add.2 (A)	--->	CERD/C/SR.946 (07-08-92)		
		CERD/C/SR.950 (11-08-92)	--->	A/47/18

** Reports submitted by the former People's Democratic Republic of Yemen

Iran

Reports		Summary Records		Observations
E/1978/8/Add.2 (withdrawn)				
(arts. 6-9)				
E/1982/3/Add.43	--->	E/C.12/1990/SR.42 (06-12-90)		
(arts. 13-15)		E/C.12/1990/SR.43 (06-12-90)		
		E/C.12/1990/SR.45 (10-12-90)	--->	E/1991/23
E/1990/5/Add.9	--->	E/C.12/1993/SR.7 (18-05-93)		

(arts. 6-12)		E/C.12/1993/SR.8 (19-05-93)		
		E/C.12/1993/SR.9 (19-05-93)		
		E/C.12/1993/SR.20 (28-05-93)	--->	E/1995/22
CCPR/C/1/Add.16				
+ Add.26 + Corr.1	--->	CCPR/C/SR.89 (20-07-78)		
		CCPR/C/SR.90 (20-07-78)		
		CCPR/C/SR.93 (24-07-78)	--->	A/33/40
CCPR/C/1/Add.58	--->	CCPR/C/SR.364 (15-07-82)		
		CCPR/C/SR.365 (15-07-82)		
		CCPR/C/SR.366 (16-07-82)		
		CCPR/C/SR.368 (19-07-82)	--->	A/37/40
CCPR/C/28/Add.15	--->	CCPR/C/SR.1193 (29-10-92)		
		CCPR/C/SR.1194 (29-10-92)		
		CCPR/C/SR.1195 (30-10-92)		
		CCPR/C/SR.1196 (30-10-92)		
		CCPR/C/SR.1230 (07-04-93)		
		CCPR/C/SR.1231 (07-04-93)		
		CCPR/C/SR.1251 (22-07-93)		
		CCPR/C/SR.1252 (23-07-93)		
		CCPR/C/SR.1253 (23-07-93)	--->	A/48/40
CERD/C/R.3/Add.1	--->	CERD/C/SR.31 (10-09-70)		
		CERD/C/SR.33 (11-09-70)		
		CERD/C/SR.56 (22-04-71)		
CERD/C/R.30/Add.3	--->	CERD/C/SR.127 (23-04-73)		
+ Add.39 + Add.45				
CERD/C/R.70/Add.1	--->	CERD/C/SR.179 (28-03-74)	--->	A/29/18
CERD/C/R.90/Add.2	--->	CERD/C/SR.279 (06-04-76)	--->	A/31/18
CERD/C/20/Add.1	--->	CERD/C/SR.371 (27-04-78)	--->	A/33/18
CERD/C/66/Add.5	--->	CERD/C/SR.472 (03-04-80)	--->	A/35/18
CERD/C/91/Add.31	--->	CERD/C/SR.615 (18-03-83)		
		CERD/C/SR.616 (18-03-83)	--->	A/38/18

CERD/C/118/Add.12	--->	CERD/C/SR.709 (11-03-85)		
		CERD/C/SR.710 (12-03-85)	--->	A/40/18
CERD/C/226/Add.8	--->	CERD/C/SR.989 (04-08-93)		
		CERD/C/SR.990 (04-08-93)		
		CERD/C/SR.1009 (18-08-93)	--->	A/48/18

F. List of other quoted documents

Amnesty International (ed.) 1987 - open. Jahresberichte.

Bundesamt für Verfassungsschutz (ed.) 1995. Verfassungsschutzbericht 1995. Cologne.

Bundesamt für Verfassungsschutz (ed.) 1996. Die "Arbeiterpartei Kurdistans" (PKK) -- Strukturen, Ziele, Aktivitäten. Cologne.

Bundesamt für Verfassungsschutz (ed.) 1996. Islamischer Extremismus und seine Auswirkungen auf die Bundesrepublik Deutschland. Cologne.

H.M Stationary Office (ed.) 1939. Report of a Committee set up to consider Certain Correspondence between Sir Henry McMahon [His Majesty's High Commissioner in Egypt] and The Sharif of Mecca in 1915 and 1916. London.

Institute for Palestine Studies (ed.) 1988. United Nations Resolutions on Palestine and the Arab-Israeli Conflict, 2 vols. Washington.

Jāmiʿat ad-duwal al-ʿarabīya, al-ʾamāna al-ʿāmma, ʾidārat aš-šuʾūn al-qānūnīya (ed.) 1985. Majmūʿat al-muʿāhadāt wa-l-ittifāqīyāt. Cairo.

United Nations, Department of Public Information (ed.) 1990. The United Nations and the Iraq-Kuwait Conflict 1990-1996. New York (= Al-ʾUmam al-muttaḥida, ʾIḍārat šuʾūn al-ʾiʿlām 1996. Al-ʾUmam al-muttaḥida wa-n-nizāʿ bayna l-ʿirāq wa-l-kuwayt 1990-1996. New York).

United Nations, Dag Hammarskjöld Library (ed.) 1993. Palestine Question. A select bibliography, 1976-1993. New York.

U.S. Department of State 1997. Country Reports on Human Rights Practices for 1996.

G. List of quoted cases, pleadings, and judgments

Mavrommatis Palestine Concessions. P.I.C.J. Series A, no. 2, 1924.

Western Sahara Advisory Opinion, I.C.J. Reports 1975.

Western Sahara Advisory Opinion, I.C.J. Pleadings 1982.

United States Diplomatic and Consular Staff in Tehran, I.C.J. Pleadings 1982.

Continental Shelf (Tunisia/Libyan Arab Jamahiriya), Application to Intervene, Judgment, I.C.J. Reports 1981.

H. Original Arabic quotations

Item (1): UN-doc. A/45/1018 = S/22655

لو أن التاريخ يعيد نفسه لن يكون لنا غير ذلك الموقف الذي اتخذناه لأن الحديث عن أن الكويت جزء من العراق لم يكن جدلا أو خيالا بل قناعة ... لقد قدمنا في أم المعارك التضحيات الغالية ولكن بجهود منظمة وبإمكانيات متواضعة لكنها متصلة، وعلينا أن نقطف ثمار هذه المعركة في المعركة القادمة والأساس الذي سنعتمد عليه هو الشعب ومن خلال قيادته الوطنية.

Item (4): Treaty of Ḥudaybīya

هذا ما صلح عليه محمد بن عبد الله سهيل بن عمرو،
اصطلحا على وضع الحرب عن الناس عشر سنين تأمن فيهن الناس ويكف بعضهم من بعضن،
على أنه من اتى محمدا من قريش بغير إذن واليه رده عليهم،
ومن جاء قريشا ممن مع محمد لم يردوه عليه،
وإن بيننا عيبة مكفوفة،
وأنه لا إسلال ولا إغلال،
وأنه من أحب أن يدخل في عقد محمد وعهده دخل فيه،
و من أحب أن يدخل في عقد قريش وعهدهم دخل فيه.

Item (6): Treaty between the Caliph ᶜUmar ibn al-Ḫaṭṭāb and the Patriarch of Jerusalem

بسم الله الرحمن الرحيم
هذا ما اعطى عبد الله عمر امير المؤمنين اهل ايلياء من الامن
اعطاهم امنا لأنفسهم واموالهم ولكنائسهم وصلبانهم وسقيمها وبريئها وسائر ملتها
انه لا تسكن كنائسهم ولا تهدم ولا ينتقص منها ولا من حيزها ولا من صليبهم ولا من شيء من اموالهم
ولا يكرهون على دينهم ولا يضار احد منهم
ولا يسكن بايلياء معهم احد من اليهود
وعلى اهل ايلياء ان يعطوا الجزية كما يعطي اهل المدائن
وعليهم ان يخرجوا منها الروم واللصوت
فمن خرج منهم فانه آمن على نفسه وماله حتى يبلغوا مأمنهم
ومن اقام منهم فهو آمن وعليه مثل ما على اهل ايلياء من الجزية
ومن احب من اهل ايلياء ان يسير بنفسه وماله مع الروم ويخلي بيعهم وصلبهم فانهم آمنون على انفسهم وعلى بيعهم وصلبهم حتى يبلغوا مأمنهم
ومن كان بها من اهل الارض قبل مقتل فلان
فمن شاء منهم قعد وعليه مثل ما على اهل ايلياء من الجزية
ومن شاء سار مع الروم
ومن شاء رجع الى اهله فانه لا يؤخذ منهم شيء حتى يحصد حصادهم
وعلى ما في هذا الكتاب عهد الله وذمة رسوله وذمة الخلفاء وذمة المؤمنين اذا اعطوا

الذي عليهم من الجزية
شهد على ذلك خالد بن الوليد وعمرو بن الآصي وعبد الرحمن بن عوف ومعاوية بن ابي سفيان
وكتب [!] وحضر سنة ١٥.

Item (8): UN-doc. S/1995/633

وحول إشارة إعلان الدول الثلاث إلى قضية الحجاج الليبيين ووصف سفرهم إلى الارض المقدسة بانه انتهاك للجزاءات المفروضة على الجماهيرية العظمى، نود ان نكرر ما سبق ان اخطرنا به رئيس لجنة الجزاءات وهو ان الجماهيرية لم ولن [!] تنتهك تلك الجزاءات، إلا ان قضية ممارسة الليبيين لمشاعرهم الدينية قضية مختلفة، فهي، في المقام الاول، ممارسة لمشاعر دينية لا تخضع لإذن من احد، لا مجلس الامن ولا العالم برمته، فهي قضي "لا طاعة لمخلوق في معصية الخالق،" وعليهم ان يدركوا بكل وضوح أن الشعب الليبي سيمارس شعائره الدينية بكل حرية ولن تثنيه عن ذلك قوة في الارض حتى يرث الله الارض ومن عليه.

Item (11): Israel and Egypt: Treaty of Peace

إن حكومة دولة إسرائيل وحكومة جمهورية مصر العربية،
اقتناعا منهما بالضرورة الماسة لاقامة سلام عادل وشامل ودائم في الشرق الاوسط وفقا لقراري مجلس الأمن ٢٤٢ و٣٣٨،
إذ تؤكدان من جديد التزامهما بـ"إطار السلام في الشرق الأوسط المتفق عليه في كامب دافيد"، المؤرخ في ١٧ سبتمبر ١٩٧٨،
وإذ تلاحظان أن الإطار المشار اليه إنما قصد به أن يكون أساسا للسلام، ليس بين إسرائيل ومصر فحسب، بل أيضا بين اسرائيل وأي من جيرانها العرب كل فيما يخصه ممن يكون على استعداد للتفاوض من أجل السلام معها على هذا الأساس
ورغبة منهما في إنهاء حالة الحرب بينهما وإقامة سلام تستطيع فيه كل دولة في المنطقة أن تعيش في أمن،
واقتناعا منهما بأن عقد معاهدة سلام بين إسرائيل ومصر يعتبر خطوة هامة في طريق السلام الشامل في المنطقة والتوصل الى تسوية للنزاع العربي الإسرائيلي بكافة نواحيه،
وإذ تدعوان الأطراف العربية الأخرى في النزاع إلى الاشتراك في عملية السلام مع إسرائيل على أساس مبادئ إطار السلام المشار اليها آنفا واسترشادا بها،
وإذ ترغبان أيضا في إنماء العلاقات الودية والتعاون بينهما وفقا لميثاق الأمم المتحدة ومبادئ القانون الدولي التي تحكم العلاقات الدولية في وقت السلام،
قد اتفقتا على الاحكام التالية بمقتضى ممارستهما الحرة لسيادتهما من أجل تنفيذ الإطار الخاص بعقد معاهدة السلام بين إسرائيل ومصر.

Item (12): Pact of the League of Arab States

إن حضرة صاحب الفخام رئيس الجمهورية السورية،
وحضرة صاحب السمو الملكي امير شرق الأردن،
وحضرة صاحب الجلالة ملك العراق،
وحضرة صاحب الجلالة ملك المملكة العربية السعودية،

وحضرة صاحب الفخامة رئيس الجمهورية اللبنانية،
وحضرة صاحب الجلالة ملك مصر،
وحضرة صاحب الجلالة ملك اليمن،
تثبيتا للعلاقات الوثيقة والروابط العديدة التي تربط بين الدول العربية،
وحرصا على دعم هذه الروابط وتوطيدها على اساس احترام استقلال تلك الدول وسيادتها،
وتوجيها لجهودها الى ما فيه خير البلاد العربية قاطبة وصلاح احوالها وتأمين مستقبلها وتحقيق امانيها وآمالها،
واستجابة للرأي العربي العام في جميع الأقطار العربية،
قد اتفقوا على عقد ميثاق لهذه الغاية [...]

Item (13): UN-doc. S/1994/928

في إطار استمرار جامعة الدول العربية في بذل جهودها بغية إيجاد تسوية سلمية للازمة الليبية مع كل من الولايات المتحدة وبريطانيا وفرنسا، وإلحاقا برسالتي الكم بتاريخ ٣/٤/٩٤ بخصوص قرار مجلس جامعة الدول العربية بهذا الشأن والمقترح الذي تضمنها هذا القرار خاصة فيما يتعلق "بإجراء محاكمة عادلة للمشتبه فيهما من قبل قضاة اسكتلنديين وفق القانون الاسكتلندي، وفي مقر محكمة عدل الدولية بلا هاي وحث مجلس الامن على اخذ هذا الاقتراح الجاد والجديد بعين الاعتبار، للبحث عن حل سلمي منعا لاي تصعيد في الموقف من شأنه زيادة التوتر في المنطقة".
وفي ضوء الموقف الليبي الملتزم بهذا القرار وما أبدته الجماهيرية الليبية من مرونة وإيجابية كبيرة في التعامل مع هذه الأزمة بغية التوصل الى تسوية سلمية لها.

أرجو منكم التكرم بعرض هذا المقترح العربي على مجلس الأمن بالشكل الذي ترتأونه وكلي ثقة أنكم ستواصلون بذل الجهود من أجل التوصل لحل سلمي لهذه الأزمة.

Item (14): Exchange of Notes between the United States of America and the Kingdom of the Yemen

لي الشرف ان أفيد سعادتكم باستلامي لخطابكم المؤرخ في ٤ مايو ١٩٤٦ الموافق ٣ جمادى الثاني ١٣٦٥ والذي نصه كما يلي:
لي الشرف ان ابين فهم حكومتي للاتفاق الذي تم بعد محادثات جرت مؤخرا في صنعاء يوم ١٤ ابريل الى ٤ مايو ١٩٤٦ بين ممثلي حكومة الولايات المتحدة الامريكية وبين حكومة مملكة اليمن بشأن التمثيل السياسي والقنصلي والصيانة القضائية والتجارية والملاحة كما هي موضحة ادناه [...].
المادة الاولى
ستتبادل الولايات المتحدة الأمريكية ومملكة اليمن الممثلين الدبلوماسيين والقنصليين وذلك في التاريخ الذي سيعين بالاتفاق بين الحكومتين[...].
وإنني بالنيابة عن حكومة اليمن أفيدكم بموافقة حكومتي على النصوص المذكورة في هذه الاتفاقية والتي تعتبر سارية المفعول من تاريخ هذا التوقيع.

Item (15): UN-doc. A/45/944

تهدي المثلية الدائمة للعراق تحياتها الى الامانة العامة للأمم المتحدة وتود أن تشير إلى الوثيقة A/45/916 المؤرخة في ٨ كانون الثاني/يناير ١٩٩١ التي تضمنت رسالة الممثل الدائم لمصر التي يعترض فيها على مذكرة وفد العراق A/45/891 وAdd.1 كما يعلن فيها تحفظ النظام المصري على أوراق تفويض الوفد العراقي.

إننا إذ نرفض مذكرة الوفد المصري نشير الى أن هذا الوفد لم يتجرأ على التحفظ على أوراق تفويض وفد الكيان الصهيوني العنصري. كما انه تمادى في موقفه الاستسلامي الى درجة تصويته لصالح الاجراء النرويجي الذي حال دون اتخاذ أي إجراء على مشروع التعديل العربي الذي طرح في الدورة السابعة للجمعية العامة، مما الحق افدح الاضرار بموقف المجموعة العربية في هذا الصدد بشكل خاص وبالقضية الفلسطينية بشكل عام.

إن وفدنا يؤكد ان قرار الوحدة الاندماجية الذي أعاد الكويت إلى وطنها الأم العراق في ثامن من آب/اغسطس ١٩٩٠ قد كرس العدالة والشرعية وأعاد الحق المغتصب للشعب العراقي، كما أنه يشكل خطوة على طريق إعادة الحقوق المغتصبة للأمة العربية في فلسطين.

نرجو أن تنشر هذه الرسالة كوثيقة من وثائق الجمعية العامة في إطار البند ٣ من جدول الاعمال.

Item (16): UN-doc. CCPR/C/82/Add. 1

يملك اليمن تاريخا حضاريا عريقا يمتد عبر الاجيال والازمان جسدت خلاله الكثير من الاعمال الانسانية والحضارية والتي لا زالت معالمها شاهدة على ذلك حتى اليوم.

إن الإسلام بالنسبة للشعب اليمني كان وما زال أساس تكوينه الفكري والروحي، فهو بمبادئه وقيمه الاخلاقية التي ترسخت لدى الانسان اليمني منذ اكثر من ١٤ قرنا من الزمن جعلته يدرك عن يقين ان الله سبحانه وتعالى كرم الإنسان وفضله على جميع مخلوقاته: حيث قال في محكم أياته "ولقد كرمنا بني آدم وحملناهم في البر والبحر ورزقناهم من الطيبات وفضلناهم على كثير ممن خلقنا تفضيلا".

إن هذه النظرة الإسلامية للإنسان تتميز بالشمول، فالإسلام لا يعني بفرد دون آخر فالكل سواسي "فلا فضل لعربي على عجمي الا بالتقوى" (حديث نبوي). والاسلام يرعى الفرد كما يرعى الجماعة كلها، فحياته وكرامته وحريته وأمنه وحقوقه تساوي في أهميتها حياة وحرية وأمن وحقوق المجتمع كله. وقد قال تعالى "ومن قتل نفسا بغير نفس او فساد في الارض فكأنما قتل الناس جميعا". وانطلاقا من هذه المعاني الكريمة والمفاهيم لقيمة الانسان وحقوقه كان جهاد ونضال اليمنيين طوال المراحل الماضية لاستعادة المكانة التاريخية والحضارية لليمن. وكان نتاج كفاح ونضال اليمنيين عبر الزمان والمكان تحقيق الوحدة اليمنية في ٢٢ ايار/مايو ١٩٩٠. وكان ذلك استجابة موضوعية لظروف العصر وسماته العامة وخصائصه البارزة التي تؤكد على نحو جلي الرغبة المتزايدة والحثيثة لدى مختلف الأمم والشعوب في تكوين الوحدات السياسية والاقتصادية الكبرى على اسس المصالح المشتركة والتكامل العلمي الواسع، وتوفيقا بين مصالح الجماعة الإنسانية ومصالح

الأفراد. وأصبحت الوحدة اليمنية هي سلح الشعب اليمني لدخول العصر القادم والتجارب مع الظروف الراهنة التي يعيشها العالم

Item (17): UN-doc. S/1994/870

وأخيرا أرجو أن تثقوا بأن بلادي سوف لن تتردد في الاستفادة من إمكانيات وخيرات الأمم المتحدة بصفة عامة، ...

Item (18): UN-doc. S/1995/633

نود أن نكرر ما سبق أن أخطرنا به رئيس لجنة الجزاءات وهو ان الجماهيرية لم ولن [!] تنتهك تلك الجزاءات [...]

Item (19): UN-doc. S/23102

سأكون ممتنا لو تفضلتم بتأمين توزيع هذه الرسالة [...] كوثيقة رسمية منوثائق مجلس الامن.

Item (20): McMahon-Ḥusayn-correspondence

ثم يجب أن لا تتعبوا أنفسكم بإرسال الطيارات او رجال الحرب، لإلقاء المناشير، وإذاعة الشائعات، كما كنتم تفعلون من قبل، لان القضية قد قررت الآن.

Item (21): UN-doc. S/1994/651

من مبلغ الكون أن الأمر مؤتمن
تبقى وتسلم في أوطاننا اليمن
دار الحضارات ذخر العرب متلدي
تاه الوجود بها واستبشر الزمن
يا دارة المجد والأذواء من يمن
قد هزني في ذراك الشوق والشجن
حملت همك إيثارا على كبر
والوجد يلظى كما تلظى بك المحن
نفح الشمال اذا ندى بصيبه
وافى الجنوب بما يهمي ويختزن
صنعاء حاضرة التاريخ غاليتي
وجنة الخلد في الطافها عدن
كلتاهما في سويدائي وفي بدني
تنزلان هما لي الروح والبدن
عيناهما في أساريري وأخيلتي
يطوف فيها الهوى والسهد والوسن
نام الخليون إلا مقلة سهرت
فما اليماني إلا الساهر الفطن
طيب اليماني في إيماض بارقه
يهمي سماحا كما تهمي الحيا المزن
ويستضيء بنور غب غربته

فما اليماني إلا الماجد الظعن
ماذا نقول لتاريخ يناشدنا
أن نرعوي فكفانا البؤس والحزن
حلم الشعوب اذا ما انداح عن غبش
فالفجر آت به الايضاح والعلن
إني أتوق الى الأهلين في يمن
ليست تمزقه الأضغان والفتن
باق على الدهر يرقى للعلى يمنا
موحدا يتسامى باسمه الوطن
شكرا لكم سيدي الرئيس على لطفكم وحسن استماعكم والسلام عليكم

Item (22): Arabie Saoudiene et Irak. Traité de fraternité arabe et d'alliance

بسم الله الرحمن الرحيم،
حضرة صاحب الجلالة ملك العراق،
حضرة صاحب الجلالة ملك المملكة العربية السعودية،
بناء على الروابط الإسلامية والوحدة القومية التي تجمعهما وبغية المحافظة على سلامة بلادهما وبناء على ما تقتضيه الحاجة الماسة للتعاون فيما بينهما والتفاهم في الشؤون التي تهم مصلحة مملكتيهما فقد اتفقا على عقد معاهدة اخوة عربية وتحالف وعينا عنهما لهذا الغرض مندوبين مفوضين:
عن حضرة صاحب الجلالة ملك العراق
صاحب الفخامة نوري باشا السعيد - وزير خارجية المملكة العراقية حامل وسام الرافدين من الدرجة الاولى ومن النوع العسكري
عن حضرة صاحب الجلالة ملك المملكة العربية السعودية
صاحب السعادة الشيخ يوسف الياسين - السكرتير الخاص لجلالة الملك ورئيس الشعبة السياسية في ديوان جلالته
وبعد ان تبادلا وثائق تفويضهما فوجداها مطابقة للاصول تحالفا وتعاهدا على المواد الآتية.

Item (23): UN-doc. 24118

هذه هي رسالتنا الى المؤتمر ونامل ان تجد الصدى المطلوب بالاتجاه الذي يحقق العدالة وينسجم مع الاهداف الانسانية لهذا المؤتمر.
والله أكبر.

Item (24): UN-doc. 21566

والله نسأل أن يخلص الأمة العربية والإسلامية من شرور هذا النظام الآثم الذي ارتكب من الجرائم في حق الشعب العراقي والشعب الكويتي بل والامة العربية ما لا يمكن حصره ولا تصوره، إنه سميع مجيب.
وسأكون ممتنا لو تفضلتم بتوزيع هذه الرسالة كوثيقة من وثائق مجلس الأمن.

Item (26): UN-doc. A/49/180 = S/1994/727

يستخدم الرئيس عرفات، عند دخوله قطاع غزة ومنطقة اريحا، لقب "رئيس السلطة الفلسطينية" او "رئيس منظمة التحرير الفلسطينية"، ولا يستخدم لقب "رئيس فلسطين".

Item (27): Israel and Egypt. Treaty of Peace

يعتبر الطرفان ان مديق تيران وخليج العقبة من الممرت المائية الدولية المفتوحة لكافة الدول دون عائق او إقاف لحرية الملاحة او العبور الجوي كما يحترم الطرفان حق كل منهما في الملاحة والعبور الجويي من والى أراضيه عبر مديق تيران وخليج العقبة.

Item (28): Security Council resolution 242

سحب القوات المسلحة الاسرائيلية من اراض احتلتها في النزاع الاخير.

Item (30): Grande Bretagne et Irak. Traité d'alliance

يوافق جلالة ملك العراق وذلك من غير مساس بنصوص المادين ١٧ و١٨ من هذه المعاهدة على ان يستدل بما يقدمه جلالة ملك بريطانية من المشورة بواسطة المعتمد السامي في جميع الشؤون المهمة التي تمس بتعهدات ومصالح جلالة ملك بريطانية الدولية والمالية وذلك طول مد هذه المعاهدة. ويستشير جلالة ملك العراق المعتمد السامي الاستشارة التامة في ما يؤدي إلى سياسة مالية ونقدية سليمة ويؤمن ثبات وحسن نظام ماليات حكومة العراق ما دامت تلك الحكومة مدوينة لحكومة جلالة ملك بريطانية.

Item (31): Qur'ān 9: 5

فإذا انسلخ الاشهر الحرم فاقتلوا المشركين حيث وجدتموهم وخذوهم واحصروهم واقعدوا لهم كل مرصد فإن تابوا واقاموا الصلوة وأتوا الزكوة فخلوا سبيلهم إن الله غفور رحيم.

Item (32): Qur'ān 9: 29

قتلوا الذين لا يؤمنون بالله ولا باليوم الاخر ولا يحرمون ما حرم الله ورسوله ولا يدينون دين الحق من الذين أوتوا الكتب حتى يعطوا الجزية عن يد وهم صغرون.

Item (33): UN-doc. S/1994/869

بناء على توجيهات من حكومتي، وبالاشارة الى رسالة الممثل الدائم لجمهورية ايران الاسلامية المؤرخة في ١٧ حزيران/ يونيا ١٩٩٤ (الوثيقة S/1994/726) نود أن نوضح أن ما ورد فيها عن حالة انتهاكة مزعومة من جانب العراق لوقف إطلاق النار بين البلدين واحكام منطقة العزل مهد اداعات دأب النظام الايراني على اختلاقها بغية خلق اجواء توتر لا مبرر لها.

Item (34): UN-doc. S/1994/761

إننا في الوقت الذي نؤكد فيه استمرار التزام قواتنا المسلحة بوقف إطلاق النار نحمل المتمردين الخارجين على الشرعية مسؤولية رفضهم لهذه المبادرة وانتهاكهم

للمرة السادسة لمحاولات تثبيت وقف إطلاق النار والضرب بعرض الحائط بكل النداءات والمساعي والمحاولات المبذولة من أجل تثبيت وقف إطلاق النار.

Item (36): UN-doc. S/21348

ومن هذا المنطلق وحده جاء تحذير السيد الرئيس صدام حسين في الاول من نسان / ابريل الماضي بأن العراق سيستعمل حقه في الدفاع الشرعي للرد على اي عدوان يتعرض له من قبل الكيان الصهيوني

Item (37): UN-doc. S/22452

بسم لله الرحمن الرحيم،
نحمد الله سبحانه وتعالى في هذا الشهر الفضيل إذ نعلن لأبناء شعب العراق العظيم نبأ القضاء التام على أعمال الفتنة والتخريب والشغب في كل مدن العراق [...]
ولم يكن من قبيل الصدفة أن تنطلق هذه الأعمال الشائنة التي هي ليست من أخلاق العراقيين ومن تقاليد نضالهم الوطني خلال العدوان الأمريكي الأطلسي الصهيوني على العراق [...]
إن بلادنا التي تعرضت إلى العدوان الامبريالي الأطلسي الصهيوني تعرضت إلى غزو آخر مشابه لغزو هولاكو لبغداد عام ١٢٥٨.

Item (38): UN-doc. S/21505

اعترف العراق في بيانه الأخير بأن احتلاله لدولة الكويت يماثل احتلال إسرائيل لبعض الأراضي العربية وهو بذلك كشف عن نفسه باعتباره يلعب نفس الدور الذي يمارسه الكيان الصهيوني في المنطقة العربية.
والنصر آت بإذن الله.

Item (39): UN-doc. CCPR/C/37/Add. 3

أم الجرائم الماسة بأمن الدولة الداخلي والتي عقوبتها الإعدام فهي [...]:
من جند او زوج مبادئ صهيونية بما في ذلك الماسونية او انتسب الى مؤسساتها (المادة ٢٠١).

Item (40): McMahon-Ḥusayn-correspondence

إن ولايتي مرسين واسكندرونة وأجزاء من بلاد الشام الواقعة في الجهة الغربية لولاية دمشق الشام وحمص وحماه وحلب لا يمكن ان يقال انها عربية محضة وعليه يجب أن تستثنى من الحدود المطلوبة.

Item (41): McMahon-Ḥusayn-correspondence

أم من خصوص ولايتي بغداد والبصرة فإن العرب تعترف ان مركز ومصالح بريطانية العظمى الموطدة هناك تستلزم اتخاذ تدابير إدارية مخصوصة لوقاية هذه الاقاليم من الاعتداء الاجنبي وزيادة خير سكانها وحماية مصالحنا الاقتصادية المتبادلة.

Item (43): Israel and Egypt. Treaty of Peace

تنتهي حالة الحرب بين الطرفين ويقام السلام بينهما عند تبادل وثائق التصديق على هذه المعاهدة.

Item (44): UN-doc. A/48/486 = S/26560

إن حكومة إسرائيل وفريق منظمة التحرير الفلسطينية (في الوفد الأردني الفلسطيني لدى مؤتمر السلام في الشرق الاوسط) ("الوفد الفلسطيني") يتفقان أن الوقت قد حان لوضع حد لعقود من المواجهة والنزاع، ويعترفان كل منهما بالحقوق المشروعة والسياسية للآخر، ويسعايان الى الحياة في تعايش سلمي وكرامة وأمن متبادلين، والى تحقيق تسوية سلمية عادلة ودائمة وشاملة، ومصالحة تاريخية عن طريق العملية السياسية المتفق عليها.

Item (45): UN-doc. A/49/300 = S/1994/939

إن الصراع الطويل العمد بين الدولتين أصبح الآن في نهايته. وبهذه الروح أنهيت حالة الحرب بين الاردن وإسرائيل.

Item (46): UN-doc. A/50/73 = S/1995/83

وإذ تأخذان بعين الاعتبار أنهما أعلنتا انتهاء حالة العداء بينهما بمجيب إعلان وشنطون الموقع في ٢٥ تموز ١٩٩٤.
وإذ تقرران إقامة سلام بينهما بمجيب معاهدة السلام هذه.

Item (48): UN-doc. S/22204

إن هذا العمل العدواني جزء من المؤامرة الامريكية الاطلسية الصهيونية للهيمنة وتثبيت النظام الستعماري الجديد في منطقة الشرق الاوسط.

Item (49): UN-doc. S/21494

بسم الله الرحمن الرحيم،

مساهمة منا في خلق اجواء سلام حقيقي في المنطقة، وتسهيلا لوضع المنطقة في حالة استقرار، وكشفا لزيف امريكا وحليفتها المسخ إسرائيل، وفضا لعملائها الصغار وجرائمهم ضد الامة وتوكيدا للحق من موقع الاقتدار المؤمن بالله والشعب والامة قررنا ان نتقدم بالمبادرة التالية. [...]:

إعداد ترتيبات انسحاب وفق مبادئ واحدة لانسحاب إسرائيل فورا وبلا شروط من الأراضي العربية المحتلة في فلسطين وسوريا ولبنان، وانسحاب سوريا من لبنان، والانسحاب بين العراق وايران، ووضع ترتيبات لحالة الكويت، وأن تنسحب الترتيبات العسكرية في توقيتاتها وكل ما يتصل بها من ترتيبات سياسية، على كل الحالات ووفق نفس الأسس والمبادئ، والمنطلقات المعتمدة، آخذين بنظر الاعتبار الحقوق التاريخية للعراق في أرضه، واختيار شعب الكويت، وأن تكون البداية في تطبيق البرنامج لما هو أسبق للاحتلال أو ما سمي احتلالا، مبتدئين بتطبيق كل ما صدر من قرارات لمجلس الأمن وهيئة الأمم المتحدة لكل الحالات، وهكذا وصولا إلى أقرب حالة فيها، وأن تطبق نفس الاجراءات التي اتخذها مجلس الأمن حيال العراق، تجاه من لا يلتزم بهذا الترتيب أو يتجاوب معه. [...]

وفي كل احوال وعندما لا تتجاوب امريكا هي وحلفاؤها الصغار من عملائها

مع مبادرتنا هذه، فإننا سنقاوم بقوة، نحن والخيرون من أبناء الامة العربية وشعب العراق العظيم، نزعاتها الشريرة ومخططاتها العدوانية، وسننتصر بعون الله، وسيندم الأشرار على فعلتهم بعد ان يخرجوا مدحورين ملعونين من المنطقة يجرون أذيال الخزي والعار.

ولله أكبر وليخسأ الخاسئون.

صدام حسين

١٣ آب\أغسطس ١٩٩٠.

٢١ محرم ١٤١١هـ

Item (50): UN-doc. S/21651

بسم الله الرحمن الرحيم

رسالة مفتوحة الى عوائل الأجانب الذين قرر ممثلو الشعب المنتخبين [sic!] "المجلس الوطني" استضافتهم في العراق حتى تنفرج الأزمة ... ومن خلالهم أخاطب الغربيين بوجه عام والأميركيين منهم بوجه خاص ...

أيها السيدات والسادة ... أيها الأطفال الأعزاء ... إنني أعرب بأنكم تتألمون لعدم السماح لذويكم بالسفر خارج العراق وإنني معكم أتألم لهذا، بل وإنني على يقين تماما بأن رئيس وأعضاء المجلس الوطني في العراق يتألمون أيضا، مثلما هو حال كل العراقيين والعرب، ذلك لأنني أعرف أن أعضاء المجلس الوطني في العراق مؤمنون بالله، ومؤمنون بحقوق الانسان لأنهم كافحوا سنين طويلة حتى يفوزوا فيما هم فيه من حال يحمدون الله عليه، وإنهم يعرفون مثلما أنا أعرف بأن بلادهم قد علمت الانسانية أول حرف وبذلك علمتهم الكتابة، وإن بلادهم علمت الانسانية أول قانون سن على وجه الأرض ذلك هو قانون حمورابي، الذي رتب فيه الحقوق والواجبات الانسانية قبل أربعة آلاف وخمسمائة سنة، ولذلك فإنهم يعرفون بأن لا قيمة للسعادة في بلادهم إن لم تفهم الانسانية كلها أن أي احتجاز لحرية أي إنسان هو ثلم للحرية الانسانية في جانب من جوانبها، وإنهم يحبون الانسان مهما تكن جنسيته ولونه وجنسه، ذلك لأنهم يحبون الله، وإن الله لا يفرق بين عباده إلا على أسس درجة الايمان ومقتضياته.

لذلك فإن أعضاء المجلس الوطني يتألمون مثلما أنتم تتألمون، ونحن جميعا آسفون للذي حصل وهو ليس من إرادتنا وإنما هو أساسا نابع من فعل إرادة أناس تجبروا وخرجوا عن إرادة الله وتعاليمه أن المسؤول المباشر عن هذا بالدرجة الأساس [sic!] هما الإدارة الأميركية والإدارة الانكليزية. كيف ذالك؟

تعرفون أيها السيدات والسادة ان العراق قد خرج من حرب دامت ثماني سنوات بينه وبين ايران وتعرفون ان تلك الحرب التي دامت ثماني سنوات كانت بين دولتين نفطيتين، وانها كانت ايضا ضمن حقول نفط الخليج، وان في هذه الحرب صادف ان دخلت الجيوش العراقية الى داخل ايران، وان دخلت الجيوش الايرانية الى داخل العراق فلماذا لم تتدخل اميركا وبريطانيا والآخرون لإيقافها ولماذا لم يهددوا من لم يلتزم بالقرارات التي اصدرها مجلس الأمن في حينه؟ إنهم لم يفعلوا ذلك لأنهم قد اسهموا في إشعالها ولأنهم هم وحلفاؤهم المتخلفون من أمثال قارون الكويت واعوانه ارادوا لها ان تستمر وان لا تتوقف حتى شاء لها الله ان تتوقف، وعندما توقفت سلطوا علينا عملاءهم في المنطقة وفي مقدمتهم قارون الكويت وزمرته ليحاربوا شعب العراق بلقمة عيشه ويحرمونه بالحرب الاقتصادية وبالاعتداء على حقول

بترولنا، من أبسط ما يليق به، وهو شعب الحضارات والأمجاد، حتى اوصلوا قيمة دينار العراق الى ما يقرب من ١ [دينار] الى ٥٤ فلس [!] من قيمة دينار الكويت، مع ان قيمة دينار العراق كانت في عام ١٩٨٠. أعلى من قيمة دينار الكويت، حتى أصبح يتعذر علينا توفير حليب لأطفالنا ونحن بلاد ما بين النهرين، بلاد الخير والعطاء، وقد لا تعرفون أيها السادة ان هذا البلد الذي تأمر من نصبوا حكاما عليه [!] هو جزء من العراق حتى عام ١٩١٣ وان العراق لم يعترف به كدولة حتى الستينات من هذا القرن وان رئيس وزراء العراق أصدر قرارا عام ١٩٦١ يقضي بضم الكويت الى العراق وأعاد الكويت كقضاء مرتبط بالبصرة، وعين شيخها قائمقاما لها مثلما كان عليه حتى قيام الحرب العالمية الاولى وان المجلس الاستشاري في الكويت قرر مرتين في الثلاثينات الوحدة مع العراق حتى حل بقرار من الأسرة الحاكمة آنذاك، وان رئيس وزراء العراق نوري السعيد طرح على حلف بغداد وبحضور ممثل اميركا في عام ١٩٥٨ الوحدة مع الكويت...

فلماذا يريد رئيس الولايات المتحدة الاميركية ورئيسة وزراء بريطانيا تجويع شعب العراق حتى الموت، خاب ما يفعلون، وماذا عمل شعب العراق غير انه وحد نفسه، ووحد شأن العواطل التي شطرها الدهر بين العراق والكويت ودافع عن نفسه وساعد في خلع شيخ الكويت المتخلف الذي لا هم له غير جمع الأموال والنساء فلماذا يفرضون الحصار على العراق ليميتوا الأطفال الرضع والشيوخ وكل الناس الذين لا يتوفر لهم الغذاء والدواء لو ان الذي تريده الإدارة الاميركية والبريطانية يتحقق! ولماذا يحشدون الأساطيل البحرية وأسراب الطائرات والقوات البرية التي يريدون باكتمال حشودها الهجوم على العراق؟ انهم قالوا بأنهم جاؤا الى هنا، وأهانوا أرض العرب ومقدسات المسلمين باحتلالهم لأرض الحجاز ونجد، ليدافعوا عن السعودية تجاه خطر العراق، وهم يكذبون لأنهم يعرفون ان العراق لا يعتدي وانما يضرب عندما يعتدى عليه. فإن لم يكن هنالك من قرر ضرب العراق فلينم مطمئنا هانئا في نومه قرير العين ...

أقول أيتها السيدات وأيها السادة ويا أحباء الله وأحبائي الأطفال الأعزاء في اوروبا واميركا ... إن وطننا كما هو واضح الكم مهدد من اميركا و بريطانيا ومن سيتورط معهما من الخائبين الأذلاء ... وإن شعبنا معرض لإيذاء شديد. وإذا ما أقدم الخاسئون على العدوان ستسقط الكثير من رؤوس الحكام عن الأكتاف، وسيموت نساء ورجال وأطفال بعشرات الألوف من الجانبين، [...]

ترك موضوع الكويت ليعالجه العرب شأن عربي، مثلما حصل في كل القضايا المماثلة، كقضية الصحراء في مغرب الوطن العربي بين المغرب وأطراف القضية، وكقضية الاحتلال السوري للبنان، وغيرها من القضايا المماثلة.

هذه هي أيتها الأخوات والإخوة وأيها الأطفال الأعزاء مبادرتنا وإنني أسألكم هل فيها ما هو مخالف للقانون الدولي او معاد للإنسانية او مناقض للمصالح المشروعة للغرب؟

فإذا كان الجواب أن المبادرة عادلة فلنتعاون جميعا لتحقيقها وبذلك يتحقق السلام للجميع وتتحقق الحرية والحياة الهانئة للجميع، فهل سيسمع الذي في أذنه وقر؟ ...

سؤال موجه الى الإدارة الاميركية بوجه خاص وبالجواب الصحيح عليه

يتحقق الكثير مما يخدم الإنسانية.
والسلام عليكم ورحمة الله وبركاته.
(توقيع) صدام حسين
١٩ آب\أغسطس ١٩٩٠.

Item (51): UN-doc. S/21790

تعقيبا على قرار مجلس الأمن ٦٦٦ في ١٣ أيلول\سبتمبر صرح ناطق رسمي باسم وزارة الخارجية بما يلي: [...]
فالاجراءات الواردة في هذا القرار هي اجراءات مهينة لشعب أبي يفخر بتراثه الإنساني ومساهمته البارزة في حضارة الإنسان. وعلى هؤلاء الذين دفعوا باتجاه إصدار هذا القرار أن يتذكروا بأن بلاد ما بين النهرين كانت مركزا للتجارة ومركزا للانتاج عندما كان أجدادهم يعيشون في الكهوف. لذلك فإن شعبنا المبدع والمنتج والواثق من نفسه والمصمم على الدفاع عن حقوقه وسيادته يرفض بإباء وصاية القوى الكبرى عليه وسيواصل كفاحه العادل والظافر متكلا على الله، وعلى ارادته الصلبة وعلى أمته العربية المجيدة وعلى الخيرين والشرفاء في العالم.

Item (52): UN-doc. S/22456

وغير أن المجلس بقراره المجحف هذا، وبالاسلوب الانتقائي الذي مارسه ضد شعب العراق أثبت الحقيقة التي أكدنا عليها باستمرار وهي أن المجلس قد تحول الى اداة طيعة في يد الولايات المتحدة لتنفيذ رغباتها وسياساتها في المنطقة، وأن الهدف الاساسي من ذلك هو حماية عدوانية إسرائيل وسياستها التوسعية برغم الكلام الذي لا يقترن بفعل حول السلم والعدالة في الشرق الاوسط الذي صدر عن هذا العضو او ذلك من أعضاء المجلس الذين صوتوا على هذا القرار.

ومن الواضح تماما لكل الشرفاء والمنصفين في العالم أن هذه الإجراءات الانتقامية والجائرة التي تتخذ ضد العراق ليست نتيجة للأحداث التي وقعت في ٢ آب/اغسطس ١٩٩٠. وبعدها بل أن السبب الجوهري الذي يمكن وراءها هو لأن العراق لم يقبل بالوضع المجحف الذي فرض على الامة العربية ودول المنطقة منذ عقود عديدة والذي جال من إسرائيل القوة العدوانية المهيمنة بما تمتلكه من أحدث وأقوى الأسلحة التقليدية وأسلحة الدمار الشامل ومنها السلاح النووي. وإن هذه الحقيقة تؤكد ما بينه العراق قبل أحداث ٢ آب/اغسطس ١٩٩٠. من أنه يتعرض الى مؤامرة تستهدف القضاء على الإمكانات التي وفرها من أجل إقامة توازن عادل في المنطقة من شأنه أن يمهد الطريق لإحلال السلم المنصف والعدالة فيها.

ومن المؤسف أن دولا لم تقصد بالأساس أن تشارك الولايات المتحدة وإسرائيل في تحقيق هذه الأهداف قد اسهمت ربما من غير قصد في تحقيق من خلال التصويت على هذا القرار الجائر.

وفي الوقت الذي يسجل فيه العراق هذه الملاحظات المبدئية والقانونية والشرعية ليحث أصحاب الضمير من أعضاء المجتمع الدولي والرأي العام العالمي على فهم الحقيقة كما هي والانتصار للحق كما ينبغي، فإن العراق يجد نفسه على خيار واحد لا غير هو القبول بهذا القرار.

أرجو تأمين توزيع هذه الرسالة كوثيقة من وثائق مجلس الأمن، وتفضلوا

بقبول وافر الاحترام.
(توقيع) أحمد حسين
وزير خارجية الجمهورية العراقية

Item (54): UN-doc. S/22629

إن المجلس باسم الشرعية الدولية يخالف جوهر هذه الشرعية ويعود الى شرعت الغاب حيث تكون القوة وليس القانون هي الحاكم المطلق. إن جوهر الشرعية سواء في القوانين الوطنية او القانون الدولي هو ليس في تطبيق القانون فقط وإنما تطبيقه بصورة سليمة تحول دون إساءة استعماله وذلك مراعاة المتطلبات القانون (due process of law).

Item (55): UN-doc. S/26887

القوى الكبرى قد تغير الجوغرافيا لكنها لا تغير التاريخ، وهذا الكلام ليس عاطفيا، والأمثلة على ذلك كثيرة، فالقضية الفلسطينية مثلا، مهما كانت هناك حلول جزئية، فهي لا تعني أن القضية الفلسطينية انتهت أساسا، وأن فلسطين انتهت. كذلك هناك أمثلة، فالصين لم تنس جزر فرموزا، والمانيا الغربية لم تنس المانيا الشرقية، والكويت كانت جزءا من العراق.

Item (56): UN-doc. S/1994/1288

امتثالا لقرار مجلس الأمن التابع للأمم المتحد رقم ٨٣٣ (١٩٩٣) تعترف جمهورية العراق بالحدود الدولية بين جمهورية العراق ودولة الكويت كما رسمتها لجنة الأمم المتحدة لترسيم الحدود بين العراق والكويت المشكلة بموجب الفقرت (٣) من القرار ٦٨٧ (١٩٩١)، وتحترم حرمة الحدود المذكورة.

Item (57): Charter of the Islamic Conference

وإذ يقررون الحفاظ على القيم الروحية والأخلاقية والاجتماعية والاقتصادية الموجودة في الإسلام، والتي تظل عاملا من العوامل الهامة لتحقيق التقدم بين أبناء البشر،
ويعيدون التأكيد بتقيدهم بميثاق الأمم المتحدة وحقوق الإنسان الأساسية التي تعتبر أغرادها ومبادئها أساسا لتعاون مثمر بين جميع الشعوب [...].

Item (58): "Project of the Arab(ic) Human Rights Charter"

وتحقيقا للمبادئ الخالدية التي أرستها الشريعة الإسلامية والديانات السماوية الأخرى في الأخوة والمساواة بين البشر.

Item (59): "Project of the Arab(ic) Human Rights Charter"

ورفضا للعنصرية والصهيونية اللتين تشكلان انتهاكا لحقوق الانسان وتهديدا للسلام العالي.
إن العنصرية والصهيونية والاحتلال والسيطرة الاجنبية هي تحد للكرامة الانسانية وعائق اساسي يحول دون الحقوق الاساسية للشعوب ومن الواجب ادانة جميع ممارساتها والعمل على ازالتها.

Item (62): UN-doc. CCPR/C/51/Add. 7

وقد جاءت الشريعة الإسلامية الغراء بقيم ومبادئ وأحكام تشكل نظاما كاملا ومتكاملا يضمن للإنسان، أي ما كانت عقيدته، حقوقه وحرياته في كافة المجالات السياسية والاجتماعية والاقتصادية وهي الحقوق والحريات التي بكتاب الله (القرآن الكريم) والسنة النبوية الشريفة منذ ظهور الإسلام منذ أربعة عشر قرنا وقبل أن يعرف العالم آنذاك منهاجا فكريا ينظم هذه الحقوق وتلك الحريات وفقا لما تسعى اليه الآن البشرية جمعاء.

Item (63): UN-doc. CEDAW/C/YEM/3 (Qurʾān 24:33)

وليستعفف الذين لا يجدون نكاحا حتى يغنيهم الله من فضله والذين يبتغون الكتاب مما ملكت أيمانكم فكاتبوهم إن علمتم فيهم خيرا وآتوهم من مال الله الذي أتاكم ولا تكرهوا فتياتكم على البغاء إن أردن تحصنا لتبتغوا عرض الحياة الدنيا ومن يكرههن فإن الله من بعد إكراههن غفور رحيم.

Item (64): UN-doc. CCPR/C/82/Add. 1

إن هذه النظرة الإسلامية للإنسان تتميز بالشمول، فالإسلام لا يعني بفرد دون آخر فالكل سواسي "فلا فضل لعربي على عجمي الا بالتقوى" (حديث نبوي)

Item (67): Yemen's instrument of ratification of CERD

وبعد إقرارنا من مجلس الشورى فقد أصدرنا القانون رقم (٣) لسنة ١٩٨٩م بالموافقة على انضمام الجمهورية العربية اليمنية الى الاتفاقية المذكورة مع التحفظ على ما جاء في الفقر (ج) في المادة الخامسة منها، وعلى ما جاء في البنود (٤ . ٦ . ٧) من المادة المذكورة الخامسة.

Item (69): UN-doc. CRC/C/3/Add. 6

ويلزم كل مصري بحمل البطاقة الشخصية، وعليه أن يقدمها عند أي تعامل مدني أو جنائي، وكل من لا يحمل البطاقة يجوز مساءلته قانونيا.

وقد نص قانون السجل المدني على تغيير نوعية البطاقة عند الزواج للذكر، فيجب أن يغير البطاقة الشخصية ببطاقت عائلية، ويثبت بها اسم الزوجة وأسماء الأولاد.

Item (71): UN-doc. CCPR/C/82/Add. 1

يشترط رضا المرأة البكر سكوتها ورضا الثيب نطقها [...].

Item (71): CRC, article 14

المادة ١٤

١ تحترم الدول الأطراف حق الطفل في حرية الفكر والوجدان والدين.

٢ تحترم الدول الأطراف حقوق وواجبات الوالدين وكذلك، تبعا للحالة، الأوصياء القانونيين عليه، في توجيه الطفل في ممارسة حقه بطريقة تنسجم مع قدرات الطفل المتطورة.

٣ لا يجوز أن يخضع الإجهار بالدين او المعتقدات إلا للقيود التي ينص عليها

القانون واللازمة لحماية السلامة العامة او النظام او الصحة او الآداب العامة او الحقوق والحريات الأساسية للآخرين.

Item (73): CEDAW, articles 9 and 16

المادة ٩

١ تمنح الدول الاطرف المرأة حقا مساويا لحق الرجل في اكتساب جنسيتها او الاحتفاظ بها او تغيرها. وتضمن بوجه خاص ألا يترتب على الزواج من أجنبي او تغيير جنسية الزوج أثناء الزواج أن تتغير تلقائيا جنسية الزوجة، او أن تصبح بلا جنسية او أن تفرض عليها جنسية الزوج.

٢ تمنح الدول الأطراف المرأة حقا مساويا لحق الرجل فيما يتعلق بجنسية أطفالها.

المادة ١٦

١ تتخذ الدول الأطراف جميع التدابير المناسبة للقضاء على التمييز ضد المرأة في كافة الأمور المتعلقة بالزواج والعلاقات الأسرية وبوجه خاص تضمن، على أساس تساوي الرجل والمرأة:

(أ) نفس الحق في عقد الزواج،

(ب) نفس الحق في حرية اختيار الزوج، وفي عدم عقد الزواج إلا برضاها الحر الكامل،

(ج) نفس الحقوق والمسؤوليات أثناء الزواج وعند فسخه،

(د) نفس الحقوق والمسؤوليات كوالدة، بغض النظر عن حالتها الزوجية، في الأمور المتعلقة بأطفالها، وفي جميع الأحوال، تكون مصالح الأطفال هي الراجحة،

(ه) نفس الحقوق في أن تقرر بحرية وبشعور من المسؤوليات عدد أطفالها والفترة بين إنجاب طفل وآخر، وفي الحصول على المعلومات والتثقيف والوسائل الكفيلة بتمكينها من ممارسة هذه الحقوق،

(و) نفس الحقوق والمسؤوليات فيما يتعلق بالولاية والقوامة والوصاية على الأطفال وتبنيهم او ما شبه ذلك من الأنظمة المؤسسية الاجتماعية، حين توجد هذه المفاهيم في التشريع الوطني، وفي جميع الأحوال تكون مصالح الأطفال هي الراجحة،

(ز) نفس الحقوق الشخصية للزوج والزوجة، بما في ذلك الحق في اختيار اللقب، والمهنة، والعمل،

(ح) نفس الحقوق لكلا الزوجين فيما يتعلق بملكية وحيازة الممتلكة، والإشراف عليها، وإدارتها، والتمتع بها، والتصرف فيها، سواء بلا مقابل او مقابل عوض ذي قيمة.

٢ لا يكون لخطوبة الطفل او زواجه اي أثر قانوني، وتتخذ جميع الإجراءات الضرورية، بما فيها التشريع، لتحديد سن أدنى للزواج ولجعل تسجيل الزواج في سجل رسمي أمرا إلزاميا.

Item (74): Egypt's reservations to CEDAW

التحفظات:

التحفظ على نص الفقرة الثانية من المادة (٩) بشأن منح المرأة حقا متساويا لحق

الرجل فيما يتعلق بجنسية أطفالها، بأن يكون ذلك دون إخلال باكتساب الطفل الناتج لجنسية أبيه، وذلك تفاديا من اكتسابه الجنسيتين في حال اختلاف جنسية الأبوين اتقاء أضرار بمستقبله، و من الجليل أن اكتساب الطفل لجنسية أبيه هو أنسب الأوضاع له ولا مساس بمبدأ المساواة بين الرجل والمرأة إذ المألوف موافقة المرأة في حالة زواجها من أجنبيا على انتساب أطفالهما لجنسية الأب.
التحفظ على نص المادة (١٦) بشأن تساوي المرأة بالرجل في كافة الأمور المتعلقة بالزواج وعلاقات الأسرة أثناء الزواج وعقد فسخه بأن يكون ذلك دون إخلال بما تكفله الشريعة الإسلامية للزوجة لحقوق مقابلة لحقوق الزوج بما يحقق التوازن العادل بينهما وذلك مراعاة بما تقوم عليه العلاقات الزوجية في مصر من قدسية مستمدة من العقائد الدينية الراسخة التي لا يجوز الخروج عليها، واعتبارا بأن من أهم الأسس التي تقوم عليها هذه العلاقات التقابل بين الحقوق والواجبات على نحو من التكامل الذي يحقق المساواة الحقيقية بين الزوجين لا مظاهر المساواة الشكلية التي لا تحقق للزوجة مصلحة نافعة من الزواج بقدر ما تثقل كاهلها من القيود. ذلك أن أحكام الشريعة الإسلامية تفرض على الزوج أداء المهر المناسب للزوجة والإنفاق عليها من ماله إنفاقا كاملا ثم أداء نفقة لها عند الطلاق في حين تحتفظ الزوجة بحقوقها على أموالها ولا تلتزم بالإنفاق منها على نفسها و[ل]ذلك قيدت الشريعة حق الزوجة في الطلاق بأن أوجبت أن يكون ذلك بحكم القضاء في حين لم تضع مثل هذا القيد على الزوج. [...]

Item (75): UN-doc. CEDAW/C/5/Add. 10

[...] لا مظاهر المساواة الشكلية التي لا تحقق للزوجة مصلحة نافعة من الزواج بقدر ما تثقل كاهلها من القيود.

Item (77): UN-doc. CCPR/C/82/Add. 1

للزوج على الزوجة حق الطاعة فيما يحقق مصلحة الأسرة وعلى الأخص فيما يلي:
(١) الانتقال معه الى منزل الزوجية ما لم تكن قد اشترطت عليه في العقد البقاء في منزلها او منزل أسرتها فيكون عليها تمكينه من السكن معه والدخول عليها.
(٢) تمكينه منها صالحه للوطء المشروع في غير حضور أحد.
(٣) امتثال أمره والقيام بعملها في بيت الزوجية مثل غيرها.
(٤) عدم الخروج من منزل الزوجية إلا بإذنه، وليس للزوج منع زوجته من الخروج لعذر شرعي او ما جرء العرف بمثله مما ليس فيه قيد الإخلال بالشرف ولا بواجباتها نحوه، وعلى الأخص الخروج في إصلاح مالها او أداء وظيفتها، ويعتبر عذر شرعي للمرأة خدمة والديها العاجزين وليس لهما من يقوم بخدمتهما او أحدهما غيرها.

Item (81): CRC, articles 20 and 21

المادة ٢٠

١ للطفل المحروم بصفة مؤقتة او دائمة من بيئته العائلية او الذي لا يسمح له، حفاظا على مصالحه الفضلى، بالبقاء في تلك البيئة، الحق في حماية ومساعدة

خاصتين توفرهما الدولة.

٢ تضمن الدول الأطراف وفقا لقوانينها الوطنية، رعاية بديلة لمثل هذا الطفل.

٣ يمكن أن تشمل هذه الرعاية، في جملة أمور، الحضانة، او الكفالة الواردة في القانون الإسلامي، او التبني، او، عند الضرورة، الإقامة في مؤسسة مناسبة لرعاية الأطفال. وعند النظر في الحلول، ينبغي إيلاء الاعتبار الواجب لاستصواب الاستمرارية في تربية الطفل ولخلفية الطفل الإثنية والدينية والثقافية واللغوية.

المادة ٢١

تضمن الدول التي تقر و/او تجيز نظام التبني إيلاء مصالح الطفل الفضلى الاعتبار الاول والقيام بما يلي:

(أ) تضمن ألا تصرح بتبني الطفل إلا السلطة المختصة التي تحدد، وفقا للقوانين والإجراءات المعمول بها وعلى أساس كل المعلومات ذات الصلة الموثوق بها، أن التبني جائز نظرا لحالة الطفل فيما يتعلق بالوالدين والأقارب، والأوصياء القانونيين وأن الأشخاص المعنيين، عند الاقتضاء، قد أعطوا عن علم موافقتهم على التبني على أساس حصولهم على ما قد يلزم من المشورة.

(ب) تعترف بأن التبني في بلد آخر يمكن اعتباره وسيلة بديلة لرعاية الطفل، إذا تعذرت إقامة الطفل لدى أسرة حاضنة او متبنية، او إذا تعذرت العناية به بأي طريقة ملائمة في وطنه.

(ج) تضمن، بالنسبة للتبني في بلد آخر، أن يستفيد الطفل من ضمانات ومعايير تعادل تلك القائمة فيما يتعلق بالتبني الوطني.

(د) تتخذ جميع التدابير المناسبة كي تضمن، بالنسبة للتبني في بلد آخر، أن عملية التبني لا تعود على أولائك المشاركين فيها بكسب مالي غير مشروع.

(ه) تعزز، عند الاقتضاء، أهداف هذه المادة بعقد ترتيبات او اتفاقات ثنائية او متعددة الأطراف، وتسعى، في هذا الإطار، الى ضمان أن يكون تبني الطفل في بلد آخر من خلال السلطات او الهيئات المختصة.

Item (82): Egypt's reservations to CRC

اعتبارا لأن الشريعة الإسلامية هي مصدر أساسي من مصادر التشريع في القانون الوضعي المصري ونظرا لأن هذه الشريعة إذ توجب توفير كافة وسائل للحماية والرعاية للأطفال بطرق ووسائل متعددة ليس من بينها نظام التبني الموجود في بعض القوانين الوضعية الأخرى فإن حكومة جمهورية مصر العربية تتحفظ على كافة النصوص والأحكام الخاصة بالتبني في هذه الاتفاقية، على وجه خاص ما ورد بشأن التبني في المادتين ٢٠ و٢١ من الاتفاقية.

Item (83): Jordan's reservations to CRC

بعد أن اطلعنا على اتفاقية حقوق الطفل التي اعتمدت من قبل الجمعية العامة للأمم المتحدة في العشرين من شهر تشرين ثاني [c!] لعام ألف وتسعمئة وتسعة وثمانين ملادية، نعلن موافقتنا وتصديقنا عليها في مجموعها وتفصيلاتها ونتعهد بأن نقوم بما ورد فيها ونلاهظ بنودها ولن نسمح بإذن الله بإخلال بها. وإن المملكة الأردنية الهاشمية تبدي تحفظها وتعتبر نفسها غير ملزمة بماورد في المواد الرابعة عشرة

والعشرين والواحدة والعشرين من الاتفاقية والتي تعطي الطفل الحق في حرية اختيار الدين، والبنود المتعلقة في قضية التبني لمعارضتها لأحكام الشريعة الإسلامية السمحة.

Item (87): UN-doc. CRC/C/3/Add.3

(ب) الجلد على سبيل التأديب لمن بلغ العاشرة بما لا يجاوز عشرين جلدة؛

Item (89): Qurʾān 4:3

وإن خفتم الا تقسطوا في اليتمى فانكحوا ما طاب لكم من النساء مثنى وثلث وربع فإن خفتم ألا تعدلوا فوحدة أو ما ملكت أيمنكم ذلك أدنى الا تعولوا.

References

A. Arabic references

ᶜAbdalbāqī, F. 1944/1945. Al-muᶜjam al-mufahras li-ʾalfāẓ al-qurʾān al-karīm. Cairo.

ᶜAbdallāh, Ḥ. 1982. A Dictionary of International Relations & Conference Terminology (Arabic: Qāmūs muṣṭalaḥāt al-ᶜalāqāt wa-l-muʾtamarāt ad-duwalīya). Beirut.

ᶜAbdarrāziq, ᶜAlī 1972. Al-ʾislām wa-ʾuṣūl al-ḥukm. Beirut.

ʾAbū Luġud, I. 1974. "As-sayṭara aṣ-ṣahyūnīya ᶜalā d-dirāsāt al-ʾislāmīya fī ʾamrīka", Al -ʾĀdāb 12/6, pp. 5ff.

ʾAbū Salāmā [no date]. An-nāsiḫ wa-l-mansūḫ, a text which appears as marginal gloss in *Nīsābūrī* [no date]. ʾAsbāb an-nuzūl.

ʾAbū Zayd, Naṣr Ḥāmid 1990. Mafhūm an-naṣṣ. Dirāsa fī ᶜulūm al-qurʾān. Cairo.

– 1994. Naqd al-ḫiṭāb ad-dīnī. Cairo.

al-ʾAḥmad, N. 1985. Filasṭīn tārīḫan wa-niḍālan. Amman.

ʾAmīn Saᶜīd [no date]. Aṯ-ṯawra al-ᶜarabīya al-kubrā, 3 vols. Cairo.

al-ᶜAẓm, Ṣ. 1981. Al-istišrāq wa-l-istišrāq maᶜkūsan. Beirut.

Bānāja, S. 1985. Al-mabādiʾ al-ʾasāsīya li-l-ᶜalāqāt ad-duwalīya wa-d-diblūmāsīya waqta s-salām wa-l-ḥarb bayna t-tašrīᶜ al-ʾislāmī wa-l-qānūn ad-duwalī l-ᶜāmm. Beirut.

Darġām, R. 1996. "Al-majmūᶜa al-ᶜarabīya fī l-ʾumam al-muttaḥida taḥtafī bi-Ġālī muʾayyidatan ʾiᶜādat intiḫābi-hī", Al-Ḥayāt, September 14, 1996, p. 7.

Didaoui, M./UNIDO (United Nations Industrial Development Organization) 1989. Dalīl al-mutarjim maᶜa tarkīz ᶜalā manẓūmat al-ʾumam al-muttaḥida (Manual for Arabic Translators with Emphasis on the Usage in the United Nations System), 2 vols. Vienna.

Fawq al-ᶜĀda, S. 1974. A Dictionary of Diplomacy and International Affairs (Arabic: Muᶜjam ad-diblūmāsīya wa-š-šuʾūn ad-duwalīya). Beirut.

Ibn Hišām / Wüstenfeld, F. (ed.) [1858]. Kitāb sīrat rasūl allāh, 2 vols. Göttingen.

Ibn Taymīya [1971]. As-siyāsa aš-šarᶜīya fī ʾiṣlāḥ ar-rāᶜī wa-r-raᶜīya. Cairo.

Maḥmūd Muḥammad Ṭāhā/an-Naᶜīm, ᶜAbdallāh ʾAḥmad (transl.) 1987. Ar-risāla aṯ-ṯāniya min al-ʾislām (= *Mahmoud Mohamed Taha*. The Second Message of Islam). Syracuse.

Muḥammad ibn ᶜAbdallāh [ca. 610-632]. Al-Qurʾān.

Nuᶜmān, A. [no date]. Al-ittijāhāt al-ᶜalmānīya fī l-ᶜālam al-ᶜarabī. Jounieh (Lebanon).

al-Qalqašandī [1913-1919]. Ṣubḥ al-ʾaᶜšā fī ṣināᶜat al-ʾinšāʾ. Cairo.

as-Saraḫsī, M. [1971/1972]. Šarḥ kitāb as-siyar al-kabīr li-Muḥammad ibn Aḥmad aš-Šaybānī. Cairo.

Šaḥrūr, M. 1992. Al-kitāb wa-l-qurʾān. Qirāʾa muᶜāṣira. Damascus.

aṭ-Ṭabarī/de Goeje, M. (ed.) [1893]. Tārīḫ ar-rusul wa-l-mulūk, series 1, vol. 5. Leiden.

B. Non-Arabic references

Abu-Sahlieh, S. 1985. "La définition internationale des droits de l'homme et l'islam", Revue générale de droit international public 89 (1985), pp. 625ff.

– 1994. Les musulmans face aux droits de l'homme. Réligion & droit & politique. Etude de documents. Bochum.

Alston, P. (ed.) 1992a. The United Nations and Human Rights. A Critical Appraisal. Oxford.

– 1992b. "The Security Council and human rights: lessons to be learned from the Iraq-Kuwait crisis and its aftermath", The Australian Year Book of International Law 13 (1992), pp. 107ff.

Amereller, F. 1995. Hintergründe des "Islamic Banking". Rechtliche Problematik des ribā-Verbotes in der Shariᶜa und seine Auswirkungen auf einzelne Rechtsordnungen arabischer Staaten. Berlin.

Andrews, P. 1989. Ethnic Groups in the Republic of Turkey. Wiesbaden.

Arzt, D. 1990. "The application of international human rights law in Islamic states", Human Rights Quarterly 12 (1990), pp. 202ff.

Atiya, A. 1986. "Ḳibṭ", The Encyclopaedia of Islam (new edition), vol. 5, pp. 90ff.

Austin, J. 1962. How to Do Things with Words. Oxford.

Ayalon, A. 1987. Language and Change in the Arab Middle East. New York/Oxford.

Aziz, Y. 1993. "Explicit and implicit reference in Arabic-English translation", Babel: International Journal of Translation 39 (1993), pp. 129ff.

Bälz, K. 1997. "Submitting faith to judicial scrutiny through the family trial: the Abū Zayd case", Die Welt des Islams 37/2 (1997), pp. 135ff.

Bailey, S. 1985. The Making of Resolution 242. Dordrecht.

Barkey, H./*Fuller*, G. 1997. "Turkey's Kurdish question: Critical turning points and missed opportunities", The Middle East Journal 51/1 (1997), pp. 59ff.

Barkho, L. 1987. "Cultural problems of Arabic-English political translation", Babel: International Journal of Translation 33 (1987), pp. 143ff.

Basset, A. 1952. La langue berbère. (Handbook of African Languages, part I). London.

Bedjaoui, M. 1992. "The Gulf War of 1980-1988 and the Islamic conception of International Law", in: *Dekker*, I./*Post*, H. (eds.) 1992. The Gulf War of 1980-1988. The Iran-Iraq War in International Legal Perspective. Dordrecht, pp. 283ff.

Bell, R. 1937. The Qur'ān. Translated, with a critical rearrangement of the Surahs, 2 vols. Edinburgh.

Bernhardt, R. 1963. Die Auslegung völkerrechtlicher Verträge insbesondere in der neueren Rechtssprechung internationaler Gerichte. Köln/Berlin.

Bielefeldt, H. 1992. "Islam und Menschenrechte. Eine Problemskizze", in: *Bielefeldt*, H./*Bohnet*, M./*Dicke*, K./*Nuscheler*/F. 1992 [ms]. "Menschenrechte und Entwicklung". Globale Politik zwischen universalen Normen und kultureller Identität, pp. 31ff.

Björkman, W. 1965. "Diplomatic", The Encyclopaedia of Islam (new edition), vol. 2, pp. 301 ff.

Blanc, H. 1964. Communal Dialects in Baghdad. Cambridge, MA.

Blau, J. 1981. The Renaissance of Modern Hebrew and Modern Standard Arabic. Parallels and Differences in the Revival of Two Semitic Languages. Berkeley.

Bois, T./*MacKenzie*, D./*Minorsky*, V. 1986. "Kurds, Kurdistan", The Encyclopaedia of Islam (new edition), vol. 5, pp. 438ff.

Boisard, M. 1979. L'humanisme de l'islam. Paris.

– 1980. "On the probable influences of Islam on Western Public and International Law", International Journal of Middle Eastern Studies 11 (1980), pp. 429ff.

Boutros-Ghali, B. 1972. Les conflits de frontières en Afrique - étude et documents. Paris.

Bowman, M./*Harris*, D. 1984. Multilateral Treaties. Index & Current Status, 2 vols. (and further fascicles). London.

Boyle, F. 1989. "International law and organizations as an approach to conflict resolution in the Middle East", in: *Buergenthal*, T. (ed.) 1989. Contemporary Issues in International Law. Essays in Honor of Louis B. Sohn. Kehl.

Bozarslan, H. 1996. "Political crisis and the Kurdish issue in Turkey", in: *Olson* (ed.) 1996, pp. 135ff.

Bozeman, A. 1971. The Future of Law in a Multicultural World. Princeton.

Bring, O. 1992. "Kurdistan and the principle of self-determination", German Yearbook of International Law 35 (1992), pp. 157ff.

Bühler, K. 1934. Sprachtheorie. Jena.

Burton, J. (ed.) 1987. Abū ᶜUbaid al-Qāsim b. Sallām's *K. al-nāsikh wa-l-mansūkh*. Cambridge.

Busse, H. 1984. "ᶜOmar b. al-Ḫaṭṭāb in Jerusalem", Jerusalem Studies in Arabic and Islam 5 (1984), pp. 73ff.

Bußmann, H. 1983. Lexikon der Sprachwissenschaft. Stuttgart.

Capotorti, F. 1991. Study on the Rights of Persons belonging to Ethnic, Religious and Linguistic Minorities. Geneva/New York.

Carter, M. 1993. "Probleme bei der Übersetzung von Fachsprache am Beispiel des Arabischen," in: *Frank*, A./*Maaß*, K./*Paul*, F./*Turk*, H. (eds.) 1993. Übersetzen, verstehen, Brücken bauen: Geisteswissenschaftliches und literarisches Übersetzen im internationalen Kulturaustausch. Berlin, pp. 130ff.

Carty, A. 1991. "Critical International Law: Recent trends in the theory of International Law", European Journal of International Law 2/1 (1991), pp. 66ff.

Chabry, L./*Chabry*, A. 1984. Politique et minorités au Proche-Orient. Les raisons d'une explosion. Paris.

Chaliand, G. (ed.) 1980. A People without a Country. The Kurds and Kurdistan. London.

Chappez, J. 1976. "L'avis consultatif de la cour internationale de justice du 16 octobre 1975 dans l'affaire du Sahara Occidental", Revue générale de droit international public 80 (1976), pp. 1132ff.

Chehata, C. 1960. "ᶜAḳd", The Encyclopaedia of Islam (new edition), vol. 1, pp. 318ff.

Childs, P./*Williams*, R. 1997. An Introduction to Post-Colonial Theory. London.

Chinkin, C. 1993. "East Timor moves into the World Cot", European Journal of International Law 4/2 (1993), pp. 206ff.

– 1997. "Reservations and objections to the Convention on the Elimination of All Forms of Discrimination against Women", in: *Gardner* (ed.) 1997, pp. 64ff.

Chomsky, N. 1983. The Fateful Triangle. The United States, Israel, and the Palestinians. Boston.

– 1987. "Rejectionism and accomodation", in: *Chomsky*, N./*Peck*, J. (eds.) 1987. The Chomsky Reader. New York, pp. 371ff.

Chyet, M. 1995. "Neo-Aramaic and Kurdish. An interdisciplinary consideration of their influence on each other", in: *Izre'el*, S./*Drory*, R. (eds.) 1995. Language and Culture in the Near East (= Israel Oriental Studies XV). Leiden , pp. 219ff.

Clark, B. 1991. "The Vienna Convention reservations régime and the Convention on Discrimination against Women (!)", American Journal of International Law 85 (1991), pp. 281ff.

Cocatre-Zilgien, A. 1955. "La comptabilité du pacte turco-irakien et des obligations internationales antérieures des états signataires", Annuaire Français de Droit International 1 (1955), pp. 158ff.

Connors, J. 1997. "The Women's Convention in the Muslim world, in: *Gardner* (ed.) 1997, pp. 85ff.

Cook, R. 1990. "Reservations to the Convention on the Elimination of All Forms of Discrimination against Women", Virginia Journal of International Law 30 (1990), pp. 643ff.

Crawford, J. 1990. "The creation of the State of Palestine: too much too soon?", European Journal of International Law 1/2 (1990), pp. 307ff.

Davies, H. 1947. Constitutions, Electoral Laws, Treaties of States in the Near and Middle East. Durham.

Despagnet, F. 1897. "Le conflit entre l'Italie et l'Abyssinie", Revue générale de droit international public 4 (1897), pp. 5ff.

Dilger, K. 1981. "Das islamische Strafrecht in der modernen Welt. Ein Beitrag zur Rechtskonzeption im Islam", Zeitschrift für die gesamte Strafrechtswissenschaft 93 (1981), pp. 1311ff.

– 1990. "Die Entwicklung des islamischen Rechts", in: *Ahmed*, M. et al. (eds.) 1990. Der Islam. III. Islamische Kultur – Zeitgenössische Strömungen – Volksfrömmigkeit. Stuttgart, pp. 60ff.

Dinstein, Y. 1981. Models of Autonomy. New Brunswick/London.

– 1987. "Anti-Semism, anti-Zionism and the United Nations", Israel Yearbook on Human Rights 17 (1987), pp. 15ff.

Doeker, G./*Melsheimer*, K./*Schröder*, D. 1973. "Berlin and the Quadripartite Agreement", American Journal of International Law 67(1973), pp. 44ff.

Dölle, H. 1961. "Zur Problematik mehrsprachiger Gesetzes- und Vertragstexte", Rabels Zeitschrift für ausländisches und internationales Privatrecht 26 (1961), pp. 4ff.

Dolph, W. 1988. "Nicht so gemeint... Die UNO-Sprache", Vereinte Nationen 6/1988, pp. 178f.

Donoho, D. 1991. "Relativism versus universalism in human rights: the search for meaningful standards", Stanford Journal of International Law 27 (1991), pp. 345ff.

D'Souza, D. 1991. Illiberal Eduacation. The Politics of Race and Sex on Campus. New York.

Ebert, H. 1996. Das Personalstatut arabischer Länder – Problemfelder, Methoden, Perspektiven. Frankfurt.

Edel, E. 1997. Der Vertrag zwischen Ramses II. von Ägypten und Ḫattušili III von Ḫatti. Berlin.

Edzard, L. 1993. United Nations Electoral Assistance: Current Issues (Rapporteur's Report on the New York Training Seminar on Electoral Assistance, 26 October - 6 November 1992). United Nations Institute for Training and Research, New York.

– 1996. "Stylistic elements in the use of Arabic as language in diplomacy: Recent developments in United Nations context", Die Welt des Islams 36/1 (1996), pp. 25ff.

– 1997. "Language as medium of legal norm: The topics "war and peace" and "human rights" in bi- and multilateral treaties with Arab states and organizations", in: *Edzard*, L./*Szyska*, C. (eds.) 1997. Encounters of Words and Texts. Intercultural Studies in Honor of Stefan Wild on the Occasion of His 60th

Birthday, March 2, 1997, Presented by His Pupils in Bonn. Hildesheim, pp. 69ff.

Eitel, T. 1992. "The escape and parole of the imprisoned God of War. An overview of the Second Gulf War from the perspective of International Law", German Yearbook of International Law 35 (1992), pp. 170ff.

Emery, P. 1989. "Legal Arabic texts: implications for translation", Babel: International Journal of Translation 35 (1989), pp. 1ff.

Ende, W. 1996. Schreckgespenst und reale Bedrohung: Der "Heilige Krieg" der Fundamentalisten. Köln.

Erlich, H. 1981. "The Eritrean Autonomy 1952 - 1962; its failure and its contribution to further escalation", in: *Dinstein*, Y. (ed.) 1981. Models of Autonomy. New Brunswick/London, pp. 171ff.

Esman, J./*Rabinovich*, I. (eds.) 1988. Ethnicity, Pluralism and the State in the Middle East. Ithaca.

Fastenrath, U. 1991. Lücken im Völkerrecht. Zu Rechtscharakter, Quellen, Systemzusammenhang, Methodenlehre und Funktionen des Völkerrechts. Berlin.

– 1993. "Relative normativity in International Law", European Journal of International Law 4/3 (1993), pp. 305ff.

Fikentscher, W. 1975-1977. Methoden des Rechts in vergleichender Darstellung, 5 vols. Tübingen.

Filip, O. "Wenn man "odsun" und "vyhnání" kreuzt, kommt "vyhánění" heraus. Der Streit um Abschiebung und Vertreibung, die philologischen Finessen und ihre glorreiche Auflösung in der deutsch-tschechischen Erklärung", Frankfurter Allgemeine Zeitung, December 24, 1996.

Finet, A. 1973. Le code de Hammurapi. Paris.

Forstner, M. 1993. "Zur Diskussion über die Menschenrechte in den arabischen Staaten", in: *Bertsch*, L./*Messer*, H. (eds.) 1993. Christen und Muslime in der Verantwortung für eine Welt- und Friedensordnung. Frankfurt, pp. 49ff.

Fox, S. 1994. "The relationship of the Eastern Neo-Aramaic dialects", Journal of the American Oriental Society 114 (1994), pp. 154ff.

Franck, T. 1976. "The stealing of the Sahara", American Journal of International Law 70 (1976), pp. 694ff.

Franz, E. 1978. Minderheiten im Vorderen Orient. Auswahlbibliographie. Hamburg.

Frege, G. 1892a. "Über Sinn und Bedeutung", Zeitschrift für Philosophie und philosophische Kritik 100 (1892), pp. 25ff.

– 1892b. "Über Begriff und Gegenstand", Zeitschrift für Philosophie und philosophische Kritik 100 (1892), pp. 51ff.

Friedmann, Y. (transl.) 1992. The History of al-Tabari. Volume XII. The Battle of al-Qadisiyyah and the Conquest of Syria and Palestine. Albany.

Friedrich, J. 1962. "Das Neusyrische als Typus einer entarteten semitischen Sprache", Annali del Istituto Orientale di Napoli (1962), pp. 95ff.

Gaja, G. 1987. "Unruly treaty reservations", in: Le droit international à l'heure de sa codification. Etudes en honneur de Roberto Ago, 2 vols. (1987), vol. 1, pp. 307ff.

Gätje, H. 1973. Zur Syntax der Determinationsverhältnisse im Arabischen. Hamburg.

Gardner, J. (ed.) 1997. Human Rights as General Norms and a State's Right to Opt out. British Institute of International and Comparative Law.

Geiger, R. 1985. Grundgesetz und Völkerrecht. Die Bezüge des Staatsrechts zum Völkerrecht und Europarecht. Munich.

Germer, P. 1970. "Interpretation of plurilingual treaties: A study of article 33 of the Vienna Convention on the Law of Treaties", Harvard International Law Journal 11 (1970), pp. 400ff.

Gnidil, A. 1987. Die völkerrechtliche Lage der ehemaligen Spanischen Sahara. Tübingen.

Gökalp, Z. 1920. Türkčülügün esāslari. Ankara. [= *Gökalp*, Z. 1968. The Principles of Turkism. Translated from the Turkish and Annotated by Robert Devereux. Leiden.]

Gray, C. 1994. "After the ceasefire: Iraq, the Security Council and the use of force", The British Yearbook of International Law 65 (1994), pp. 135ff.

Gruenwald, I. 1994. "The Other Self: Introductory notes", in: *Alon*, I./*Gruenwald*, I./*Singer*, I. (eds.) 1994. Concepts of the Other in Near Eastern Religions (= Israel Oriental Studies XIV), pp. 7ff.

Gully, A. 1993. "The changing face of modern written Arabic: an update", Al-ᶜArabiyya 26 (1993), pp. 19ff.

Gürbey, G. 1996. "The Kurdish nationalist movement in Turkey since the 1980s", in: *Olson* (ed.) 1996, pp. 9ff.

Habermas, J. 1985. Theorie des kommunikativen Handelns, 2 vols., 3rd ed. Frankfurt.

Hamui, M. 1949. Diplomatic Terms. English-Arabic. Damascus.

Hardy, J. 1961. "The interpretation of plurilingual treaties by international courts and tribunals", The British Yearbook of International Law 37 (1961), pp. 72ff.

Hartmann, K. 1980. Untersuchungen zur Sozialgeographie christlicher Minderheiten im Vorderen Orient. Wiesbaden.

Hary, B. 1992. Multiglossia in Judeo-Arabic. Leiden.

Heper, M. 1997. "Islam and democracy in Turkey: Toward a reconciliation", The Middle East Journal 51/1 (1997), pp. 32ff.

Hilf, M. 1973. Die Auslegung mehrsprachiger Verträge. Eine Untersuchung zum Völkerrecht und zum Staatsrecht der Bundesrepublik Deutschland. Berlin.

Hourani, A. 1983. Arabic Thought in the Liberal Age 1798-1939. Cambridge.

Hummer, W./*Schweitzer*, M. 1994. "Chapter VIII. Regional Arrangements", in: *Simma*, B. (ed.) 1994. The Charter of the United Nations. A Commentary. Oxford, pp. 679ff.

Huntington, S. 1996. The Clash of Civilizations and the Remaking of World Order. New York.

Hurewitz, J. 1956. Diplomacy in the Near and Middle East. A Documentary Record: 1914-1956, 2 vols. Princeton.

– 1975/1979. The Middle East and North Africa in World Politics. A Documentary Record, 2 vols. New Haven.

Issawi, C. 1967. "European loan-words in contemporary Arabic writing: a case-study in modernization", Middle Eastern Studies 3 (1967), pp. 110ff.

Jastrow, O. 1967. Laut- und Formenlehre des neuaramäischen Dialekts von Midin im Ṭur ᶜAbdin. Bamberg.

Johnstone, T. 1975. The Modern South Arabian Languages (= Afroasiatic Linguistics 1/5). Malibu.

Kaikobad, K. 1980. The Shatt al-Arab Boundary Question. A Legal Approach. Oxford.

– 1992. "Self-defence, enforcement action and the Gulf Wars 1980-88 and 1990-91", The British Yearbook of International Law 63 (1992), pp. 299ff.

Kapeliuk, O. 1996. "Is Modern Hebrew the only "Indo-Europeanized" Semitic language? And what about Neo-Aramaic?", in: *Izre'el*, S./*Raz*, S. (eds.) 1996. Studies in Modern Semitic Languages (= Israel Oriental Studies 16). Leiden, pp. 59ff.

Kedourie, E. 1976. In the Anglo-Arab Labyrinth. The McMahon-Husayn Correspondence and its Interpretations 1914-1939. Cambridge.

– 1988. "Ethnicity, majority, and minority in the Middle East", in: *Esman/Rabinovich* (eds.) 1988, pp. 25ff.

Khadduri, M. 1955. War and Peace in the Law of Islam. Baltimore.

– 1966. The Islamic Law of Nations. Shaybānī's Siyar. Baltimore.

– 1972. Major Middle Eastern Problems in International Law. Washington.

Khalil, M. 1962. The Arab States and the Arab League, 2 vols. Beirut.

Khan, K./*Matthies*, V. (eds.) 1981. Regionalkonflikte in der Dritten Welt. Ursachen. Verlauf. Internationalisierung. Lösungsansätze. München/Köln/London.

Klein-Franke, A. 1997. "Zum Rechtsstatus der Juden im Jemen", Die Welt des Islams 37/2 (1997), pp. 178ff.

Kramer, H. 1996. "Die Türkei unter Erbakan. Kontinuität und islamistischer Wandel", Außenpolitik 4/96, pp. 379ff.

Kratochwil, G. 1996. Die Berber in der historischen Entwicklung Algeriens von 1949 bis 1990. Zur Konstruktion einer ethnischen Identität. Berlin.

Krawietz, B. 1991. Die Ḥurma. Schariarechtlicher Schutz vor Eingriffen in die körperliche Unversehrtheit nach arabischen Fatwas des 20. Jahrhunderts. Berlin.

Kreyenbroek, G./*Sperl*, S. (eds.) 1992. The Kurds. A Contemporary Overview. London/New York.

Krüger, H. 1987. "Überblick über das Privatrecht der Staaten des ägyptischen Rechtskreises", Recht van de Islam 5 (1987), pp. 98ff.

Kühnhardt, L. 1987. Die Universalität der Menschenrechte. Studien zur ideengeschichtlichen Bestimmung eines politischen Schlüsselbegriffs. München.

Kuner, C. 1991. "The interpretation of multilingual treaties. Comparison of texts versus the assumption of similar meaning", International and Comparative Law Quarterly 40 (1991), pp. 953ff.

Landau, J. 1993. "Mu^{c}āhada", The Encyclopaedia of Islam (new edition), vol. 7, pp. 250ff.

Langdon, S./*Gardiner*, A. 1920. The treaty of alliance between Hattušili, King of the Hittites, and the Pharaoh Ramesses II, Journal of Egyptian Archeology 6 (1920), pp. 179ff.

Lapidoth, R. 1970. "La résolution du Conseil de sécurité du 22 novembre 1967 au sujet du Moyen Orient", Revue générale de droit international public 74 (1970), pp. 289ff.

– 1983. "The Strait of Tiran, the Gulf of Aqaba, and the 1979 Treaty of Peace between Egypt and Israel", American Journal of International Law 77 (1983), pp. 84ff.

Lapidoth, R./*Hirsch*, M. (eds.) 1992. The Arab-Israeli Conflict and its Resolution: Selected Documents. Dordrecht/Boston/London.

Laqueur, W./*Rubin*, B. (eds.) 1984 (4th ed.). The Israel-Arab Reader. A Documentary History of the Middle East Conflict. New York.

Lauterpacht, E. et al. (eds.) 1991. The Kuwait Crisis. Basic Documents, 3 vols. Cambridge.

Lerch, W. 1996. "Alle unter einer Sonne. Linguistik als Politik: Wie die Türkei das Kurdische verdrängt", Frankfurter Allgemeine Zeitung, April 2, 1996, p. 39.

Leslau, W. 1987. Comparative Dictionary of Ge^{c}ez. Wiesbaden.

Lewis, B. 1956. A Handbook of Diplomatic and Political Arabic. London.

– 1974a. Islam from the Prophet Muhammad to the Capture of Constantinople, 2 vols. New York.

– 1974b. "On some modern Arabic political terms", in: *Barral*, J. (ed.) 1974. Orientalia Hispanica sive studia F. M. Pareja Octogenario [de]dicata. Leiden, vol. 1, pp. 465ff.

– 1980. "Translation from Arabic", Proceedings [of the American Philosophical Society] 4, no. 1 (Februar 1980), pp. 41ff, reprinted in: *Lewis*, B. 1993a. Islam and the West. New York/Oxford, pp. 61ff.

– 1984. The Jews of Islam. Princeton.

– 1986. Semites and Anti-Semites. An Inquiry into Conflict and Prejudice. New York.

– 1988. The Political Language of Islam. Chicago.

– 1990a. Race and Slavery in the Middle East. New York.

– 1990b. "The roots of Muslim rage: Why so many Muslims deeply resent the West and why their bitterness will not be easily mollified", Atlantic Monthly 266 (1990).

– 1993a. Islam and the West. New York/Oxford.

– 1993b. "Orientalist notes on the Soviet-United Arab Republic Treaty of 27 May 1971", Princeton Papers in Near Eastern Studies 2 (1993), pp. 57ff.

– 1995. "The other Middle East problems", in: *Kramer*, M. (ed.) 1995. Middle Eastern Lectures. Number One. 1995. Tel Aviv, pp.45ff.

Lijnzaad, L. 1995. Reservations to Human Rights Treaties: Ratify and Ruin. Dordrecht.

Lord Caradon et al. 1981. U.N. Security Council Resolution 242: A Case Study in Diplomatic Ambiguity. Institute for the Study of Diplomacy, Edmund A. Walsh School of Foreign Service, Georgetown University, Washington.

Lyons, J. 1977. Semantics, 2 vols. Cambridge.

Maffei, M. 1993. "The case of East Timor before the International Court of Justice – some tentative comments", European Journal of International Law 4/2 (1993), pp. 223ff.

Makarov, A. 1968. "Zur Auslegung mehrsprachiger Staatsverträge", in: Recueil d'études de droit international en hommage à Paul Guggenheim. Genf 1968, pp. 403ff.

Malanczuk, P. 1991. "The Kurdish crisis and allied intervention in the aftermath of the Second Gulf War", European Journal of International Law 2/1 (1991), pp. 114ff.

– 1996. "Some basic aspects of the agreements between Israel and the PLO from the perspective of International Law", European Journal of International Law 7/2 (1996), pp. 485ff.

Mansoor, M. 1965. Legal and Documentary Arabic Reader (Arabic: Qirāʾāt mina l-ʿarabīya al-qaḍāʾīya wa-l-waṯāʾiqīya). Leiden.

Marwick, L. 1980. Diplomatic Hebrew. A Glossary of Current Terminology. Washington.

Mayer, A. 1980. "Libyan legislation in defense of Arabo-Islamic sexual mores", The American Journal of Comparative Law 28 (1980), pp. 287ff.

– 1987. "Law and religion in the Muslim Middle East", The American Journal of Comparative Law 35 (1987), pp. 127ff.

– 1991a. Islam and Human Rights. Boulder/San Francisco/London.

– 1991b. "War and peace in the Islamic tradition and in International Law, in: *Kelsay*, J./*Johnson*, J. (eds.) 1991. Just War and Jihad. New York, pp. 195ff.

– 1994. "Universal versus Islamic human rights: a clash of cultures or clash with a construct", Michigan Journal of International Law 15 (1994), pp. 307ff.

McLaurin, R. (ed.) 1976. The Political Role of Minority Groups in the Middle East. New York.

Menashri, D. 1988. "Khomeini's policy toward ethnic and religious minorities", in: *Esman/Rabinovich* (eds.) 1988, pp. 215ff.

Mendelson, M./*Hulton*, S. 1993. The Iraq-Kuwait boundary", The British Yearbook of International Law 64 (1993), pp. 135ff.

Monteil, V. 1960. L'arabe moderne. Paris.

Moore, J. (ed.) 1974-1981. The Arab-Israeli Conflict, 4 vols. Princeton.

Mössner, J. 1968. Die Völkerrechtspersönlichkeit und die Völkerrechtspraxis der Barbareskenstaaten. Berlin.

– 1972. "Die Auslegung mehrsprachiger Staatsverträge. Bemerkungen zu Artikel 33 der Wiener Konvention über das Recht der Verträge", Archiv des Völkerrechts 15/3 (1972), pp. 273ff.

Muranyi, M. 1987. "Fiqh", in: *Gätje*, H. (ed.) 1987. Grundriß der arabischen Philologie, Band II: Literaturwissenschaft. Wiesbaden, pp. 299ff.

Na'im, A. (transl.) 1987a. The Second Message of Islam. Mahmoud Mohamed Taha. Syracuse.

– 1987b. "Islamic law, international relations, and human rights: challenge and response", Cornell International Law Journal 20 (1987), pp. 317ff.

– 1988. "Islamic ambivalence to political violence: Islamic law and international terrorism", German Yearbook of International Law 31 (1988), pp. 307ff.

– 1990. Toward an Islamic Reformation: Civil Liberties, Human Rights, and International Law. Syracuse.

Nasir, J. 1990. The Status of Women under Islamic Law and under Modern Islamic Legislation. London/Dordrecht/Boston.

Nelson, L. 1986. "The drafting committee of the third United Nations Conference on the Law of the Sea: The implications of multilingual texts", The British Yearbook of International Law 57 (1986), pp. 171ff.

Nisan, M. 1991. Minorities in the Middle East. A History of Struggle and Self-Expression. Jefferson, N.C.

Noth, A. 1980. "Die Scharia, das religiöse Gesetz des Islam -- Wandlungsmöglichkeiten, Anwendung und Wirkung", in: *Fikentscher*, W./*Franke*, H./*Köhler*, O. (eds.) 1980. Entstehung und Wandel rechtlicher Traditionen. Freiburg/Munich, pp. 415ff.

Odio Benito, E. 1989. Elimination of All Forms of Intolerance and Discrimination Based on Religion or Belief. Geneva/New York.

Oeter, S. 1986. "Die Entwicklung der Westsahara-Frage unter besonderer Berücksichtigung der völkerrechtlichen Anerkennung", Zeitschrift für ausländisches öffentliches Recht und Völkerrecht 46 (1986), pp. 48ff.

Olmert, Y. 1986. Mi'utim ba-mizrakh ha-tikhon. Tel Aviv.

Olson, R. 1989. The Emergence of Kurdish Nationalism and the Sheikh Said Rebellion, 1880-1925. Austin, Texas.

– (ed.) 1996. The Kurdish Nationalist Movement in the 1990s. Its Impact on Turkey and the Middle East. Lexington, Kentucky.

Onuf, N. 1985. "Do rules say what they do? From ordinary language to International Law", Harvard International Law Journal 26 (1985), pp. 385ff.

Osmańczyk, E. 1990. Encyclopedia of the United Nations and International Agreements. New York.

Ostrower, A. 1965. Language, Law, and Diplomacy. A Study of Linguistic Diversity in Official International Relations and International Law, 2 vols. Philadelphia.

Paqué, R. 1980. Sprachen und Sprachendienste der Vereinten Nationen, Vereinte Nationen 5/1980, pp. 165ff.

Payne Smith, R. 1903. A Compendious Syriac Dictionary. Oxford.

Piamenta, M. 1979. Islam in Everyday Arabic Speech. Leiden.

Pitamić, L. 1971. "Linguistik im Völkerrecht", Österreichische Zeitschrift für Öffentliches Recht 21 (1971), pp. 305ff.

Podlech, A. 1976. "Rechtslinguistik", in: *Grimm*, D. (ed.) 1976. Rechtswissenschaft und Nachbarwissenschaften, 2 vols. Munich, vol. 2, pp. 105ff.

Pohl, D. 1988. Islam und Friedensvölkerrechtsordnung. Die dogmatischen Grundlagen der Teilnahme eines islamischen Staates am modernen Völkerrechtssystem am Beispiel Ägyptens. Vienna/New York.

Prévost, J. 1976. "Observations sur l'avis consultatif de la Cour Internationale de Justice relatif au Sahara occidental", Journal de droit international (Clunet) 103 (1976), S. 831ff.

Rebhan, H. 1986. Geschichte und Funktion einiger politischer Termini im Arabischen des 19. Jahrhunderts (1798-1882). Wiesbaden.

Redden, K. (ed.) 1990. Modern Legal Systems Cyclopedia, vol. 5/5A (Middle East) and vol. 6/6A (Africa).

Renteln, A. 1990. International Human Rights. Universalism vs. Relativism. Newberry Park.

Reuter, P. 1970. "Quelques réflexions sur le vocabulaire du droit international", in: Mélanges offerts à Monsieur le Doyen Trotabas. Paris, pp. 423ff.

Riedel, E. 1976. "Confrontation in Western Sahara in the light of the advisory opinion of the International Court of Justice of 16 October 1975", German Yearbook of International Law 19 (1976), pp. 405ff.

Roeder, G. 1919. Ägypter und Hethiter, Der Alte Orient 20 (1919), pp. 1ff.

Rohn, P. 1984. World Treaty Index, 5 vols., 2nd edition. Santa Barbara.

Rosén, H. 1977. Contemporary Hebrew. The Hague.

Rosenne, S. 1951. Israel's Armistice Agreements with the Arab States. Jerusalem.

- "On multi-lingual interpretation", in: *Moore*, J. (ed.) 1974-1991, The Arab-Israeli Conflict, 4 vols. Princeton, vol. 2, pp. 906ff.

- 1983. "The meaning of "Authentic Text" in modern treaty law", in: *Bernhardt*, R./*Geck*, W./*Jaenicke*, G./*Steinberger*, M. (eds.) 1983. Völkerrecht als Rechtsordnung. Internationale Gerichtsbarkeit. Menschenrechte. Festschrift für Hermann Mosler. Berlin/Heidelberg/New York, pp. 759ff.

Rosenthal, F. 1997. "The stranger in medieval Islam", Arabica 44/1 (1997), pp. 35ff.

Rousseau, C. 1944. Principes généraux de droit international public. Paris.

Rubenson, S. 1964. Wichale XVII. The Attempt to Establish a Protectorate over Ethiopia. Addis Abeba.

Rudolf, W. 1972. Die Sprache in der Diplomatie und internationalen Verträgen. Frankfurt.

Russell, B. 1905. "On denoting", Mind 14 (1905), pp. 479ff.

Saeed, A. 1996. Islamic Banking and Interest. A Study of the Prohibition of Riba and its Contemporary Interpretation. Leiden.

Sasse, H. 1981a. "Afroasiatisch", in: *Heine*, B./*Schadeberg*, T./*Wolff*, E. (eds.) 1981. Die Sprachen Afrikas. Hamburg , pp. 129ff.

– 1981b. "Semitisch", in: *Heine*, B./*Schadeberg*, T./*Wolff*, E. (eds.) 1981, pp. 225ff.

Satow, E. 1957 (4th ed.). A Guide to Diplomatic Practice. London.

Schacht, J. 1964. An Introduction to Islamic Law. Oxford.

Schaefer, M. 1981. Die Funktionsfähigkeit des Sicherheitsmechanismus der Vereinten Nationen. Berlin.

Scheffler, T. 1990. Ethnisch-religiöse Konflikte und gesellschaftliche Integration im Vorderen Orient. Berlin.

Schiedermair, H. 1975, Der völkerrechtliche Status Berlins nach dem Viermächte-Abkommen vom 3. September 1971. Berlin.

Schimmel, A. 1989. Islamic Names. Edinburgh.

Schneider, H. 1992. "Die sprachlichen Annahmen der Sprechakttheorie", in: *Dascal*, M./*Gerhardus*, D./*Lorenz*, K./*Meggle*, G. (eds.) 1992. Sprachphilosophie. Berlin, pp. 761ff.

Schulze, R. 1992. "Islam und Herrschaft. Zur politischen Instrumentalisierung einer Religion", in: *Lüders*, M. (ed.) 1992. Der Islam im Aufbruch. Perspektiven der arabischen Welt. Munich, pp. 94ff.

– 1994. Geschichte der islamischen Welt im 20. Jahrhundert. Munich.

Searle, J. 1969. Speech Acts. An Essay in the Philosophy of Language. Cambridge.

Shaked, H. 1981. "Anatomy of an autonomy", in: *Dinstein*, Y. 1981. Models of Autonomy. New Brunswick/London 1981, pp. 151ff.

Sharabi, H. 1966. Nationalism and Revolution in the Arab World. Princeton.

Shaw, M. 1978. "The Western Sahara case", The British Yearbook of International Law 49 (1978), pp. 119ff.

Shouby, E. 1951. "The influence of the Arabic language on the psychology of the Arabs", Middle East Journal, summer 1951, pp. 284ff.

Stegmüller, W. 1978/1986. Hauptströmungen der Gegenwartsphilosophie, vol. 1, 6th ed., vol. 2, 7th ed., vol. 3, 7th ed. Stuttgart.

Stetkevych, J. 1970. The Modern Arabic Literary Language. Lexical and Stylistic Developments. Chicago.

Szalay, L./*Abu-Hilal*, A./*Strohl*, J./*Mason*, J./*Goodison*, R. 1978. U.S.-Arabic Communication Lexicon of Cultural Meanings. Washington.

Tabory, M. 1980a. Multilingualism in International Law and Institutions. Princeton.

– 1980b. "Language rights as human rights", Israel Yearbook on Human Rights 10 (1980), pp. 167ff.

– 1982. "Recent developments in United Nations treaty registration and publication practices", The American Journal of International Law 76 (1982), pp. 350ff.

Tabouillot, W. 1989. Der grüne Marsch im Lichte des Völkerrechts. Ein Beitrag zum territorialen Status der ehemaligen Spanischen Sahara. Innsbruck.

Tankut, H. 1937. Günes-dil teorisinin izahi. Istanbul.

Tapper, R. (ed.) 1992. Some Minorities in the Middle East. London: SOAS.

Tellenbach, S. 1996. Strafgesetze der Islamischen Republik Iran. Berlin/New York.

Thornberry, P. 1991. International Law and the Protection of Minorities. Oxford.

Tibi, B. 1980. "Islam and secularization. Religion and the functional differentiation of the social system", Archiv für Rechts- und Sozialphilosophie 66 (1980), pp. 207ff.

– 1995. Krieg der Zivilisationen. Politik und Religion zwischen Vernunft und Fundamentalismus. Hamburg.

Tomuschat, C. 1983. "Protection of minorities under article 27 of the International Covenant on Civil and Political Rights", in: *Bernhardt*, R./*Geck*, W./*Jaenicke*, G./*Steinberger*, M. (eds.) 1983. Völkerrecht als Rechtsordnung. Internationale Gerichtsbarkeit. Menschenrechte. Festschrift für Hermann Mosler. Berlin/Heidelberg/New York, pp. 949ff.

Tsereteli, K. 1978. Grammatik der modernen assyrischen Sprache. Leipzig.

Ulkan, M. 1992. Zur Klassifikation von Sprechakten. Eine grundlagentheoretische Fallstudie. Tübingen.

Valdès, T. 1977. "The authoritativeness of the English and French texts of the Security Council Resolution 242 (1967) on the situation in the Middle East", American Journal of International Law 71 (1977), pp. 311ff.

Vennemann, T. 1986. Neuere Entwicklungen in der Phonologie. Berlin.

Verdross, A./*Simma*, B. 1984. Universelles Völkerrecht - Theorie und Praxis, 3rd ed. Berlin.

Volle, A./*Weidenfeld*, W. (eds.) 1997. Frieden im Nahen Osten? Chancen, Gefahren, Perspektiven. Bonn.

Wagner, H. 1971. Der Arabisch-Israelische Konflikt im Völkerrecht. Berlin.

Watt, M. 1971. "Al-Ḥudaybīya", The Encyclopaedia of Islam (new edition), vol. 3, p. 539.

Watzlawick, P. 1978. Gebrauchsanweisung für Amerika. Munich.

Wedel, H. 1991. Der türkische Weg zwischen Laizismus und Islam. Opladen.

Weil, P. 1983. "Towards relative normativity in International Law", American Journal of International Law 77 (1983), pp. 413ff.

Weisgerber, L. 1961. Vertragstexte als sprachliche Aufgabe. Formulierungs-, Auslegungs- und Übersetzungsprobleme des Südtirol-Abkommens von 1946. Bonn.

Wensinck, A. 1936-1988. Concordance et indices de la tradition musulmane, 8 vols. Leiden.

Wexler, P. 1990. The Schizoid Nature of Modern Hebrew: Slavic Language in Search of a Semitic Past. Wiesbaden.

Wild, S. 1969. ""Das Kapital" in arabischen Übersetzungen", in: *Fischer*, W. (ed.) 1969. Festgabe für Hans Wehr. Wiesbaden, pp. 97ff.

- 1975a. Sprachpolitik und Nationalismus. Arabisch und Ivrit. Leiden.
- 1975b. "Ist Ivrit eine semitische Sprache?", in: *Voigt*, W. (ed.) 1977. XIX. Deutscher Orientalistentag. Wiesbaden, pp. 757ff.
- 1982a. "Arabische Eigennamen", in: *Fischer*, W. (ed.) 1982. Grundriß der Arabischen Philologie. Band I: Sprachwissenschaft. Wiesbaden, pp. 154ff.
- 1982b. "Die arabische Schriftsprache der Gegenwart", in: *Fischer*, W. (ed.) 1982, pp. 51ff.
- 1993. "Zum Selbstverständnis palästinensisch-arabischer Nationalität", in: *Mejcher*, H. (ed.) 1993. Die Palästina-Frage 1917-1948. Paderborn, pp. 75ff.
- 1994. "Anfang und Ende von arabischen Texten", in: *Bellmann*, D. (ed.) 1994. Gedenkschrift Wolfgang Reuschel. Stuttgart, pp. 305ff.

Work, E. 1935. Ethiopia, a Pawn in European Diplomacy. New Concord (Ohio).

Yalcin-Heckmann, L. 1997. "Zur Kurdenproblematik in der Türkei", Aus Politik und Zeitgeschichte. Beilage zur Wochenzeitung Das Parlament B 11-12/97, March 7, 1997, pp. 41ff.

Yasseen, M. 1976. "L'interprétation des traités d'après la convention de Vienne sur le droit de traités", Recueil des Cours de l'Académie de Droit International 151 (1976), pp. 1ff.

Al-Zwaini, L./*Peters*, R. 1994. A Bibliography of Islamic Law, 1980-1993. Leiden.

Index

A. Index of names

[1] Arabic names are listed in the order of the English alphabet, irrespective of diacritical marks. For the structure of Arabic names, cf. *Wild* 1982a.

B. Index of subjects

[2] For a glossary of Arabic terms, cf. pp. 187ff. Arabic terms are listed in the order of the English alphabet, irrespective of diacritical marks.

MIX
Papier aus verantwortungsvollen Quellen
Paper from responsible sources
FSC® C105338

Printed by Libri Plureos GmbH
in Hamburg, Germany